PRAISE FOR *WILD MATERIALISM*

"An urgently contemporary study of the relation between 'terror' as a state of expectancy in relation to an event to come, and 'terrorism' as the deadly deployment of force in situations of radical exploitation and oppression."—Julia Lupton, University of California, Irvine

"Jacques Lezra has written what is undoubtedly the most nuanced and complex analysis of the relation between terror, terrorism, and republicanism that we have today. Through a dazzling highway of theoretical engagements with the most important ethical and political thinkers of our day, Lezra brilliantly defends his own notion of positive freedom, which turns on an allegory of a wounded sovereignty. Wounded, in that 'the city' no longer walls itself off from that which would pierce its walls and its defenses. Lezra seeks to keep us awake at night by powerfully reminding us of our 'terrible' responsibility in an unjust world, where we truly leave ourselves open to an encounter with the suffering of others. Lezra also engages with the major works of Western literature from Greek tragedy on, to show us the pervasiveness of the theme of what happens to the city when it fails to live up to its own image. If this were not enough, Lezra's careful enunciation of the difference between terror, terrible responsibility, and terrorism explores the political and ethical significance of both the actuality of terrorist acts and their phantasized presentation in the media, which leads them to become a justification for the protection of the city through grossly immoral acts, such as acts of torture. This is an extraordinarily rich and fearless book that will be must-reading in disciplines from law and politics to media studies and comparative literature."—Drucilla Cornell

"Lezra sketches a fascinating trip from the archaic scene of Oedipus, beyond the time of the founding of the individual and collective subject, to the events of September 11, at the threshold of our contingent future. *Wild Materialism*'s path leads through the Paris of the fifteenth century, the Spanish empire, the war in Algeria, and on to the contemporary world, and delivers an analysis of the production of universals in and of political space, that prior instant from which dualisms and differences flow— inside/out, friend/enemy, private/public, terror/terrorism—divisions and reconstitutions of what is held in common. This is a work that refuses finally to dissolve politics into aesthetics and seeks out an innovative, apt vocabulary for the tasks of ethics and politics, far from the fiction of sovereign, constituting power. *Wild Materialism* revises the sense of radical republicanism, basing itself in a fascinating interpretation of Levinas, Althusser, and Freud, which forces us to rethink the classic arguments of the twentieth century, from Arendt to Schmitt, from Koselleck to Habermas, Derrida to Negri."—José Luis Villacañas, Universidad Complutense de Madrid

WILD MATERIALISM

Wild Materialism

THE ETHIC OF TERROR
AND THE MODERN REPUBLIC

JACQUES LEZRA

FORDHAM UNIVERSITY PRESS

New York 2010

Library of Congress Cataloging-in-Publication Data

Lezra, Jacques, 1960-
Wild materialism : the ethic of terror and the modern
republic / Jacques Lezra.—1st ed.
p.   cm.
Includes bibliographical references and index.
ISBN 978-0-8232-3235-2 (cloth : alk. paper)—ISBN 978-0-
8232-3236-9 (pbk. : alk. paper)—ISBN 978-0-8232-3237-6
(ebook)
1. Political science—Philosophy.   2. Terrorism.   I. Title.
JA71.L49   2010
320.01—dc22
2010011758

Printed in the United States of America
12   11   10   5   4   3   2   1
First edition

CONTENTS

Illustrations   vii

Acknowledgments   ix

Introduction: Terrible Ethics   1

1.   The Ethic of Terror   34

2.   *Phares*; or, Divisible Sovereignty   63

3.   The Logic of Sovereignty   88

4.   *Materia* in the Critique of Autonomy   110

5.   A Sadean Community   150

6.   Three Women, Three Bombs   173

Conclusion: Distracted Republic   202

Notes   223

Bibliography   285

Index   309

ILLUSTRATIONS

1. Calle Claudio Coello, Madrid, December 20, 1973.   44

2. Diagram of the path of Carrero's car. From Sebastián
    Galdós and Gastón Pardo, *Cómo ejecutamos a Carrero
    Blanco* (México: Editores Asociados, 1975).   47

3. "Excerpt from 'Information Bulletin No. 7/74.'" From
    Eva Forest (writing as Julen Agirre), *Operation Ogro: The
    Execution of Admiral Luis Carrero Blanco*, trans. Barbara
    Probst Solomon (New York: Quadrangle/NY Times
    Book Co., 1975).   48

4a–c. Ralph Lever, *The Arte of Reason, Rightly Termed, Witcraft*
    (London, 1573), details of 114–15.   82

5a–e. The mirror shot, *The Battle of Algiers*.   180

6a–h. The mirror shot, *Le petit soldat*.   181

7. Eugène Delacroix, *Algerian Women in Their Apartments.*
    Courtesy of Réunion des Musées Nationaux/Art
    Resource, NY.   182

8a–d. The closing tracking shot, *Night and Fog*.   196

9a–c. The tracking shot in *Kapo*.   197

10. Proclaiming the Republic in Cullera.   203

11. Diego de Saavedra Fajardo, *Idea de un príncipe político
    cristiano* (1640), emblem 21.   206

ACKNOWLEDGMENTS

A manuscript on the topic of this book was on my desk, almost finished, in August 2001. I've spent time since then rethinking, writing and rewriting in light of the events, public and private, following that grim fall.

I had help. My students in Madison and for a term at Harvard were my constant, demanding interlocutors; this book is the record of our long conversations and our continuing friendship. I am delighted to acknowledge the support of the University of Wisconsin–Madison Graduate School, which provided me with the time I needed to write and revise. A grant from the Humanities Initiative at New York University made it possible for me to add the illustrations: my thanks.

Portions of Chapter 1 appeared as "The Ethic of Terror in Radical Democracy," in *Arizona Journal of Hispanic Cultural Studies* 7 (2003): 173–93. A version of Chapter 2 was published as *"Phares*, or *Divisible* Sovereignty," in *Sovereigns, Citizens, and Saints: Political Theology and Renaissance Literature*, ed. Julia Reinhard Lupton and Graham Hammill, special issue, *Religion and Literature* 38, no. 3 (Autumn 2006): 13–39. My "Labors of Reading," in *Depositions: Althusser, Balibar, Macherey, and the Labor of Reading*, ed. Jacques Lezra, special issue, *Yale French Studies* 88 (1995): 78–117, is the archaic precursor of Chapter 4; Chapters 5 and 6 draw upon material I published in "Sade on Pontecorvo," *Discourse* 26, no. 3 (Fall 2005): 48–75. Sections of the Conclusion to *Wild Materialism* appeared as my "Introduction" to *Spanish Republic*, special issue, *Journal of Spanish Cultural Studies* 6, no. 2 (2005).

Susanne, Gabe, and Nat are written into these pages somehow and constantly. Without them, nothing.

This book is for Mauricio and Giggy, who live in Madrid.

WILD MATERIALISM

Introduction:
Terrible Ethics

To an anomalous species of terror I found him a bounden slave.

—EDGAR ALLAN POE, "The Fall of the House of Usher"

They were creating not just terror; they were creating images.

—NEIL GABLER, "This Time, The Scene Was Real,"
New York Times, September 16, 2001

There is an old kinship between terror, judgment, and the city. That relation and the promises it may hold for the almost equally old concept *republicanism*, are the subject of this book.

This is how the story starts. It is 1982. A city's survival is at stake, and everything depends on our decision: this is what the philosopher Michael Levin invites us to imagine. Levin gives us a particular city; it stands in for any other. His famous fable terrifies, but it is a pedagogical, or better yet, a *civic* experience that he intends. (If we are terrified enough, we will be moved to act in defense of the city.) The story he tells bears on the relation between ethical judgments and political interests, and he gives it the shape that the conflict between globalization and national interest assumes in the metropolitan imaginary. "Suppose," Levin writes:

a terrorist has hidden an atomic bomb on Manhattan Island which will detonate at noon on July 4 unless . . . (here follow the usual demands for money and release of his friends from jail). Suppose, further, that he is caught at 10 A.M. of the fateful day, but—preferring death to failure—won't disclose where the bomb is. What do we do? If we follow due process—wait for his lawyer, arraign him—millions of people will die. If the only way to save those lives is to subject the terrorist to the most excruciating possible

I

pain, what grounds can there be for not doing so? I suggest there are none. In any case, I ask you to face the question with an open mind.

Torturing the terrorist is unconstitutional? Probably. But millions of lives surely outweigh constitutionality. Torture is barbaric? Mass murder is far more barbaric. Indeed, letting millions of innocents die in deference to one who flaunts his guilt is moral cowardice, an unwillingness to dirty one's hands. If you caught the terrorist, could you sleep nights knowing that millions died because you couldn't bring yourself to apply the electrodes?[1]

No counterargument has prevailed, certainly not in the media or in the political idiom in the United States in the past quarter century, and a fortiori after September 11, 2001. Not even the scandals of Abu Ghraib and Guantánamo or the disclosure of the United States' practices of prisoner rendition and "enhanced interrogation" have made much of an impact—juridically, legally, or culturally. Within the academy Levin's controversial scenario has fared only marginally less well; the essay's presence on the syllabi of any number of writing or rhetoric classes attests more to the luridness and sad topicality of its thesis, images, and techniques than to its coherence.[2] The utilitarian argument based upon the "ticking-bomb" scenario is stark indeed, and, as recent TV shows like "24" suggest, the proposition that the greater good of greater numbers trumps any particular interest, and some general ones as well (for instance, the abstract social interest in the preservation of law and "constitutionality"), has an undeniable commercial cachet. The most effective objections to Levin's scenario are practical ones (for example: the argument that the practice of torture does not work, because it does not produce the effects required or produces undesirable additional effects; or the argument that the practice of torture licenses others to employ torture against U.S. forces; or the argument that torture lowers international opinion of the United States; etc.). Deontology, value ethics, religious morality—no ethical argument against torture and state terror has standing when the city is imagined to be in peril. The city's walls protect us from enemies, keep us from terror, close the circle of our friends, define the practices, habits, and idioms that determine us. Within the city walls, we are all humanitarians; rights are equally protected; a measure of political autonomy is presumed. When we allow those practices to cross the walls and apply them, extramurally, to those who do not accept the idioms of the city, who seek, indeed, to destroy it—then we are guilty of "moral cowardice."

Let's stop here a moment longer. A more detailed reading of Levin's position shows us that it depends on what is either an incoherent or an impracticable account of judgment. In the first place, the truth-seeking function of acts of torture, which in Levin's description makes these acts permissible, may not be separated from secondary and tertiary functions that in themselves cannot be (and which would then require balancing against the primary goal, presuming it has been achieved). Two examples. Acts of torture that produce "truth" (if they do) necessarily also produce a reflexive justification for these acts. If we succeed in saving the city, then we were justified in proceeding as we did; if we do not succeed, we are at least not guilty of "moral cowardice," even if we are guilty of something else: our heroism here is of the tragic variety. The principle that torture is permissible because it works is not disproved—quite the contrary: perhaps we had the wrong terrorist (*someone* knew where the bomb was planted), or we did not apply sufficient pain to the right one. This second, self-legitimating, heroic function is not morally permissible as a *goal* of torture, but it cannot be separated from the first function. And acts of torture also have what one could call secondary *lexical* consequences: if I can bring myself to apply the electrodes, then I have become something other than what I was (I may, for instance, have purchased a sort of extra-constitutional heroism by the gesture), and the city I have saved now shelters its walls behind a set of extra-mural, extra-judicial walls different from the ones that defined and guarded it before. Just as there is no single, discrete act of torture, but rather a plurality of acts involving the gestures, decisions, and applications of instruments by different hands, stretching across the city and across time, so there is no simple product of acts of torture (truth telling is also an act of revenge, for example).

This promiscuity of the act, its division and seepage across spaces, agents, and times, also holds in the second place, where the act of uttering a statement under torture is concerned. A confession, the statement of a location, a plan, a name: these will not yet count as true, not until the conditions of veridification have been satisfied. Is the utterance what it appears to be? What if it is true, but incomplete? That is, it is true that the bomb is in place X, but I haven't told you how to disarm it. (Terrorists are diabolically clever.) For instance: tell me where the bomb is; the bomb is at X location, at the Air France ticket office, say, but that statement, even if it should prove to be true, isn't sufficient to prevent the device from exploding. A further answer is required, pending a further question. (How is it to be disarmed?) From a juridical perspective, another class of questions and answers is presupposed, the sorts of questions that establish that this is indeed the terrorist whose knowledge we must extract (and not just a traveler seeking to cross into the city). Questions breed others and entail further ones. The difficulty is conceptual as well as practical: one needs to stipulate too much before one begins asking the question, and there is no *single* question adequate to the scenario Levin envisions. Questions too are promiscuous.

The fantasy of the single, master question rests on, and is indissociable from, a chronological fantasy as well. Think of another, ancient story—set this time among the Theban hills, where two roads cross near the city, where a great, unsolved crime occurred alongside a private, unremembered one (the abandonment of a child), where both still poison the city. By uttering the name of the person who gave him the baby, the shepherd makes the plague disappear, or rather, he also names the plague and by naming ends it. Like Sophocles', Levin's fable has a mythological horizon: when the terrorist utters the word elicited by the most excruciating possible pain, the threat disappears. Indeed, we judge that it was the right word because we recognize that the threat has disappeared (and not till then). Or because the answer was known in advance (the day, as in Levin's example, is known to be "fated"; Oedipus's parentage, like the facts that the "terrorist" is a "terrorist" and that his information will ipso facto save the city, is known by the gods, by the Sphinx, by Teiresias, by Oedipus, by the audience). "Of course, *that's* where the device is, we knew it all along," we say, and the device is no longer there, or no longer active. Without this mythological recognition effect, the horizon of the acts of torture is not the production of truth and the salvation of the city—that is an indirect consequence of my use of the information (though it may be the one I intend). It is, rather, the production of an utterance, whose truth or falsehood is to be determined in the event: what Aristotelian logicians would call a *future contingent*. (These are truth-neutral or undecided statements, which escape from the Aristotelian principle of bivalence—the requirement that propositions must be either true or false. The most famous is Aristotle's own "A sea battle will take place tomorrow." Like Aristotle's example, the statement "A bomb located in Manhattan will go off 'at noon on July 4'" is not yet true or false: it merely becomes one or the other.) In the interim, between the utterance and its veridification, as between the act and its consequences, my judgment is also neutral, undecided, suspended. And how, after all, am I, or the community, supposed to assess an action, a decision, a state of affairs—if not in relation to its foreseeable or inferred outcome, or to what it *is* intrinsically, or to agreed-upon, explicit norms or rules of association that constitute the community?[3]

One cannot justify an act (or a set of acts: torture) on *both* consequentialist and truth-neutral, contingent grounds; one cannot stipulate which consequences of acts will be subject to ethical judgment and which will be merely incidental; or rather, one can, but only in a very restricted sense indeed. A literary example may be useful: another story. This is *Purgatory*, and Virgil is instructing Dante the pilgrim how to read the *tormento*, the scenes of torture and retribution passing before him:

> Li occhi miei, ch'a mirare eran contenti
> per veder novitadi ond' e' son vaghi,
> volgendosi ver' lui non furon lenti.
> Non vo' però, lettor, che tu ti smaghi
> di buon proponimento per udire
> come Dio vuol che 'l debito si paghi.
> Non attender la forma del martìre:
> pensa la succession; pensa ch'al peggio
> oltre la gran sentenza non può ire.
>
> *My eyes, which were looking intently,*
> *eager for any new thing they could see,*
> *were not slow in turning towards him.*
> *Reader, I would not have you fall away*
> *from your good resolution to hear the way*
> *God wills that what is owed is to be paid.*
> *Do not linger on the form of the torment.*
> *Think of what follows it. At the worst, think*
> *it cannot go beyond the great judgment.*[4]

The scene is distracting enough that Dante the poet in turn instructs his readers, from the retrospective vantage of the journey's end, how to understand the torment he witnessed with Virgil's aid. "Pensa la succession," he tells his reader: think about what follows and think about *la gran sentenza*, the Last Judgment. To attend to the form that torture takes is to be guilty of misplaced compassion or of "moral cowardice." It's only from the perspective of the outcome or the event (a good, strong translation of *succession*), from the Olympian standpoint reserved for those who know not only that days and acts have consequences but which acts serve to pay what debts, or save the city or the soul, that one can truly judge. Dante doubles his verb for emphasis: it is thought, *il pensier*, rather than vision or imagination, that helps us derive from torments we see or imagine outcomes that justify them. Consequentialist thought can ward off the risk that an example will become a bad example, or the risk that too much interest, pleasure, or content, *contento*, will be generated by (say) the spectacle of the pain of another's *tormento*, or the risk that what we see or what we imagine will parasitically overtake all *buon proponimento* and, Medusa-like, astonish our judgment and arrest the pilgrim. Levin's fable both requires of his readers the mythological perspective of the event and offers it as the ground on which the city is built, on which membership in the community is to be assessed. Civic judgments thought under the aspect of the Last Judgment, subject to its sovereign integrity. Sovereign thought, banning from the city's gates what we merely see and merely imagine. The city is an eschatology. Is there another way of imagining the relation between terror, judgment, and the city?

Before the City

Let's begin the story differently. It's still an archaic scene, an old tragedy: famine, blight, a plague; their causes unknown. The city, *polis*, the institutions and communal practices that support it and that its solid walls make possible, and the life of the city dwellers—all are in peril. On this ancient stage two stories cross, the story of the city's suffering and the story of its ruler's origins. Where they meet, the sovereign addresses the slave; a man (who is at first silent out of—what, reticence? decorum? loyalty?) is forced to speak: violently. For the chorus of citizens, always at hand, this scene has a shape that Sophocles' or Seneca's modern reader may find unfamiliar. For instance: we, the modern readers or viewers of these old tragedies, believe that the stories crossing before the chorus and before us should be different from each other because one concerns public matters, the other private ones. And we believe that the moral grounds for locating sovereignty—understood both as self-possession, as the capacity to decide autonomously whether one enters into one or another course of action, and as political sovereignty—in an office or an individual, or for distributing it across groups, depend upon a distinction between the interests of the city and those of the individuals within it. And—again—we may ask whether there are secular, noneschatological grounds on which to ground judgments concerning the admissibility of acts undertaken in the city's name. Finally, we believe that, even if we acknowledge that the city cannot survive without the slave's tale and further grant that to this end the slave (or the terrorist) can be "subject . . . to the most excruciating possible pain," as Levin says, we will also conclude that the city will not be the same afterwards, that aspects of its self-understanding cannot survive when it elicits violently the tale that will save it. (It is no longer, for example, a "constitutional" society; its values are no longer universal or universally applied.)

None of these four objections pertains when this old story begins: public and private interests have not taken on their modern, distinct, correlative and contrastive form, and the distinction between them has no normative value. The slave's tale is not his own but the city's, and its standing in public matters is a consequence of the very violence that a contemporary viewpoint might find disabling, even self-stultifying; the vast, inefficient, and subtle machinery of secularization has as yet no purchase.[5] In Sophocles, even in Seneca, there is no secular stance from which a character, a member of the chorus, or, indeed, a member of the audience might ask whether the city will survive the Shepherd's story and the violence required to elicit it or might judge whether the interests of the collective warrant the sacrifice of the individual (the slave or the sovereign). No ostensible concepts—like "the city," "the individual," or their relation, citizenship—stand apart, free from the plague that threatens the city and its citizens from within and without, by which one might judge whether (or command that) one or another course of action should be followed, by whom, and under what circumstances and then describe and set rules prescribing what "following a course of action" means. No grounded position from which minimal ethical or political judgments might be made—and no position from which their relation might be assessed. There is no stance from which to decide whether the decision to accept the city's laws precedes or follows from the city's laws themselves, or to seek to determine whether in fact it is a decision at all: an absence on which the Socratic theory of the state articulated in the *Apology* will turn.[6]

Here, then, is the archaic scene I have been conjuring. It is one of the points at which the public or political story in Sophocles' *Oedipus* touches the private story, and by no means the most explicitly violent one. Or rather, it is violent in a different way from the enraged interrogation of Teiresias, or from Oedipus's confrontation with Creon, or from the radical but offstage physicalization of the encounter, the touch, of those two accounts: Oedipus's blows to his own eyes, a gesture that sutures one story to the other forever, his blinded sockets marking the two points where the city's story, its sovereign's, and every citizen's knowledge of these are held together; blind spots, crossroads, impasses. The interest of the city, the city's health, its very survival: these are explicitly at stake as the play opens (Oedipus to the suppliants and chorus: "Your pain comes on each of you for himself alone, and for no other, but my soul is in pain at once for the city, for myself, and for you," ll. 60ff) but not in this climactic scene.

Oedipus does not appeal to the servant on political grounds; a different logic is now at work:

> MESSENGER: Come, tell me now: do you remember having given me a boy in those days, to be reared as my own foster-son?
> SHEPHERD: What now? Why do you ask?
> MESSENGER: This man, my friend, is he who then was young.
> SHEPHERD: Damn you! Be silent once and for all!
> OEDIPUS: Do not rebuke him, old man. Your words need rebuking more than his.
> SHEPHERD: And in what way, most noble master, do I offend?
> OEDIPUS: In not telling of the boy about whom he asks.
> SHEPHERD: He speaks without knowledge, but is busy to no purpose.
> OEDIPUS: You will not speak with good grace, but will in pain.
> SHEPHERD: No, in the name of the gods, do not mistreat an old man.
> OEDIPUS: Someone, quick—tie his hands behind [*apostrephō*: "to turn or twist the hands behind"] him this instant!
> SHEPHERD: Alas, why?[7] [*dustēnos anti tou*]

Small editorial disagreements tug at these lines. The Shepherd's exclamation— *dustēnos*, "wretched, disastrous, miserable"—has generally been read as applying to himself, though some editors point out that the adjective may also describe Oedipus: the term floats between the slave and the sovereign, lighting on both. Nor is there consensus about the import of Oedipus's lines, "Someone, quick—tie his hands behind him this instant!" which can be understood either as a threat (binding the Shepherd's hands in preparation for other, unnamed torments to come) or as commanding that the pain begin by means of the binding back of the Shepherd's hands (the twisting of the hands is part of the torture to which the Shepherd is put).

The exchange has thus provoked two sorts of staging, one suggesting that the mere fear of pain is enough to elicit the Shepherd's story, the other placing the character's pain on display: the first, in line with the play's consistent relegation of the spectacle of violence to the imaginary, offstage realm (the murder of Laius, Jocasta's suicide, Oedipus's blinding); the second, threatening to bring it onstage. Seneca's version favors the second. His Oedipus interrogates Phorbas, the shepherd who cares for Thebes' royal flocks:

> OEDIPUS: [*Aside*] Why search further? Now destiny comes close. [*To Phorbas*] Tell me fully, who was the baby?
> PHORBAS: My loyalty forbids. [*Prohibet fides.*]

OEDIPUS: Bring fire, one of you! Flames will soon drive out loyalty. [*Huc aliquis ignem! Flamma iam excutiet fidem.*]

PHORBAS: Is truth to be sought by such bloody means? Forgive me, I beg you. [*Per tam cruentas vera quaerentur vias?*]

OEDIPUS: If you think me cruel and ruthless, you have vengeance ready to hand: tell me the truth! [*Si ferus videor tibi/Et impotens, parata vindicta in manu est:/Dic vera.*][8]

Neither Sophocles' commands ("Tell the story" or "Tie his hands behind him this instant!") nor Seneca's ("Dic vera!," "Tell the truth!") stand upon a firm distinction between the interest of the city and the interest of the citizen. It is not possible at this point in either version of *Oedipus* to distinguish abidingly or consistently between the desire that the sovereign expresses (as a son, a husband, a possible murderer, a man betrayed; as a man acting freely; as a man following, blindly, a destiny laid out for him by others) and the interest of the city. Although they are determining in the fields to which the plays compare them (in drawing familial or generational distinctions; in distinguishing between a stranger and a relative, between a slave and a citizen, between the sovereign and the citizen, or between the present and the past; or in determining whether one's apparently free act in fact obeys an older logic), the distinctions are both fundamental and impossible to draw in the domain of political or even of ethical judgments.[9]

Along the arc that these two plays trace, one form of ethico-political logic declines and another arises, as if in compensation. By the end of Sophocles' play and *as a result of the play*, what it means to be part of a city or what it means to be a citizen, a sovereign, or a member of the chorus or of the audience has changed profoundly. As the responsibility for different aspects of the ruler's and the city's story is distributed across the citizenry, so the relations between the citizens are resemanticized, reconfigured, mediated, shifted. Just as Oedipus's and Creon's familial relations are, as well. Sophocles' *Oedipus* closes on a series of demands, made on different levels and based in different normative frames. Two are particularly striking. The Chorus, displaying the blind Oedipus to its audiences (the Theban citizenry as well as the play's audience), reminds them of the eager imitation, even envy, that the sovereign's good fortune (*ēn tuchais*, a clear, ironic reference to Oedipus's claim, at l. 1080, that he is the "son of Fortune," *paida tēs tukhēs*) once elicited (*hou tis ou zēlōi politōn ē n tuchais epiblepōn*), then famously draws from Oedipus's fall the injunction to the residents of Thebes (*ō patras Thēbēs enoikoi*) that they withhold judgment concerning the happiness or unhappiness of any mortal till after his or her death (ll. 1524–30). The difference between the "resident" of Thebes, *enoikos*, and the "citizen," *politēs*, is notable. *Enoikos* is unusual in Sophocles, and indeed more generally; its only other occurrence in Sophocles is in the *Trachiniae*, where it is used not of a man but about an animal, the Nemean lion (*hoi pote Nemeas enoikon*); in the *Crito* (113c), Plato uses the term to characterize the Atlantidean autochthon Evenor. The demand that the Chorus places upon the audience transforms the audience, and the Thebans, into mere residents of a space. They are inhabitants, not citizens (*politēs*); theirs is the bare life of the animal or the autochthon; the city is now understood to be a place inhabited by beasts. More properly: a zoo. And when Oedipus appeals to Creon to protect and shelter Antigone and Ismene, to lay his hand upon them (*xunneuson, ō gennaie, sēi psausas cheri*) he has no grounds beyond their kinship; the demand is not made on the basis of a social, ethical, or political norm. In Sophocles, the painful disclosure of the Shepherd's story spells the end of the city's *political* life, now fatally divided between interests aimed at mere dwelling, and the aristocratic requirements of the family. With the expulsion of Oedipus, Thebes regains its health, exiles the terrors of Sphinx and plague, and loses, too, what has properly made the city a *political* space: the sovereign's wounds, his susceptibility to fortune, *tukhē*, and mere contingency, the distribution of his weakness over the whole city. "An infamous double bond," as Jocasta says of her relation with Oedipus: the sacrificial exile of the wounded sovereign saves and condemns the city, and briefly opens the possibility of imagining an alternative, a sovereignty whose woundedness, division, and contingency are not expelled but assumed by the city, distributed across the citizenry. Remembered, repeated, worked through.

Seneca's reading of Sophocles is precise and consequential; we hardly miss the small ambiguities of the earlier text, or its hesitations (Will the spectacle of violence be brought before us, or remain hidden? Is it to come, or has it already begun?), or the questions Sophocles raises but does not answer: What sort of decision, or foundational act, or mere happenstance lies at the origin of citizenship? Can there be an inaugural decision that is not already a repetition and that does not draw its intelligibility from its status as a repetition? From a structure of return and recognition? In what relation to ethical judgments does that decision stand? To political judgments? We remark four important differences between the two works, though.

In the first place, Seneca's brief observations about the "truth" of truth telling in the city (for the city) glaringly set on stage matters that Sophocles leaves obscure. Senecan truth, it appears, lies at the end of a cruel path. It wars with loyalty. And torture, the cruel path that the true story takes in appearing, that the true story takes in order to save the city, makes truth an instrument of revenge: to tell the truth is effectively to repay cruelty with cruelty, to balance pain with pain.[10] These Senecan observations about the "truth" of truth-telling under torture (about the uses and structure of truth) are not subordinated to each other or to a normative conception of truth-telling, moral or epistemological; they are not even correlated observations. The scene's interest lies in the contrast between these jostling observations and the sphere that Seneca sketches in Oedipus's aside: "(*Aside*) Why search further? Now destiny comes close (*Quid quaeris ultra? Fata iam accedunt prope*)." The truth of the story is the place to which it was destined, fated; when the true story appears, it is, if not already known, at any rate recognized. This, then, is why the story Phorbas tells is immediately understood, and understood to be true: the Shepherd's story repeats a story that Oedipus knows in some way, has been telling himself, has already been fearing. The truth of truth-telling in and for the Senecan city is linked, in brief, to its repetition and to its recognition. (We might say: in the Senecan city truth is always a myth, a communally agreed-upon story recalled and repeated.

In the second place, in Seneca's *Oedipus* the truth of "truth-telling" is also linked to an embryonic sense of the character's interiority. Oedipus experiences his story in advance, and the city's as well, and Seneca structures this repetition as a characterological feature (the ruler is torturing himself; he is the city's pollution; torturing Phorbas is a way of externalizing a psychological state of affairs), an interior representation to which the staged stories can then be shown to correspond. An audience, attuned to the irony of a scene in which the threat or experience of torture both represents the anguish the ruler has been feeling (and causing himself) and anticipates the torments he will experience, will understand its own awareness of the earlier iterations of the play in the same vein, but with an inverted affect: as a memory to which the play may or may not correspond, to which the play alludes, from which it draws its identity—a communal identity drawn from the spectacle of the sovereign's wounds.

In the third place—and relatedly—remark the relation between Oedipus and the Chorus. Where Sophocles' Chorus stands in for the city, voices its interests to the king directly, and is addressed directly, as a group of citizens, by the king, Seneca's Chorus does not. A font of moralizing generalities, the Senecan Chorus is an uncomfortable, belated, one might almost say vestigial convention, soon to be abandoned in the history of drama. As dramatic space comes to be understood to stand in for psychological space, this story goes, the Chorus's function is absorbed by characterological devices and conventions.

And finally, on this same characterological note, there is Seneca's Oedipus himself—a welter of sacrificial self-pity, vastly stressing just one of the attributes that Sophocles gives his Oedipus. Here is Seneca's Oedipus, addressing the audience:

> All you who are weak at heart and heavy with sickness, dragging frames only half alive, see, I am leaving for exile: lift up your heads, a kindlier condition of the skies will come in behind me. You who feebly retain the breath of life on your sickbeds may freely take in life-giving draughts of air. Go, bring help to those abandoned to die: I am drawing with me the deadly maladies of the land. Savage Fates, the shuddering tremor of Disease, Wasting and black Plague and ravening Pain, come with me, come with me: I rejoice to have guides such as these.[11]

We see none of the ambivalence one finds at the close of Sophocles' *Oedipus*: here exile is reward and cure; the wounded sovereign's departure entails the health and prosperity of the city, its survival.

Seneca's *Oedipus*, in short, translates the impasses that Sophocles devises from the domain of political ontology to that of aesthetics and addresses them at that level. Sophoclean tragedy—the loss of the political that is entailed in the city's survival—is converted to Senecan comedy. The strategy only partly succeeds, but it lies wholly behind the eschatology of the city that we find in arguments like Levin's.

It is not a question, for us, of a "return to Sophocles" (whatever that might mean) but rather of seeking behind contemporary representations of the city's interest, and of the ethical disposition that those interests require, the archaic shape of another stance—a noneschatological, nonheroic, nonsacrificial, which is to say, a properly *political* stance—from which to decide where ethical judgments stand, before the city. Is it possible to derive norms for judging whether this or that act or circumstance accords with the rules of the city *without* recourse to a regulative idea, to an aesthetic displacement of the question of the political, to a concept, or to a fantasy (for example, the idea, concept, or fantasy of what such a city or community might be, or might require)? What might be entailed in the rather allegorical image of an introjected, wounded sovereignty?

Toward Defective Universals

> There are moments when, even to the sober eye of Reason, the world
> of our sad Humanity may assume the semblance of a Hell—but the

imagination of man is no Carathis, to explore with impunity its every
cavern. Alas! The grim legion of sepulchral terrors cannot be regarded
as altogether fanciful—but, like the Demons in whose company
Afrasiab made his voyage down the Oxus, they must sleep, or they will
devour us—they must be suffered to slumber, or we perish.

EDGAR ALLAN POE, "The Premature Burial"

Let me begin again, on different ground. Think of a modern scene (the
scene, if you will, of modernity). In place of a physical city—call it Thebes,
Athens, or Alexandria—imagine a sphere of deliberation and action suited
to the resolution of conflict, to the negotiation of differences, to mediation
between competing interests. Imagine a public sphere sheltered by the
idea of comity and reconciliation, and regulated according to norms
derived from that idea: what classical sociology might call *Gemeinschaft*.
Or what the sociologists Luc Boltanski and Eve Chiapello call the "projective city," "simultaneously [an] operator of justification and [a] critical
operator . . . a *self-referential critical mechanism*, internal to and immanent
in a world that is in the process of coming into being, and must limit itself
if it is to last."[12] Plague, blight, and famine, taken literally or not, threaten
and conspire to make impossible anything like classical citizenship (the
deliberate and conscious participation in the community according to the
rules of association that define it, rules that may be, as in Boltanski and
Chiapello's model, partly autopoetic, self-reproducing as well as self-limiting). The threats arise from within as well as from without: indeed, as in
the archaic scene they recall, they bear on the distinction itself, on the
immanent processes of self-reflection and self-limiting that will make it
last. (Physiology again: the political disease of modernity is an autoim-
mune condition, Derrida's last works argue.) What I say and what I do are
understood within as well as without the city, inside as well as outside of
political idiom or deliberation. Different rules of association (we might
also say: different ideas of what is public, different language games at play,
alternative responsibilities) are sovereign, or rather, they are *also* sovereign; other cities (or an empire, say) are imagined within and across these
walls, other citizenships acknowledged and performed, other responsibilities attended to. The sheltered community now suffers from the globalization of corporate capital and the dispersal of traditional notions of class
interest and class identity that flows from the "large is beautiful" socioeco-
nomic model, from the economic and ideological consolidation of the
media, from the creation of self-sustaining politico-bureaucratic classes,
and from the devaluation of the idea of the public sphere as a domain in

which these trends might be subject to debate or reflection.[13] A restricted economy; a general economy. A projective city, a world system.

Where the sovereign and the slave meet, the plays come to a crossroads. With Sophocles' characters, his spectators, and their choral proxies on stage, we find ourselves where the domain of decisions opens onto the landscape of the city, where ethical judgments and political interest meet. We recall that a man died earlier, at a crossroads. But every crossroads differs from every other; that the city does not survive in one sense does not mean that we will not survive, we its citizens, in another sense; we draw comfort from these observations. Sophocles has taken one path: the path of the transformation of associative politics into either mere dwelling, the transformation of the city's space into an animal habitat (a zoo, an animal park, a *Menschenpark*; lions and men live there) or into mere familial obligation. Seneca takes another path, generating an early form of interiority for his sovereign and his play (external events are repetitions of interior intuitions), aestheticizing the city's political relations, and side-stepping the troubling questions his precursor raises.

Let's return to the primitive form of the question (to the Shepherd's cry at the city's heart), bearing in mind the mediations that flow from Sophocles' recasting of it (the direction of citizenship as either mere dwelling or mere kinship) and from Seneca's answer (the Stoic valorization of interiority). How is our responsibility for the city's survival imagined? This is to ask three sorts of questions.

In the first place, what does it mean to accept responsibility for (an aspect of) the city, for the sovereign, and for the slave and the slave's story? Are we making a decision? Can I ever *decide*, autonomously, to enter the city? Are we registering or acquiescing in an event? The decision, if it is one, is the condition for belonging to the city: it founds the city. It is constitutive of the domain of the political; it provides my identity as a citizen. Can one take this class of events or decisions from outside the city? What standing does ethical judgment have before (from outside the walls of, in advance of the founding of) the polis?

In the second place, to ask how we are responsible for the city's survival is to ask where we stand with regard to those who are not citizens and yet constitute us as citizens: to ask where we stand with regard to the sovereign and the slave, and to the violence of their encounter, where we stand with regard to dissidence, to governance, to subjection, and to abjection.

Finally, it is to ask how we—the spectators at this archaic, primal scene—can distribute the twin, exceptional positions of the sovereign and the slave (the position of abject dispossession before the law) across the city. A scattering of problems: *Can* these positions be distributed? Are they divisible? If we determine that they are—and the answer is by no means self-evident—what means will we employ to carry out this distribution? What sort of task does this responsibility demand? How will we understand the pock-marked spots where this double distribution won't take— the marks of dehiscence, of the refusal of this double distribution, of the enemy?

"The task confronting democracy," Chantal Mouffe argues in *The Democratic Paradox*, is "to transform the potential antagonism existing in human relations into an agonism."[14] This is capacious, even vague enough to include the many tasks set in and by most political philosophies since the fall of European socialism and the eclipse of dialectical materialism. Mouffe is among a small number, however, who stand aside from the prevailing "ethical" perspective on the democratic transformation of antagonism. In her description, "ethics"—virtue ethics, classical deontological ethics, and what Mouffe calls "postmodern" ethics (which celebrates "the possibility of plurality without antagonism")—falls short because it cannot account for the constitutive character of social antagonism and the necessary violence it entails. Like other forms of dialectical thought, these "ethical" perspectives seek to set in place a formal identity of social interests that regulates the agon of political encounters, and, in order to achieve this political goal, they displace, rename, or render merely abstract any number of substantial differences (of interest, identity, desire) that would tend to disaggregate the community. Pluralist democracies, Mouffe and a number of radical democratic thinkers suggest, are or should be made up of and responsive to divided subjectivities and incomplete autonomies; they should recognize that political interests are never the same as subjective desires; and they start from the premise that ethics and politics cannot be reconciled to each other. This description gives rise to a number of difficulties. Just how and at what level (institutional? intersubjective?), if different social interests and demands are constitutively antagonistic, can social "unity . . . [emerge] out of heterogeneity," as Ernesto Laclau asks?[15] (Mouffe speaks of the potential antagonism that exists in human relations: the modal difference does not alter the claim, or the objection.) On the shoulders, it appears, of a "psychoanalytic ethics of the Real" or, as Simon Critchley has argued, of a strong account of hegemony.[16] Social unity then requires (at both the intersubjective and the institutional levels) corresponding universals—in the shape, minimally, of an encompassing conception of the psychic apparatus or of "hegemony," but the lexicon of radical democracy is shot through with quasi- or para-universal formulations and operators: antagonism, articulation, human relations, and so on. What are these universals, where are they found, how are they constructed?[17] How do they differ from normative terms drawn from the idiom of classical ethics: autonomy, value, consequence, utility? Finally and most broadly, how must the concept of democracy be revised in response to the twin phenomena of economic globalization and religious, ethnic, and national fundamentalisms?

The keenest answers to these questions have come recently from the encounter between two "ethical" perspectives in radical democratic thought, both flowing roughly from Jürgen Habermas's conception of classical republican politics:

> On the 'republican' view . . . politics is constitutive of the process of society
> as a whole. [It] is conceived as the reflective form of substantial ethical life,
> namely as the medium in which the members of somehow solitary commu-
> nities become aware of their dependence on one another and, acting with
> full deliberation as citizens, further shape and develop existing relations of
> reciprocal recognition into an association of free and equal consociates
> under law.[18]

On the one hand, we find the argument that a postmetaphysical version of Hegel's "struggle for recognition" (supplementing that inchoate argument from the early Jena writings with a distinctly pragmatic anthropology drawn from George Herbert Meade as well as from Habermas) provides the norms for what Axel Honneth calls a "formal conception of ethical life [*Sittlichkeit*]."[19] On the other stands an argument that works not from a monist but from a dualist perspective: setting the task of the redistribution of rights and economic and social capital alongside the claims of recognition or, even more stringently, integrating the two by devising in the moral sphere, as Nancy Fraser puts it, "an overarching conception of justice that can accommodate both defensible claims for social equality and defensible claims for the recognition of difference."[20]

The two positions entail quite different programs, and although they flow from common sources and concerns, they seem in important ways opposed, except on the broadest and least useful level: for instance, one could confidently assert that both Fraser and Honneth seek to devise models of social relation that account for and seek to overcome both existing inequalities and structural problems leading to differential access to the sphere of rights. Nevertheless, the recognitionist and redistributionist positions share a significant difficulty—an incapacity to account for (or to resolve, bypass, or capitalize upon) a tension between two aspects of their arguments. The broadly recognitionist and redistributionist camps make a central aspect of their ethico-political frame the critique of formal regimes of rights and theories of justice based on symmetrical recognition (this interest group recognizes another in relation to itself and stipulates that the other group recognize it in the same way, that is, also in relation to itself, or that both recognize each other reciprocally according to a set of neutral criteria, rules, or a grammar for what constitutes "interest," "identity," or "citizenship").[21] Such symmetries (or neutral criteria for designating what counts as recognition) are fundamentally ahistorical, and, as Patchen Markell has recently observed, they are "at least in part cultivated by (and centered around) the institutions of the putatively sovereign state."[22] Their use presumes that an equal, abstract access to the lexicon of recognition and "esteem," as Honneth puts it, either "really exists" or exists *in posse*; this normative belief constrains all prospective changes in the concepts of "interest," "value," or "identity" that might substantially alter or even destroy relations of recognition and redistribution.

Both the redistributionist and the recognitionist camps are aware of this objection, and they make similar methodological choices to address it. Fraser writes:

> Both Honneth and I reject the strong internalism of historicist hermeneutics. Not content merely to explicate the meanings sedimented in given traditions, both of us assume that critique can harbor a radical potential only if the gap between norm and the given is kept open. And we both assume that valid norms transcend the immediate context that generates them. Thus, far from restricting ourselves to criticism that is strictly internal, we both seek concepts with "surplus validity."[23]

And Honneth clarifies, using the example of Fraser's use of the "notion of a successive 'expansion' of the equality principle," a thesis, he says, "which can only mean that the idea of social equality in a certain way possesses a semantic surplus, which is gradually revealed by innovative interpretations without ever being completely or clearly determinable."[24]

This point of methodological agreement is illusory, however. The notions of the "surplus validity" of normative concepts (that is, their transcendence of the immediate contexts that generate them: we might say, of the language game in which they are first used) and the "semantic surplus" of "ideas" are contradictory rather than synonymous, at least in this formulation. For Honneth, the task of "innovative interpretation" of ideas is imagined to reveal an always already existing semantic surplus, presumably without ever revealing all of it (otherwise it would be "completely or clearly determinable," if not in advance then sub specie aeternitatis: the full unfolding of a concept's semantic surplus exists *in posse*; critique is a form of entelechy). For Fraser, the surplus is immanent not within the concept but in its relation of excess or deficiency to the immediate context that generates it; the task she imagines involves the mutual modification of contexts and concept, and it is a distinctly interminable task. ("Validity" is a relational concept.) The ethico-political model that flows from Honneth's notion of surplus is eschatological, even apocalyptic. (Althusser might say: "semantic excess" falls under the normative rule of the last instance.) The ethico-political model that flows from Fraser's notion of surplus is mechanistic, almost physiological: it imagines a homeostatic relation between normative concepts and their normative contexts. Both entail a sharp redefinition of the domain of freedom, at least as it is classically understood. "Innovative interpretations" are regulated by the shadow of the fully unfolded semantic field: critique is responsible to that fully unfolded field; the "surplus validity" of concepts with respect to originating contexts, discursive as well as material, generates further contexts and further concepts: critique is responsible to that movement.

For an alternative that preserves the critique of symmetrical recognition without recourse either to an apocalyptic immanence or to a form of mechanism, for a radically *republican* alternative, in short, a different account of "surplus value"—semantic or conceptual—must be articulated, and a different understanding of the ontological status of normative contexts must be furnished. Simon Critchley has called recently for the "cultivation of what might be called *politicities*, zones of hegemonic struggle that work against the consensual idyll of the state . . . linked to the cultivation of an anarchic multiplicity."[25] The term *republic* may seem controversial in this context, inasmuch as in my usage it appears to designate no positive regime or disposition (civility, respect, recognition) but only a division or a group of relations. Furthermore, the frisson-inducing modifier *radical* may strike some as superfluous, portentous, or meretricious. Going to the *root* of this or that means, among other things, that such a thing *has* a root, a source, a point of sustenance—and is not itself a root, for instance, or another sort of organic or semiorganic system, a rhizome, say, or a machine, as in Marx and Deleuze.

And yet I sense that what is at stake in contemporary accounts of political organization is precisely the difficult assertion of relation (in the nominative as well as the verbal senses) as the practice of positive freedom. The modern republic is not, in the description I will advance, a regime of laws that promote civic recognition and allow "someone," as Philip Pettit has defined it, "to enjoy non-domination . . . [to] live among others [in such a way that] . . . no other has the capacity to interfere on an arbitrary basis in their choices."[26] Neither is it a modality of communitarianism that seeks (promotes, relies upon) participatory actualization, as it is for John Pocock.[27] It accepts what Antonio Negri takes to be its principal disqualification: "Despite its merits," he says, "republican discourse remains linked to the transcendental tradition." This link is indeed critical. (The claim that one has successfully unlinked oneself from the "transcendental tradition" seems to me a gross form of disavowal in general and a striking instance of bad faith in Negri's work, as I will try to show below.) The debt republicanism bears, in my description, to the transcendental tradition manifests itself not as affirmation but as the explicit engagement with and displacement of what Negri goes on to call "the philosophy of the One, of a reduction of multiplicity, and of the alienation of the subject through mechanisms of representation."[28] Radical republicanism is superficially closer to the political position described by value pluralists in the tradition of Isaiah Berlin, Thomas Nagel, and Judith Thomson, for whom values are genuinely heterogeneous and incompatible. A value-pluralist account of modern republicanism thus acknowledges the need for political institutions to be flexible and capacious enough to permit fundamentally incompatible values to be exercised with a minimum of social violence (coercion, policing, surveillance).[29]

These three accounts of republicanism seem to me tellingly negative, or importantly vacuous. "Only connect!"—the aesthetico-humanistic principle of high modernism—translates violently into political practice: "Only relate!" where the stress falls on the first term, "*only* relate." (*Only* provide a frame where the positive freedom to create relations—libidinal, political, economic—is freed from constraint, the institution itself functioning negatively or passively with respect to the relations thus generated). *Pace* Pettit, the role of the *radical* republic—the gory modifier seems to me required here—flows precisely from the irreducible capacity that others have, both as political agents and as objects in the world, "to interfere on an arbitrary basis" with every other—that is, to provoke terror in me. To guard and promote in each political subject and in each body of the republic as such, as the defining condition of political subjectivity, the capacity to interfere, the right to arbitrariness (that is, to understand mute or immanent capacity in the form of a claim or an interest) is the positive ethico-political norm of the radical republic.

Let me try to be more precise before I turn to fleshing out this positive norm. I would like to consider very briefly two lines of thought that bear a different relation to what Poe calls "the imagination of man" than the tradition of critique, lines of thought or lexicons in which a different model of "surplus value" is at work and where the relation of normative contexts to normative concepts in use (of the domain of rule giving to that of rule following) is not imagined as one of ontological, logical, or temporal priority. Together, they will give a better sense of the ethical, psychological, and political axes on which I am projecting the shape of this modern, radical republic.

Emmanuel Levinas's famous, and famously reticent, definition of responsibility runs like this: "Responsibility prior to any free commitment, the oneself outside of all the tropes of essence, would be responsibility for the freedom of the others. The irremissible guilt with regard to the neighbor is like a Nessus tunic my skin would be."[30] This is not, of course, Levinas's only brush with skin, always a freighted figure in his lexicon.[31] ("How strangely beautiful are these pages that celebrate the beauty of the skin 'with wrinkles, a trace of itself,'" exclaims Paul Ricoeur about Levinas's *Otherwise than Being.*[32]) We are far here from contemplating or caressing the skin's beauty, though the symbolic pathos of the experience is much the same whether the skin burns and kills us or exposes us to the other's loving touch.

Here the weight of the argument is in part borne by the explicit allusion to the story of Nessus, Herakles, and Deianira, famous from (among many other places) Sohocles' *Trachiniae.*[33] This is how Herakles describes the "binding net" the cloak has become for him, "woven by furies, in which [he is] dying." It is surely one of the most enduring representations of pain—of what Levin calls "the most excruciating possible pain"—we have. It is surely not irrelevant to Levinas's argument, and certainly not to my own, that the torture Herakles is put to has no truth-revealing function whatsoever, that his suffering is, in that sense, meaningless.[34] Purely and posthumously retributive, a blind and mechanical force, the gift of the centaur's blood avenges Nessus long after his death; Deianira is his unknowing instrument and his victim. To whom, then, is Herakles responsible? For which of his sins is he paying so terrible a price?

> Glued to my sides, [the tunic] eats my flesh away
> deep down within, and dwells inside my lungs
> choking my breath: already it has drunk
> my fresh warm blood and wasted my whole body,
> binding me with unutterable chains [*aphrastōi tēide cheirōtheis pedēi*].[35]

Beyond the allusion to this appalling scene—to which I will return in brief—Levinas's argument is partly carried in his aphorism's prepositional phrases ("Responsabilité *anterieure à* . . . , le soi-même *en dehors de* . . . , la *responsabilité pour.* . . . L'irremisible culpabilité *à l'egard du* prochain"), for indeed it is the relative position of self and other (others, my neighbor: *les autres, le prochain,* the one who is close at hand), of oneself and the tropes of essence that might be applied to oneself and to others, that is in play. Responsibility is *pre*-positional: it is the ground on which the positions that we occupy with respect to each other and with respect to being are drawn, occupied, contested. Understanding this pre-positionality, Levinas's lines show, requires addressing two classes of ambiguity coordinated in the aphorism.[36] Note in the first place the awkward, almost appositional "my skin would be": the clause translates *comme la tunique de Nessus de ma peau,* intelligently capturing the double ambivalence of Levinas's *de*: responsibility is like the tunic, which is what my skin *is* (and this skin-tunic, the trace of another's poisoned blood and of another's love, is irremissibly and terminally attached to the other me that lies below this skin-tunic), or responsibility is like the tunic that my skin *wears* (that I wear over my skin), the skin of my skin, a covering, a shelter, an outer form, or a substitute, a trope or a figure cloaking and revealing the shape of my skin, a trope of essence.

Levinas's mythological language, sheltered behind two "likes," is not a cloak or a tunic that one can strip from the (skin of the) aphorism, any more than the aphorism and the allusion can be stripped from the body of *Otherwise than Being*; it is not a trope, or not only a trope, a concrete term substituting for a concept on the basis of some likeness that obscures but also reveals that concept's essence. And, simultaneously, it *is* a cloak or tunic, made of a different material from my skin (from the argument's concepts), bearing the traces of my enemy's blood, a gift intended to preserve my love—traces of my guilt with respect to others. The mythology of Nessus's tunic (the clutch of stories, characters, literatures the name evokes) is, in short, both like a normative context that sets the criteria for understanding Levinas's argument concerning the normative concept of responsibility and like that concept itself: like its borders, the walls sheltering it, a deadly and foreign part of its skin. Responsibility not only stands outside of the tropes of essence (before, in advance of; it is presupposed), but exists otherwise than (as) being, *autrement qu'être ou au-delà de l'essence.* It is, in the term that Sophocles' Herakles uses to designate the deadly intimacy that Nessus's cloak bears to his skin, *aphrastos*: unutterable, marvelous, inexpressible, too wonderful for words; incomprehensible; beyond thought.[37]

Unspeakable.

Levinas achieves three goals, linked but distinct. They operate on different levels. He shows, in the first place, that the "surplus validity" or "semantic excess" of normative ethical concepts (for instance, responsibility) can be regulated only according to a normative dimension or context that is also (but in a different way) excessive. But in the second place, and relatedly, Levinas also shows the instability of the distinction between the concrete instance of judgment (this or that circumstance arises and a decision must be taken: for instance, the decision to sacrifice constitutionality to the life of the city, as Levin might phrase it, or the decision to entertain the supposititious scenario he outlines in the first place), the normative concept we apply in making the decision (responsibility, or the possibility and value of weighing one life and many), and the normative context stipulating the uses of that concept. The lexicon of positionality is inadequate to the distinction; so is the lexicon of ontology. Statements, including the minimal assertion required to designate a concept as a concept, that is, the assertion of self-identity that underlies any sort of predication (a city is a city, or it is other than a city; a citizen is a citizen, or he is not; an act is an act, or it is something else; a decision is a decision; and so forth), are both tropes of essence (substitutes for an essence: "like" being, "like" the being of the concept) and the concept's essential expression (its skin: what marks it off from contiguous concepts; a city's walls).

What lexicon is adequate to the ethical task? Levinas's final step is to link the paradoxical ontology of the norm (the normative ethical concept, the normative context regulating its use) to the domain of mythology. We see a similar gesture in Husserl, some ten years earlier; in Levinas the link is necessarily a weak one ("The irremissible guilt with regard to the neighbor is *like* a Nessus tunic my skin would be")—or rather, what is pertinent in his work (as distinct from Husserl's treatment of mythology, to which I will return in my conclusion) is the double gesture that mythology requires. On the one hand, there is a weakening of the normative element, precisely because the myth is never one: the variety of interpretations the myth requires, its cultural mediations, its fictionality, the uncertainty of its sources—all ensure that mythic names are not, in a classic sense, tropes of something else, transports from the abstract domain of the concept (for instance, in this case, guilt, or love, or responsibility, or revenge) to the concrete domain of teachable images. The story of the cloak of Nessus thematizes this dispersing of the myth's unity, and it is in part for this reason that it so complexly figures the problem of responsibility. Levinas refers to it as *Nessus's* cloak, but of course it is not the centaur's at all, both because the centaur is already dead and because it is Deianira's cloak to give, a gift in return for the gift Herakles has sent her, the slave-princess Iole, for whose love Herakles destroyed her parents' city, and because the poisoned blood upon the cloak is the trace not just of what was most intimately proper to the centaur but also of what was most alien to him, the poison that ended Nessus's life, as it must, directly or indirectly, end Herakles'.[38]

Every gift has more than one function—life giving, life ending. Every myth, every name that names a myth, does as well. It is impossible to decide, and the *Trachiniae* derives its enduring power from this undecidability, whether the centaur's blood acts as a figure and a vehicle of retribution for Herakles' guilt in the centaur's death, or in the betrayal of Deianeira, or in the destruction of Trachis. And yet these are three extraordinarily different crimes, if they even are crimes—private, ceremonial, civic, with consequences on very different levels. In the cloak of Nessus, which both is and is not the centaur's, which will guarantee that Herakles will never love another as he does Deianeira (because it binds him to her with deadly, unspeakable ties), the dispersal of responsibility for another's life and death loses its bounds. The deadly, unutterable bond of the centaur's blood spreads beyond the skin of Herakles and, touched by it as well, Sophocles' audience henceforth wears like a skin the ingrowing skin of others' blood.

For—and this is the second gesture that the mythological norm requires—the quality of anteriority and cultural sanction that the myth provides, *despite or because of its lack of normative coherence, and distinct from its disputed content*, stands precisely in the place of a norm, the defective cultural universalism provided by received names and languages (fictions, stories, myths), also the dissemination of guilt, the movement beyond responsibility for one another: *res publica*.[39]

The word I will use to designate the defective universal on which ethical judgments and political interests may be coordinated is *terror*; *terror* is also the name for both the class of defective universals and the experience that this class of terms elicits in and for the city. I am borrowing the term from the languages of political philosophy and aesthetics; the links between revolutionary Terror and the dynamics of the sublime—par excellence, the aesthetic experience of the unutterable, the marvelous, the inexpressible, and so on—have been well studied. In associating terror with the possibility of unutterable but radically democratic binds, I am seeking, however, to activate a different group of normative contexts. (Different language games, different sets of conventions, themselves also highly inflected by Romantic aesthetics.)

"How does Levinasian subjectivity look," Simon Critchley has asked, "from the perspective of the second Freudian topography?"[40] It might look something like what follows. (My second tack into the ethics of terror.)

Recall the dissonant chord that Sigmund Freud plays, at the beginning of his 1920 work *Beyond the Pleasure Principle*, in the shadow of a war that had rung the first knell on the fantasy that European "culture" was indeed "one," let alone universal.[41] The context is a discussion of the relation between the neuroses that attend "severe mechanical concussions," including war traumas—"shell-shock," or what today we would call post-traumatic stress disorders provoked by accidents, the shock of war, sudden emergencies—and what Freud helpfully calls the "traumatic neuroses of peace."[42] The latter are characterized, he tells us, by their suddenness and by the surprise, fright, or terror (*Schreck*) that attend them. He continues:

> Fright [*Schreck*], fear [*Furcht*] and anxiety [*Angst*] are improperly used as synonymous expressions; they are in fact capable of clear distinction in their relation to danger [*Gefahr*]. "Anxiety" describes a particular state of expecting the danger or preparing for it, even though it may be an unknown one. "Fear" requires a definite object of which to be afraid. "Fright" (or terror), however, is the name we give to the state a person gets into when he has run into danger without being prepared for it; it emphasizes the factor of surprise [*betont das Moment der Überraschung*]. . . . There is something about anxiety that protects its subject against fright and so against fright-neuroses.[43]

Just how fraught the diagnosis and treatment of "war neuroses" was, not just for the societies facing the return of soldiers afflicted with a variety of intractable "nervous" conditions but also for the medical establishment, may be judged by the number of editorials both the popular and the professional press, on the Continent and in England, devoted to the subject. The most famous is perhaps "Neurasthenia and Shell Shock," a piece that *The Lancet* devoted in March 1916 to patients who could not be called either "sane or insane," inhabitants of a "no-man's-land, a *regnum protisti-cum*, which really defies definition. This nebulous zone shelters many among the sad examples of nervous trouble sent home from the front."[44]

Let's set aside, for the moment, the question whether Freud's description of the etiology of traumatic neuroses is medically correct; let's ignore for now the objection that the "clear distinction" between "states" cannot carry the weight that Freud seems to want it to. Indeed, it's worth remembering that the distinction does not have much currency outside the pages of *Beyond the Pleasure Principle*: Freud roughly sketches it out but does not pursue it systematically, and after *Beyond the Pleasure Principle* he not infrequently returns to the habit of using *Angst*, "anxiety," to designate what here he calls *Schreck*, "fright" or "terror."[45] The term *Schreck* is nicely ambiguous, covering a range of senses, which run from horror to pleasant surprise. What most importantly distinguishes "fear" and "anxiety" from "fright" or "terror," though, is the status of the object or circumstance that causes the affect. Fear is a state of mind caused by distinct objects (as in I am afraid of my cousin's knife, I am afraid of spiders); anxiety is caused by the apprehension of a particular temporal relation to a state of affairs (I am apprehensive about something, even if I don't know what it is, because I reckon that it lies before me, awaits me, will cross my path in the future). Finally, *Schreck*, "fright" or "terror," is attached neither to a distinct object or a particular state of affairs nor to a particular apprehension of time but instead to the disconcerting encounter with something for which one was not prepared, whose "object-ness" or "state-of-affairsness" is not given, defined, or established. Terror: I have suddenly encountered something—I don't know what it is, and I don't know what my encountering it means, and as a result I don't know what this encounter then may signify for every other encounter I can imagine, which is to say that this surprise encounter may not be a surprising moment at all but may extend to all the other moments that make up what I remember and to all those that make up what I foresee for myself.

One understands why Freud tends to forget that he has drawn this "clear distinction": he's onto something very troubling indeed—troubling to his readers, but also troubling to his efforts to come up with a methodical description of the psychic apparatus. But one also understands why he is forced into it: of the distinct affects or experiences he is distinguishing, only what he calls "terror" seems to respond to the situation that *The Lancet* described in the returning soldiers. In the absence of an object or an event that provokes terror, no provision can be made against it (since it's caused by an encounter that's unforeseeable), and in the immediate instance no therapeutic means of overcoming terror present themselves. Terror's effects cannot be assessed against my past or against the future outcome of my actions; the possibility of terror is itself, one might say, a source of anxiety. Once my fright is over in this or that instance, the terrifying circumstances interpreted, assimilated to a state of affairs, *objectified*, then I may say in retrospect that I feared this or that object or circumstance. But to be terrified is to lack both fear and anxiety: to be in terror is to be without an object one can reckon with and without a time one can assess. The terror of the encounter extends beyond the encounter; indeed, it threatens to become not an anomalous species of but the norm for every encounter, another name for the *event*.

I opened this Introduction by glancing at the second normative context in which the word *terror* operates today: the context of the "terrorist" threat to the city (to the nation, to liberal democratic values, to the West) and of the "war on terror." The construction of terror that I am suggesting—of the city, of biopolitical and ethico-political life, and of the relations among them—is necessarily inflected by this context. But "terrorism" is not "terror," though what are vulgarly called "acts of terror" or "terrorism" can produce "terror" in the sense I intend it. Incidentally, however. The term *terrorism* works in part—by association, by contamination, by displacement—to obscure the necessary work of terror in the modern republic. Take Levin's brief example. Everything about it tends away from the terrible ethos that I am describing: the consolidation of a normative context (the "atomic bomb on Manhattan Island . . . at noon on July 4 . . . the fateful day") by appeal to a mythic but immediate and immediately communicative collection of tropes ("July 4"), the appeal to the equally mythic vantage of the outcome to justify torture in the present (a doctrine of preemptive torture is implied, judgments without contingency), the insularity of the city, sheltered behind physical as well as conceptual walls (an island, and an exemplary space), the foreclosure of "semantic excess" (a "terrorist" is a "terrorist," a city a city, the information elicited by torture is ipso facto the salvation of the city); the objectivity, or rather, the objectality of the scenario: what terrifies us about the terrorist is known in advance (it is entailed in his identity: a terrorist makes the usual threats, with the usual outcomes). The figure of the terrorist, abjectly embodied, displayed imaginatively for us here in pain, connected fluidly, electrically, to our own, shelters our imagination from more unsettling thoughts. We apply the electrodes to the terrorist, and the current flows in both directions, though always (our fantasy is a prophylactic: terrorism is prophylaxis) with different signs, different effects. "Our" active, deciding body—our ethico-political body—comes to life alongside the body we are tormenting; modern political subjectivity flows from the decision to subject another to "the most excruciating possible pain." A Gothic scenario: a biopolitics that draws its life from abjection; a necropolitics.

Terror works otherwise, and must be thought otherwise. For me to tie myself to another today or to find myself bound to him or her, with unutterable or unspeakable links, rather than with the current of necropolitical subjection-subjectification requires that I distribute responsibility for the survival of ethico-political life and that I attend to and guard the occurring of that distribution. Both of these are ethico-political tasks, roughly of a public and a private sort, respectively; each is both (in Berlin's sense) a positive as well as a negative task, entered into both affirmatively and passively. (The line between the four modifying terms—*public, private, positive, negative*—is not, of course, given.) The public task involves devising formal regimes that both recognize and distribute the exceptional positions of slave and sovereign across citizenship, that design and shelter a wounded and divided sovereignty. The private task entails a different sort of work—hermeneutic, destructive, or rather, deconstructive, dispositional. Not *cura sui*, as Foucault would have it, but rather the cultivation of *insecuritas sui*.

Taken together, the two may be conceived to promote "terror"—a description, however, too lurid to be terribly useful, and in any case misleading to the extent that it invites confusions that my argument works to dispel. (Between "terror" and "terrorism," between the forms of agency attributable to each, and so on.) Each task alone and both together (and they can only be undertaken together) require concepts or para-concepts whose "surplus validity" or "semantic excess" is regulated neither immanently nor mechanistically but according to defective universals. Seen in this light, terror is not, as it is for Hannah Arendt or Adriana Cavarero, "the essence of totalitarian domination," the "realization" and the "execution" of what Arendt calls the "law of movement"—a tendency of thought characteristic of the great ideologies of the mid-nineteenth century, consisting in "the refusal to view or accept anything 'as it is' and in the consistent interpretation of everything as being only a stage of some future development."[46]

To be "in terror" or "terrified," to promote "terror" in the special sense I intend, entails decoupling Arendt's two propositions and fashioning a sort of thought between refusal and providentialism, on the edge of or in the fissure between the two terms. (A visual, linguistic echo: the "barely perceptible fissure, which, extending from the roof of the [House of Usher] in front, made its way down the wall in a zigzag direction, until it became lost in the sullen waters of the tarn."[47]) Here thought thinks through, experiences, is responsible for and to, and guards the failure of the objectality of objects (things become other things, or their borders become unfixed and encroach upon others, on oneself), the failure of the discreteness (the calculability, the regularity, the spatiality) of being in time, the failure of the rough closure of concepts (whose borders also become unfixed and irregular). Here thought distributes divided sovereignty across the wounded concept of the class of subjects.

Roderick Usher, a "bounden slave" to "an anomalous species of terror," finds in it a crippling pathology, misanthropy, a heightened aesthetic awareness, finally, death. As a ground for judgment and as a ground for envisioning the new republic, being in "terror," being "terrified," is indispensable.

My argumentation is, accordingly, inclined to *provoke failures* and to guard and keep them: to rub histories and genres against the grain, interjecting vestigial genealogies and dividing, always dividing. I treat familiar texts and rather arcane ones—canonical works, firmly hedged behind thickets of received interpretations and conventional evaluations; but also texts and works that lie aslant governing traditions. Well-known local stories (often English, German, French: hegemonic stories, their borders well guarded, saturated, semantically unfolded) jostle up against unfamiliar ones (the case of Spain, that liminal ground for Europe, recurs; Algeria's ghostly shape in the European postwar imaginary; the United States). Established histories, too: a Sophoclean Oedipus proves more our contemporary than his successor, Seneca's; Derrida's analysis of sovereignty passes necessarily through those of Shakespeare and Robert Persons; Agamben's topology runs through Louvain and Toledo; Husserl's late melancholia comes up against the work of his contemporary, the Spanish philosopher María Zambrano. This divisive, aleatory path seeks to hinge ethical judgment to an unfinished concept of the political under the aspect, not of *tukhē*, "fate," but of contingency, the encounter. "It could have been otherwise!" cries the philosopher in Althusser's late rendering of what he calls the "subterranean current of the materialism of the encounter." It *is*, otherwise.

The chapters that follow proceed in a roughly chronological order and make what can be called a historical argument. European "modernity," one line of historiography has suggested, is tied to the coincidence of, or to the interaction between, secularization and mercantilism. The sixteenth century is the stage on which this encounter takes place; the results—proto-national formations, the rise of *jus publicum europaeum*, the desacralization of sovereignty—register unevenly throughout Europe and over the succeeding centuries, and only come to a full and stable articulation in the wake of the French Revolution. Political theology asks: What residues of an incomplete secularization, and an incomplete desacralization of the sovereign's body, haunt European modernity? The story I tell here is punctual, as well—it moves between the period of early modernity, the late Enlightenment, and the struggles of European decolonization in the mid-twentieth century. The argument, however, does not primarily concern residual or emergent cultural formations. One could summarize it in this way: "The modern experience of 'terror' is the residue, or marks the reemergence, of an incomplete desacralization of the 'terror' invested in, and provoked by, the sovereign body in premodernity." My goal is to provide an answer on a different level to these two questions: What form of political association is appropriate to the smoothed, radically deterritorialized landscape of the postnational age? How does ethico-political life learn to *guard* terror? What I call the *modern republic*—Sadean, terrible—is the answer I propose to the first question; as an answer to the second, I suggest the methodological principle this book seeks to outline and to practice: a *wild materialism*, nondialectical, historical, aleatory.

I begin by drawing some distinctions, genealogical as well as conceptual. In Chapter 1, "The Ethic of Terror," I show how terror can be distinguished from terrorism. The chapter opens by analyzing the persistence and function of organic models of association in the work of Slavoj Žižek and then proposes an alternative account based on a close analysis of the discursive construction of one of the best-known acts of targeted terrorism of the twentieth century, the assassination by ETA in 1973 of the Spanish president, Admiral Luis Carrero Blanco. The event provoked wide comment at the time and was the subject of a number of journalistic accounts and of *Operación Ogro*, a 1979 film by Gillo Pontecorvo. The chapter traces the event's imaginary reconstruction through automobile advertisements, photographs, newspaper reports, historiographies, Franco's address to the nation at year's end, and the memoirs of the ETA team that carried out the assassination. The complex of accounts, I argue, constructs the event of the assassination according to a logic that confirms the organic conception of the state promoted by the Spanish Falange under Franco, furnishes an instrumental, heroic counternarrative still loosely expressed in the Falange's conceptual lexicon, and also, simultaneously, describes a remarkable domain (a time; a physical, urban space; an epistemological epoch) of objectless anxiety—of terror—on which a concept of an-organic sociality can be imagined.

Chapters 2 and 3, "*Phares*; or, Divisible Sovereignty" and "The Logic of Sovereignty," provide an account of the concept of wounded sovereignty. They focus on the logico-political imaginaries of European early modernity, the moment when, as Carl Schmitt and his closest readers have suggested, the secularization of theological concepts, in particular the concept of sovereignty, is articulated with the hypothesis of its indivisibility and begins its slow refiguration of the concept of the political. In Chapter 2, "*Phares*; or, Divisible Sovereignty," I distinguish between the Christological, heroic, and sacrificial division of substance that Jean-Luc Nancy associates with community—which tends to reinstate the sovereignty of an indivisible act of decision governing the sharing, *partage*, of power—and a pharisaical division of matter, which does not. The former rests upon the determining, Bodinian claim that sovereignty is necessarily (logically as well as practically) indivisible. The latter, by contrast, rests upon what Derrida calls, in his last works, not a logic but an "aporetic of divisible sovereignty." In Chapter 3, "The Logic of Sovereignty," I focus on what Giorgio Agamben calls the logical "zone of indistinction" on which sovereign decisions stand. The scenes that I treat—one historically documented, the so-called conflict of Louvain regarding future contingents, between the rhetorician Pierre de Rivo and the theologian Henri de Zomeren (the conflict stretches roughly from 1465 to 1479); the other perhaps mythological, Archbishop of Toledo Juan Martínez Guijarro's ill-fated 1546 effort to demystify the legend of the so-called Cave of Hercules, as narrated in 1671 by Cristóbal de Lozano—provide a complex picture of the strange logic of sovereignty and of the logic of historiography that seeks to account for its emergence and "modern" characteristics. They are also linked documents in the earliest conceptualization of the relation between governance, logic, and the experience of terror.

What does it mean to live in and according to terror? What sort of concept is terror? In what way can it provide a social frame, rules to live by, an aporetic, an ethos? For whom? The following two chapters engage these questions in the historical frame afforded by the Enlightenment and its most severe contemporaneous critics—Sade and Marx. In Chapter 4, "*Materia* in the Critique of Autonomy," I study the way that the Idealist philosophical tradition imagines the emergence of philosophical concepts. I tack into the matter through the work of Louis Althusser, for whom the question takes shape at the nexus of a particularly rich set of problems: how to imagine historical events (including the appearing of a concept) outside the Hegelian "absorption of the *e*-vent by the notion of *Ad*-vent," as he puts it in his thesis for Gaston Bachelard at the École normale supérieure, "Du contenu dans la pensée de G. W. F. Hegel" ("On Content in the Thought of G. W. F. Hegel," 1947); whether concepts are produced (and if so, what sort of labor is entailed in that production), or discovered, or posited, or arise contingently; whether the "effectivity" of a concept can be read in a particular discourse despite the absence of that concept (the concept of the relation between a structure—economic, social—and its elements, for instance); whether life, or *a* life, can be said to have a concept. "*Materia* in the Critique of Autonomy" shows that Althusser's account of the emergence and circulation of concepts entails a dramatic redefinition of the term: concepts (for example, the concept of the common good or the concept of sovereignty) are no longer (as in Kant) *raepresentationes comunes* but emerge as nonrepresentational expressions, in line with a specifically literary materialism the chapter finds in and sketches through the highly overdetermined encounter between Marx and Hegel on the nature of the state. Terror, I suggest, is a concept of this sort, but also a name we can give to the class of paradoxically open, non–self-identical concepts, produced according to the spontaneous rules that govern the emergence and circulation of Althusserian or (better) *material* concepts and regulative of conduct and thought on the model of the same paradoxically spontaneous rules.

Chapter 5, "A Sadean Community," considers three ways one might seek to describe this class of material concepts (that is, to define "terror" in this sense), in such a way that they can become an alternative to instrumental, foundational logics of association. The first is the radical democratic challenge to "dialectical logics" found in the line of thinkers who in this respect follow Horkheimer and Adorno (Mouffe and Laclau, Hardt and Negri). The second is the pragmatic, liberal democratic alternative proposed by Richard Rorty. Both, I argue, depend upon two insufficiently elaborated concepts, which work in part by reinforcing each other, in part by returning to an inadequate representational logic: on one side, what could be called a weak account of contingency (antagonistic social interests and forces are irreducible; nevertheless, a formal political or juridical frame can be generated for converting antagonism into agonism); on the other, a heroic account of the function of culture in suturing irreducible social antagonisms. Narratives allow us to redescribe ourselves, Rorty proposes; the "political process of constitution," Hardt and Negri conclude, "will have to take place on this open terrain of forces with a positive logic"—an imaginary terrain produced culturally before it is defended politically. The third alternative to instrumental logics of association, a radical republicanism based in the notion of distributed, sovereign pleasure, does not suffer from this double weakness. Both the strong account of contingency one finds in Sade's *La philosophie dans le boudoir* (*Philosophy in the Bedroom*) and that work's critique of cultural heroism take shape in a new pedagogy imagined to be prior (logically as well as chronologically) to any political account of association—Dolmancé standing in place of Diotima, as Lacan has it.

In Chapter 6, "Three Women, Three Bombs," *Wild Materialism* returns to the immediate historical context with which the book opens— the ticking-bomb scenario, the assassination of Spain's president in 1973. It treats the imbrication of the phenomenon of European decolonization with the emergence of the specific form of terrorism that occupies the media and much of the cultural imaginary today: the fantasmatic figure of fundamentalist Islamic terrorism, as embodied in the figure of the veiled female bomber. I turn to two of Gillo Pontecorvo's films, *Kapo* (1960) and the much better-known *The Battle of Algiers* (1965–66). The chapter opens by discussing the seeming evenhandedness with which *The Battle of Algiers* balances the atrocities of the French *paras* and the FLN's bombs. I then place the ethical stance that this seeming objectivity implies in three con- texts: the cultural-historical context of the debate, in Algerian and in main- stream French culture of the late 1950s and early 1960s, over the role of the *haik* or veil worn by traditional Muslim women; the Orientalizing visual tradition (following Delacroix and others) that depicts, in postcards, erotic *curiosa*, and works of high art, the moment of the Algerian woman's unveiling; and the context provided by the critical-philosophic contrast established by Jacques Rivette, Serge Daney, and others between Ponte- corvo's film technique in representing "historical" events (the women's concentration camp in *Kapo*, as well as *The Battle of Algiers*) and that of Alain Resnais, particularly in *Night and Fog*. The two small cultural storms at issue—one over the strategic function that lay intellectuals (Pierre Bourdieu, in dialogue with Franz Fanon) ascribed to Algerian women's reassumption of the veil, the other over the aestheticizing technique that came to be called, eponymously, "the tracking shot in *Kapo*"—inflect the "three women, three bombs" montage representing the terrorist bomb- ings at the heart of *The Battle of Algiers*. The requirement of representabil- ity, ethical as well as technical, leads to an "abject" logic (Rivette, referring to *Kapo*), to a kind of concentration-camp pornography.[48] *The Battle of Algiers*, which famously and controversially appears to stage the conflict between two instrumental logics, the logic of torture (the ticking-bomb scenario) and the instrumental use of terrorism, shows how the opposition between these two logics reaches a common limit at the unrepresentable.

Wild Materialism concludes with a concrete treatment of the conceptual scenarios the book has set out. In "Distracted Republic," the radical republicanism one finds in Sade, the wild materialism of the Althusserian concept of the political, the critique of the suturing function of the cultural sphere, and the aporetics of divisible sovereignty are conjugated in an analysis of the concept of the republic taken from twentieth-century political history: from the tragic failure of the republican model with the defeat of the Spanish Republic in 1939. The chapter reads the work of the Spanish republican philosopher María Zambrano alongside Husserl's 1935 "Vienna Lecture." Zambrano's melancholic account envisions the republic as an unfinished *empresa*, a labor to be carried out but also a regulative image or representation; her paradoxical analysis contrasts to the mythic "heroism of reason" that Husserl envisions will lead Europe out of the darkness of fascism. The form of association that guards and stands on friable, paradoxical, weak universals settles neither in the melancholic disposition nor in the heroic. It does not correspond to either of these, nor does it result from them. It passes instead through the *relation* between the two and seeks to extend the time and purchase of that unsettled and unsettling movement. The modern republic is (it begins with, it ends upon) the regime of this movement. The effort to become "republican" in this sense is an effort to live in and distribute, share, and extend the strong terror of weak concepts.

CHAPTER I

The Ethic of Terror

Movement is the indefiniteness and imperfection of every politics. It
always leaves a residue. . . . the movement is that which if it is, is as if
it wasn't, it lacks itself [*manca a se stesso*], and if it isn't, is as if it was,
it exceeds itself. It is the threshold of indeterminacy between an excess
and a deficiency which marks the limit of every politics in its
constitutive imperfection.

—GIORGIO AGAMBEN, "Movement"

It might seem superfluous to talk about the motives of jokes, since the
aim of getting pleasure must be recognized as a sufficient motive for
the joke work. . . . The second fact which makes an enquiry into the
subjective determination of jokes necessary is the generally
recognized experience that no one can be content with having made
a joke for himself alone. An urge to tell the joke to someone is
inextricably bound up with the joke-work.

—SIGMUND FREUD, *Jokes and their Relation to the Unconscious*

In the right of sovereignty, death was the moment of the most obvious
and the most spectacular manifestation of the absolute power of the
sovereign; death now becomes, in contrast, the moment when the
individual escapes all power, falls back on himself and retreats, so to
speak, into his own privacy. Power no longer recognizes death. Power
literally ignores death. To symbolize all this, let's take, if you will, the
death of Franco, which is after all a very, very interesting event.

—MICHEL FOUCAULT, *Society Must Be Defended*

Why Jokes Must Be Defended

Here's a joke with a trick to it.

Francisco Franco spoke with a magisterial "we" that some found pleas-
antly archaic, others rather sinister. Taken with the syncopating hand
movements that punctuated his speeches, the collective pronoun irresist-
ibly wed the notional corporate body of the Spanish state to Franco's own.
In the early 1970s Franco is reputed to have announced the beginning of

34

a new economic movement intended to catalyze the Spanish economy, which was threatening to stagnate after the brief boom of the 1960s. News of the announcement took the shape of this *chiste*, to be told with the Caudillo's ponderous diction and mimicking the up-and-down movements of his hand: "After thirty years of a postwar state, we have decided to change our movement [or "the direction of our movement," or "our political program," or "our political allegiance"; *hemos decidido cambiar de movimiento*],"—a phrase to be accompanied, midway, by a change in the direction of the joker's hand, interrupted in its vertical flight and now made to move horizontally, with an equally stolid side-to-side rhythm.

This was neither the first nor the best joke told about Franco, but it may be among the most subversive, since it requires the person telling it to envision what for many was the moment's most pressing political fantasy, the promise of a change of political movement or of the political direction to be given the country upon the dictator's death, by assuming the character of the Caudillo in word as well as gesture.[1] To the cultural critic, the *chiste* furnishes a royal road into the remarkable association between the Falangist imaginary and the figure of the hand.[2] A political historian turns to it for an example of the migration of the term *Movimiento* during the Spanish postwar era, from its more or less proper historical use in the expression *Movimiento Falangista*, the Fascist-inspired movement founded by José Antonio Primo de Rivera, to the Movimiento Nacional after the nationalist victory in 1939, then to the entirely abstract *movimiento* found in the dictator's speeches after the Matesa scandal in 1969. (That was a massive, well-publicized corruption case involving an important textile company, one of Spain's largest public banks, three of Franco's former ministers and appointees, and the sitting minister of development, Laureano López Rodó, who owed his appointment to Carrero.[3]) For our notional political historian, the semantic movements of *movimiento* marked Franco's effort to distance himself from the Falange and in the early 1970s from its heirs, Manuel Fraga, José Solís, and Fernando María Castiella.[4]

Those keen to understand the shapes taken by Spanish cultural anxieties today, on the country's joining the European Union and renegotiating matters long cherished as the prerogative of national sovereignty, must puzzle out the emergence of popular cultural treatments of the years of transition alongside institutional efforts to rescue the material traces of events long repressed: the opening of mass graves, the consolidation and democratization of access to Civil War archives, the surprising success of television serials like *Cuéntame cómo pasó* (*Tell Me How It All Happened*), the long-running serial chronicling a Madrid family's experience of the decades from the mid 1960s through Franco's death and the transition to democracy, etc. And, of course, the resuscitation of old jokes, which now circulate with a nostalgic surplus value hard at times to square with their sharply satiric beginnings.

Finally, a cultural anthropologist might note that the moving hand speaks to the way in which political change is imagined at a moment when the concept of political movement and the signifier *movimiento* remain tied to the corporatist model of association—indeed, to the very body—that this notional movement might seek to abandon. Or one might, in an attempt at disciplinary synthesis, put the matter like this. For Spanish society since 1989, economic and social integration into the EU is shaped by a troubled recollection of the "transition," the movement from forty years of authoritarian rule to a constitutional democracy federating weakly autonomous regions under a nominal monarchy. The shapes that this recollection takes are tricky to describe, because for the Spain that lived that transition, thinking "beyond" the "movement" so as to "change movements" decisively—thinking through a transition still to be recollected— meant assuming the figure and gestures of the Caudillo so as to work the violence of a gesture upon his body or, less allegorically, assuming the burden of political terror so as to escape or profit from it, so as to work it through reflexively, introject it, consume it. To attach to the hand of the Caudillo the form that retrospective thought about political change can take is to stress the ghostly influence that Franco's body has after its own passing, furnishing a recent history preserved under the entailing shadow of the Movimiento's *mort-main*, or *ley de manos muertas*, as the legislation is called in Spain.[5]

This collection of observations, jokes, and micro-arguments has implications beyond the borders of the Spanish peninsula. Let me group these under three headings.

The first is, broadly speaking, *genealogical*, or better yet, *transitional*. Tracking the emergence of a historical formation, whether social, political, or economic, means not just addressing the transition from one constituted *movimiento* to another one, and not just identifying and describing (in Raymond Williams's wonderful, defining terms) the "structures of feelings" behind these transitions (behind the emergence of one or another form, or the domination of one by another, or the repetition or reconstitution of a residual form), "thought as felt and feeling as thought: practical consciousness of a present kind, in a living and inter-relating continuity."[6] The trick of the matter is to understand what it is that is *present* about "practical consciousness," which is to say, to understand the form and functions that "thought" and "feeling" assume today with regard to this or that historical formation (for instance, with regard to the decline of state fascism in Europe and the emergence of cultural fascism of different sorts in the United States, the Middle East, and Europe as well). To approach the thought and feeling behind emergent historical formations under the aspect of their social and conceptual uses, fantasmatic and practical, here and now, is to understand them as part of a constituent logic that may or may not be explicitly acknowledged (which may or may not be properly thought or felt). Whether it acknowledges the task or not, transitional thought opens on the question posed here by Franco's wandering hand: Do representations of political change ever become detached from sublime bodies? In what ways, under what conditions, do sublime political bodies suffer dematerializations or resemanticizations that effectively change their movements (direction, value—a whole microphysics is entailed here)?

The second, general level on which Franco's hand waves from within this joke is topographical and bears precisely on what we call *thought* and on what we call *feeling*. Much of the work that this joke does—and that many others that it stands for here do as well—appears to happen just where Williams locates the "structures of feeling": where "thought" is "as felt" and "feeling" is "as thought." Williams provocatively and accurately places "art and literature" in this stressing, intermediate location, where they function to articulate structures of feeling—and Franco's wandering hand, too, articulates something about Spanish society in the mid 1970s.[7] But the function of mediation that characterizes Williams's understanding of articulation is controversial when applied to art and literature, and clearly inadequate to the strange work of the joke. Neither jokes nor art and literature can be reduced to the articulation of "practical consciousness of a present kind," to the articulation of thought and feeling, without putting considerable stress on conventional definitions of all the concepts at issue, as Freud's *Jokes and Their Relation to the Unconscious* makes clear—without, in fact, threatening to disarticulate the lot. No other model of articulation—most prominently, the one set forth as early as *Hegemony and Socialist Strategy* by Laclau and Mouffe, and then independently developed by each—has succeeded any better than Williams's in accounting for the complex function of art and literature, and the joke-work companionably associated with them: a function of articulating and disarticulating thought from feeling and of threatening the integrity of each from within as well as from without. What and how does Franco's hand articulate? Where is it, and where, more generally, are speech acts like it located with respect to thought and to feeling?

The third problem I'd like to draw out of this thin joke might be said to flow from the oddly social context that Freud remarks in the joke-work in general, the "urge to tell the joke *to someone* (that is) inextricably bound up with the joke-work."[8] For Freud, as is well known, this "urge [*Drang*]" derives from our anticipation of the pleasure we expect to take in the relief at discharging the pent-up, chary, "economic" condensations (of words, images, notions) that make up the first, private moment of the joke-work. Jokes are not one social process among others: the binding of economy and discharge they embody verbally and conceptually marks for Freud the opening of the "first person" to the "interpolated third person [*eingescho-benen dritten Person*]."[9] What sort of community, what sort of political association, does the joke entail?

Why the Sphincter Is Sublime

Let's say that the accepted story of the establishment of European nation-alisms and of their apparent, imminent subsumption in meta-national organisms shadows closely the story of the desacralization, politicization, and depoliticization of the notion of terror. One might gloss the story in this way. In accounts of the phenomenology of national or proto-national consciousness, the experience of terror, an affect traditionally restricted to private, aesthetic, or physiological domains, moves suddenly, and to some extent on account of the Enlightenment's normativization of those domains, into the public sphere. The aesthetic vehicle for this movement is the language of the sublime, tied as early as Burke to a reflection on the circumstance of political revolution;[10] its cultural-journalistic vehicle can be found in the eponymous characterization of the Robespierrian revolu-tion as "the Terror," an over-concretization that apotropaically restricts to a particular moment and to a particularly egregious set of behaviors what is in fact a general condition of representative government.[11]

The early national *crainte des masses*, as Balibar calls it, is experienced in both subjective and objective forms, both as the fear that the masses expe-rience toward the forms of identification newly available to them and as the fear that the emergent political establishments experience toward the masses they nominally represent.[12] On the one hand, we might range the social anxieties classically said to follow on the development of modern

forms of identification: anxiety over the first definitions and almost correlative subsumption of a notional private sphere in a public one or vice versa;
more generally, anxiety over the subsumption (facilitated by changes in
communications and technology, the increased ease of movement of persons and capital, etc.) of local modalities of identification—ethnic, geo-
graphical, economic, religious—in larger or differently organized national
ones: in brief, social anxiety expressed as terror of the political and, incidentally, apotropaically, as terror of and resistance to the political classes.
Consider, on the other hand, how, called to administer these larger or
differently organized forms of identification, required to represent a
volonté générale in the face of a *volonté particulière*, a general will in the
face of particular wills forever both subsumed in the public sphere and
irreducible to it, the modern political classes encountered in the masses
and in the "citizen subject" an *extimate* knot of familiar and unfamiliar
interests, interests reducible to political or other representation and interests exceeding these reductions. The terror of the intimately alien mass
and of the citizen-subject (in this case, the genitives are subjective) comes
to be expressed practically as greater or lesser degrees of repression prac-
ticed by the political classes—as political terror, in brief—and in the language of political economics in the commodification of terms intended to
negotiate between particular and collective interests, or between repre-
sentable and unrepresentable interests: the "spirit" of laws or of nations,
the voluntary surrender of the will, the inevitable globalization of capital.

A successful republicanism, it turns out, does not minimize but instead
seeks to understand, guard, and administer these intimate, asymmetrical
terrors and their practical and politico-philosophical expressions: resistance and repression, Schumacherite relocalization (what we might call
small-is-beautification) and economic globalization. We might put it
polemically: radical democratic republicanism nurtures and depends upon
the experience of social terror. This is not a claim that anyone living and
writing after the events of September 11, 2001, can make lightly. Social
terrors, which appear as the critical-epistemological devices on which
republican ethics are to be founded, must be distinguished from the phenomenon of terrorism. This turns out to be a particularly delicate task; it
is not, on that account, any less pressing. Consider Saint-Just's famous
proposition "A republican government has virtue as its principle; otherwise, it has terror."[13] Here the relation between governance and principle
is not political but foundational, the sort of mythic posit that Catherine
Kinztler calls a metaphysical "moving force located beyond the political,
understood as a machine."[14] In Saint-Just, the principles of republican

government reveal themselves to be mythic posits, that is, to be precisely not republican, when the mechanicity of political institutions is laid bare: when the formal devices of republican representation fail to map the field of political interests, when an impasse or a differend arises between the claims of right and the formality of law, or when virtue is not a perspicuous, given term but the opaque occasion of administrative disagreement or, indeed, the contested ground of semantic battles as terrible as the literal ones that they support. In this instance the experience of terror, because it evokes what Kintzler calls "the scenario of an abolition or suspension of the [political] machine," a scenario "equivalent to that of its foundation," becomes not the exceptional but the normative cause for critical reflection on the principles of republican government, in particular, on the sublime asymmetry between the principles and means of government.[15] Deplorable as it may seem, the breaks in the fabric of social experience revealed by the experience of terror become defining attributes of genuinely open, radically democratic states whose institutions seek to negotiate the constitutive antagonism between interest-governed doctrines of right and law.[16]

In this description, social terror becomes the privileged cause of reflection on the status of political principles, and the disruptive and disrupted phenomenology of terror becomes the privileged trope for postnational principles of association. But can social terror also serve as a model for this reflection? Not, seemingly, without assuming the form of a terrorist act. Consider now these pseudo-syllogistic lines from a communiqué that ETA-V published in *Hautsi* in 1973:

> What tactics can the Vietnamese, the Irish, the Basques, etc. rely upon in their fight, when they have been denied every legal and democratic avenue of combating for legitimate rights, under a legal system that is foreign to them? Our objectives are to favor the organization of the working class and of the people, so that the latter, directed by the former, can carry out the revolutionary fight for the national and social liberation of our people. At the same time, revolutionary activities will be directed at dividing and isolating the oppressors, in an effort to radicalize the contradictions that exist in the breast of the exploiting classes [*en el seno de las clases explotadoras*]. . . . This is not terrorism. We are not attacking indiscriminately, but rather attacking selected people, well-defined inasmuch as they are leading members of an oppressor class, or of the repressive apparatus.[17]

ETA's effort to distinguish between the "indiscriminate" attack (terrorism) and the representative act of violence (a justifiable military tactic undertaken in the context of a foreign legal system that sacrifices rights to law) rests on an unstable principle closely related to Saint-Just's wobbly distinction between "terror" and "virtue." The impasse here is both strategic and analytic. To the extent that the "oppressor class" or the "repressive apparatus" are taken to be given, perspicuous terms, then the "terrorist" organization relinquishes the vanguardist function of "laying bare" the mechanicity of a repressive state or conceptual apparatus—purchasing thereby a rationale for every act at the cost of the epistemologically and politically critical function of revealing the mythic foundations of the contradictions in the "oppressors' breast." But say, by contrast, that an organization like ETA seeks to lay bare and exacerbate these contradictions by taking as its target civilians selected precisely because their "representativeness" is *not* self-evident, but must be made manifest. In this case, the organization purchases a critical function at the expense of any immediate political representativeness of its own. The less evident the target's membership in the "repressive apparatus," the more the act's didactic function, which is to make manifest retrospectively the rationale for choosing the target, itself appears as an arbitrary resemanticization, a form of "terrorism" conducted at the level of the sign.

This impasse at the heart of ETA's communiqué allows me to return to my question: Can the experience of social terror serve noninstrumentally as a model for reflecting on political principles obscured by the mechanics of government? If the postnational models of radical democracy that emerge in the shadow of state and/or revolutionary terror nurture and guard an explicit and historical relation to the experience and cultural affect-value of terror (as a cause of reflection, as a trope for an unsutured and open social field, perhaps as a model for reflection upon the political more broadly), then brokering postnational forms of association means opening to scrutiny the double bind of terror disclosed by its instrumentalized form, that is, by what we call terrorism. The double bind consists in this. For the terrorist, the opacity of the relation between individuals and the class interests they represent or can be made to represent must, on the one hand, be maintained: the didactic function of the act of terror being to construct that relation *après coup*, to generate after a first, inexplicable blow a second one in the form of what could be called a political "Aha!"-phenomenon, (re)cognition of the "representativeness" or collusion of the target of the first blow in a repressive apparatus. Yet on the other hand, it must be undermined, in the form of the assertion of the self-evident transparency of the relation between the individual and the class or conceptual interests he or she represents. The logic of terrorism oscillates between the poles of this antinomy, as its tactics move between what Carlos Marighella calls the precision of the guerrilla's "shot" and the "irreparable damage" caused by the terrorist's less discriminating bomb.[18] Radical democratic, republican terror—the affirmative terror of (again, both forms of the genitive govern) postnational, nonconceptual, unevenly deterritorialized and unevenly reterritorializing forms of association—takes shape when this oscillation no longer obtains between the poles of a conceptual antinomy describing "the political" but constitutes the substance of the political itself.

What might it mean, then, to submit the logic of terrorism—as state terrorism, or acts of terrorism against the state, or, as in Al-Qaeda's case, attacks against civilians weakly representative of broad cultural and economic formations—to a critique rooted in the thought of terror? And vice versa: What might it mean to submit republican terror to the strong solvent of terrorism? To turn to the legacies of terrorism so as to make evident the conceptual instability that, nurtured at the heart of the philosophy of terror, remains necessary to a radical democratic postnationalism? Say one associates the cultural experience of political terror with the somaticization of the corporate nation-state (an embodied concept is heir to all the outrages that afflict the flesh: hence the two bodies Kantorowicz famously imagined for the king or the bodies that Franco sports in my opening *chiste*). Here again the case of Spain proves instructive. In the Catholic-mystical form it took for the Falange, the organicism of the state is best summarized in the words of José Antonio Primo de Rivera:

> The Fatherland is a total unity, in which individuals and classes are integrated; the Fatherland cannot be in the hands of the strongest class, nor of the best-organized Party. The Fatherland is a transcendent synthesis, an indivisible synthesis, with its own ends to accomplish. And what we would like is for the movement of today, and the State that it creates, to be the effective, authoritative and authoritarian instrument, in the service of an indisputable unity, of that permanent unity, that irrevocable unity, called Fatherland.[19]

Note two things. First is the paradox that haunts populist authoritarianism: the fatherland is not in the hands of the strongest or the best organized—not because it is in everyone's hands, as it putatively is in a democratic society, but because being *in hands*, being concretely used as a form of concrete power, cannot be an attribute of the transcendent. On the one hand, "movement" and "state" relate to this transcendent synthesis entirely contingently (concrete institutions cannot be said to act for the fatherland, in the sense of having it in their hands) but also as parts of its irrevocable unity. But on the other hand, the "movement of today" imagines the state as the "end" of the fatherland and seeks to fashion the state in that model: the movement, in other words, is conflated with the transcendent, as what accomplishes *fines propios*. The movement serves the fatherland by making its "own ends" available to it, by making certain that the state is the end of the fatherland. The bind is a difficult one: either the movement is unnecessary, because the transcendent synthesis of the fatherland already exists and will produce from itself a material match to its ideality, or else the party is the instrument by means of which the fatherland builds the state in its image, in which case the preexistence of the fatherland is not an a priori but an accidental aspect of the fatherland, one requiring technique, handling, an instrument, a slave. Note, second, that the distinction between state and fatherland (*Estado, Patria*) is a temporal as well as an ontological one. The Falangist state remains to come, but the fatherland is permanent, irrevocable, a concept rather than a materialization; the movement is an instrument both for the creation of the state, for the reconciliation of the matter to the concept, state to fatherland; and, in the resulting state, for the service of the fatherland. In other words, the transcendental synthesis attributed to the party and its goals both exists independently of the concretization of the party and requires the party as its instrument.

Imagine, then, that this unstable relation between party and state becomes a strategic element in an ideology that both identifies *movimiento* with *Patria* and makes the first the means to achieve the true spirit of the latter. Imagine, too, that the fantasy of a rupture in the organicist nation-state model locates that rupture precisely at the point of the greatest mystification of that strategic element: where the "transcendent synthesis" of the party's political apparatus with the state's conceptual extension takes concrete form, that is, in the homology between the concrete shape of the party leadership and the conceptual extension of the fatherland. In Franco's hand, in short—executive, hortatory, indexical, monitory, and, above all, uncannily both a concrete and an entirely allegorical organ.

Here is an example of an act of terrorism that attaches to that homology. I'm turning to it in part for its spectacular shape, in part because it furnishes an example of an act of violence whose target seems so well selected, so distinct, as to obscure rather than facilitate reflection on the state's contradictions, and in part because of the privileged place granted this event in the histories of Spain's transition from authoritarian rule to democracy. But what principally governs my choice of examples is this: as

Spain seeks to devise for itself a postnational, "European" identity, the interests at war in the death of Admiral Luis Carrero Blanco still define the relation between local nationalism and state interest. That event, and the specific conflict it represents, mark in ways as yet unacknowledged the limit of the capacious, liberal democratic, "European" social imaginary.[20]

In 1973, in the waning days of Franco's regime, Carrero, the president of the Spanish government and the anointed successor to the Generalísimo, stepped out of the church of San Francisco de Borja in Madrid, where he regularly attended Mass, and into his official car. Minutes later there was a huge explosion. The first news reports that day stated that a gas main had exploded, causing no injuries but digging up a huge trench on the street, Claudio Coello. In fact, the President's car had not been found immediately. Blown over the façade of the church by a bomb that commandos had planted, the limousine was discovered some moments later by a priest, who was reading and made his way to the balcony of an inner courtyard, where he discovered the car, deformed into a V-shape, resting in such a way that he could see only the hands of the occupants. To these hands he administered the last rites. "And with this event," writes Josep Carles Clemente, "the transition to democracy begins [*Empieza la transición*]."[21]

1. Calle Claudio Coello, Madrid, December 20, 1973.

Both the timing and the target of the attempt were, in a way, entirely foreseeable. The bombing took place on the day in which the elaborately prepared *proceso 1001*, the trial of ten imprisoned leaders of the underground Communist union Comisiones Obreras, was to begin. Carrero, Franco's longest-standing deputy, was known to be in charge of the political *relevo* envisioned for the time of Franco's death and had recently—in June 1973—been appointed president by Franco and charged with forming a cabinet. ETA made the argument in this way:

> From 1951 on Carrero was for all practical purposes the Chief of Government of the regime. Carrero more than any one else symbolized the figure of "pure Franquismo." His police force managed to insert itself in all the apparatus of Franco's government. He thus became the key element of the system, and the most basic piece in the political game of the oligarchy. Everybody knows that the Spanish oligarchy was counting on Carrero to insure a smooth transition to a "franquismo" without Franco.[22]

The assassination provoked an immediate—or almost immediate—crisis, both political and social. A number of theories explaining who really killed Carrero surfaced and remain the subject of some (at times absurdly heated) discussion; a subclass of jokes about the assassination and a cotillion of rather morbid parlor games made the rounds. The political result of the attack was the return to power of the hard-line Falangist faction that had been replaced after the Matesa scandal. Still, the event's epistemological and one might say psycho-social consequences were in their way quite a bit more important. Here are two moments in Teresa Vilarós's description of the assassination's outcome:

> The complicated inweaving and unraveling that the political and the affective responses [to Carrero's assassination] underwent in the palace of El Pardo partially reflect what the Spanish social body also suffered at the time, equally and conflictedly entangled between affect and politics, feeling in part a surge of hope at what the magnicide might imply, and in part horrified at the violence that political change demands. . . . But in addition to marking the end and the beginning of an era, the assassination also marks the beginning of the process of historical encryption with which the fabric of Spanish society reacts to the magnicide.[23]

Remark, in the spirit of decryption to which the event invites us, the mediations (temporal, institutional, symbolic) between the bombing and its social (re)construction. In the hours and days immediately after the assassination, the resemanticization of Carrero's body proceeded frantically and unevenly, following official and unofficial channels, according to voluntary and involuntary mechanisms. The "news-bomb delivered in small doses," as Campo Vidal calls it, was doled out to and by the media in an atmosphere that *El País*'s investigation some years later would call *hermetismo informativo*;[24] a smattering of alternative accounts filtered into Spain from France. *Operación Ogro*, Eva Forest's 1974 interviews with the ETA commando responsible for the attack, gave the event a narrative shape it has not yet shed and a heroic cast confirmed in Pontecorvo's version of Forest's account, the film *Ogro*. Even today it seems difficult to tell the story without importing oddly discrepant elements. In a recent history of the period, a merely evocative animism employed to naturalize Carrero's vehicle oddly flows into terminology drawn from the field of competitive diving: "The street pavement disintegrated under the wheels of the official vehicle, which suddenly interrupted its slow horizontal movement to rocket up over thirty-five meters. It was a clean jump. On its descent—which was too vertical—the car scratched the border of the overhanging roof."[25]

What socio-cultural work do these accounts carry out? Here is Forest's transcription of a conversation in which two members of the group recall how they dug the tunnel in which the explosives were placed:

> We could just manage to get one arm through the hole and start digging dirt out with the other hand. . . . The stink was atrocious! As soon as we hit earth, it began to reek of escaping gas—the earth was impregnated with gas. It was soft, greasy, humid earth. And every time we pulled the toilet chain in the water-closet—*hombre!*—there was a stench that just about knocked us out. When we dug through the sewage, we must have opened one of the conduits to the toilet disposal. It was impossible to withstand that stink.[26]

The stress in these lines falls largely on the multiplying analogies between the terrorist's (bowel, or at any rate excretory) movements, the pulling of the chain, the stench, and the expulsion, from the analized body of the street of Claudio Coello, of the president's car.[27] The mechanism of the analogy is, again, all too evident: nothing could seem more repugnant than the stench from a toilet; nothing more routine, more natural than the various digestive and muscular processes that lead to "pulling the toilet chain in the water-closet." (The Spanish makes the analogy even bolder. "[C]ada vez que daban la bomba del piso de arriba salía por allí un tufo que no se podía aguantar": the echo of *bomba*, pump or flushing mechanism, and *bomba*, bomb, is unmistakable).[28] Once established, the cloacal analogy forms the basis of the pseudo-syllogism for the "natural" necessity

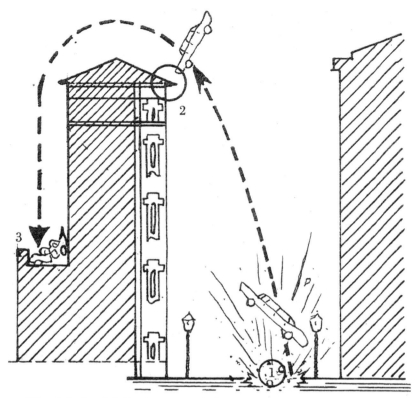

El vehículo del Presidente del Gobierno, con sus tres ocupantes dentro fué lanzado por la explosión (1) hacia el aire, chocó con el alerón (2) del edificio de cinco pisos, saltó sobre el tejado y fué a caer en la terraza (3) que rodea el patio interior, quedando destrozado en forma de V.

2. Diagram of the path of Carrero's car. From Sebastián Galdós and Gastón Pardo, *Cómo ejecutamos a Carrero Blanco* (México: Editores Asociados, 1975).

of eliminating or expelling Carrero, the toilet chain and *la bomba del piso de arriba* operating much as the *bomba* planted below the *piso de abajo* would, the president a stand-in for the fecal material that forms the panorama of Madrid's *cloacas*, and vice versa. The argument's rhetorical work of bridging carries an additional conceptual value: the expulsion of Carrero reverses the antifederalism of the Falange, which refused to acknowledge the "foreignness" of the Basque country to the Spanish state, by showing explosively that the Castilianizing ideology of the Franco regime can itself be symbolically and quite literally detached from the body of the city, of the state, of Spain.

EXCERPT FROM "INFORMATION BULLETIN NO. 7/74," REPORT FROM THE SPANISH POLICE:

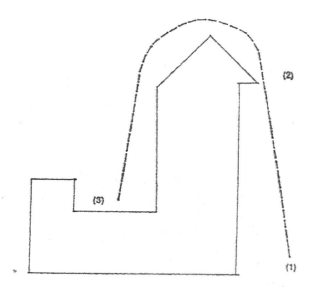

The vehicle of the President of the Government, with its three occupants inside, was hurled up in the air by the explosion (1), collided with the top edge (2) of the five-story building, cleared the roof-top and landed on the terrace (3) that surrounds the interior patio, folding into the shape of a "V". . . .

The President, the Police Inspector, and the driver were quickly taken to the Francisco Franco Health Center; Mr. Carrero Blanco and Mr. Bueno Fernandez were admitted dead on arrival.

OPERATION OGRO

The book that was banned in France—outlawed in Spain—"A GRIPPING STORY."

—*Foreign Affairs*

3. "Excerpt from 'Information Bulletin No. 7/74.'" From Eva Forest (writing as Julen Agirre), *Operation Ogro: The Execution of Admiral Luis Carrero Blanco*, trans. Barbara Probst Solomon (New York: Quadrangle/NY Times Book Co., 1975).

What Forest's analogy deliberately loses is precisely what Luis Herrero's description provides in his droll characterization of a car "interrupting its movement," "jumping or diving [*salto*]," and finally "scratching" the roof: the element of the will that the body or mind exercises in pulling the chain, *deciding* to interrupt its movement (its *movimiento* or its *desplazamiento*), to dive, to scratch—an act of will animistically supplied to the president's car. This displacement compensates for the violence with which Carrero's own will, whatever it might have been, was shown to be beside the point. These lines from *Operation Ogro* powerfully envision the loss of his will: the bomb blocks the passage from *decisión* to *movimiento*. By means of ETA's "operation" or "execution," the corporate body of the state loses the immediacy of its limbs to its will, or, to put it differently, the terrorist shows that the exercise of a corporate will is never direct but always mediate and interruptible, that an element of the involuntary or of the merely reflexive inhabits the "transcendent union" between the "symbol" and the concept of *franquismo*, as between the movement and the state, or indeed between "Spain" and the intimately alien province of the Basque country. One set of explanations for the overdetermination of the Ogro story now becomes patent: the issue is not only the fecalization of Carrero, the analization of the city, the eroticizing of the terrorist's strategy of introjection and expulsion. Forest's interviews show explicitly what popular historiography also suggests: that the construction of Carrero's assassination represents the denial of a form of closure to the conceptual body that the state ascribes to itself, and locates that resistance to closure in the body's lack of control, in its absence of will, in the recourse to reflexive action cut from reflection that the state suffers in managing the economy of the body's surfaces and borders, internal (the surface of Madrid suddenly revealing a thick, unsuspected, and threatening material panorama) as well as external (the border between the Basque country and France being at this time hardly subject to Spanish control).

This, at any rate, is how Franco himself construed ETA's attack on Carrero. In the complex, much-debated "Mensaje de fin de año" that Franco delivered some two weeks after the assassination, the inside-outside logic that would be appropriated in ETA's account in *Operation Ogro* is significantly recast. Characterizing the attack, opaquely but fascinatingly, with the words "there is no evil that does not result from good [*No hay mal que por bien no venga*]," Franco proposed that:

> The violence of a minority, supported and encouraged from outside the country, a minority that represents no-one and nothing, drowns itself in

the maturity of the Spanish people. The institutions have worked from within our people. . . . We have not even had to turn to the exceptional measures that the law provides for, since the confidence and hopes of the Spanish people insured that order and peace would prevail. Peoples cannot be judged by the external appearances of consumer society, or by the frivolity of a part of their social classes. There exists in them [*ellas*] what cannot be seen, what the ideals of our Movement have engraved [or "infused" or "mined": *calar*] in the good Spanish people, that which makes itself manifest on all great occasions.[29]

The relation that Franco's words establish between the open frontier and the effect of the bomb is double. On the one hand, the attack on Carrero reveals the existence of a porous border, a way in which the external can influence the state—the city—from outside its walls. But on the other hand, and correspondingly, the effect of the bomb is to close the state in upon itself, to reassert its fundamental laws and to provoke the closed defense of those ideals. On the one hand, the attack and social reaction to the attack reveal the external frivolity of the commercial classes, the classes of consumer society; on the other, they suggest the existence of what is not seen, the soul, the ideals, or the character of the people. The argument is complex, and in at least one sense quite troubling. "Revealing" what the Movement has inscribed within the "buen pueblo español" (as "madurez," "serenidad," "confianza," and respect for "los órganos del estado") is clearly desirable here—on the more or less Hegelian grounds that recognizing the aspect of "el buen pueblo" that on occasion "makes itself manifest" for "el buen pueblo" to see is the condition for "el pueblo's" twin awareness, of itself *as pueblo* and of itself as the object of the Movement's work of inscription and formation: its *cala*. But if this is so, then the assassination of Carrero, precisely one such "gran ocasión," cannot be entirely condemned. Instead, the bombing and its sequel must be, as it were, introjected or consumed (to use Franco's word), must be turned to advantage, must reveal themselves as a case, to reverse the movement of Franco's aphorism, of "no hay bien que por mal no venga," the emergence of a "good"—the externalization of the Movement's mark upon the people, the concretization of a border that had become all too porous, the reassertion of a Falangist hard line endangered by the technocratic government that Carrero had sought to install—out of an "evil." ETA, in brief, reveals itself the witting or unwitting agent of the Falangist state's self-recognition, the agent of the dialectical reassertion of a mediate but decisive—read willed—relation between the people and the party, as the party reveals itself deeply marked—*calado*—within the substance of the people.

Or say this: in Franco's words the concepts of terrorism and the foreign arise before the act that they characterize, as the place to which the act is destined in the field of the social as the outside of that field. This predestination of the act of resistance to the state's internal outside means, naturally, that the state generates the names and the categories of terrorism and the foreign for the purposes of imposing its will, of holding and making use of the chain that will expel what the social body cannot entirely consume. A familiar, coercive pattern ensues, whose immediate effect is to preempt genuine dissent by associating it with an arbitrary "foreignness" but whose more interesting and far-reaching consequence is to generate (nominally as well as practically) excessive acts of terror to which a strong state and a nation unified internally by a patterned "outside" can respond as one. Because this patterned outside then also stands as a product of the strong state and of the national character, as the concretization of what most intimately defines the State's interior, the topology of Franco's *mensaje* and of ETA's account assume in relation to each other the ghostly, mirroring shape that Begoña Aretxaga has sketched, in discussing "narrative excess" in accounts of state terror in the Basque country:

> the *feeling* body of the state becomes real, not so much through the confluence of reason and violence that is the hallmark of the modern state, as through the performance of mimetic violence against a fantasized enemy. The state is constituted through the narrative proliferation of excess, [and] as nothing but excess. Nationalist activists are constituted as political subjects in an imaginary relation to the state, just as the state is constituted in an imaginary relation to the phantom Basque terrorist.[30]

In Franco's argument, the state's "feeling body" becomes real in his key verb *calar*, in its own slim way the bearer of deeply excessive narratives. Meaning "to saturate some matter completely, to mark or enter deeply into something," *calar* here describes the work of ideology in the formation of the people's self-recognition. In its substantive form, the verb *calar* becomes a *cala*, the hole, cut, or incision made in a surface—a wall or the pavement of a street, say—to determine its thickness, its composition, and to find what lies beneath. But *calar* also means "to embroider" or "to stitch together according to a pattern"—in its antithetical condensation a wonderfully compact description of the desuturing and resuturing movement by means of which, in Franco's account, the movement of *mal* and *bien*, of externalization and internalization, of terrorism and reason of state in the social fabric are reducible to a closed and regulated economy. Franco's phrase carefully designs and follows a syntactical and conceptual border defined by these three senses and by the distinct topologies they envision: "What the ideals of our Movement have engraved [or "infused" or "mined": *calar*] in the good Spanish people" suggests the bore, the core sample that the Movement draws from the depths of the Spanish people and then introjects, a *movimiento* whose ideology thus comes to reflect the core values of the people it governs; it suggests the infusing of the Movement's ideology within the matter of the Spanish people, the insertion into or impregnation of that interiority by volatile ideals from without (inherited, for instance, from Italian fascism or from the vanguardist cadre of the Falange itself); and it suggests the superficial patterning that guides the needle's incision, a map upon the skin of the "buen pueblo español." Poised within, without, and upon the very skin of this "good people," Franco's words define the counter-erotic economy of a corporate state body at whose well-policed borders allopaths of every description—immigrants, subversive ideas, commercial products that threaten the competitiveness of local merchandise, etc.—can be turned back.

Or let in at will, of course. Aretxaga's careful analysis of the narratives of state terror closes on a note of qualification that turns out to be particularly apt here. In the mirroring constitution of facing subjectivities "as fetishes of each other," "neither the state nor radical nationalists constitute a homogeneous or coherent subject."[31] If this is so, then we can expect to find, in cultural narratives that link social terror and state or separatist terrorism in a correspondingly mimetic relation, what we could call an *excess of excess* in the project of mutual fetishization—an enigmatic double to the part that narrative excess plays in constituting terror as the inside of the terrorist act and vice versa, or in constituting terrorism as the intimate outside of the strong state (and vice versa).

Strong as it turns out to be, Franco's account leaves untouched an aspect of ETA's version of the assassination that cannot be traded in the counter-erotic economy that his remarks set in place. With the occlusion of the corporate will, the immediate exhaustion of "Carrero" in his symbolic function and the critical rematerialization of Carrero's symbolic body, the story of Carrero's assassination reveals itself to do too much and too little work for the process of inscription and reinscription—undertaken by ETA, Franco, and Campo Vidal's government-informed *circuitos informativos*—to succeed: the grim story *tiene chiste*; it has a trick to it, we might say, or it hides a joke. This unstable an-economy of semiotic and conceptual lack and excess opens the logic of terrorism to a different construction of lived terror. It has lodged *en el seno*, in the breast, of the vocabularies of transition and movement ever since Carrero's assassination and is the proper object for our reflection here.

Think about what might be doubly excessive or doubly lacking in accounts of the assassination of Carrero. By this I don't mean to ask whether the act itself is to be condemned or not, or on what grounds—those are crucial questions, but of a different order from the ones I have in mind. Nor do I mean, exactly, the strangely unclosed aspect of the assassination itself—the complex repetitions to which it became susceptible, under one sign or another.[32] I mean, instead, to draw attention to the aspects of the *story* of the assassination that exceed its fashionings by Franco, ETA, and others or that fall short of the story's ideological reconstruction and of the oedipalized "process of historical encryption" that Vilarós has described. If either Franco's *cala* and ETA's *bomba* proves inadequate to the event of Carrero's assassination, it may be because the moment of social terror cannot itself be fashioned—though its immediate consequences can to some extent be managed (to this or that end). The resistance that the social experience of terror opposes to the borders that one or another organization may draw for it (whether as a form of desuturing or as a means of resuturing the social field) itself becomes the source of a sort of tertiary terror, the affect-form in which the critical unveiling of the mechanical principles of state and party fascism—their *chiste*, if you will—is at length undertaken.

What are we to make, for instance, of the extraordinary literality of the assassination? Everything about Carrero's assassination seems to take place between instances of reading and of writing, or between tropically substituted symbols—parts (the parts of bodies) taken for wholes, bodies (those of Carrero and his entourage; those of the ETA commando) emblematically or mistakenly taken for others (for the body of Franco or the conceptual body of the central state; of course, the terrorists were also taken to be sculptors), events substituted counterphobically for others (the explosion of a gas main for the assassination). The ETA brigade that planted the bomb marked the spot with a red spot of paint; the priest who turned from reading on hearing the blast said he saw a car deformed by the explosion into the shape of a letter—the letter *U* or *V*—flying outside the window; the tunnel in which the explosives were hidden below the street was described as having the shape of the letter *T*.

Note the perverse multiplication of body parts throughout descriptions of the event: remember how it was the victims' hands alone that Father Jiménez Berzal saw when he first ran to the crushed car and to which he administered the last rites; that the name of the street in which the assassination occurred bears a cryptic, entirely accidental relation to this *sparagmos*—the pronunciation of the word *Coello* in *Claudio Coello* opens from the closed *O* toward the sound of the *U*—the shape of the blasted car—and toward *cuello*, "the neck." Recall the odd animism still at work in descriptions of the event: the car's "jump," its animalization (still clearer in the Spanish: *arañar*, "to scratch," refers us to another figure of aesthetic metamorphosis, Arachne, *arañada* in an even more primitive sense), its personification. Carrero's assassination was not only foreseeable; it was not destined to be the mere object of intense written and visual polemic. The attack was always already "written" and took place, as it were. within the space of a certain aesthetic construction (of the state, of the city, of the relation between concrete bodies and what they represent). Or rather: the radical re-materialization of the state that ETA's bomb provoked and revealed opened contiguous figures, names, spaces, and geographies to this process of rematerialization. The bomb that killed Carrero scattered the cityscape and animated it with a flurry of broken names, bodies, and senses, partial ghosts whose hauntings no *cala* or *corte* could hope to describe or contain.

Take now one of these ghosts: Carrero's car. Campo Vidal excerpts, with signs of dismay (he calls it "**s**hocking, even inconceivable . . . bordering upon the irreverent [*chocante, inconcebible incluso . . . rayana en la irreverencia*]"), the publicity campaign that Chrysler España launched after the assassination. "The vehicle has certainly demonstrated its solidity and strength," ran the advertisement, "since it bore rather well the tremendous explosion that took place right under it, which launched the car to the height of some twenty-five meters."

> The president's car not only did not disintegrate (as we are sure would have happened to many other cars of different national or international origins, including some more expensive than the Dodge 3700): its doors did not open in its jump to the terrace, thus avoiding that the occupants' bodies should have flown out, which would have increased the drama of the events. . . . What is more, we have heard that *when the car had landed on the terrace, one of its turning lights was still blinking.*[33]

The grim device of this advertisement is the link it forges between the integrity of the car's body, the solidity of the *fabricación española* (the Dodge, although a foreign car, was made in Spain—*fabricado en Villaverde*, a town near Madrid where the Dodge factory was indeed housed), and the inviolability of the state and the market: the strength of the president's car embodies and libidinizes the solid value of the state he heads and to buy (or acquiesce in the political legitimacy of) the one is to acquiesce in the political legitimacy of (or to consume) the other. The underscored, climactic detail—that the car's turning signal was still on after the explosion—thus becomes a peculiarly uncanny sign, no longer indicating a (spatial or political) *cambio de movimiento*, but instead signaling the opposite: the signal's little light insistently makes manifest the internal solidity of the car, its internal and external spaces at one under its driver's still hand, still safe from the drama that might have opened another car to lurid interest or critical scrutiny. Marked by this turning sign and by the gesturing hand of the Caudillo, inside and outside, *movimiento* and *cambio de movimiento* are sutured together and held apart even and especially when an incision—*corte* or *cala*—has been made in the body politic.

The economization of the Dodge's fragile but persistent turning signal, however, not only confirms Franco's subtle regulation of inside-outside tropes in his "Mensaje de fin de año," it also dramatically unbalances it. How, after all, does one regulate this excess value added to the narrative detail? To the letter? Note again the terms that Campo Vidal uses to express his shock: the advertisement is "inconcebible," its tone "rayana en la irreverencia." The mechanisms that Franco deploys in his "Mensaje de fin de año" are indeed these triplets of Enlightenment political economy: the doctrine of *reverence* for a *concept* (the state, say, or "el buen pueblo español") depending for its definition on established and well-policed *borders—rayas*, in the topology of this example, or the inviolable interior of the president's car. In the libidinization of this triplet emerges the field in which Carrero's assassination will be most thoroughly and unpredictably absorbed, the field of a desire-driven commodity culture no less shocking, inconceivable, and irreverent with respect to the conceptual topology of national identity than the field of terrorist acts it so avidly consumes. The advertising copy for Chrysler España *tiene chiste*: it sings out the unforeseeable and unregulated, excess affect-investment that undefines the corporate state body whose outline it draws and capitalizes upon.

Involuntary Contractions; or, The Limits of Reflexive Populism

Here, in conclusion, is another ghost—this time, the reawakened ghost for which Carrero substituted, Franco's gesturing body. I have suggested that the attack on the president emblematized in the cultural and political imaginary of the early 1970s the threat and pleasures of a lack of ideological, economic, cultural, and physical closure, and produced in the languages of the political establishment, in particular in Franco's determining reconstruction of the event, a compensatory counter-eroticization of the reflexive borders that keep the inner and outer spaces of the state's, people's, or party's body under the sway of a corporate will. This ghostly emblematizing proves increasingly ungovernable: the content of the assassination is rendered too literal to be exhausted by the mechanics of ETA's substitutive logic, but not literal enough to attach only to a single, given, and unrepresentative body—too easily consumed to be restricted to a regulated economy, but never entirely consumed in its circulations in emergent commodity culture. It is ungovernable, too, in any conventional historiographical sense, for by now the chronological borders of the assassination have themselves become strangely porous. We are not surprised to find, for example, that ETA's blow against Franco's deputy in 1973 repeated, in the form of tragedy, a more or less farcical blow that Franco had suffered in a hunting accident in 1961. Spaniards were made aware of the accident by means of a bulletin announcing that "While hunting this afternoon in El Pardo, His Excellency the Head of State suffered slight wounds in his left hand through an accident of his hunting rifle." Some days later the daily *ABC* announced that Franco had been released from hospital and printed an interview with Vicente Gil, Franco's personal physician and a participant in the hunt at which the head of state had suffered his accident. Here again the strange logic of the Caudillo's "Mensaje de fin de año" of a decade later is anticipated, in quite a different key—almost, one suspects, *de chiste*:

   —Did the Caudillo say anything?
   —[Dr. Gil]: When I said to him, "This is exciting," he answered simply
      that "People are good."
   —Do you know the specifications of the rifle that failed?
   —Not exactly; but it certainly isn't a Spanish rifle.[34]

Gil's "desde luego"—"it *certainly* isn't a Spanish rifle"—captures marvelously the tautologous arrangement of foreign and national, outer and inner identities played out in Franco's words and policies in the nearly two decades that followed. And yet the incident's connection to Carrero's assassination is not as tenuous as it might seem. This early and accidental threat to the Caudillo's control of the state was among the principal reasons given for passing the legislation that eventually stipulated the form that the transition would take on Franco's death—legislation that Carrero was instrumental in crafting and consolidating, legislation from which he had stood to profit so signally. That afternoon in El Pardo, the threat concerned the Caudillo's wounded hand, but also (and much more importantly) quite a different set of organs. Ramón Soriano recalls Franco's doctors commenting to the Marquis of Villaverde, Franco's son-in-law, that: "'It's only a hand. We recently did a check-up on the Generalísimo, and everything was normal. The only exception," they continued:

> "is that he tends to digest food slowly." This observation, which to the lay person might seem a trivial enough detail, was worth keeping in mind for the team of doctors. When under anaesthetic, a body's reflexes disappear, and particularly those that block the entrance of foreign bodies into the lungs and windpipe. In these circumstances, if the patient regurgitates, the contents of the stomach can invade the lungs and choke the patient.. . . . The fact that the Generalísimo had suffered the accident some two hours after lunch made it probable that the stomach contained something.[35]

The incidental similarities between the accident and the assassination are less significant than the political continuities between the two crises, of course—and yet it is hard to settle on precisely the criteria to be used to distinguish between "accidental" and "deliberate" or "necessary" similarities or entailments, between the political content of the event and the merely aesthetic matter in which it is couched, which may threaten to invade, perhaps even to choke it when anaesthetic is applied. Consider that matter for a moment—for instance, the overdetermined wound to the Caudillo's hand, tropically wounded again in 1973 and reemerging in the truncated (and doubled) form of the chauffeur's dead hands, posed upon the steering wheel of the president's car; consider how the foreign gun's backfiring finds its aesthetic complement in the failure of foreign elements—ETA—to disrupt the characteristics that "el buen pueblo español" carries treasured within its breast, like the grim body of Carrero within the inviolate Dodge 3700; consider that the president's car was made in the very town—Villaverde—we come to associate with the name of the Marquis to whom the Caudillo's doctors reported Franco's rather slow digestion.[36] These are surely trivial enough details to the lay person—but they reveal alternative, perhaps even foreign contents within the political content that ostensibly joins the hunting accident to the political assassination: for instance, the cryptic collusion between the Spanish aristocracy (the Marquis of Villaverde), the incipient globalization of labor markets signaled by the location of Chrysler's assembly plant in Spain ("fabricado en Villaverde"), and the trial of leaders of independent trade unions, scheduled to begin on the day of Carrero's assassination. They invite us to ask whether Carrero's assassination should not be understood both as *a reflexive act* and as an event flowing from the "disappearance" of the body politic's "reflexes." The political distinction is critical: either Carrero's death represents the Falange turning upon itself by means of ETA, wounding itself with (a proxy of) itself, as if the Caudillo's right-hand man were foreign to him and to the Movement, so that the assassination becomes a form of self-mutilation rather than an attack from outside; or else Carrero's death represents the failure of the political body's most basic forms of self-regulation.

This suggestion might be given a slightly more formal shape. Here, then, would be a way of speaking to the event from the vantage of the detail and of sketching out thereby the shape we might ascribe to a transitional thought that arises conditioned by the movement it rejects and yet remains radically external to that movement: thought at the point of the an-aesthetic. Where ETA eroticized the sphincter, analized the street of Claudio Coello, reembodied Madrid as a body parasitized by a foreign state, and made this body's reflexive, expulsive function the natural figure for the assassination of Carrero, the medical reconstruction of Franco's operation a decade earlier had sought to control and de-eroticize the invasion and expulsion of what the head of state had consumed and of the foreign gun that had backfired. When Franco's doctors physically sought to suture the wound to his hand and aesthetically to dress the second wound caused to the "transcendent synthesis" of party, state, nation, and ruler by the threat to Franco's life, they anticipated unknowingly but with an exemplary clarity the cultural functions of Franco's year-end message—principally, the regulation of exchanges between the inner and outer surfaces of "el buen pueblo español" and the policing of the borders, or *rayas*, of a concept irreverently breached by ETA. The danger then posed by the anaesthetic lies just where ETA's treatment of the assassination also dwells, just where the reflex movement that keeps an event's political content from being contaminated by its aesthetic expression or vitiated by "trivial enough details" both begins and falters: in the failure of corporate mechanisms for regulating the passage from external to internal organs, from the outside of the body to its interior. It becomes difficult, indeed formally impossible, to distinguish between "accidental" and "deliberate" or "necessary" aspects of the event, between reflexive and unreflective acts or thoughts, between the political content of the event and the merely aesthetic matter in which it is couched, just at the spot where the logic of biopolitics finds its limits in the logic of autoimmunity, and vice versa.

I am making neither an intentionalist nor a causal argument. ETA's rationale in the 1973 bombing does not follow in deed or word the description of Franco's operation; the organization does not envision the attack on Carrero in relation to the market processes that Chrysler España would exploit; the linguistic dissemination of partial ghosts across the geography of the city and across Spain's recent cultural history was not ETA's goal. The assassination of Carrero works culturally as an un-bounded event or a defective object rather than as a bounded sign or act. It produces languages that designate it and histories that explain it—the anatomies, ideologies, temporality, and economies of its sense; it exposes an underdetermination of social intent and an excess of social affect radi-cally irreducible to any definition of political interest; it changes the past no less than the present and the future; it unbounds the instant. To put it more compactly: in the domains of Spain's political imaginary, of its eco-nomic symbology, and of the narratives forming its national history, the unbounding of terror is a form of thought as well as a model of ethico-political intervention. This unbounding thought subjects terrorism to the rigors of terror and subjects the mystification and paralysis to which such terror becomes bound (as the sublimity of one or another corporate form) to the ethico-political demands posed in the terrorist act.

I'd like to conclude this chapter by mentioning briefly and by contrast one of the sequels to Carrero's assassination, ETA's murder of Miguel Ángel Blanco in Ermua, in July 1997. The two events were of course very different, as were the circumstances in which they took place—the wan-ing days of Franco's regime on the one hand, a robust, if young, largely social-democratic government, on the other. (I say "largely social-demo-cratic," though the party in power in 1997 was José María Aznar's center-right Partido Popular.) ETA's targets were nearly incommensurable, symbolically and politically—a head of state, on the one hand, an obscure city councilman, on the other. The results of the two assassinations, too, were different—though perhaps not quite so profoundly so as it might seem. With Carrero's death, as we have seen, the transition to democracy seems to begin. With Miguel Ángel Blanco's death, the longer, less punc-tual transition to a society free from terrorism was announced, even appeared imminent. It was possible in the days and months that followed Blanco's assassination to believe that the moving images of silently marching crowds protesting the killing marked the exhaustion of the instrumental logic of nationalist terrorism. *ABC* put it this way: "A cry for peace has broken out across Spain. Miguel Ángel Blanco's death has not been in vain: his memory has joined the conscience of millions of Spaniards, disregarding ideological differences. Yesterday, only one voice sounded, thunderously: 'All of us are Miguel Ángel.'" The first sentence of the daily *El País*'s lead article the day after Blanco's death was equally stark: "Yesterday, all of Spain became an immense referendum in favor of peace [*un inmenso plebiscito por la paz*, the word *plebiscito* being much more firmly anchored in the lexicon of democratic institutions than my "referendum"].''[37]

In the symbolic economy of these images of protest and outrage, tongue and hand acted in unison, spontaneous affect met mass mobilization, the affective movement or disposition of individual shock organized itself (became organized), and all took expression in the cultural and social material that lay at hand. Naturally, this entailed not just refunctionalizing and resemanticizing the available cultural and social tropes but erasing, bracketing, or forgetting their long and different histories. The crowd's hands, for instance, outstretched in the gesture popularly called *manos blancas* ("white or clean hands"), condensed the claim of corporate, social innocence and the name of the victim, Miguel Ángel Blanco. The *manos blancas* slogan, devised to protest ETA's killing a year earlier of Francisco Tomás y Valiente, a law professor in Madrid, draws on popular culture (a traditional saw: *las blancas manos no agravian, mas duelen*, "white hands cannot cause an affront, but they do cause pain," generally taken to mean "a woman's slights do not wound the honor of a man," as the venerable *Diccionario de las metáforas y refranes de la lengua castellana* puts it), as well as high culture (the title of an almost unperformable but well-known honor play by Calderón).[38] "See," the demonstrators seemed to say, "*our* hands are unspotted, and so should yours be—you the terrorists, and your nationalist supporters, and those who stand outside or against this new movement guarded in the breast of the Spanish people." "See," the journalistic gloss of the images read, "we take our identity and our voice from this gesture, from these hands we raise together. See, we have emptied the sign of the raised hand of its historical content and left it blank, all white, *blanco* or *blanca*: its vacuity is the ground on which we form our corporate identity, beyond ideology and partisan interests. See, this corporate identity is what you, ETA, have produced, what the sacrifice of Blanco has brought about. *No hay bien que por mal no venga*, but also *no hay mal que por bien no venga* ["there is no good that does not result from evil," but also "there is no evil that does not result from good"]." The idiom is reminiscent of the expressions of outrage the international media reported following the September 11, 2001, attacks and of solidarity with the city and inhabitants of New York: "We are all New Yorkers, we are all Americans," the pronoun "we" blanked out, emptied, vacuous for the nonce.

It made sense at the time of the assassinations of Tomás y Valiente and Blanco for the media to tell two stories in one stroke, compactly, symbolically: the story of Spain's transition from Franco's regime to the formal, more or less federal democracy the country was devising; and the story of the spontaneous corporatization of the Spanish population, stepping forth beyond partisanship and ideologies, out of the long and still-slumbering shadow of the Civil War, on the shoulders of a common rejection of terrorist violence. Told following the lines of a hand, *las rayas de la mano*, the double story reached across sixty years, from the first *falanges* to the Caudillo's hunting accident, the death of Carrero, his right-hand man, his *mano derecha*, to the murders of Tomás y Valiente and Miguel Ángel Blanco. The community formed around the terrorist act, brought into symbolic coherence by the vacuous signifier of the white hands, forms itself reflexively, even spontaneously, into the corporate shape shared by the two braided strands of Spanish fascism. One voice, one hand, one memory, one name. The echoes of ETA's and the Falange's inside-outside topology are unmistakable: to believe that such topologies exhaust themselves, that they can be erased or refunctionalized, or that the clear boundary of the instant or the moment can be redrawn around them is to set back in place Primo de Rivera's organic, corporativist fantasy of the "síntesis trascendente e indivisible, con fines propios que cumplir" ("a transcendent synthesis, an indivisible synthesis, with its own ends to accomplish"). In its pathological form—as a fantasy—this belief rebuilds the act, encloses and immediately exhausts it in a sense given it by the institutional forms that produce it. The reflexive closure of the political body results in the mute, motionless, numerical ontology of the mass, which is to say, in a radically *non*political, abstract association. In terrorism.

Say, however, that we propose an alternative to spontaneous populist reason and to building populist corporatization upon a notionally empty signifier. We describe our alternative approach as a work of suturing and desuturing socio-cultural wounds, of tracking the unbounding movement of cultural resemanticizations within and across historical moments, of making space in political thought for the habitation of social terror. We call this an-aesthetic thought. We will have escaped the trap into which the populist response falls, but only because we have fallen into another, perhaps more dangerous one. Where the fantasy of a single, corporate response to the terrorist act becomes the blank numerical ontology of the mutely nonpolitical, we erect a second fantasy, the fantasy that the philosophically minded critic can act immediately outside the corporatization of popular and university culture, beyond the material determinations that bind and bound his or her speech; the fantasy, in short, that transitional, moving, an-aesthetic thought acts as explosively as a bomb, suddenly or spontaneously, with the effect of fully saturating and effectively changing the sense of the semantic and political fields it enters. A heroism of critical thought: the an-aesthetic thinker as terrorist.

Radical democratic republican thought escapes these twin traps and assumes its most responsible form—as an ethic of terror—when it takes the nonpolitical and heroic, populist and vanguardist, turbulent and elite fantasies of spontaneity, collectivization or corporatization, and symbolic resemanticization as its condition of possibility but also and simultaneously as the irreducible objects of its critique. "To think" here means to guard terror as one keeps and shares a joke. (Terrorism is not a joke, but perhaps, and this may well be crucial, terror *is*.) We will find in the next chapters that "thinking" in this sense has a special, highly destabilizing relation to three lexical fields from which the modern state-form takes its claims to legitimacy: the fields of political theology, logic, and mythic historiography.

CHAPTER 2

Phares; or, Divisible Sovereignty

The special difficulty of these analyses lies in the patient's horror at
violating a parent's or a family's guarded secret, even though the
secret's text and context are inscribed within the patient's own
unconscious. The horror of transgression, in the strict sense of the
term, is compounded by the risk of undermining the fictitious yet
necessary integrity of the parental figure in question.

—NICOLAS ABRAHAM, "Notes on the Phantom"

Grant me, for now, the distinction between the terrorist and the foundational terror that radical democratic republicanism guards—the condition
of its ethical form, the weak concept or the weak norm at its breast. Converting ungovernable semantic excess into a weak norm for thought and
conduct seems a tolerable, if still fairly abstract program. Certainly, it
would appear to be a distinctively modern one: inseparable from a post-
Romantic literary-political lexicon, specific to a transitional state form,
pertinent at one time but not all. My example has been the construction
of political movement in the postwar Spanish imaginary: a Falangist state
officially laying claim to modernization; an armed nationalist, separatist
movement momentarily in line with the forces of political dissidence; an
economy making the transition to a specific form of consumer capitalism;
a labile society, opening borders on some levels, closing them on others—
all particular circumstances. My claim is broader, though. The mystical
body of the Caudillo, subject to fluxes, depositions, substitutions, wounds,
and delegations, also stands sublimely beyond these merely accidental
eventualities. The flickering border between the sovereign's mystical and
material bodies is the trace—one of them, the most spectacular—of discontinuous processes of secularization and modernization whose pas de
deux long precedes Romanticism and the Enlightenment. The diagnostic,

exemplary movement from one postwar state form to another trails other
movements that may partially determine it and that will necessarily provide a broader palette from which to draw the "innovative interpretations"
and expanded "concepts with 'surplus validity'" that Honneth and Fraser
require.[1] The border between modern interpretations and concepts, modern events and archaic or future ones, is as labile and indecisive as the
porous frontiers of Spain's imaginary postwar state, or the body of its Caudillo. The concept of sovereignty that partially governs, partially results
from these asynchronous movements has a history and a particular logic
of expression, a grammar and indeed a literature of its own. The weak
pseudo-concept "terror" emerges and subsists in this history, in the logic
of expression, in the grammar and literature of modern sovereignty. In
this chapter and the next I turn to consider the genealogy of the ethic of
terror.

Theoretical Sovereignty: Fatherhood

> Hence the necessity of another problematic, in truth, an aporetic, of
> divisible sovereignty. For a long time now, at least since the end of
> the nineteenth century, people have spoken of nation-states with
> "limited" or "shared" sovereignty. But is not the very essence of the
> principle of sovereignty, everywhere and in every case, precisely its
> exceptional indivisibility, its illimitation, its integral integrity?
> Sovereignty is undivided, unshared, or it is not. The division of the
> indivisible, the sharing of what cannot be shared: that is the possibility
> of the impossible.
>
> —JACQUES DERRIDA, "Provocation: Forewords"

The two-step project that Derrida announces—describing and displac-
ing the "integral integrity" on which sovereignty turns, setting out an
"aporetic of divisible sovereignty" yet to come—remains incomplete. His
last works, in dialogue with Giorgio Agamben, Carl Schmitt, Jean-Luc
Nancy, and others, sketch its contours and furnish a basket of concepts,
here advanced in their briefest, most paradoxical, and most spectacular
shape: a "*division of the indivisible, the sharing of what cannot be shared . . .
the possibility of the impossible.*" The string of aporias will let us approach
not only the limited, shared distribution of state sovereignty but also the
prior, Bodinian distinctions between delegated power and sovereignty, on
the one hand, and between derived and posited sovereignty on the other.

Less gaudy and less controversial is Derrida's guarded historical assertion that a certain idiom—"speaking" of limited or shared sovereignty in
the case of nation-states—has been in use "at least since the end of the
nineteenth century." To pose the matter in this way—to remark that Derrida is both fashioning a number of aporetic concepts and making a brief
historical argument concerning their emergence and use—is to walk hand
in hand with Schmitt, who suggests, famously, that "all significant concepts
of the modern theory of the state are secularized theological concepts" and
also that this circumstance obtains "not only because of their historical
development . . . but also because of their systematic structure."[2] A string
of questions follows this encounter between Derrida's argument and
Schmitt's—hard questions even to pose, for we inhabit the time of the
nation-state, and thus we imagine the idioms of sovereignty, its logics and
aporetics, in step with that time. What is the relation between the "historical development" of an "aporetic of divisible sovereignty" and its "systematic structure"? Was there not an "aporetic of divisible sovereignty" before
what we call the nation-state emerges—for instance, when Jean Bodin published *Les six livres de la république*? In what time or history will "another
problematic, in truth, an aporetic" emerge? And on a different level: What
does an assertion about the historical standing of an idiom, or indeed, an
assertion about the historicity of an assertion like "sovereignty can be
shared" or "an aporetic of divisible sovereignty is necessary" share with
the "aporetic" of divisible sovereignty? According to what logic (to what
standards of coherence, correspondence, relevance, reference) will we assess
the claims of divisible sovereignty? In what ways is the secularization of
theological concepts registered or produced in the cultural sphere of early
European modernity?

For Schmitt, let us recall, the indivisibility of sovereignty (in Bodin,
Hobbes, Machiavelli, and others) is expressed in the power to decide on
exceptions—the power to decide who is the state's enemy, for instance—
and established when that power is itself exceptional, in being underived
and undelegated. Here is the pertinent passage from the first English
translation of Bodin's *The Six Books of a Commonweale*:

> if the high and absolute power graunted by a prince to his lieutenant should
> of right be called Soueraigntie, he might use the same against his prince, to
> whome nothing was left but the bare name of a prince, standing but for a
> cipher: so should the subject command his Soueraigne, the seruant his mas-
> ter, than which nothing could be more absurd: considering that in all power
> graunted unto magistrates, or priuat men, the person of the prince is always

to be excepted [*attendu que la personne du souverain est toujours exceptée en termes de droit, quelque puissance & auctorité qu'il donne à autruy*]; who neuer giueth so much power unto another, but that hee always keepeth more unto himselfe; neither is ever to be thought so depriued of his soueraigne power, but that he may take unto himself the examination and deciding of such things as he hath committed unto his magistrates or officers . . . from whom he may also take the power giuen them by virtue of their commission or institution.[3]

With the emergence of *jus publicum europaeum* in the period between the Peace of Augsburg (1555) and the edict of Nantes (1598), Schmitt argues, the exceptional sovereignty that Bodin here grants to the prince comes to be located in the state—for in this fifty-year period European states begin to assume responsive, mutually recognizable corporate-administrative identities, the different institutions that make up particular states working in coordination internally with each other and externally with other states. Alongside the exceptional right to recognize enemies as *public* enemies, the emergent European state builds the right to recognize other states as friends or as nonenemies, overlooking bitter differences of economic and political interest, religious cult, or tradition out of a polite, modern princi-ple of comity and respect for sovereignty, *comiter maiestatem conseruare*, the principle that in cases of differences between state sovereigns they should first strive "courteously to preserue the maiestie of the greater" sovereign, as Bodin's translator has it.[4] Schmitt mentions, among other examples, Elizabeth I's compromises concerning religion between 1559 and 1563.

As in Derrida's much briefer comments, two sorts of arguments are marshaled in Schmitt's *The Concept of the Political* and *Political Theology*: an argument from the empirical situation of the early modern European state's relative, emergent equilibrium and an argument from the concept of "the political." The former is provocative but weak, on the face of it. The characterization of the political secularization of early modern European regimes that one finds in *The Concept of the Political* and *Political Theology* seems partial, uneven, even reductive. One might quickly glance at Spain, for instance, where the stormy co-existence of the *morisco* popu-lation and the Hapsburg monarchy suffered every sort of mediation—and could hardly be said to serve as an example of the "conjoining" of institu-tions, given that different sectors of the Church, the local nobility, and the court were at each other's throats for more than forty years on the matter by the time of the *morisco* expulsion in 1609–10. One might also object that in lionizing Elizabeth I's early religious tolerance Schmitt is ignoring her own and her successor's later intolerance (as signaled, for instance, by the Oath of Allegiance, the treatment of recusants, the expulsion of the Jesuit order, and so on); or that the secularization thesis overlooks crying failures of state comity and *jus publicum europaeum* in the period. Such failures often took the shape of non-negotiable differends. Take the 1588 Armada. In one description, the crisis arises in the refusal of one state—Spain—to abide by the genteel protocol of *comiter maiestatem conseruare*. In another, incompatible description, it arises from *Britain's* refusal to do the same, by supporting privateering and piratical ventures against the Spanish economy, as well as the insurrection against Spain in the Netherlands.

The deployment of religious exile as an instrument of state policy in Britain, Spain, and France between 1555 and 1610 signals at least this: that the displacement of state sovereignty from theologico-political to nominally secular-administrative institutions was linked tightly to the violent exclusion from those states of alternative interests and identities that might not have been amenable to a single secular-administrative regime. That the secularization thesis—in Schmitt and in his followers—usually neglects to address the costs of European state consolidation in early modernity reminds us to what extent the notions of the conjoined sovereign state and *jus publicum europaeum* are retrospective fantasy, compensation for the evident failure of European civil society in the first quarter of the twentieth century: a managed forgetting, whose consequences twentieth-century European society would soon experience.

Schmitt's second argument, a formal argument from the concept or the structure of the political rather than from the empirical development of modern political systems, has the tricky task of coordinating two defining circumstances—we might say, of coordinating two predicates in one concept—that only *look* synonymous or correlative: sovereignty is located in the entity that can decide who the enemy is, or who the friend is, or who or what institutions can substitute asymmetrically (that is, without being able to claim a reciprocal power of substitution, as Bodin points out) for the prince (that is, "sovereignty" derives from a decision); and only the sovereign can make this class of decisions (that is, the exceptional decision is a decision, rather than a description or a fantasy or a mere representation, by virtue of being the will of a constituted sovereign subject or state). The difficulty—and it is one that neither Bodin nor Schmitt quite acknowledges—centers upon the derivation of the claim to sovereignty, upon its timing and structure, upon its structure as a speech act. Sovereign power, we understand, is unconditioned, exempted from all laws ("the

chiefe power giuen unto a prince with charge and condition, is not properly soveraigntie, not power absolute"[5]): power given unconditionally
erases the obligation or charge the sovereign may feel to the entity (institution, circumstances) from which he receives it. Or rather: that conditioning or charge remains (the sovereign must, for reasons practical as well
as historical, be distinguished from the tyrant), but it is displaced—
elevated or abstracted. Bodin continues: "such charge or condition . . .
[must] be directly comprehended within the lawes of God and nature . . .
[sovereign power] hath no condition annexed thereunto, other than is by
the law of God and nature commaunded." It would hardly be unusual to
imagine the administration of power to be divided between competing
institutions (as, for instance, if the Church were said to be in charge of
regulating the "lawes of God" and the monarch those pertaining to civil
institutions). The status of these underived, conditioning laws, divine and
natural, is stipulated rather than explored—but the division between underived and conditioning laws, on the one hand, and, on the other, derived
and constituting power (for instance, a community or another corporate
entity, which may delegate, grant, or "give" sovereignty, but only when
that act is erased *in advance*, envisioned as creating no obligation or charge,
leaving no trace) itself has no clear standing in Bodin or in Schmitt. In
whose hands, then, does this division rest? What is its logical status?

This is how Derrida approaches the matter in *Rogues*; his formulation
is almost identical to the one we find in "Provocation: Forewords":

> A pure sovereignty is indivisible or it is not, as all the theoreticians of sover-
> eignty have rightly recognized, and that is what links it to the decisionist
> exceptionality spoken of by Schmitt. This indivisibility excludes it in princi-
> ple from being shared, from time and from language. From time, from the
> temporalization that it infinitely contracts, and thus, paradoxically, from
> history. In a certain way, then, sovereignty is ahistorical; it is the contract
> contracted with a history that retracts in the instantaneous event of the
> deciding exception, an event that is without any temporal or historical
> thickness.[6]

The fantasy of the "instantaneity" of the event (perhaps even, to borrow
Nicolas Abraham's words, its "fictitious yet necessary integrity") is a
matter of old concern to Derrida—one thinks of *Speech and Phenomena*,
for instance, or, more recently, of *Politics of Friendship*—and here it joins
a running discussion of Nancy's important work on the notion of community, which for Nancy turns upon a remarkable form of primary, traumatic sharing or dividing (*partage*).[7] *Partage* flows from a Freudian

account of the sharing of the father's body, familiar from *Totem and Taboo*, for instance (one thinks, likewise, of Frazer). Fraternity—and hence, Nancy argues, community and in particular the paradoxical notion of communal or fraternal sovereignty—emerges from and depends upon the primary sacrifice and sharing of the father's body. Derrida rightly associates the mystical form of this whole, paternal body with a Christological discourse and the event of its sharing with the equally mystical indivisibility of the exceptional decision: in Schmitt, and in theoretical accounts of pure sovereignty, the event of the decision (to divide) is undivided, just as the event of the dividing or sharing of the father's body is itself singular and indivisible (that is to say, it is, as Nancy puts it, "le partage de l'incommensurable").

To read Nancy with Schmitt, as Derrida does in *Rogues*, makes the difficulties in each position patent: sovereignty is pure to the extent that the exceptional decision equally divides the indivisible (of the father's body); it is pure when it rests upon an event distinguished, which is to say, divided from historical experience (which is always already shared, partial, divided) in being unshared, impartial, and indivisible. Nancy makes no claims to the anthropological or historical accuracy of his account, any more than *Totem and Taboo* does (in its more careful moments) to its own tale of fraternal parricide. Like the sharing of the father that is its content, or like the division or dividing of conditioning, underived, natural or theological laws from the constituting, self-erasing gifts of sovereign power that we find in Bodin, the (event of the) sovereign decision may be a sort of fiction, cultural or individual, an oedipalized fantasy of such a sharing. Nevertheless, the function of this cultural or individual fantasy is to rescue the idea of the father, the idea of the indivisible event, the idea of the exceptional decision, the "integrity of the parental figure" from the sharing, the publication, the communal divisions and fraternal negotiations that Nancy imagines. This totemic sharing and ideal reconstituting of the father's body remain a matter of necessity in Nancy's account, not so much an attribute or an accidental quality of the (event of the) decision as its very substance. The integrity of the sovereign and spontaneous decision to share the father's body takes the place of that shared, consumed, sacramentalized body, becomes the substance of the unwrought community, its shared memory, its immanent law. And as indivisible substance, the sovereign decision falls outside of language, time, and history.

At this point in Derrida's redaction, the distinctly Scholastic tropes employed throughout Nancy's work reach a kind of exasperated impasse. For *as* indivisible substance, stripped of the attribute—divisibility—that makes him a father, the sacrificed father always falls outside of the community of his successors: he alone cannot share his divided body. The father-ideal or imago reconstituted from the indivisible event of his dividing, his sacrifice, becomes manifestly, classically the onto-theological ground for community—a community that shares, consumes, and includes him but that he cannot join, can be no part of. Nancy, Derrida suggests, can neither step beyond this impasse nor evade it because Nancy is too close, or not quite close enough, to the classic, "theoretical" view of sovereignty.

Recall how Derrida phrases that view, both in "Provocation: Forewords" and in *Rogues*: "Pure sovereignty is indivisible or it is not, as all theorists of sovereignty have rightly recognized, and that's what ties it to the exceptionality of decision that Schmitt discusses." Set aside, for the moment, the perplexing modifier *pure*. In *Rogues*, and much more briefly in "Provocations," the proposition that "all theorists of sovereignty have recognized," that "pure sovereignty is indivisible or it is not," is divided, to use the Boethian and the Scholastic term, into a few alternatives. "Pure sovereignty," the little logical table undergirding Derrida's argument might run, "is indivisible or it is not (sovereignty)," an ontological claim; "pure sovereignty is indivisible or it is not (pure)," a Platonic claim; "pure sovereignty is indivisible or it is not (indivisible)," a claim having the form of the basic logical necessity P is S or it is not S; in no case can P be both S and not-S. Attributes or predicates—divisibility or indivisibility, say—may be imagined on the model of accidents—for instance, as if one said "A table is round" and meant by this that all tables are round, when only some are. Or they may be imagined as subject to historical variation (for instance, "The sun revolves around the earth"). Finally, one might imagine "indivisibility" to be predicated of sovereignty on the model of an attribute that cannot be removed from, divided from, the entity of which it is predicated.

The class of essential attributes or predicates, to which "indivisibility" must be assumed to belong, is a matter of long-standing interest to early modern logicians, who generally followed Aristotle's *Posterior Analytics* and Boethius's commentary in distinguishing three forms, essential predication *de omni*, *per se*, and *universale*.[8] In all three cases, and more generally underlying all of these divided forms of the proposition, the limit-form of essential attribution is tautology: "the sun is the sun"; "a table is a table"; "sovereignty is sovereignty." It is with respect to this class of essential attributes, because they are explicitly undergirded by a tautologous logic of identity, that early modern logicians make the key association between predication and sovereignty—a purely theoretical association that establishes and protects the theoretical view of both logic and sovereignty in early modernity, in Bodin, in Schmitt, and in Nancy.

Take Thomas Blundeville's *Art of Logike* of 1599, for instance. "Essentiall predication," he writes, is:

> a naturall & usuall kinde of speech, whereby one thing is naturally & properly spoken of another, or as the Logitians say, when words superior are spoken of their inferiors being of one self affinity as when the generall kind is spoken of any his speciall kindes, or the special kinde of any his Individuums . . . for such speeches are both naturall and of necessitie, because the predicat is aptly applied to his subject.[9]

The analogy between the hierarchy of kinds (universal, genus, species, individual) and a rough social organization is primitive, but it is explicitly naturalized ("naturall & usuall," "naturally & properly spoken," "both naturall and of necessitie") and hard to miss. The proposition that "words superior are spoken of their inferior" governs the subsequent couples, genus-species and species-individual; the companion stipulation, that this difference in level (in generality) obtain between "words" "of one self affinity" hardly registers. It seems an entirely formal requirement, designating only that upper-level words can be predicated only of lower-level words related to them as species to universal or genus to species and so on. No breaches of affinity or of hierarchy are countenanced or even imaginable: a proposition like "sovereignty is indivisible" depends on a prior affirmation that "sovereignty is sovereignty," which establishes both the self-identity of the class to which the word belongs (a universal is a universal and nothing else; a species a species, and so on) and the identity of "self affinity" (a word is a member of one of those self-identical classes, and no more). Remark that Bundeville's exaggerated naturalization of the logic of sovereignty ("naturall & usuall," "naturally & properly spoken," "both naturall and of necessitie") in some respects undercuts his argument—or at least tends to tinge it with the colors of compensation. Blundeville's "nature" is always restrained by an additional, supplementary word: *usual, proper, necessary*—surely because "nature" is in this period a domain in which classification is not just unsystematic but also under extraordinary Mandevillean pressures, external as well as internal, from natural philosophy, a flourishing trade in exotic cultural tropes in conjunction with equally exotic, hitherto unseen commodities, travel narratives, marvelous accounts of voyages of discovery. A "natural" logic unrestrained by use, propriety, and necessity (and even one restrained in these ways) could and

did countenance uncategorizable or over-categorizable affinities, amphib-
ologous words belonging to more than one class or terms both predicated
of and serving to predicate more than one subject, serving and mastering
two or more masters: hypogriffs, and "Anthropophagi, and men whose
heads/Do grow beneath their shoulders," as Othello puts it (1.3.143–44).
A "natural" logic like that Blundeville invokes could and did countenance
paradoxes of subordination and predication, aporias rigorously excluded
from classical, even Ramist logic: propositions like "pure sovereignty is
indivisible and it is not sovereignty" or "sovereignty is indivisible and it is
not indivisible."

"Divided, in their dire division"

The impasses that Blundeville's account discloses in the logic of sovereignty and in the sovereignty of logic take shape not in the theoretical and
practical treatises on logic and sovereignty of the period but more vividly
and consequentially among the hypogriffs and anthropophagi of what I've
referred to as the early modern sphere of cultural production. It is here
that we should look for early traces of the "aporetic of divisible sovereignty" that Derrida sets before his twenty-first-century readers, whose
archaic form we saw in Sophocles' injunction that the wounded sovereign
be guarded in the city, not sacrificed.

My subtitle, "Divided, in their dire division," comes from Richmond's
famous lines closing *Richard III*—perhaps the least equivocal assertion of
the so-called Tudor myth of history to be found in Shakespeare's work
and surely his most obscure treatment of political division. The battle is
won; the "bloody dog" lies dead; the dreadful, traumatic wars of the Roses
draw to a close; the victorious Richmond—the future Henry VII, grand-
father of Elizabeth I—is presented by Stanley with the "long-usurped roy-
alty" "plucked" from Richard's "dead temples." Richmond's words run
like this:

> Inter their bodies as become their Births.
> Proclaim a pardon to the soldiers fled
> That in submission will return to us;
> And then, as we have ta'en the sacrament,
> We will unite the white rose and the red.
> Smile, heaven, upon this fair conjunction,
> That long have frown'd upon their enmity:

What traitor hears me and says not Amen?
England hath long been mad, and scarr'd herself;
The brother blindly shed the brother's blood;
The father rashly slaughter'd his own son;
The son, compell'd, been butcher to the sire.
All this divided York and Lancaster,
Divided, in their dire division.
O now let *Richmond* and *Elizabeth*,
The true succeeders of each royal House,
By God's fair ordinance conjoin together,
And let their heirs, God, if Thy will be so,
Enrich the time to come with smooth-fac'd peace,
With smiling plenty, and fair prosperous days.
(Folio: "And let thy Heires [God if thy will be so]
Enrich the time to come, with Smooth-fac'd Peace,
With smiling Plenty, and faire Prosperous dayes.")[10]

The mild controversy that attends the impenetrable phrase "All this divided York and Lancaster,/Divided, in their dire division" flows in part from a slight divergence between the Folio and the Quarto versions. The Quarto spelling renders "devided" and "devision," with a nice play on *device*, and suppresses the comma after Richmond's second "devided"; "We have nothing but the reported Q1 to rely upon here, and the F. compositor is being wretchedly careless," J. Dover Wilson complained. The line's obscurity irritates because it crops up, clotted in alliteration and doubled "divisions," just as the clear tones of providence sound out, retrospect and prospect chiming in unison, the kingdom's fate riding on Richmond's tongue. Deciding just what "Divided, in their dire division" might mean, if indeed it means anything, appears trivial enough when weighed against "all this" that once divided York and Lancaster, which has been the subject of the play, or against the "conjoining" of the two houses that "now" takes the place of those old divisions. "All this," what we have just heard recounted by Richmond, what we recollect from the cycle of plays that now concludes, "All this divided York and Lancaster," not only against each other but also within each camp, divided them against themselves. Surely this would suggest, not that "dire division" divided the two camps, but rather that York and Lancaster *shared* at least this: that both camps were divided, each within each, each against the other. And so the Oxford and Norton editions of the play reasonably replace the divisive Folio and Quarto "Divided, in their dire division" with

"United in their dire division," helpfully glossed in *The Norton Shakespeare* as "Joined by hatred, having nothing in common but mutual antagonism."[11] For the only "division" that matters as *Richard III* draws to a close is the one marked by the crown's return to its proper place, a division now overcome, conjoined, united: Richard's brief reign divided a long, legitimate line, now restored. We who listen to Richmond are in consequence divided from Richard's division and from the divisions shared by York and Lancaster, apart from them and united as a result of this division from division.

Recall Richmond's closing lines. His orders to "Inter their bodies as become their Births" and his proclamations of pardon distinguishing those who return "in submission" from those who will not are mixed speech acts expressing corporate wishes ("Smile, heaven, upon this fair conjunction"; "O now let *Richmond* and *Elizabeth*, . . ./By God's fair ordinance conjoin together,/And let their heirs, God, if Thy will be so,/Enrich the time"). These proclamations, orders, vows, and manifestations of hope work because the truth of Richmond and Elizabeth's succession chimes with "God's fair ordinance" and the sovereign will that they express echoes God's own.[12] The "dire" political division between York and Lancaster and within each camp has now been replaced by the union of two distinct orders of submission: the submission of a subject to the sovereign, and the submission of his or her speech to the "fair ordinance" and the "will" of God. Richard's genius, we reflect, lay in making the first appear to be proof of the second; Richmond now seeks to make the second the grounds for the first. The complex negotiation staged in these lines between "united" orders of "division" and corresponding (if indeed they do correspond) forms of submission represents *in nuce* the cultural mechanism by means of which a theological-administrative conception of sovereignty begins a slow migration into the domain of the political-administrative.

But just how sharp this "dire division" can be remains a matter of uncertainty. Although the perspective that Richmond assumes and holds out to us appears safe from the limitations on sovereignty so nervously envisioned and rigorously excluded by the theoretical treatments that Derrida recalls, there is much in Richmond's words to suggest that the exercise of sovereignty will depend, even in the "enriched" future time that *Richard III* envisions, upon divisions every bit as dire as those that set York against Lancaster in the first place. Let me return to Richmond's "division." The obscure crux we have been teasing, the line "Divided, in their dire division," evokes the secondary, now archaic musical sense of *division* as a descant, the execution of a melodic transition between longer notes achieved by dividing each of them into shorter notes.[13] The shorter the interval, the more divided the melodic line, the better—the more virtuosic, the closer too to mimicking the continuous, undivided, smooth transition that certain nonpercussive instruments, and the human voice, can achieve.[14] The "smooth" face of peace, amiable Plenty, and fair Prosperity not only serve to contrast Richard's disfigured body but token the shape assumed by Richmond's brief history, "smooth" in having refigured "dire division" as the regulated elaboration of a patterned progress. The trauma of "dire division" (or rather, the division that Richard provoked in the fabric of British history, which Richmond now heals) works "now," in retrospect, merely as a "smooth" transition between historical periods, as between points in a melody. Richmond's form of sovereignty replaces Richard's but cannot be divided from it without retaining the very notion of an unregulated division, an unsmoothing of the face of providence. Richmond's words work not only as Shakespeare's description of a state of affairs, one might say, but as a sort of fantasy or as a vehicle for forgetting. We must be "divided" from the "dire division" represented by civil war—and this dividing must be both an example of the new order and yet "divided" from "dire division" *direly*: absolutely, unambiguously, unbridgeably. Because it is precisely the instrument of iniquity, the means of corrupting sovereignty, of unsmoothing what is "fair," Richard's moralizing must be buried, forgotten—with consequent danger to the play, which lives, in a sense, from staging it.

If Richmond's perspective, editorial as well as providential, appears suddenly quite a bit less divided from Richard's divisions, it is surely in part because *Richard III* plays on the different idioms and circumstances that inflect the concept of division in the sphere of cultural production midway through Elizabeth's reign—religious, political, musical, even pedagogical idioms and circumstances, determining and overdetermining each other and the closing lines of *Richard III*, immensely complicating the task of conjoining our time to Elizabeth's, or Shakespeare's to Richard III's. I've suggested how the musical sense of *division* may begin to thicken Shakespeare's understanding of political division at the play's end; here, stenographically, is a quick survey of *division*'s companion registers.

Richard III plays obviously on the cultural association of "division" with the interruption of political succession, a matter of increasing anxiety in British court and popular culture as the childless Elizabeth aged, especially in the years directly after the defeat of the Spanish Armada.[15] Shakespeare's inquiry into the legitimacy of "Heaven's substitutes," as John of Gaunt puts it in *Richard II*, and a fortiori of their substitutes, the usurping

Richards and Claudiuses, the Angelos, Hotspurs, and so on, draws much
of its urgency from the threat these deputies, surrogates, and usurpers pose
to smooth succession in both the genealogical and the temporal sense.[16]
Richmond's distinctly apocalyptic tone is strategic—it reinforces the association of Richard's reign with upheavals and divisions to be healed by a
revealed order, here taking Richmond's shape.

It also echoes an important line of patristic glosses on *division* that link
the notion to a millenarian prophetic idiom, to sectarian disagreements
within the established church, and to political schism. The text to which
these glosses attach is the Book of Daniel; Daniel, whose role as a figure
of justice Shakespeare elsewhere invokes explicitly, for instance, in *The
Merchant of Venice*, stands implicitly behind Richmond's "conjoining"; the
"dire division" he describes and seeks to set behind all England evokes the
division that Daniel reads upon Belshaz'zar's wall and in his future. *Phares*,
the last word that the mysterious hand writes on the Biblical wall, means
divisio (for instance, in Isidore, who links the term *phares* etymologically to
the Pharisees, and in the Vulgate), or, less commonly, *fragmentum* (Petrus
Comestor); the King James Bible specifies that Belshaz'zar's kingdom "is
divided, and given to the Medes and Persians." More proximately, the
Jesuit leader Robert Persons's influential treatise *A Christian Directorie
Guiding Men to Their Saluation* (1585) makes explicit the connection
between the patristic construction of the scene from the Book of Daniel
and the schism that had already driven Persons and so many other English
Jesuits into exile. (The years between 1580, the date of Edmund Campi-
on's *Challenge to the Privy Council*, and 1585, when an act was proclaimed
designating all Jesuits who sought to enter England traitors, present what
Persons's biographer rather understatedly calls a "depressing picture of
persecution" of Catholics, Jesuits in particular, under Elizabeth.[17]) After
explaining that "Balsasar king of Babylon, sitting at his banket merry upon
a tyme, espied suddainlie, certaine fingares without a hande, that wrote in
the wall" and briefly glossing the three baffling words written there, Persons exclaims:

> Oh, that thes three golden and most significant wordes, ingrauen by
> th'angel upon Balsasars wall, were redesteredi upon everie dore and poste
> in Christiandome, or rather imprinted in the harte of eche Christian. . . .
> What shall we expect, that haue not onlie lesse weight then we should haue,
> but no weight at all, in the most of our actions? What may such men (I
> saye) expecte, but only that most terrible threat of diuision made unto
> Balsasar, (or rather worse if worse may be,) that is, to be deuided from God

and his Angels; from participation with our Saueour; from communion of Sainctes; from hope of our inheritance; from our portion celestial, and life euerlasting? According to th'expresse declaration, made hereof by Christ himself in thes wordes, to the negligent seruant: *The Lord of such a servant, shall come at a daye when he hopeth not, and at an houre that he knoweth not; and shal devide him out, and assigne his parte with hypocrites, wher shal be weeping and gnashing of teeth.*[18]

As Persons's words suggest, "that most terrible threat of diuision" from "participation," "communion," "hope," and "life everlasting" not only marks out the Christian from the non-Christian but also stands in for the equally sharp division between those Christians on whose heart the Book of Daniel's words are truly engraved and those who "haue . . . lesse weight" than they should, or none at all: between the Roman Catholic and the Anglican and Reformed churches. Liturgically, this distinction turns in part on a further division, indeed on the *divisibility* of certain sacraments—for Persons is describing nothing less than the participation in or the apportioning of the Eucharist. The restored monarchy is indeed announced in a sacramental scene: "Proclaim a pardon to the soldiers fled," Richmond announces, "That in submission will return to us;/And then, as we have ta'en the sacrament,/We will unite the white rose and the red."[19] Thus Bishop Thomas Bilson's 1585 *The True Difference Betweene Christian Subiection and Unchristian Rebellion* argues the Anglican position on the sacrament of communion—at its most radical, the distribution of the officiating function across the entire congregation, indeed across the universal congregation of the faithful—like this: "our Sauiour appointed neither time, nor place, to be respected in his supper, but the word & elements: charging vs to do what he did, which is to breake & giue, that all may be partakers of one bread; to diuide the cup, that all may drincke thereof."[20]

The extraordinary density of "division's" overdeterminations should not surprise us. As Lacan also saw, the scene from the Book of Daniel on which Persons's gloss turns and which stands behind Richmond's closing words serves as something like the primal scene of textual exegesis for the patristic tradition and its early modern epigones. Jerome's famous gloss to Daniel is explicit: the words on Belshaz'zar's wall provoke "a need not only for reading the inscription but also for interpreting what had been read, in order that it might be understood what these words were announcing"—a need for interpretation that rings out, expressly, in *Richard III's* closing construction of sovereignty.[21] The small obscurity in Richmond's words—dividing and doubling division—is written upon the wall of theoretical approaches to sovereignty: in it the correspondence between political sovereignty and the sovereignty of interpretive rules governing logical division is both asserted and revealed to be inadequate. Neither the negotiation amongst "division" that *Richard III* or Richmond alone appears to offer a public weary of war nor the discursive determinations and overdeterminations of the concept of division, is governed by a perspicuous, constituted word: the play offers no agreed-upon set of rules or principles, either theologically set or pragmatically derived, according to which a reader or an interpreter might decide whether submission to a sovereign stands upon, or instead legitimates, or bears neither relation to, the submission of the sovereign to "fair ordnance," whether divine or constitutional.

The stakes are high indeed, for the analogy between logical and political submission (if it is an analogy) flows in both directions: rule following in interpretation and in argument derives its authority, in practice and theoretically (in pedagogy and conceptually) from the indivisible, which we now understand to be uninterpretable or unanalyzable, sovereignty of the rule (of a rule). Political sovereignty in turn derives its authority in some measure, in practice and theoretically, from the structure of rule following that Scholasticism assigns to the procedures of logical division and analysis. Hence the strange, reflexive repetitiousness of Richmond's lines; hence the invaginating shift in levels of analysis and predication that we encounter in the patristic gloss on Daniel's division (of division): "division" is a synonym for a dilemma (for instance, the dilemma posed to Shakespeare's readers and audience by Richmond's words, or to Belshaz'-zar's court by the hand's mysterious script) and also for the logical procedures invoked in resolving dilemmas—a synonymy not infrequently manifest in the same work.

Take, for example, George Abbot's *An Exposition vpon the Prophet Ionah*, in which, discussing (of all things) seaweed, Abbot declares that "Experience hath confirmed this in the huge Atlantike sea, as men saile to America, whereout doth grow a very strange Dilemma or Diuision, because either they [the seaweed] be there without any rootes at all, and that is very maruellous, or because the rootes do go downe exceeding deepe in the water, which is not otherwise affoorded by nature in thinne spindie bodies."[22] A bit farther along, Abbot clarifies: "My charge at this time is, to shew the meanes of [Jonah's] deliuerance, which is set downe so briefly, and plainely in my text, that the words do neither need diuision, nor much interpretation."[23] Or again: "What is Division?" asks Blundevil-le's *Art of Logike*. "Division is the parting or dividing of a word or thing that is more generall unto other wordes or things lesse generall. . . . [It is] said to be the division of a name . . . when some Equivoke or doubtfull word is divided into his manifold significations." And later: division "helpeth to teach playnely to define, and to make thinges that be compound intricate or confused, to appear simple, playne and certayne."[24] What might appear a logical weakness—a term or word figuring in the predicate as well as the subject role, governing but also governed, and hence in no way identical to itself, ambiguously part of the class of terms to which it seems to belong, yet integral to that class as well—is turned to advantage, in Richmond's words as in their overdetermined cultural context. The motility of division rather than its indivisibility serves to suture the governance of logical rules and political sovereignty: it is no easier, however, to determine what sort of predicate "motility" can be than it is to determine what sort of subject, or what sort of word, "division" is.

Motility, or Logic in Exile

Father Robert Persons, whom we last encountered as author of the 1585 *A Christian Directorie Guiding Men to their Saluation*, published anonymously some years later a treatise titled *Newes from Spayne and Holland*, consisting of "An information of Inglish affayres in Spayne with a conference made thereupon in Amsterdame of Holland." The treatise, one of a number of Persons's writings from exile that respond to the new constraints on English Catholics following the 1588 Armada, was published in 1593, almost exactly contemporaneous with the redaction of *Richard III*. Written in the aftermath of the Armada, which the English Jesuit mission had supported, a support Persons had a small hand in conveying to King Philip II of Spain, it is a document quite different from *A Christian Directorie* in its treatment of history, forgetting, and of the indivisibility of sovereignty. In *Newes*, Persons details for a nameless correspondent his recent travels from England to Holland, south to Lisbon, then through Spain. He takes the opportunity to describe the English colleges in Spain, to relate with charming tendentiousness how British prisoners in Spain would come to embrace Catholicism, and to convey the strange, reverse Mariolatry that filled discussions of Elizabeth's policies among English and continental Catholics. A "Second Parte of this letter, conteyning certaine considerations of State upon the former relation," written, Persons tells us, on his return to Holland, serves as a gloss and epilogue to *Newes*.

Newes from Spayne and Holland is a deeply peculiar document, a bit of a hippogriff in its own way—a travelogue, a homily, a political and religious tract, a commonplace book, a school inspector's almanac or report. It includes, among other notable *varia*, the transcript of a letter from the Grand Turk to Elizabeth I, as well as a disputation set in Amsterdam among "divers gentlemen, captaynes, schollers, and others, as well Inglish, Scottish, Irish & French, as also some Italians & Dutchmen" concerning "certaine considerations of State upon the former relation."[25] At the center of *Newes* we find a remarkable account of Persons's visit to a newly founded Jesuit school in Seville, one of a number of such colleges that Persons had helped make possible throughout Europe. Persons, arriving in Seville from Lisbon, tells his notional correspondent that he finds there "a goodly English Seminarie newly begone."[26] It is, of course, disingenuous for Persons to speak of "finding" this school, which he had been at great pains to see founded and endowed. The seminary, the School of Saint Gregory, called "de los ingleses," has been by far the least studied of Spain's Jesuit colleges (the ones in Valladolid and Madrid having garnered most of the attention, in part because their archives are more thoroughly preserved, in part because the Colegio de los ingleses survived a much briefer period). And Persons's visit seems unexceptional. It coincides, he tells his reader, with "certaine feastes and excercises of learning which these young men made upon certaine daies" before a number of the city's luminaries (the Cardinal Archbishop don Rodrigo de Castro, the governor and noble men of the city, "as also before the whole university and cleargie of Sivil").[27] At a certain point in his description of the festivities "of St. Thomas of Canterbery," celebrated on December 29, 1592 (a sermon in Latin on the life of St. Thomas, followed by its English version and an account of his martyrdom, followed by a second sermon, in Spanish and not transcribed, but serving, Persons tells his reader, "to give the people a reason of so many Inglish mens coming forth of Ingland in these days"), Persons stops, addresses his reader, and confesses to having—almost—forgotten to record for him "a certayne fayre paper set up this day in the Inglish Colledge emongst other poemes, and lerned devises of the schollers."[28] This "fayre paper" represents "the antithesis or contrary procedinges of two King Henries of England, to witt, king Henry the second . . . who persecuted S. Thomas of Canterbury in his life, but after repented . . . and king Henry the eight who fower hundred yeares after his death cited and condemned him and destroyed his sepulcre."[29]

It is not entirely clear just what this "paper" actually was—a broadsheet? Another poem or "devise"? A theatrical backdrop, with accompanying text? At any rate, it is the occasion for one of Persons's most striking

accounts of the derivation of political sovereignty, an extraordinary combination of ecphrasis and argumentation, dramatics and architecture,
homiletics and didactics—a sort of monster within the generically heterogeneous body of *Newes*. Persons describes the "fayre paper" in detail. He
says he believes "The Representation of the Two Persecutions by the Two
King Henryes of Ingland Against S. Thomas of Canterbury" has recently
been "engraved and printed"; perhaps to add to the anecdote's realism, he
notes for his readers the colors of the sketches, the arrangement of "large
and fayrely paynted" images and text on the folios, etc. Directly under the
title, this image sets out the "antithesis" that the pamphlet will then follow
through:

> king Henry the second on the right hand armed and angry and striking at
> S. Thomas that was paynted before him, flying away and falling downe on
> his knees, and over the kings head is written *Henricus Secundus Angliae Rex*,
> and between him and S. Thomas was written, *Persequitur vivum & fugien-*
> *tem*, he pursueth him in his life flying from him: On the left side is paynted
> king Henry the eight very fat and furious and S. Thomas lying before him
> with the ensigns of glory, and over the king is written, *Henricus octavus*
> *Angliae Rex*, and between them is written, *Persequitur mortuum & regnan-*
> *tem*. He pursueth him dead and rayning in heaven.[30]

Masques and "representations," occasional, ceremonial works of school
theater performed on saints' days or to mark other festivities, were common in colleges (by no means just Jesuit colleges) throughout Spain and
Europe, of course—and the colleges in Seville were no exception.[31] The
best-known surviving Spanish work of school-theater, for instance, is a
Tragœdia Divi Ermenegildi Regis, or *Tragedia de San Hermenegildo*, performed in Seville at the principal Jesuit college some two years before
"The Two Persecutions" was performed, enacted, or merely posted as part
of the extended festivities inaugurating the Colegio de San Gregorio.[32]
Painted scenarios or "devises" served as backdrops or as tableaux decorat-
ing the hall in which the various celebratory sermons and disputations
were held. This was certainly the case with the *Tragedia de San Hermene-*
gildo, by all accounts an enormously splashy, long, and ostentatious affair,
with spectacular, three-dimensional backdrops and settings, which would,
one supposes, have served as both a model for, and a bit of a gall to the
more modest ceremonies opening the much less wealthy Colegio de San
Gregorio.

Persons's account of the "paper" representing "The Two Persecutions," scrupulous in its detail, is also precise in employing a lexicon at

once spatial and recognizably pedagogical. The "devise," he tells his reader, is organized along a series of "rancks," which play out the little allegory set forth at the beginning of the "Representation." One imagines a sort of large-scale graphic novel, consisting of a series of panels, sequentially organized.

Ranck, the term Persons uses to suggest the architecture of the "devise," here intends, clearly, to evoke the perspectival sense of depth sought by contemporary stage sets and notoriously achieved in the production of the *Tragedia de San Hermenegildo*. But the word has some trouble, as it were, not breaking ranks—as we might expect of so generically mixed a text. *Ranck* is also a word used in contemporary logical treatises as a synonym for "class," "kind," or "set" and to designate—to map, in some cases—the parts of a syllogism and the relation and function of those parts. In the idiosyncratic lexicon of "strange, and new devised termes" that we find in Ralph Lever's 1573 *The Arte of Reason, Rightly Termed, Witcraft* (where we encounter the neologism *backset* for "predicate," *saywhat* for "definition," *storehouse* for "attribute," *seate* for *modus*), *ranke* stands for *figura*, the Scholastic term employed to classify syllogisms according to the distribution of their premises and conclusions.[33] Thus "a reason in Barbara," the first of the Scholastic logical figures (or, in Lever's idiom, "a reason in the fyrste seate of the first ranke"), "concluding that the first terme is generally sayde of the thirde," may be represented in this way (where the letter *a* stands, conventionally, for a universal affirmative).

Lever envisions three "rankes," based on permutations of the general, proving, and special terms; in this way his *Witcraft* is considerably simpler

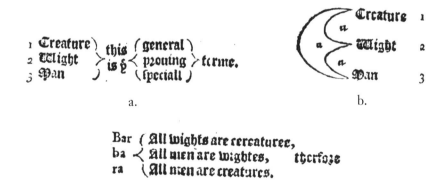

a.   b.

c.

4a–c. Ralph Lever, *The Arte of Reason, Rightly Termed, Witcraft* (London, 1573), details of 114–15

than the most exhaustive of the Scholastic tables of figures. The scheme's particulars are of less interest than its topology, whose oddity Persons's account of the "ranck" of representations in "The Two Persecutions" shares: the semicircle whose base is defined by two semicircles, designating a spatial relation of inclusion or interiority. "Wights" are included in the circle or set, one might say, of creatures, and men in the set of "wights," hence men are also included in the set of creatures. The limits of the spatial representation of logical forms are as evident here as they are in Lever's predecessors, Ramist as well as Aristotelian, British as well as continental.[34] The direction of the predication—"witcraft's" movement—and its quality (what kind of predication it is: *a*, all members of the class of "man," or "wights," or "creatures") are governed by a supplementary numerology (1, 2, 3) and lexicon (*a* stands for "universal affirmative"), whose senses cannot be derived from the scheme itself and require an additional, sovereign "ranck," as it were, of a different order entirely.

How one might visualize this additional "ranck" and how one might understand its relation to the figures it governs is thus not only the subject of debate in treatises such as the *Grammatographia* of Jacques Lefèvre d'Étaples or the *Mnemonic Logic* of Thomas Murner. It has crept into the language with which Persons reflects upon the pedagogical value of the allegorical "Representation," of the secondary, visual depiction of that play, and of his own account of both—and upon the form that the representation of sovereignty can take in these three related spaces: the space of the "Representation," the space of the "large and fayrely paynted" images before which the play is to be represented, and the seeming space of Persons's own *Newes*. The third "ranck" of "The Two Persecutions" thus proceeds: "in the middle is paynted Queene Elizabeth beholding sadly the one and the other example, & ouer her head is written, *Elizabetha Henricorum filia*, for that she is discended of both these Henryes, and the sentence written beneth is *E duobus elige*, choose which you wil of thes two."[35]

The little allegory's religious-political sense is clear enough. The students at the English college invite Elizabeth to choose her example, to choose her father and her relation to a traumatic history—and they understand the legitimacy of her claim to sovereignty to flow from this choice, from this decision. Furthermore, the choice facing the queen is not simply between two policies regarding the state's Catholic population, but also between two dispositions toward history. One can assume responsibility for this or that past event (the killing of Saint Thomas, say), repent it, and thereby memorialize it, or one can repeat the injury it entailed by seeking to erase its memorialization. The startling image of Henry VIII digging up Thomas's bones "with a pickaxe" and scattering his ashes serves to represent the Anglican effort to deconsecrate the saint, to erase the history of his martyrdom and burial—but also to attest to the hold that the past has, *as a tomb*, upon the present. Like the college's students, we presume, Persons hopes that the printed "paper" of this representation will have the effect of conveying "newes" to Elizabethan society, perhaps with the intent of inclining the Queen's choice toward one Henry rather than the other, one form of remembering rather than the other, toward legitimate sovereignty rather than tyranny.

But Persons's description goes awry with this third "ranck." Just how is Elizabeth beholding "the one and the other example"? Is she doing it at the same time? How would one represent that, in "large and fayrely paynted" images? Is she viewing her two ancestors sequentially? How would the paper represent that? To what sort of vision are Persons's reader and the audience of St. Gregory's college in the early 1590s invited? No *realistic* form of representation, on stage or page, can possibly capture this sort of divided vision and divided decision; no conventional logic, no topology can supply it. A supplementary lexicon and numerology are required, as in Lever's *Witcraft*, to translate an intractably unrepresentable topology or *grammatography*, to use Lefèvre's wonderful term, into a plausible phenomenology, to move from "antithesis," as *Newes* puts it, to choosing "which you wil." To this end, Persons adds a fourth, concluding "ranck" to the allegory, as if realizing not only that the decision offered to Elizabeth, however strongly weighted visually by the various demons dragging Henry VIII to hell and elevating Henry II to heaven, or semantically by the glosses promising damnation to the first, salvation to the second, may yet go against the Catholic camp—but also that the argumentative shape of his embedded "Representation" is slipping from his grasp. In this fourth "ranck" Persons gives us two "inglish students in their Colledg garments, one on the one side of the paper and the other on the other, holding up the said paper," each "ottring" Latin verses to Elizabeth "for explication of their meaning in this representation," urging her, in sum, "rather to follow the example of king Henry the second, that repented his sinnes, then king Henry the eight that died in the same." This is conventional and wholly unsurprising, the "explication" furnished by this last "ranck" serving as it were to divide, gloss, or interpret the allegory Persons has just presented to us, to help readers and audience alike move from the impasse—the dire division, the civil strife—of mere "antithesis" toward a providential outcome: the decision on which a legitimate claim to sovereignty can be founded, the choice of the right genealogy. So conventional is it, indeed, that the structure of a "representation" followed by a gloss may be said also to apply to *Newes* itself, whose first, generically fantastical section is followed by a commentary and interpretation. But to achieve this end, Persons's last "ranck" steps entirely outside of conventional space: the scene suddenly seems to fold in upon itself, to divide itself, the two students represented as standing within the paper but also outside of it, holding up "the said paper," not only uttering verses but uttering verses intended "for explication of their meaning in this representation"—where "their meaning" refers opaquely to the verses themselves (why would one need to explain, gloss or "divide" their meaning in the representation? surely the verses are intended to explicate the representation, to divide its words, as Blundeville's *Logike* might put it—or are the students so uncertain about their explication of the representation that they must explicate their explication? divide their division?), to the students (whose "meaning" in the representation certainly needs explicating, if the students are both within it and without it—but whose meaning is hardly likely to be clarified by an explication whose object is itself unclear), and most distantly to the figures of the two Henries (who by this time stand least in need of any explicating at all).

With this last, strange image—students inside as well as outside of the text they are explicating, if that indeed is what their poems do, inside as well as outside of their own history, divided between acting and holding up the representation of their acting—with this last "ranck" Persons is accomplishing a number of things. For one, he provides a rather moving analogue to the strange situation of "so many Inglish men . . . com[e] forth of Ingland in these days," the college's students and Persons himself: exiles, not wholly alien to what is properly English (they remain "Inglish men") but unable to return to England, wholly external to the sovereign, official conception of the state. This little story that Persons almost forgets to tell is also a story about forms of remembering—remembering the land from which one is exiled, to be sure, or pleading for the privilege of one recollection (Henry) over another (Henry). But it is also about memory's double difficulty: on the one hand, the impossibility of regarding *at the same time* two recollections, as if the "antithesis" between the two Henries required two consciousnesses; on the other hand, the supplement of "explication" intended to prove the superiority of one memory over the other as a reigning or governing or sovereign trope or model for imitation. Persons is also proposing for the explication of the representation this same complex logical position, within as well as without, part of the meta-discourse but also of the "Representation's" object discourse.

Persons conveys something of the historical paradox that attends theories of sovereignty based in the exceptional decision, in the ideal moment of the decision. His *Newes*, like Richmond's complex closing speech acts, seeks to show that sovereignty is a derived concept; to suggest that there's something peculiar about the nature of this concept (that there are members of the class described by that concept that fall within as well as without the concept: exiles); to suggest that this logically distributed sovereignty allows for a form of divisibility that does not return to hierarchy (which does not embed an underived moment: which is, or could be, radically republican); and to outline the aporetics of that divisible sovereignty. Where the triumphalist conclusion to *Richard III* embeds this radical historicization of sovereignty within the divisions that Richmond's words run on Richard's example, Persons embeds the derivation of sovereignty in an account of the paradoxical temporal topology linking representation to explication (In what way is the explication sovereign over the representation or the recollection of the father, if there is no generic division between the two?), example to *exemplum*, the inside of a representation to its outside. Conceptually as well as temporally, *Newes* renders it impossible to grant privilege to one over the other. For Persons, Elizabeth's sovereignty is most truly exercised when she gazes sadly, impossibly, passively, at both her fathers, at both her histories, gazing at both simultaneously and sequentially. In 1592, hers is the sovereignty of a nonchoosing, the disposition toward a nonchoice, a dwelling in dire division. Its emblem is the device of the two-headed monarch, divided between two fathers, each soliciting from his child her choice, her love, her obligation, and his fantasmatic but necessary integrity, a Janus-headed sovereign facing a divided and shared figure whose integral integrity is reborn in the single body of the monarchy. *Newes* furnishes the exile's alternative: in place of Elizabeth's structural passivity, the exacerbation of division, the radical distribution of sovereignty. This distribution of sovereignty, Persons tells his readers, is not to be understood as the mere partition of an integral attribute or a substance among a constituted class of terms or subjects: sovereignty's "shared indivisibility" is not the division of a predicate, indivisibility, within the same logical "ranck," within a class of terms "of one self affinity," as Blundeville puts it. The fourth "ranck" of Persons's *Newes*, the rank that stands outside of his representation and also within it, dividing the division that it represents, provides the pharisaical emblem of divisible sovereignty: ranks folding into and across ranks, attributes conditioning subjects and interpretations their objects, the supplementary lexicons, histories, and numerologies governing thought's movement enfolded in and excluded from the "self affinity" of thought. The emergence, in short, of a secularized, mobile, incomplete, and radically republican sovereign imaginary.

CHAPTER 3

The Logic of Sovereignty

Llegóse luego don Quijote y dijo:
—Dime tú, el que respondes: ¿fue verdad, o fue sueño lo que yo cuento
que me pasó en la cueva de Montesinos? ¿Serán ciertos los azotes de
Sancho mi escudero? ¿Tendrá efeto el desencanto de Dulcinea?
—A lo de la cueva—respondieron—,
hay mucho que decir: de todo tiene.

Now came Don Quixote, and said, "Tell me, thou that answerest, was
it true, or a dream, that (as I recount) befel me in Montesinos' Cave?
shall Sancho my squire's whipping be accomplished? shall Dulcinea
be disenchanted?" "For that of the cave," quoth the answerer, "there
is much to be said, it partakes of all."

—MIGUEL DE CERVANTES, *Don Quixote* II, chap. 72 (trans. Thomas Shelton)

Si vis vaticinari quot scuta sunt in marsupio tui socii,
hac arte procedendum est.

If you wish to predict how many coins are in the purse of your friend,
you must proceed by means of this art.

—JUAN MARTÍNEZ SILÍCEO, *Arithmetica Ioannis Martini, Scilicei, in theoricen
et praxim scissa* (1519)

A group of men enter a famous, forbidden cave located in the cellar of a tower—or is it a church? a house?—in a city on a hill. The date—sometime in the year 1546. The new ruler has sent the adventurers to look for something—treasure, perhaps. They were told, "In the cave you will find something." They return to the surface much later, terrified and empty-handed, giving strange and contradictory accounts of what they saw underground: vast caverns, animated statues, rivers, mysterious roaring winds. Many of them die soon after. The cave is sealed by the powerful ruler who sent them below, never to be reopened. The ruler goes on to become famous for his cruelty and his generosity.

The stuff of myths, no doubt. Even the questions it raises seem archaic. By what authority were they dispatched? Did they or did they not find the treasure they were promised, or just told about: told to seek, or advised they would not find? What sort of promise—or threat, or order—took them below? What did they see there? The story is also, in the version that I will set before you in this chapter, the ground on which an influential account of modernity is founded—the account that places in the early modern period the subtle emergence of secular political concepts from a historical substrate in which they were imagined theologically and linked to a new conceptualization of the experience of terror. Sovereignty, in particular the time or times of sovereignty, is my topic in this chapter, and the argument I will make, as well as the stories I will tell, concern not just the logical grounds on which modern sovereignty is established—its divisibility or indivisibility, its topology and topography—but also when historically modern sovereignty arises and when (at what time) we can designate that time. I will link the logic of sovereignty, an experience that we will learn to call "terror," the temporal conditions and horizons of sovereignty, and the conditions of our recognition or stipulation that here, at this point, something like a modern conception of sovereignty can be located, defined, or described.

As I did in thinking about Robert Person's strange conception of divisible sovereignty, I will put a great deal of weight upon a single word, the historicizing term *modern*. I am obviously echoing, once again, Schmitt's lapidary observation that "All significant concepts of the modern theory of the state are secularized theological concepts,"[1] but with a difference. To the extent that we are Schmittians—to the extent that we inhabit the modernity he describes, which is hardly uncontroversial—we are all nominalists as regards the time and the boundaries not just of sovereignty but of modernity as well: we take all significant concepts of modernity more broadly to be secularized theological concepts, relics of the stuff of myth, divine, providential, or universal histories washed in the prosaic bath of modernization, enlightenment, contingency. Disenchanted, Husserl would say. Three corollaries. First, concepts that represent, mark, or police the limits of "theology"—for example, with respect to companion disciplines with different histories, truth claims, and practices—are also limit-concepts for the modern theory of the state. Second, and vice versa, concepts that represent or mark the limits of the modern theory of the state, for example, with respect to fellow-traveling disciplines such as economics, sociology, anthropology, etc.—are also limit-concepts for theology. Finally, these reflexive limit-concepts are at issue when our modernity seeks out its historical antecedents or seeks to recognize itself in and by means of a past it forms or finds for itself.

The story at hand concerns the mutual limit that theology, the modern theory of the state, and secularized historiography find in a particularly complex logical problem and in an affect associated with it. From the phrase that I put in my imagined sovereign's mouth—the assertion to his servants "In this cave you will find something, a treasure or the absence of a treasure"—it may be clear that I am talking about the problem of future contingents. It is an inelegant name for a tricky problem, akin to the ones posed by the sorts of prophetic or oracular speech that Michael Wood has studied in his recent *Road to Delphi*.[2] I won't yet venture a definition of what future-contingent propositions are. Remark, however, that the sovereign is not a prophet or an oracle: when he asserts, "In this cave you will find something," he is doing something other than what the *pythia* did at Delphi, where another traveler might have heard "At the crossroads you will kill a man." He is also doing something other than what a logician or a philosopher does when he utters the same phrase, handling it as an example or a case of a nasty sort of truth-neutral proposition: "In this cave you will find something" or "There will be a sea battle tomorrow." The sovereign is doing something other than guessing or predicting, as the schoolboy in the epigraph to this chapter does, "how many coins are in a neighbor's pocket." Finally, he is doing something different from what Christ does in the garden when he says to Peter, "You will deny me thrice."

What, exactly, is the difference? Presumably the sovereign doesn't need to promise or to give examples. Nor does he require a method, a whole arithmetic, for knowing or foretelling. (Methods can be taught broadly, after all.) When he says, "Go into the cave," he does not need to explain why ("I want the treasure that you will find" or "I want the legend of the existence of treasure disproved") or to tell his subject how he knows what secrets lie underground, in the earth's pocket. What makes him sovereign is precisely that he guards, and by virtue of this guarding is perceived to possess, as one would a treasure, that which makes explanation unnecessary. It is *this* treasure, one might say, that Lear squanders through public division: the disposition to reason the need (2.2.439) behind his commands grows in his daughters and in his kingdom broadly, on ground tilled by the ceremonial acts of allegiance that open the play, and reveal the public logic of his sovereign decision to "express [his] darker purpose" (1.1.36).[3] That way, Shakespeare seems to suggest, madness lies—madness for the state and for the crown. Sovereign is he who treasures his "darker purposes" and allows and needs no expeditions into the shadowy caves of his motives. In my story, madness lies in the cave under the house, tower, church, or hill—or its causes, at any rate, appear to lie there. What might the relation be between the raving, varied accounts of the ill-fated expedition and the sovereign's promise, order, or proposition?

A couple of assertions, then—to be proven in the event. The problem of future contingents forms the border—or I should say *a* border—between philosophical, theological, and political discourse. And this border shifts remarkably, decisively, in the period Schmitt identifies as critical to the secularization of theological concepts: the period of early modernity.

The present-day shape of my cave and treasure story can be found in lines in which Agamben gives us something like a definition of sovereign power. For now, remark two things. First, the "definition" serves to define the period of Schmittian modernity, of *jus publicum europaeum*, a period that opens roughly in the early modern period and that is *now*—in Schmitt's and Agamben's chronology, a "now" that begins roughly at the end of the First World War—giving way to a new *nomos* of the Earth. And second, Agamben's definition has as weird a shape—it concerns as indeterminate a topology—as my cave and treasure tale. Here is Agamben's definition:

> The state of nature and the state of exception are nothing but two sides of
> a single topological process in which what was presupposed as external (the
> state of nature) now reappears [*ricompare ora*], as in a Möbius strip or a
> Leyden jar, in the inside (as state of exception), and the sovereign power is
> this [*questa*] very impossibility of distinguishing between outside and inside,
> nature and exception, *physis* and *nomos*. The state of exception is thus not
> so much a spatiotemporal suspension as a complex topological figure in
> which not only the exception and the rule but also the state of nature and
> law [*diritto*], outside and inside, pass through one another.[4]

I will return to this "complex topological figure" or "single topological process" or "topological zone of indistinction [*zona topologica di indistinzione*]"; for now, keep in mind the as yet unproven suggestion that Agamben inherits this zone from the classic problem of future contingents.

Agamben's gesture toward a definition of sovereign power seems to me less than satisfying, and the fully developed definition one finds in his recent work—whatever the nuance and historical precision it adds—still turns on the same lexicon and structure.[5] *Homo Sacer* becomes a work about the relation between governmentality and economy (in a very special sense), but it begins as an argument concerning the problem of definition, the definition of life we inherit from Greece—and it opens with the question of the relation between the terms for "life," *bios* and *zoē*, and the range of senses and uses each term designates, at certain times and to certain ends. One can thus legitimately ask whether Agamben has a consistent definition of "sovereign power." When we do so, we find not only a certain number of different definitions but also and more importantly a rather hesitant relation between the lexical-philosophic process of definition and the concept of sovereign power. This is not news. Foucault, who is Agamben's main interlocutor when it comes to the matter of power, notoriously resists providing any recognizable definition of power: what he calls an "analytic of power"—as opposed to a "theory" of power, for instance—is an account of cases of power use at one or another moment, grouped lexically and genealogically under certain conditions and for certain purposes. Foucault's modified nominalism permits him to use the term *power* without implying the existence, either transhistorically, universally, or ideally, of a subsistent substance or substantive called "power." Compare statements like this well-known one from *The History of Sexuality*: power is "the name that one attributes to a complex strategic situation in a particular society."[6] Or these: "power means relations, a more or less organized, hierarchical, coordinated cluster of relations," and power is "an open, more-or-less coordinated (in the event, no doubt, ill-coordinated) cluster of relations."[7] Expressions of this sort are not so much definitions as ways of describing or locating an act (the acts of attributing or designating) carried out felicitously by someone, under certain conditions and at certain times (in a particular society), with respect to a different strategic situation.[8]

Agamben, however, does provide a definition of power—and a logically peculiar one at that, what Wittgenstein might call a *queer* definition. "Sovereign power," Agamben says, "is this very impossibility of distinguishing [*discernere*] between outside and inside, nature and exception, *physis* and *nomos*." This is—even taking into account the difference between the terms *distinguishing* and *discerning*, *discernere*—in most ways both a confusing definition and a confusing way to define. (I'm using "confusing" not as an evaluative but rather as a descriptive term.) The definition is confusing on two grounds. First, it correlates an abstract noun or a nominal phrase, *sovereign power*, with a substantivized verbal expression, "distinguishing" or, in Italian, *discernere*, "discerning." Such substantivizations retain, willy-nilly, a trace of the act or event that the verb indicates, and they thus color the definition of the abstract noun with a particular "spatiotemporal suspension": with a normative case, the *nomos* in this instance too "passing through" *physis*.

A primitive version of Agamben's confusion might be represented by the pseudo-definitions "Love means never having to say you're sorry," or "Pleasure is eating a madeleine," or, as in Clarice Lispector's startling combination of the two, "Love is not to be devoured."[9] Here, "eating a madeleine" is surely a physical case or an instance of pleasure, rather than a definition of that abstract noun (if this were a definition rather than an instance, then other things that give pleasure would be found either not to give pleasure or to do so only by analogy to "eating a madeleine" or "not saying one is sorry"); "never having to say you're sorry," a sorry excuse for a definition of anything, is a particular pathology (or the particular privilege) of "love" or *noblesse obligée* that flowers in red-brick college quadrangles; and, finally, "not being eaten" is a form of "unrefined" love, Lispector's mysterious narrator tells us, proper to the "humidity of the jungle," where the "cruel refinements" of more "civilized" definitions do not apply. *Physis*, the "humidity of the jungle," or the red brick of Boston Brahmin circles, or even the flavor of a madeleine colors every definition with the particular case. When Agamben defines sovereign power as "this very impossibility of distinguishing between outside and inside, nature and exception, *physis* and *nomos*," the shadow of a particular case—of *this* effort to draw a distinction (and no other, or of any other only by analogy to the one I am pointing out), of *this* failed act of discernment (and no other)— falls upon the norm.

One understands that Agamben is not being gratuitously confusing but is in this shadowy way applying to the definition itself the topology that the definition describes. A definition is, one might say, the basic form of the proposition. A definition shapes the outline, the limits or *fines*, of the Venn diagram. "Sovereign power" is . . . , we might begin, defining "sovereign power," and what follows "is" is a finished, closed, limited, and immanently related set of properties, which, taken as a set, are the equivalent of "sovereign power." To this set of properties there corresponds a second set of cases of the exercise of sovereign power—what "sovereign power" is *in act*, in *physis*: historical instances, identified now and imagined here. Of course, this second set is closed as well, but in a different sense.

The lexicon of set theory is useful, but finally and importantly misleading. We could say, for example, that the set of cases of the exercise of "sovereign power" is infinite but countable, and has the same cardinality [$\aleph_0$] as the set of natural numbers we could use to count it, human "history" being in principle infinite, unrolling before and behind us unendingly, safe from genesis and providential ending. Membership in this set of cases is governed precisely by application of the conditions set forth in the first set, which determines which instances or events can be said to belong to the history of the exercise of "sovereign power."

The construction of a closed but infinite, hence countable set whose range is *governed* by another set is one minimal topological description or definition of a surface. Notice that by introducing the word *governance* I have pointed to the place—to one of the two places; I'll mention the other briefly—where the logic of projections and what Agamben calls "the modern theory of the state" join hands. The person—or the function—that decides the inclusion or exclusion of a case, an act, an instance in a surface-set is indeed "sovereign" with respect to that surface-set, even when the identity of that sovereign person or function is derived, through analysis or induction, from that surface-set.

However, when it comes to sovereign power, which is in part the power to include or exclude defining properties and cases of what is defined, the lexicon of topology runs into symptomatic difficulties. "Sovereign power," Agamben tells us, "is . . ." and some of what follows lies within as well as without the range of cases of the exercise of sovereign power, and within as well as without the set of properties that, taken as a set, are the equivalent of sovereign power. The definition of sovereign power is normative with respect to the cases it defines, but it is also a case subject to the norm; it can be counted within one or the other set, or both; and it cannot be counted. It is not true *or* false to say of sovereign power that it is or is not a norm for, or a case of, the exercise of sovereign power. We wouldn't be far off in recognizing here the outline of Russell's paradox. It might go something like this. Take the defining characteristics of sovereign power— and by this we mean that sovereign power is not sovereign power, is not itself, if it does not manifest this necessary attribute. One of the necessary elements in the set of normative qualities that governs the range of cases of the exercise of sovereign power (the *physis*, the evential set or articulation of sovereign power, its historical surface) lies outside of the normative set (is a mere case of sovereign decision) as well as inside of it.

What looks like a productive topological invagination is also close to a tautology. "Sovereign power *is* . . ." both the governing term for and a governed term within the definition and the set of cases: sovereign power is among the things that sovereign power is (hence it just is: sovereign power is sovereign power or it is nothing); and sovereign power is a case or an example of sovereign power (a case where sovereign power is exercised is [just] a case of the exercise of sovereign power). The Möbius strip structure proper to sovereign power is proper, at the point of definition, at least, to the definition of sovereign power as well. But at the point of definition, sovereign power cannot truthfully be said to fall within or without that one-sided, continuous surface. It is an utterly inclusive, continuous surface-set, a surface-set that is incomplete inasmuch as it is logically incoherent.

Here's another way to put it. Recall that *Homo Sacer* dwells on Schmitt's definition of sovereignty—or rather, of the sovereign individual, the figure in whom the power of sovereignty is invested: sovereign is he who has the power to decide the exception. "Sovereign power *is* . . ." the power to decide the exception. That power, the sovereign's power to decide, to act, to cut, to distinguish, to discern, is exercised from within and from without the bounds of the city, on the basis of a within-without that isn't stable (it is a "topological *process*"), a within-without founded in but also metaleptically granting legitimacy to the sovereign decision. The mere difficulty one might have in telling inside from outside in this or that case is not at issue. It is, rather, the structural, necessary impossibility of discerning or distinguishing one space from the other that concerns Schmitt, and Agamben after him—or perhaps more accurately, the structural impossibility of making statements about the extension of such spaces that are decidably true or false: one cannot say that it is either true or false that something is or is not within or without the space of exception. And not just any old thing: it is the very governing decision, the defining quality of the set of necessary attributes comprising sovereign power, the sovereign power to define, that is itself indeterminately both *physis* and *nomos*, that lies on one side of the surface and on the other, on one side of the city's boundaries and on the other.

The easiest way to keep the productive invagination of Agamben's—and Schmitt's—definitions of sovereignty from lapsing into mere tautology is to reintroduce the matter of time, sequencing, and entailment. Take Schmitt's definition first. Because an exception only counts as such (it can only be defined as an exception) against the background of a constituted norm, one might be inclined to distinguish on chronological or on logical grounds between the two. First, we might say, we have the rule-giving, set-constituting sovereignty of the definition or of the mathematical function—on the order of "Murder is wrong," or "The set of logical propositions is the set of propositions that are either true or false" (the classical Aristotelian principle of bivalence); or, indeed, something like my own reflexive assertions: "concepts that represent the limits of theology are also limit-concepts for the modern theory of the state." And then we find the exception-establishing power of the sovereign individual: the use of force is illegitimate, *except* that it is legitimate when administered by the state, the sovereign, or the executioner. "Murder is wrong, *except* when it is sanctioned." "Torture is wrong, except when it sanctioned," or, more provocatively, "Torture (or murder) is wrong, and yet it is sanctioned." A proposition must be either true or false, *except* inasmuch as it refers to an outcome not yet known.

This sort of temporal distinction between a constituted, normative base and an exceptional decision that follows it is a weak one. It is probably better to imagine the confusing relation that I am describing as one of mutual and simultaneous constitution: rule and exception are correlatively or reflexively related. But Schmitt hangs his definition of sovereign power upon this very weakness, and Agamben follows him, though with a productive twist. Recall Agamben's insistence on what sovereign power *is not*. It is not a spatiotemporal suspension, but rather a particular use or aspect of spatiality, a process expressed as, or mapped onto, a space or *a figure*. Not the suspension or interruption of the coordinated mapping of temporal succession on a line or on a Euclidean surface, and not the logical time of entailment (an exception supposes a norm), but rather a process of folding-reversing-looping that brings every point back to where it began, but reversed (in value, in sense: however one might want to construe the two sides of a surface that ends up having only one), and then, after a second iteration, back to where it started.

Möbius strips, Leyden jars, or Klein bottles do indeed express, complexly, the limits of the inside-outside metaphor on which premodern sovereignty, sovereign power, depends, but the temporal experiences that they map are fundamentally, almost psychotically closed. In *Homo Sacer*, Agamben's "complex topological figures" are not just mathematically and logically recursive. They are modes of repetition, or better, of *rhythm*. This mapping power is also incoherent; its rhythm also fails. The notion of a "topological zone of indistinction" is Agamben's effort to mask this incoherence. The concept—this "topological zone of indistinction"— seeks to describe a distinct, bordered zone, a concept, in short, in which "indistinction" can be distinctly located. What happens when, after visiting this zone, we return? Are its borders as closed as Agamben's argument requires? Think back to the city at the heart of Agamben's sketch: what sort of urban law, *nomos*, guards the borders of this zone? This neighborhood or ghetto? This cave?

I'm sheltering my own storytelling—my own plot—in a figure not unlike Agamben's, of course—so let me begin again. I opened with a bald, archaic fable, then provided what I take to be one of its most important modern iterations, *Homo Sacer's* complex, rhythmic repetition of a different, equally archaic story. Both my little fable and Agamben's are stories about the emergence of the indeterminate in the field of logic. Both tell us how the first flickers of the limitation, if you will, on the sovereignty of logic also mark the limits of the concept of an indivisible sovereignty. For our time as for the period of early modernity, the story really begins—to the extent that a story wound upon itself, mapped on a continuous surface-set such as I have been describing, can be said to begin at all—in a passage in Aristotle's *De interpretatione* or *Peri hermeneia*. The *De interpretatione* has nothing to do, overtly at least, with the question of sovereign power; what I want next to consider is how, in the rhythmic loops the story undergoes between *De interpretatione* and *Homo Sacer*, on this surface without a surface, the story becomes about (or just becomes) the theo-political.

It is a passage long known to be formative in the even longer history of crossings between philosophical inquiry and theology. The primitive axioms of Aristotelian logic include what has come to be called the principle of bivalence—the principle, flowing from the axiomatic laws of non-contradiction and of the excluded middle, that all propositions are either true of false, or, as Aristotle puts it in the *Metaphysics*, the principle that "there cannot be an intermediate between contradictories, but of one subject we must either affirm or deny any one predicate."[10] An example might be "Giorgio Agamben is the author of *Homo Sacer*," or "In the cave there is treasure," or "The creation of Camp X-Ray at Guantánamo is a case of the exercise of sovereign power"—propositions that are only, it would appear, either true or false. The exception, Aristotle suggests in the treatise on interpretation, is to be found in predications that concern future contingents—statements like "Jacques' car will not start tomorrow," or "In the cave you will find treasure," or "A sea battle will take place tomorrow." This is Aristotle:

> Everything must either be or not be, whether in the present or in the future, but it is not always possible to distinguish and state determinately which of these alternatives must necessarily come about. Let me illustrate. A sea-fight must either take place to-morrow or not, but it is not necessary that it should take place to-morrow, neither is it necessary that it should not take place, yet it is necessary that it either should or should not take place to-morrow. Since propositions correspond with facts, it is evident that when in future events there is a real alternative, and a potentiality in contrary directions, the corresponding affirmation and denial have the same character.[11]

For Aristotle this class of statements does not fall under the principle of bivalence, or not simply: it is neither true *nor* false that my car won't start or that it will start tomorrow, that the expedition will or will not find treasure in the cave, or that a sea battle will take place or not. Or minimally: future contingent propositions are not *determinately* true or false, or not *necessarily* true or false, or not *yet* (for us) true or false, though one or another outcome will prove itself to be or to become true, with the possible consequence of retroactively showing one or the other alternative to have been, as it were, *destined* to be true. One may say, as Aristotle seems to do, that it is necessarily true that my car will start or it will not start, that there will or will not be a sea battle tomorrow, that is, that it is necessarily true that one or the other be true, so long as that necessity applies to the disjunction and is not distributed to each of the two statements that form it—that is, so long as each disjunct is neither true nor false. I say to the expedition: "In the cave you will find treasure." The truth or falsehood of my statement will arrive in the event. It is exactly—from a logical, not a persuasive point of view—as if I had said to them: "In the cave you may find treasure, but you may not." We may say that this class of statements or propositions is, as the Epicureans put it, neutral with respect to truth or falsehood, or indeterminate. In either case we have moved from a bivalent to at least a three-value logic (a proposition can be true, false, or either neutral or indeterminate); at its most sweeping, this line of analysis of Aristotle's brief example has yielded nondeterministic logics, like Jan Lukasiewicz's, or multiple-value, or modal, or fuzzy logics. (My term *may* is the minimal marker of a modal logic.)

In the great literature on Aristotle's sea-battle example—which includes influential works by Aquinas, Boethius, Ockham, Buridan, and many, many others—the matter of sovereignty wafts at us merely and trivially from the content of Aristotle's example: a sea battle seems to imply the shock of battalions, matters of policy, Homeric heroics, generals or admirals, more than one city, a decision—in short, a cultural lexicon in which a "sea battle" is a recognizable event, and recognizable as an event. But nothing more, really. Except structurally. The sovereign act—and this is the second place at which the matter of sovereignty and the field of logic touch—is always prospective: it is an act or a decision (the creation of an exception, the assertion of the inclusion-exclusion of a case in a set) valid for the future, an act whose effectivity (and hence whose belonging to the historical *surface* of "cases of sovereign power") is subject to outcomes.

Every sovereign act—for example, the command that we take to the ships in order to fight our battle tomorrow, or the assertion, obviously subject to the principle of bivalence, that this command is a case of the exercise of sovereign power (the *assertion* is subject to the principle of bivalence: it either is or is not an assertion), or the assertion that there will be a sea battle tomorrow, or the assertion that in this or that cave you will find something—all of these, though in slightly different ways, are *cases*, I assert, of prospective acts. Call them orders, descriptions, promises; locate them (with Machiavelli, with Nietzsche, or with Schmitt) in a single, deciding will or (with Marx and Arendt) in the "case of many men mutually bound by promises," as Arendt says, or in the perception of common class interests.[12] All entail a disposition toward futurity or a threat that is necessarily future oriented: "Take to the ships . . . (or else)"; "Seek out the treasure (or else)."

A sovereign decision—for instance, a definition—is both a performative act or utterance (which is to say, an act that absolutely inhabits the present) and an indeterminate act or utterance subject to veridification, neutral (for now and for us) with respect to its truth value. Such acts, again in Arendt's words, "dispose of the future as though it were the present . . . [and] enlarge . . . the very dimension in which power can be effective."[13] They are always, as to their *logical* structure, future-contingent propositions. And from this double aspect—performatives haunted by their veridification, *nomos* by *physis*—infelicities and unpredictabilities threaten the "new" dimension of effective power. Unless I, or the group of which I am a part, have providential insight—unless we borrow the ground of our disposing from onto-theology, and our acts, definitions, or "dispositions" are verified ipso facto in the utterance—unless politics is, in short, also and necessarily a theology, matters could turn out otherwise than I, or the group of which I am a part, decide, describe, or dispose. Here intervenes the possibility of resistance; there, a contingent matter: the weather delays the sea battle that I, or we, ordered for tomorrow; we may promise to others or to ourselves, as Machiavelli's prince does, in bad faith. And something may happen in the cave that makes it impossible for us to tell whether we found something or not.

Let's set the modern retelling of Aristotle's story in 1465, at the recently founded University of Louvain. This is the period, even the moment, when the matter of future contingents began to attach to the problem of sovereignty in a recognizably *modern* way. I am choosing this moment for three reasons: because it is a case of the exercise of sovereign power; because it is normative with respect to such power (normative in the sense that the story is about an effort to create a norm for the exercise of sovereign power); and because these two—its historical content and its exemplary, determining function—are logically in conflict. It is here, in this conflict, that the secularization of the theologico-political opens, here that future contingents drift out of the bag of technical side-notes in the history of classical logic and into more violent battlegrounds. Can God know the outcome to a future contingent if human freedom is to be preserved? Did God know—the question pressed upon Catholic theologians like Pedro de Ribadeneira in the wake of the defeat of the Spanish Armada—the outcome of that sea battle? If, from the perspective of eternity, from a *nunc stans* beyond the passing of time, God already knows whether the sea battle will take place—if, indeed, he knows the outcome already, knows, for instance, that a storm will drive the Spanish fleet aground or off course—then my freedom to decide whether to command the forces or not, participate or not in the battle, dispose of this or that matter in one or another way, is eliminated. A fortiori, of course, this is the question of whether God was behind the Protestant Wind, as it was sometimes called, that wrecked the Spanish ships. *Flavit Jehovah et Dissipati Sunt*, read the commemorative medals that Elizabeth had struck in 1588 to celebrate the English victory: Jehovah blew, and they were destroyed. In brief, if I, or we, ground human sovereignty in providential onto-theology, then the sovereign decision can have no future. The decision to define sovereign power in one way or another, for example, to establish the normative set of qualities governing the set of cases of the exercise of sovereign power, is already and exclusively sovereign because it is a case of the exercise of constituted sovereign power. Always and already.

Back to Louvain, where a member of the Faculty of Arts, the professor of Rhetoric Pierre de Rivo, takes the floor in a *quodlibetal* disputation to address the following question: "Was it in Peter's power to deny Christ after Christ had said to him, 'Thou wilt deny me thrice'?" Pierre de Rivo's answer to the problem of future contingents is that "Contingency is among the things manifest per se, which is impeded neither by the truth of propositions about future contingents because there is no truth in them; nor by fated dispositions or natural instincts because they are all impedible; nor by divine foreknowledge because it is immediately present and not expectative of future things."[14] This modified Aristotelian position— that there "is no truth" in future contingents—derives from the work of the Franciscan theologian and logician Peter Auriol, who wrote and taught at the University of Paris in the early fourteenth century. Auriol's theses, as de Rivo explains and expands them, border on heresy in more places than one. Take, for instance, de Rivo's solution to the *quodlibetal* problem.

His account of "unimpeded," "manifest" contingency distinguishes between two modes of providence or foreknowledge: the divine, nonexpectative, and immediately present knowledge that God has of outcomes, which presumably makes Christ's phrase to Peter a description of a state of affairs rather than a prophecy, a promise, or any other sort of sovereign act subject to the vicissitudes of the outcome; and the expectative sort of foreknowledge that attends upon outcomes for its veridification, the sort of providential knowledge that human decisions or dispositions can hope to achieve. The content of expectative foreknowledge may not be necessarily true yet (it is a genuine future contingent). This, of course, does not entail that it is false or nonexistent, but sounds as though it might be either, thus moving strikingly beyond the principle of bivalence. But the principal difficulty comes from the loss of freedom for the sovereign in the first, "immediately present" form of foreknowledge, the loss of the prospective faculty of the will. The problem is not that Peter could not have done otherwise than he did, once Christ predicted his betrayal, but that Christ himself could not have changed the outcome—not then, not ever; could not even have willed the outcome otherwise. Christ's plea that the "cup should pass from him" is, from this perspective, nonsensical.[15]

De Rivo incensed the members of the Faculty of Theology at Louvain, particularly as, in closing his disputation, he allowed himself some remarks regarding the "uncreated Truth" on which articles of faith or divine foreknowledge of future contingents must rest, since they could not be "necessary" truths. (Articles of faith are also logical propositions, or stipulations—but a number of them are future disposed. "The dead shall be raised" is an example; so is "Antichrist will be born," as de Rivo explains.[16]) These are the lovely lines with which de Rivo seeks to convey tropically how expectant foreknowledge differs from its intuitive, immediate divine counterpart. What is most striking is the fundamentally mechanical idiom that haunts this early version of a self-reflective, self-containing, single-sided surface:

> Because all things that in the course of time are past, present, or future are, with respect to their real existence, immediately present to God, therefore the divine essence is, as it were, an image of them. For just as images of things in a mirror are immediate to themselves, so it is in God. Therefore the divine view, which is turned toward its own essence as toward its primary object, looking upon it as an example of all existing things, is said to be aware of all things, even those that in the course of time are future, not indeed with expectative cognition, for in respect of God no things are

future nor are any expected to come about. Indeed such cognition is, rather, intuitive, not in such a way that it is fixed directly upon the thing, but upon his own essence exemplifying the thing. Whence God is to be understood as a sort of mirror in which all things succeeding one another in the whole course of time have images shining back, a mirror indeed directly beholding itself and all the images existing in it.[17]

The stakes were high, as both sides in the Louvain debate understood: the content of the debate was nothing less than the double conflict between, on the one hand, Peter's freedom and Christ's knowledge or foreknowledge, and, on the other, between Christ's foreknowledge and his freedom. This debate anticipated, *in nuce*, the Reformation debates that flamed up fifty years later: the logical and theological status of prophetic language was in contention; the allocation of power and disciplinary legitimacy within the university was the debate's immediate practical context; the status, indeed, the ownership, of logic, a term common to the Faculties of Theology and Art, was in dispute, as was the privilege a rhetorician might have to address theological matters. In short, the rock on which Peter's power rested—the rock under the rock of Christ's church—was in play. For roughly the next decade, accusations, clarifications, and denunciations piled up. De Rivo's principal opponent, the theologian Henri de Zomeren, was dismissed from the university, appealed to the newly elected Pope Sixtus IV, denounced de Rivo, and found himself reinstated in his chair at Louvain. The matter was settled, theologically, when de Rivo, summoned to the Holy See in late 1472 on de Zomeren's denunciation, was forced to retract his theses before returning to teach at Louvain. The retraction doesn't seem to have taken: four years later, in 1476, de Rivo was forced to sign another one—though not before the conflict had spread from Louvain to Paris, where a cadre of realist theologians, reacting to the pope's bull condemning de Rivo's position on future contingents, managed to persuade King Louis XI to condemn the so-called nominalist faction who supported de Zomeren's cause against de Rivo's. A highly technical doctrinal disagreement, in short, served to condense and inflame existing contradictions within and between church and state.

Of course, stories like this don't really end, certainly not where one might expect them to. This story, for example, carries on into early modernity and beyond, jumping over the bounds of discipline, nation, and chronology, never constrained to France or to the old disputes between theology and philosophy, rhetoric and logic. As a way of trying to put a finger on the rhythmic articulation of indeterminacy with the limit of sovereign power, imagine the next iteration of the "quarrel of Louvain."

Imagine the Gothic story I opened with, now fleshed in: still a case of the exercise of sovereign power, whose content is the legitimacy and the time of the sovereign decision. It's a lurid tale, told by one Cristóbal de Lozano in 1671. The events it narrates are purported to have occurred in 1546, when the newly named archbishop of Toledo organized an expedition into the so-called Cave of Hercules, located mythically below the cellars of the Church of San Ginés in Toledo, or in the basement of the "Torre de Hercules," or below the "casa de Hercules," also in Toledo. Hercules is reputed to be the founder of Spain, or one of them. (The chronicles have Hercules defeating Helion, the last of the descendants of Espan, the discoverer and first settler of Spain.) And his tower or house, on which the Church of San Ginés may be built, houses any number of mythic objects— Solomon's table, a magic talking head, robotic golden statues, rivers, great caverns, winds.

Expeditions to this cave already had a wide notoriety in Toledo. The one in 1546, like many before it, was a resounding failure, even though the archbishop undertook it, or so Lozano believed, "in order to disabuse the populace and by means of the truth to remove all the stories and rumors that people were telling and recounting about this cave" and not "on the pretext adduced by King Roderick, who opened the cave to find out if there was treasure in it—instead, to treasure it [the cave or the cave's treasure], as did his people [King Roderick's people or the archbishop's?] in the chests of the poor."[18] Lozano's prose goes topologically and topographically opaque just where the location of the treasure, if it is one, and its historical placement are at issue. Is it King Roderick's men or the archbishop's who "treasure" the cave, or its treasure? This strange indeterminacy—grammatical as well as locational and topological—saturates the story and the tradition. The cave's location (high, in a tower; low, in a cellar; inside, but possessed of vast caverns, great rivers, winds; empty, but replete with treasure and peril), as well as the location of the *story* of the cave (within the sovereign, within the expedition he sends) seems unstable, a topological zone of indistinction, Agamben might say: the treasure of the sovereign's proposition is held within and without the subject; the sovereign's power to command, for example, to command us to seek out something (a treasure, for instance), derives from but also seeks to confirm the existence or nonexistence of a treasure treasured elsewhere, in a vast, unreasoned repository of cultural value, the storehouse of cultural bric-a-brac under the surface of the city.

Lozano continues his narrative. The expedition goes terribly awry when the explorers find some bronze statues, set upon a table as if it were an altar, and [as they were] setting about inspecting one of them, which looked out severely from its pedestal, the statue fell down and made an enormous noise, causing great fear in the explorers. There may have been no more statues than this one, and the fear they felt made it seem like many more, as sometimes happens, and it must have been what King Roderick found, with his mace of office.

The explorers press on, though they are terrified. They run into a huge underground river, which "filled them completely with fear, up to their eyes." Distraught, "perturbed . . . terrified, . . . with the face of corpses," they emerge from the cave, scaring the crowd waiting for them. Lozano notes finally: "They were so overcome with fear that many of them died." This is hardly the sort of thing destined to lay to rest the strange stories that surrounded the cave, so the archbishop has the cave locked up and bricked off.

What was it that they saw? And on whose orders? The name of this enterprising archbishop is none other than Juan Martínez Guijarro, who would be elected Cardinal Silíceo, preceptor to the future King Philip II, and who was from roughly 1496 to 1505 a student of logic and theology at the University of Paris.[19] Silíceo belonged to the nominalist faction in Paris—the group that had, not quite a generation before, backed de Zomeren against de Rivo on the question of future contingents—and who studied philosophy under the terminist logician and mathematical physicist Jean Dullaert (also known as Jean de Jaldun). On Silíceo's return to Spain, he edited, in Salamanca, *Questiones super duos libros Peri hermeneias Aristotelis,* an edition, with Dullaert's commentary, of Aristotle's *De interpretatione.*[20] Silíceo, who published a number of other important works, notably in arithmetic (his 1514 *Ars Arithmetica in Theoricen et Praxim Scissa* remained a standard school-text), is most enduringly remembered as the author, in 1547, of the famous "Estatuto de Limpieza," the statute of clean blood he imposed on the Cathedral of Toledo, which required that all persons holding any office in the cathedral be of nonconverso blood. It was at the time by far the most radical statement of the dogma of "cleanliness" that had been first promulgated in Toledo in 1449, though not granted papal sanction until 1495.[21] Silíceo's *estatuto* produced immediate outrage in humanist and reformation circles, but to no avail: Silíceo's influence with the emperor and later with his successor, Silíceo's former student Philip II, was determining. By 1559 Silíceo's statute had spread across much of Spain.[22]

The story of Silíceo's expedition into the cave of Hercules knots together a number of the strands I've loosely been setting out. But in order to make a little clearer the stakes of my argument—to say nothing of the weirdly recursive structure of my story—I'll need to pull another rabbit from my hat: this time in the shape of a gloss on the twice-repeated allusion to a certain "Rey Rodrigo" (King Roderick), who had once before opened this same cave in search of treasure, with apparently disastrous consequences. Lozano is referring to a cluster of legends that originate, so far as literary history can tell, among the earliest chronicles of the Arab invasion of Spain and that already figure in the *Crónica* attributed to the tenth-century historian Ahmed Ar-Razi, better known by the name that his *crónica* is given in a 1344 version, *el moro Rasis*. By 1499 these legends were the subject of Pedro de Corral's vastly influential *Crónica del Rey Don Rodrigo*, or *Crónica sarracida* or *sarracena*.[23] The tales circulated broadly as part of the extensive *romancero* culture of the day, as well as in the theater. They show up, barely transmuted, in *Don Quixote*, and they have a curious afterlife in Washington Irving's *Legends of the Conquest of Spain*, in the novels of Juan Goytisolo, and in Carlos Saura's 2001 film *Buñuel y la mesa del rey Salomón*. In the romances, as in Corral's *Crónica*, King Roderick defies the tradition his forebears had studiously observed ("That he [should] place a padlock upon the ancient House of Hercules, as his ancestors used to do," as one of the romances puts it), and, rather than lock up the entrance to the cave of Hercules in Toledo (or, alternatively, the tower of Hercules, in whose basement is found a locked cave—a fascinatingly and characteristically antithetical amalgam of high and low), he breaks all the locks previously set there by the generations of kings before him, enters the cave, and, like Silíceo's band of men, finds not treasure but disaster—in this case, of a very particular sort. The romance (from *Romancero general*) goes like this:

Don Rodrigo, rey de España,
Por la su corona honrar,
Un torneo en Toledo
Ha mandado pregonar:
Sesenta mil caballeros
En él se han ido a juntar.
Bastecido el gran torneo,
Queriéndole comenzar,
Vino gente de Toledo
Por le haber de suplicar

Que a la antigua casa de Hércules
Quisiese un candado echar,
Como sus antepasados
Lo solían acostumbrar.
El Rey no puso el candado,
Mas todos los fue a quebrar,
Pensando que gran tesoro
Hércules debía dejar.
Entrando dentro en la casa
Nada otro fue hallar
Sino letras que decían
"Rey has sido por tu mal.
Que el que esta casa abriere
A España tiene quemar."
Un cofre de gran riqueza
Hallaron dentro un pilar,
Dentro dél nuevas banderas
Con figuras de espantar;
Alárabes de caballo
Sin poderse menear,
Con espadas a los cuellos,
Ballestas de bien tirar.

Don Rodrigo, King of Spain, has ordered that a joust be held in Toledo. Sixty thousand knights have gathered for the tourney. When the tourney had been provisioned and set to begin, citizens from Toledo came to the king to beg that he place a padlock upon the ancient House of Hercules, as his ancestors used to do. The king did not place the padlock, but instead broke all the ones there, thinking that Hercules must have left a great treasure. When he entered the house, he found nothing there but some writings, which said: "You have been king for your misfortune. For he who should open this house will burn Spain." A rich chest was found inside a column, and in it new flags, on which were frightening figures; Arabs on horseback, unable to move; with swords at their necks, and well-aiming cross-bows.[24]

A second, more compact version of the prophecy can be found in another of the romances. This one reads:

Un paño dentro se ha hallado, con unas letras Latinas
Que dicen en castellano:
"Cuando aquestas cerraduras

Que cierran estos candados
Fueren abiertas, y visto,
Lo que en el paño dibujado,
España será perdida
Y en ella todo asolado.
Ganarála gente extraña,
Como aquí está figurado,
Los rostros muy denegridos,
Los brazos arremangados,
Muchas colores vestidas,
En las cabezas tocados:
Alzadas traerán sus señas
En caballos cabalgando,
En sus manos largas lanzas,
Con espadas en su lado.
Alárabes se dirán
Y de aquellas tierras extraños;
Perderáse toda España.

Inside, a cloth was found. On it, in Castilian and in Roman letters, these words: "When these locks, shut with padlocks, are opened, and what is drawn on this cloth has been seen, Spain will be lost, and everything in her destroyed. Strangers will win her, as is shown here: with darkened faces, arms bared, dressed in many colors, their heads turbaned. They will hold their standards high, galloping upon horses, long spears in their hands and swords at their sides. They will be called [or "they will call themselves"] Arabs, and strangers to those lands: all Spain will be lost."

Perderáse toda España. This is precisely the tenor of Silíceo's letters to Charles V and to Phillip II in defense of the *estatuto de limpieza:* if the cleanliness statute is not enacted, then all Spain will be lost to "strange," foreign peoples. The cultural material—Lozano's account of the expedition, the *romancero* tradition, the *crónicas* that tradition echoes—yields a prophecy retroactively confirmed, a prophecy concerning the *loss of all Spain* to *gente extraña*, with "blackened" faces. The legends of Spain's fall to the Arab invaders arise after the invasion, and attribute the defeat to venal, individual motives and decisions. The historical truth of the situation (the invasion) is then mapped metaleptically onto the explanation of its cause: it is distributed to it, looped back upon it. The occurrence of the naval battle, in short, serves to confirm the truth claim of one of the disjuncts of the contingent proposition, "Tomorrow there will be a sea battle" or, in this case, "When these locks, shut with padlocks, are opened, and what is drawn on this cloth has been seen, Spain will be lost."

The *romancero*'s diction is extraordinarily precise here: the prophecy, "Spain will be lost," can refer either to a future moment (the moment at which Spain will be lost as a result of what is seen in the cave) or, in a formulation that was equally acceptable in early modern Spanish, to a present moment: Spain will (already) be vanquished, at the very moment when the cave is opened, when the canvas or *escrito* is seen and the "strangers" "figured" on the canvas identified as "Alárabes," Arabs. The conflation of time future and time present nods, of course, to the strange retrospection of a prophetic idiom generated retroactively and confirmed by the outcome, by the present from which it is spoken: it is uttered in an indeterminate temporal voice, we might say.

But for Silíceo this indeterminacy has a significance that is additional to, and cannot theologically be squared with, the one that, as a confirmed nominalist, he would have taken from his years in Paris. His expedition into the cave reads as a repetition or a recursion, as an effort to take up the position of King Roderick's father in the first chronicles of the unlucky king's venture into the cave-tower of Hercules, a father who was, as Silíceo had just become, the archbishop of Toledo and whose warnings the young king did not heed—Roderick or Philip II. This strange repetition seeks, under the guise of debunking superstition, to undo that king's fateful trip, to undecide the first sovereign decision, that is, to show, retrospectively, that the metaleptically confirmed prophecy was false. Silíceo's expedition expresses the fantasy that an act of will can "enlarge . . . the very dimension in which power can be effective," to return to Arendt's words, the fantasy that the sovereign can indeed have power over the past. In Lozano's account, the archbishop's fantasy is expressed in the idiom of benevolent enlightenment, the desire to rid the people of Toledo of a merely superstitious, or merely mythic, attachment to history, the desire to rid his archdiocese once and for all of a perniciously repeating history—the history, precisely, of the terrible consequences that attend upon the failure to repeat a custom, here the sovereign custom of ceremonially locking the cave of Hercules.[25] This purging of the past has a companion, prospective aspect, as well—the prospective effort to ensure that the church retains ownership of the truth of future contingents: that the church is able, by demonstrating the falsehood of the first prophecy (or rather, by demonstrating that the first prophecy was not prophetic at all but a retroactive formation amenable, one might say, to analysis: a pathology of repetition to be cured), to retain control over the future. A church able, on the shoulders of its princes, to step into the place of the sovereign, to take back a power that the popular imagination had retroactively granted to the king, to King Roderick, even if in a negative sense.

The logic of sovereignty cannot rest in its structure as a future contingent, a performative act that, outside of the onto-theological horizon to which it aspires and on which it models itself, is always subject to veridification, infelicity, contingency. The logic of sovereignty requires, as it were on its other surface, what we can now call a past contingent: the capacity to make statements of fact or descriptions, like "Spain was invaded by the Arabs" or "Peter will betray Christ" (which, from the onto-theological *nunc stans* that Aquinas reserves for God or from the "immediate" and nonexpectant foreknowledge that de Rivo built in Louvain two generations before Silíceo, has the shape "Peter has always betrayed Christ already") into propositions susceptible of revision: because it could have happened otherwise, an act or a decision that I now take, or that the group I am part of now takes, can make it have happened otherwise. The tense form is impossible; the concept, unthinkable. And yet it is this radical unthinkability that Silíceo's expedition seeks to achieve. To think the single surface of the logic of sovereignty in the moment of its secularization, in the moment of the incipient decoupling of the claims of sovereignty from the onto-theology its performance requires, is to invite madness, conflicting stories, the over- and underdetermination of cultural narratives, mere literature. To invite, solicit, even to *create* the modern experience of terror.

CHAPTER 4

Materia in the Critique of Autonomy

Althusser's enterprise . . . is marked throughout by the dread of the
Marxist intellectual, the dread of the intellectual fallen prey to
politics: not to make "literature," not to address letters without
addressee; not to be Don Quixote, the fine soul who fights against
windmills; not to be alone, not to be the voice of one crying out in
the wilderness, an activity by which one loses one's head, literally as
well as figuratively.

—JACQUES RANCIÈRE, "Althusser, Don Quixote, and the Stage of the Text"

[Philip II:] Terror alone can tie rebellion's hands:
Compassion would be madness.

—FRIEDRICH SCHILLER, *Don Karlos*

To distinguish between the terror of sovereign power and weak or defective concepts that shelter the terror of association and provide grounds for
a critique of terrorism. To imagine and provide, as it were, the concept of
these weak or defective concepts, then the means for their actualization—
these are tasks that take thought beyond the stultifying opposition to
imagination and vision that Dante the poet enjoins upon us when he urges
his readers not to attend to the form of torture and to consider instead its
theological consequences and justification—*la gran sentenza*. What exactly
constitutes a weak concept, however, is not clear. The topology of weak
concepts, like the logic of sovereignty, is paradoxical. "Terror" is the content sheltered by such concepts, whose formal weakness makes manifest
that content. Their principle of closure is neither internal nor external to
them. What makes this or that weak concept a concept is intimately foreign to it—*extimate*, the Lacanian idiom might say. But are there such
things as strong concepts?

Nor is it clear how a weak concept might be produced. Do I mean
"produce" in the sense in which one speaks of producing a commodity?
Producing a rabbit from a hat? Producing a film? Indeed, there's more
than a hint of contradiction in the expression itself. *Production* is a term
generally reserved for material objects, and concepts—weak, strong, or

neither—are largely understood to be immaterial, numinous, abstract. The concept of matter is not itself material, for instance, or so it must surely appear.

Finally, it is not clear what sort of normative value weak concepts might have. They pertain to three types of instance. First, they apply to a classically conceived, autonomous ethical subject, one who enjoins upon himself, for instance, the rules "Do not steal," "Do not kill," and so on. Is there a weak concept to match the injunction "Do not do" this or that? Second, they pertain to rules of association. What sort of standing would a weak concept of society have—for instance, one based on nonidentitarian, nonrecognitionist paradigms? What would be its normative force? Finally, they apply to the relation between autonomy, understood to designate the ethical subject's rule granting and rule following, and association.

I am going to come at the matter of rule following from an unusual perspective, on the margins of traditional ethico-political thought—a route dictated by the queer understanding of concepts I am developing. I will refer to but set aside two objections to the question "What are weak or defective concepts of association?" I will not be proposing, first, that weak concepts of association are proxies for contracts or structured as contracts and that following the rules one sets oneself or following broader rules of association should be understood in the way that a contractual agreement is understood. This is an obvious, venerable, and attractive avenue, but an insufficient one. Obvious, because to the extent that contractarianism is based on outcomes—an exchange of my liberty in this domain for security in that, say—my commitment extends only as far as the return upon the contract. At the point where my security is no longer guaranteed, my agreement to limit my liberty can become void. And since that point is always possible (security is never guaranteed, no matter how thoroughly my environment is mapped and policed), my acquiescence to the norms of the contract is always provisional, always marked by a possible void. That provisionality—the shadow cast upon the norm by the contingency of outcomes—might seem as good a way as any to render the concept of weak or defective concepts of association.

The second objection is, roughly speaking, Wittgensteinian. In this approach, the requirement that concepts in general, and concepts of association or ethical behavior in particular, be strong or weak is nonsensical—if by "strong" we mean something like "distinct," "clearly bounded," "universally agreed upon," or any cognate marker of immanence or transcendence and by "weak" the opposite of these terms. It is improper to distinguish between concepts on the grounds that some are strong and others weak or defective, inasmuch as *all* concepts are equally defective and nondefective, all strong or not in much the same way, because concepts are fundamentally transactional, subject to and produced by and as rules of language use in determined circumstances and to specific ends. In this approach, again, the concept of "following a rule," whether this is imagined to be a contract one makes with oneself or with the state, or a duty assumed because following a rule is deemed a virtuous act, or obedience to a transcendent imperative of some sort, is no weaker or stronger than any other concept. One follows a rule to achieve an end, and if the rule is found to be inadcquate, it is changed or exchanged for another, as one would set down one screwdriver and pick up a different one. This line of thought seems to me suggestive in ways that complement the contractarian approach I have just sketched. An ethical or political view of rule following based in a contractual model necessarily entertains the void of a breach of contract on one side or the other; a view of rule following based in a transactional account of language necessarily entertains the possibility of misuse, abuse, and nonsense, as well as the practical requirement that rules be tested against outcomes. Both go some distance toward stripping the concept of its old dignities, its sovereign glories, and toward furnishing what, following Hilary Putnam, one might call a politics without onto-theology.

Some distance. But these may not be altogether the right ways to imagine concepts of association. The drive to shed the hoary majesty of the concept leads, on the one hand, to a classical principle of rational autonomy. That principle is the ground on which I choose to enter into or to break this or that contract, whether this is a contract I make with myself, as it were, or with another, or with the state, or with an idea of civil society. On the other hand, a transactionalist approach to the problem of the concept and to the concept of rule following that attaches to it may lead, paradoxically, away from transactionalism and (as in Wittgenstein's early work) to setting in place, as the criterion for judging any transaction, an entirely external, individual, even private "experience" of the "miracle of the existence of the world," an experience of "the existence of language" as the "expression in language" of that miracle.[1] The contractarian principle devolves into philosophies of rational choice, and Wittgenstein's account of ethics (at any rate, that of the *Tractatus* and the "Lecture on Ethics"), into a hypostasis of the "nonsensicality" of ethical and religious expressions (the necessary persistence of "absolute judgments" in the face of their nonsensicality): into "paradox," "perfect, absolute hopelessness," "respect," and companion expressions that convey the miracle of the existence of the world precisely by making us aware of the existence of language.[2]

A different approach, then—one that keeps in sight, when possible, the contractarian and Wittgensteinian critiques of the philosophy of the concept but seeks to avoid the traps of the ontologization of language, on the one hand, and of the reaffirmation of classical autonomy, on the other. This will turn out to be a path through what Étienne Balibar has called the "ontology of relations" in Marx's work, as this ontology of relations manifests itself, rather differently, in the work of Louis Althusser.[3]

Here is the pivotal project that the essays collected in *Reading 'Capital'* set for themselves: to "illuminate . . . from within [*Capital*], as the exact measurement of a disconcerting but inevitable absence, the absence of the concept . . . of the effectivity of a structure on its elements which is the visible/invisible, absent/present keystone of [Marx's] whole work."[4] "Structure" here can mean class, city, any form of collective identification; and "elements" can mean individual, worker, citizen, and so on. What's missing from *Capital*, *Reading 'Capital'* proposes, is an account of how, say, one's economic identity (membership in a class) affects one as a member of that class and how one passes from occupying a position as an individual to being part of a class, and as a member of a class, a part of a society. The trajectory that leads from "individual" to "member of a class" to "society" is evidently an ideological after-effect or (the Freudian lexicon is crucial to *Reading 'Capital'*) a secondary revision—but also a means for obscuring the much more unpredictable directions in which the flows between these concepts occur and the resulting instability of the concepts themselves. There is no doubt that such reciprocal influences—reciprocal determinations and under- and overdeterminations is better—exist and are everywhere at work in Marx's work or in the work of the collective authors of *Reading 'Capital.'*[5] The uncertainties flow from two directions. In the first place, from the rather awkward term *effectivity*, especially in its use to link the notion of structure with what Ben Brewster translates as "element." *L'efficace*, Althusser's term for "effectivity," is a rather literary version of the more common noun *efficacité*, roughly speaking, "acting upon," or "effectiveness," or in German *Wirkung*. Althusser's phrase is manifestly and symptomatically opaque; Brewster's determining translation of *Lire 'le Capital'* twice renders as "the concept . . . of the effectivity of a structure on its elements" Althusser's "concept de l'efficace d'une structure sur ses effets"—not a trivial error, since the "effects" of a structure need not, in Althusser's reading of Marx, be elements of that structure at all. A structure can, indeed, be imagined to be autotelic if it has the characteristic of producing and reproducing its elements, which would then be part of a reciprocal definition, a structure being that which has constitutive effects on its elements, and the elements of a structure being by definition those individuals affected, acted upon, interpellated by that structure. (In this case, the terms *structure*, *element*, and *constitutive effect* could be translated into the terms *set*, *member of a set*, and *conditions for belonging to a set*.) A structure, however, can also, as the French makes clear, produce effects that fall outside of it, effects that do not, one might say, conform to its concept or necessarily follow its rules—or that, more troublingly still, fall outside of it (are not elements, though they are effects) precisely because they follow the rules.

The text of *Reading 'Capital'* envisions both alternatives, though only the first, the one Brewster's translation underscores, seems to be developed explicitly. It is the first of these arguments that underlies what one might call, adopting Althusser's terms for the classical reading practices he seeks to unseat, the "religious myth" of Althusser's own development. This "myth," largely abandoned since the publication of the works on "aleatory materialism," stresses what Laclau and Mouffe described as "a growing closure [in Althusser's thought which] led to the installation of a new variant of essentialism. This process . . . was to culminate in *Reading Capital*."[6] A functionalist, "essentialist," or "structural" (as Steven Smith and Gregory Elliott term it) Marxism is entailed by Brewster's translation—a particularly good translation, then, inasmuch as its symptomatic error captures one great thrust of *Reading 'Capital,'* the effort to articulate structure and elements according to a normative and normatively produced concept that is itself an element and an effect of the structure.[7] It is also, of course, an egregiously faulty translation, since Brewster's "elements" excludes, as does this larger aspect of the argument of *Reading 'Capital,'* everything that Althusser begins to develop, concurrently but covertly, in the writings that become what has been called the "philosophy of the encounter" (a Spinozist reading of Marx, a Machiavellian . . .). That a structure can have effects that are not elements of that structure or understandable according to elements of that structure, and indeed may not even therefore register as effects at all for the elements of that structure—this means that an aleatory relation exists between structure and element and between structure and effect. (Another name for this aleatory relation would be *metonymic causality*, about which more below.) The result is a topological paradox—the possibility of elements that are also not elements, hence of a structure (or a set) that both is and is not closed and of rules that are simultaneously the rules of closure for such a structure the rules of its unfinishing.

The symptomatic opacity of Althusser's phrase corresponds to ᴜᴄ argumentative blind-spot that *Reading 'Capital'* diagnoses in *Capital*, the "disconcerting but inevitable absence" of the concept of the emergence of effectivity. This absence makes it impossible to answer, conceptually or systematically, questions of the sort "How do collective concepts arise in *Capital*?" or to assess at that level, systematically or conceptually, just how structures work upon (regulate, determine, build) their effects or the elements that constitute them. The searching inquiry into the nature of determination that we find in Althusser and his school is fueled in great part by this absence and by the epistemological impasses it entails.[8] The troubled concept *of concept* is to Althusser's work what the "concept . . . of the effectivity of a structure on its elements" or on its *effects* is to Marx's: a keystone, friable as well as solid, a point of closure and aperture, construction and deconstruction.[9]

More importantly, much of what is most disturbing—"traumatic" is Slavoj Žižek's word—but also most useful about the project that *Reading 'Capital'* opens, useful in clarifying how communal concepts (sovereignty, the city) and concepts of association (citizenship) can be produced, useful in designating in concepts a quality of "weakness" that nonetheless *works*, flows from the effort in *Reading 'Capital'* to address a profound hesitation in the *historicity* of concepts. By "historicity" I mean in part the circumstances that determine their production, circulation, ownership, uses, absorption, and disappearance: the *ecology* of concepts, always a good subject for grand, mythical narratives. But I also mean something different: to address the historicity of concepts means to attend to the contingency of their emergence, flows, and effects, and to the expression of that element of contingency in a simultaneous over- and underlegibility of the texts that mark these concepts' emergence. The weakness of concepts is entailed by their double historicity, or, to make the same point on a different argumentative level, it is entailed in the facts, both historical and logical, that structures have effects that fall outside of the structure's elements and that concepts are both elements and nonelemental effects (in this topologically paradoxical sense) of structures.[10]

What's Begriff *When It's at Home?*

First, a sketch of the philosophical landscape in which Althusser and his school mount the project of *Reading 'Capital.'* It's a craggy, ancient, ample, and discontinuous landscape, and I'll stress just one of its elements. It is hardly controversial to say that the history of philosophy, the history of the production and constitution of the concept of philosophy, is the history of the battles waged over the concept itself. The term holds in postwar philosophical debate the contested place that came to be occupied in the social sciences by the words *structure* and *function*; indeed, the crises of each discipline can be charted in the changing destinies and unhappy marriages of the three terms.[11] The contest is older (a reasonable genealogy of the concept takes account of the terms *idea*, *form*, *entity*, *essence*, and so on, mapping their differences, relations, kinship networks, conflicts), but the modern era of thought about the concept probably opens with Kant's well-known statement toward the beginning of the "Transcendental Analytic," in the *Critique of Pure Reason*. He is describing the a priori grounds upon which abstraction or synthesis—our knowledge, human judgment—must rest[12]:

> No knowledge is possible without a concept . . . and a concept is always, with regard to its form, something general, something that can serve as a rule [*Regel*]. Thus the concept of body [*vom Körper*] serves as a rule to our knowledge of external phenomena, according to the unity of the manifold which is thought by it. It can only be such a rule of intuitions because representing, in any given phenomena, the necessary reproduction of their manifold elements, or the synthetical unity in our consciousness of them [*daß er bei gegebenen Erscheinungen die notwendige Reproduktion des Mannigfaltigen derselben, mithin die synthetische Einheit in ihrem Bewußtsein, vorstellt*].[13]

Representation—*Vorstellung*—has a distinct sense here. A concept—for instance, the concept of body or of the city, "represents" the common elements in manifold phenomena, but not as some common aspect derived, upon inspection, from the way that they present themselves to my senses. (I see a group of things, I compare them, find a common element—their "embodiment," say—and then represent that embodiment to myself, making it an object of thought.) Instead, the concept represents the condition under which I am able to assign to phenomena their presentability. (They are not phenomena that I can think about or understand as phenomena unless they appear in a relation to each other; that appearing in a concrete relation is the *rule* of their presentation, and as such it is the subsistent concept.) The concept, the condition of the presentability of phenomena to thought, is necessarily always, in its form, what can serve as a rule (*zur Regel dient*) uniting concrete contents, a peculiar servant or handmaiden (*Diener*, *Dienerin*) who is herself abstractly the concrete rules she makes.

In all this the function of the rule is confounding. (Rules, as the First Critique says elsewhere, powerfully, are a riddle [*Rätsel*].) Certain concepts are regulative with respect to the field of human activity—concepts like association, freedom, responsibility, or the city's welfare. In the more or less Kantian description I have just given, though, *all* concepts are in a formal sense regulative, inasmuch as they are the condition under which manifold phenomena appear as related to one another. We might thus be distinguishing between a first, "empirical" account of the regulative aspect of certain concepts (but not all), and a second, "transcendental" account of the regulative aspect of concepts as such, of all concepts. Here, some concepts (but not all) represent and serve as norms for certain facts, understood to mean actually existing states of affairs; but there, it is a proper and necessary aspect of the concept of concept, an *analytic* requirement (again, in Kant's rather restricted use of the term), that concepts be regulative not with respect to facts or actually existing states of affairs but a priori, with respect to the possibility of the presentation of facts or states of affairs as such. Hegel's various definitions of the concept accept Kant's distinction, but set the stress on disclosing the relation between analytic, or transcendental, and empirical regulation. The key problem Hegel derives from Kant's distinction, then, will be how to understand the movement, if there is one, between these two regulative aspects of the concept—and in consequence to establish what concrete embodiments this movement might have in the history of consciousness and in the history of human institutions. Take, for example, the apodictic passage in the lesser *Logic*. This, the most notorious of Hegel's definitions of the concept, asserts that "The Concept is the principle of freedom, the power of substance self-realized." That rather gnomic phrase functions both as a definition and as a way of anticipating the ethico-political elaboration of the logic of essence to be found in the *Philosophy of Right*.[14] The attributes of this "principle of freedom" include, among others, its distinction from both the mere representation and the Idea of a thing, as well as its "onward movement," or development from substance to the truth of substance.

Still, it is the aspect of self-realization (*die für sie seiende substantielle Macht*) proper to the concept that proved most influential, and most troubling. The being-for-itself of the concept, which the *Logic* describes as "an independence which, though self-repulsive into distinct independent elements, yet in that repulsion is self-identical, and in the movement of reciprocity still at home and conversant only with itself," sketches by means of this movement the complex dialectical oscillation between attribution and essence, between *concretum* and *generalia*, that is the condition of possibility of judgment and individuality.[15] This movement, Hegel argues, constitutes a form of totality "in which each of its constituent functions is the very total which the concept is."[16] The moment of individuality, which is embodied in the form of the judgment (*Urteil*) linking subject and predicate, depends upon this relation of mediated identity to the concept of which it is a moment.

Indeterminate Determination (Suture and "the Totality of Effects")

One can see the attraction of this doctrine of the concept for the younger Marx, and as a result why the absence of the concept of effectivity from his work becomes doubly enigmatic—inasmuch as it is the keystone of the argument and inasmuch as it is a moment in a movement, a part that is both absent only as a part and, since in the context of the movement between moments any part, any single concept, and a fortiori the keystone concept of the argument, is also the "very total which the concept is," as the totality itself. Because the individual judgment bears a relation of mediated identity to the concept (of class, for instance, or party, or historical moment), it becomes possible to describe concrete situations (again, both historical and philosophical) as having a greater or lesser degree of identity with the abstract determinants of that situation. The Hegelian argument maintains that this contradictory identity can be assessed by and is constitutive of consciousness; the Lukácsian outcome is a "poor man's Hegelianism," a sort of Stalinism, Althusser argues. His own solution—obscure in its initial formulations, by now overused and misconstrued to such a degree that it is hard to reconstruct its initial promise, challenges, or function—is to maintain that the contradictory identity of concrete situations and their abstract determinants is only determinate in the last instance. Especially in this schematic version, but even if we grant that the last instance exists only as a virtual point or regulative horizon, Althusser's solution suggests a mythic historiography all too easily squared with the teleological historicity of the materialist dialectic.[17] But what if the last instance is not an *element* of the history of consciousness? (It may or may not be an effect, along the lines I outlined above.) We might then call the last instance something like a *determining fantasy*, or a point of *suture*. For it is precisely in its connection to fantasy that the term *determination* ceases to provide the determinable sense of ideological closure that these critical fictions, religious myths, or critical lives urgently require. How do fantasy and suture step in where determination, in its various forms, fails?

Let me return, as a way into this question, to the religious myth of Althusser's life and works that prevailed until the mid 1990s. Laclau and Mouffe, we saw, narrate that trajectory compactly, and Gregory Elliott has retold it, drawing a parallel with Althusser's shifting account of Marx's trajectory that is none the less striking and elegant for being fairly predictable.[18] As far as Laclau and Mouffe are concerned (the date, recall, is 1985), the trajectory of Althusser's thought about social relations is a descent or retreat from the possibilities opened by the concept of overdetermination. The story is especially important for them, as for a number of writers since then, because in it Althusser functions as a synecdoche for Marxist thought more generally, with the exception, perhaps, of Gramsci, but including their own work prior to *Hegemony and Socialist Strategy*. As a result of its analytic rigor, the story goes, Althusser's thought is able to posit the indeterminacy of the category of totality, but it must retreat from that indeterminacy for reasons that are not only pragmatic but also theoretical. I want to linger for a moment, however, on the most economical of their formulations of this scheme:

> the most profound *potential* meaning of Althusser's statement that everything existing in the social is overdetermined, is the assertion that the social constitutes itself as a symbolic order. The symbolic—i.e., overdetermined—character of social relations therefore implies that they lack an ultimate literality which would reduce them to necessary moments of an immanent law. . . . This analysis seemed to open up the possibility of elaborating a new concept of articulation, which would start from the overdetermined character of social relations. But this did not occur. The concept of overdetermination tended to disappear from Althusserian discourse, and a growing closure led to the installation of a new variant of essentialism. This process . . . was to culminate in *Reading Capital*.[19]

So, in any case, the story goes.[20]

Two things about this description are immediately striking. First, the stress on overdetermination as the defining characteristic of the symbolic does some violence to the elaboration in Althusser of the companion concept of underdetermination, especially as it is described in "Is It Simple to Be a Marxist in Philosophy?"[21] Second, the assimilation of the field of the symbolic to the "lack of an ultimate literality" is posed as enabling the undoing of reduction to an immanent law. These tactics significantly, and characteristically, assimilate the concept of literality to that of essence by means of the term *determination*, which is understood to condense a set of parallel determinations: the semantic determination of the figurative by the literal; of the representation by the concept and ultimately by the referent; of "articulation" (Laclau and Mouffe) by precisely the sort of "articulating subject" that seems banished from Althusser.

And yet as surely as the literality of a symbol is not the same as its essence, the horizon of the ultimate lack of literality of the symbolic does not in itself guarantee that a different order of literality cannot install other variants of essentialism (including an essentialism of the figure, for instance). If social relations "lack an ultimate literality," this is to say that the process by which they can be said to stand for something—other social relations, relations of power, the effectivity of a structure, etc.—will always be interminable. Thus the project of "elaborating a new concept of articulation" will also always be interminable—unless the elaboration of the new concept occurs independently of (that is, cannot be determined on the basis of) the semiotic aspect of social relations. Laclau and Mouffe continue:

> If the concept of overdetermination was unable to produce the totality of its deconstructive effects within Marxist discourse, this was because, from the very beginning, an attempt was made to render it compatible with another central moment in Althusserian discourse that is, strictly speaking, incompatible with the first: namely, determination in the last instance by the economy.

It is here that the originality of Laclau and Mouffe's project becomes clear and that their distance from Barry Hindess and Paul Hirst is most strongly marked. Associated throughout *Hegemony and Socialist Strategy* with an occlusive sense of *determination*, totality is reintroduced as a desirable possibility—the "totality of deconstructive effects." To produce this paradoxical totality of effects requires, presumably, that no effort be made to make the overdetermination of the symbolic compatible with the order of determination in the last instance and that the interminability of elaboration be understood not as what Hegel calls a "bad infinity," susceptible of no understanding and of no totalization, but as a "good" one: the simplest form of subsumption of difference or contradiction into identity, the "simple infinity" also called the "absolute Concept" in the *Phenomenology*.[22] The difficulties that such an effort poses are perhaps too evident: if "the last instance" can be understood to be the horizon of any act of judgment, then assigning it a concrete condition of possibility (determination by the economic) seems to require us to subordinate to those conditions what we experience and understand as the present constellation of social relations. The overdetermination of these relations is secondary, from the point of view of judgment, to their predetermination. And yet, from the point of view of experience (that is, from the point of view of the phenomenology of the subject), the predetermination of social relations remains permanently a matter of hypothesis, their secondariness itself secondary to an experience of actually existing social relations. It is ideology, then, that steps into this sharp disjoining of the conditions of possibility of judgment and of experience, making them compatible both in principle and in the last instance.

"Incompatibility" differs in this way from the more productive sense of a rupture or a contingent judgment that Laclau and Mouffe outline, but any reliance upon the notion will reintroduce categories perhaps best abandoned. Incompatibility, which becomes merely a first moment in the inevitable production and reproduction of ideology, bears for this reason an uncomfortable similarity to the organicist determinism of a work like Lukács's *History and Class Consciousness*. For if *Hegemony and Socialist Strategy* is to "elaborate a new concept of articulation" without making that process of elaboration into a form of determination or of ideology, it must retain the disruptive force of incompatibility without subordinating it to the organicism of a theory of production or reproduction or to an interminableness that relies, finally, upon a good infinity linked indissociably to the doctrine of bad totalities Laclau and Mouffe seek to avoid. It must retain incompatibility, then, without severing judgment from experience—that is, without abandoning the possibility of the production of the concept.

Into this knot, and in the place occupied in Althusserian epistemology by the notion of ideology, Laclau and Mouffe introduce the psychoanalytic process of quilting or suturing, which Jacques-Alain Miller elaborates, in "Suture (Elements of the Logic of the Signifier)," on the basis of the work of Lacan.[23] Statements about suture necessarily bear marks of syntactical strain (*embarras* is Alain Badiou's word for it), since the elaboration of its concept takes place only in and as the paradoxical combination of future and perfected past, and since it is a relational term that, as Badiou puts it in his analysis of the function of suture in Althusser's work, "makes uncomfortably readable its two borders," in Althusser's case "philosophy" and "the privileged condition."[24] "Suture," Miller says, "if it is not named explicitly as such by Jacques Lacan, is constantly present in his system." It thus occupies very much the same place with regard to Lacan's work as "the concept . . . of the effectivity of a structure on its elements [effects]," that "visible/invisible, absent/present keystone of [Marx's] whole work," to recall Althusser's words. Suture, it seems, is not a form of determination. It is not "an attempt [by a subject] to make compatible" a structure with its elements or effects, but a node of fantasy that produces the subject position. And it is not yet an "object of knowledge"—that is, a concept. It must, instead, be understood as the improperly conceived ground upon which a miscognized (*méconnu*) subject is enacted and can act, can affirm within a contingent, rather than a determined, horizon. For this reason, the marks of suture do not make a determined totality of the overdetermined field of symbolic social relations. Fantasies or symptoms elaborated at the level of the cultural or social signifier, rather than at the level of an "ultimate literality" that "would reduce them to necessary moments of an immanent law," mark the unforeseeable locations at which different, often competing, discourses devoted to describing the field of social relations (the languages of feminism, of cultural materialism, of aesthetics, of epistemology) will suddenly show themselves to have become articulated.[25]

The fullest development of Miller's discussion of suture has been in the arena of psychoanalytic vocabulary, from which it derives, and in the film theory of the Cahiers du cinéma . . . and Screen groups.[26] The concept also seems to provide a promising way of understanding the position I have been sketching for the ethico-political subject, located both within and without the field of social relations: the principle of closure for the totality of those relations, but also the contingent shape of its openness; both autonomous and heteronomous; giving itself rules for thought and conduct from a position those rules fashion, defectively, a posteriori.[27] Suture, a para-concept basic to thought about the possibility of totality, rests upon an elision that is clear in its initial formulation. Miller, opening his influential essay, links his discussion of Frege to the relation between objects, concepts, and the process of determination. In fact, Kant's discussion of the concept is very much at issue in Miller's argument:

> An object only has existence in so far as it falls under a concept, there being no other determination involved in its logical existence, so that the object takes its meaning from its difference to the thing integrated, by its spatio-temporal localisation, to the real. Whence you can see the disappearance of the thing which must be effected in order for it to appear as object—which is *the thing in so far as it is one.* It is clear that the concept that operates in the system, formed solely through the determination of subsumption, is a redoubled concept: *the concept of identity to a concept.*[28]

Miller goes on to identify this redoubled concept with the zero in Frege's numerical system—the place of a lack, and a lack that is the suturing point at which the subject, or what can be called subject effects, can appear. The distance from Hegel seems unbreachable: the disappearing of the thing (*chose*), insofar as it is one, is not the disappearance of the immediate object-for-itself, to be subsumed in a mediate object-for-consciousness; much less does the ex-centricity of the thing with respect to the object become in its turn determinable, thinkable, for a subject.[29] And yet the "determination of subsumption" that Miller describes retains an unmistakable kinship to Hegel's apparent solution to the problem posed by the unknowable formality of the concept. The phenomenological integration of the thing into the real erases it as thing and produces it as integer, but only insofar as this disappearance is both retained (as producing "meaning": the meaning that the object takes from its difference from the thing) and erased (the "identity to the concept" of the object requires that the thing that the object replaces appear nowhere as an unsubsumed aspect or representation of the object). The complexities and the success of Miller's position derive, again as in the Vienna *Logic*'s definition of the concept, from the ease with which the nature of the object shifts: the concrete object that "falls under a concept" is of a different order from the object's "identity to a concept." The second is a thing only by virtue of the effacement of the difference between thing and object in its case. For Miller's analysis to proceed, "identity to a concept" has to be both thing and object, both phenomenalized ("localised") and made to "fall under a concept," that is, abstracted. Abstraction and phenomenalization are here elided, principally so that the function of taking meaning from a difference that is both preserved and erased can itself be preserved. The ellipsis, accomplished here upon one signifier that covers two concepts, splitting the concept of object to which the term *object* refers, instances the logic of condensation that the essay goes on to elaborate, but only after making it clear that the "concept of identity to a concept" operates in the "system" as a concept precisely not identical to itself—that is, in a formal sense, identity (to a concept) does not exist, although it does occur.

Transference

The difficulties in Miller's description of the redoubling of the concept surface acutely when that redoubling is extended to the language of political agency. If suture, fantasy, and the unsutured are not forms of determination, they nevertheless remain linked subtly and explicitly to a notion of totality of effects, to the perfection (in the verbal sense) of effects in and as the field of the social. This promise of perfection, even in its defective or weakened shape—the perfection afforded by a principle of closure that is also a principle of opening or unfinishing, of imperfection—derives in great measure from an analogy between the process of conceptual embodiment and the process of symbolic or social materialization in and as social organizations or institutions—the relation, say, between the will and the law.

This is not, of course, just any instance. From Hegel to Althusser, the reach and implications of the analogy between conceptual embodiment and institutionalization will be determined by its association with an impasse dating to Rousseau: whether the concept of the collective will is produced spontaneously from or preexists the definition of a collectivity of individual wills.[30] The question notoriously and symptomatically bedevils Engels, and Althusser returns to it as early as his essay "Contradiction and Overdetermination." His question there forcefully echoes the concern in *Reading 'Capital'* with the "effectivity of structures on their parts": "Why," Althusser asks in "Contradiction and Overdetermination," "is everything so clear and harmonious at the level of individual wills, whereas beneath this level or beyond it, all becomes either empty or tautological?" The very transparency of the problem becoming the index of its ideological stakes, Althusser concludes that Engels is forced by the obstacles it poses into the realm of fiction:

> a fiction quite as optimistic as the fiction of bourgeois economics, a fiction closer to Locke and Rousseau than to Marx, . . . [proposing] that the resultant of all the individual wills, and the resultant of these resultants, actually has a general content, really embodies determination in the last instance by the economic (I am thinking of Rousseau, whose dearest wish was that the particular wills, cut off from one another, might come together in a fair vote, producing that miraculous Minerva, the general will!).[31]

As the ironic stress on "actual" and "real" suggests, this formulation marks a moment when Althusser is beginning to shape the contrasting thesis that ideology, that "resultant of these resultants," is their imaginary embodiment. The complex geometry of the social produces something other than a concrete content, or the content produced is not susceptible to embodiment. Engels's naïve, optimistic fiction retreats from the rigor of Marx's position to the notion that "determination in the last instance" by the economy is actually embodied in the resultant of the individual wills as their concrete content, an argument that crucially links a pedagogical notion of influence to a form of historical embodiment or identification, opposing, on the one hand, Rousseau and Engels (who does not learn from his teacher's errors) and, on the other, Marx and Althusser, who do. The error at issue, for Althusser and Marx as for Hegel (who in an important note to the *Logic* comments on Rousseau's incapacity to keep "before his eyes" the distinction between the concept, the *volonté générale*, and its particular special clauses, the laws that govern the *volonté de tous*), has to do with the phenomenology of embodiment: the embodying of the concept as concrete content, that is, the production of the concept from and within the material, cannot be the same as the production of the material—the concrete—from the concept. Within the language provided by the *Social Contract*, the solution to the aporias of production, bordering conceptual embodiment and institutionalization, occurs as the spontaneous work of a miracle—that is, as a fantasy, a delusion, or a work of literature.[32]

Yet the lesson to be drawn from this observation is far from clear. Althusser, who uses Rousseau here as the exemplary instance of the thinker in whom conceptual embodiment is fundamentally mythic, also suggests approvingly that Rousseau is exceptional among "eighteenth-century ideologues" in wanting his wish to be "productive"—that is, to have a material effect. In Althusser's parenthesis, the production or birth of "marvelous Minerva," martial wisdom fully armed springing from the forehead of Jupiter to defend Genevan republicanism as she had once protected Athenian democracy, itself embodies, with characteristic terseness, the strategic value of fiction: fiction is both embodiment or figure and critique of embodiment. Although it cannot, it seems, be construed as a material effect of the *Social Contract*, the set of determinants or *repraesentationes communes* that Rousseau proposes is an ideological effect, with distinct material consequences (the French Revolution, in one reading). The indecision marks a shift both in the understanding of Rousseau, reflected in an ambivalence in the descriptions of the law and of theological language (as an ideological apparatus), on the one hand, and of the notions of matter, effect, and body, on the other. When Althusser takes up again the form that this "dearest wish" has for Rousseau, he does so by returning to the status of the "necessary fiction," considering again its possible relation to material effect.

In his analysis of the *Social Contract* ("Sur le 'Contrat Social' [les Décalages]"; 1966), Althusser suggests that Rousseau builds a theoretical argument about a chain of *décalages*—displacements, breaks, or impasses whose solutions, in turn, generate further, slightly more general impasses. (Ben Brewster translates *décalage* as "discrepancy."[33]) Each of these impasses poses a genuine threat to the possibility of a generalized notion of the social: thus the *décalage* between the "total alienation" of the slave and the total alienation required to enter into a social contract is resolved as the difference but also identity between the two parties to the contract, the individual and the social body; this position then reveals a *décalage* between alienation and advantageous exchange, which in turn becomes the problem of the relation between the general will and the particular will, that is, the problem of the law. Rousseau both solves and displaces this last contradiction, as he does the previous ones, by means, Althusser argues, of wordplay. "We have a total contradiction," Althusser writes. "Particular interest is the essence of the general interest, but it is also the obstacle to it; now, the whole secret of this contradiction lies in a '*play*' on words in which Rousseau calls the *particular* interest of each individual in isolation and the *particular* interest of social groups *by the same name*."[34] But this solution obeys an important imperative, for if these problems are not solved, the *décalages* become confrontations, descriptions of impasses, in such a way that the act of naming returns to the originating moment at the heart of the "Discourse on Language," an act that produces what it names.

The dismissal of Rousseau's fictionalizing in "Contradiction and Overdetermination" has by this point changed substantially, although the structure of Althusser's argument remains profoundly dialectical, and the wish (Althusser's as well as Rousseau's) for the appearance of a "miraculous Minerva" of material effects persists, though remarkably transformed. The movement toward a *décalage* and the regression from it, *fuite et regression*, remain posed as operating within a discontinuity between the theoretical and the real.[35] It is when the last discontinuity shows itself to resist a theoretical solution that Althusser opens the possibility of discussing the fictional Rousseau as an allegory of the failure of the political or theoretical one:

> If there is no possibility of further Discrepancies—since they would no longer be of any use in the theoretical order which has done nothing but live on these Discrepancies, chasing before it its problems and their solutions to the point where it reaches the real, insoluble problem, there is still one recourse, but one of a different kind: a transfer, this time, the transfer of the impossible theoretical solution into the alternative to theory, literature. The admirable "fictional triumph" of an unprecedented writing [*écriture*]: *La Nouvelle Héloïse*, *Émile*, the *Confessions*. That they are unprecedented may be not unconnected with the admirable "failure" of an unprecedented theory: the Social Contract.[36]

The movement from Rousseau's theory to his fiction—the therapeutic completing of the project and this determining of each by the other—is a

transference in the shape of a narrative: the narrative of a victory, a determining narrative of determination as the appearance of a recognizable fiction. In this sense, Althusser proposes to understand fiction or literature
as the region of a double, paradoxical embodiment. It is able to express as
fiction the persistent troubling of cause and effect—the production—that
cannot operate "in theory," and it arrives at this fiction by means not of a
conceptual but of a literary movement. For this reason, fiction or literature—aesthetics—is the labor of the concept, the form and direction of its
transference from theoretical failure to fictional success. But the specific
means by which the *décalages* take place in this essay argues for another
engagement as well. The terms *flight, regression, wordplay,* and, finally, the
transference to the *other* of theory suggest that Althusser was seeking to
articulate this flight in the language of psychoanalysis, the displacement
from the theoretical region of the *décalages* to the region of fiction having
the structure of a recognizable analytic movement: the externalization-
projection by means of which a therapeutic fantasy can be represented, the
"real embodiment" of what remains unconscious, or the dynamic of the
transference.

This marked turn toward the language of psychoanalysis is not in itself
surprising—"Sur le 'Contrat Social' (les Décalages)," was, after all, first
published in *Cahiers pour l'analyse*, and at a time when Althusser's engagement with Lacan was almost constant. Some of what it suggests about
Althusser's theoretical as well as his biographical or literary trajectory is
immediately problematic, however.[37] In the first place, the pedagogical
model of historical influence at issue in "Contradiction and Overdetermination" is recast here, by virtue of the seemingly open sequence of *transferts*, as a question of identity: the problematic identity or supplementarity,
in the first instance, of the "admirable 'fictitious triumph' of a writing
without precedents" with the "admirable 'failure' of a theory without
precedents"; the equally problematic identity or supplementarity of the
Rousseau of the *Social Contract* with respect to the Rousseau of *La Nouvelle
Héloïse, Emile,* and especially the *Confessions*; and, finally, the complex identification, at issue already in "Contradiction and Overdetermination,"
between Althusser and the figure or figures of Rousseau. We cannot be
blind to the pathos of the essay's concluding lines. The topos of the flight
from reason—*theoria*—to "an avenue of recourse, but of a different sort"
is not only the narrative of the birth and the therapeutic necessity of fiction
or literature, or the narrative of the failure of all merely theoreticist positions whose effectivity must be completed or supplemented by a passage
or transference into the material region of theoretical practice. (Marx:

"Philosophers have interpreted the world; the point, however, is to change it.") It is also, as its roots in Romanticism serve to remind us, the narrative of a flight into madness. The flight or regression into fiction described for Rousseau—the flight from theoretical impasses—can also be read as the fundamental moment of this identification between Althusser and Rousseau: the recourse of madness, which derives theoretically from the effort to overcome *décalages* internal to the genealogy of the concept and biographically from the conditions described in the autobiographies and condensed, with the rigor of denegation, in its opening pages: "Alas," Althusser writes in *The Future Lasts Forever*:

> I am no Rousseau. But in planning to write about myself and the dramatic events I lived through and live with still, I often thought about his unprecedented boldness. Not that I would ever claim as he did at the beginning of the *Confessions*: "I am embarking on something which has never been done before." Certainly not. But I can in all honesty subscribe to the following declaration of his: "I shall say openly what I did, what I thought, what I was."[38]

But in the second place, and to a great extent by contrast, the dynamic of transference, for all its descriptive power and suggestiveness for the question of identity, poses fundamental problems. *Transfert* in "Rousseau: The Social Contract" conveniently straddles the field of intentional acts as well as nonintentional events, for important theoretical reasons: the movement toward resolving the last, most stubborn *décalage* in Rousseau is not Rousseau's own, "proper" act or decision, nor does it obey a structural necessity that might immediately have produced the literary recourse out of the failure of the theoretical. Instead, and as the strikingly depersonalized grammar of the last sentences conveys, the *transfert* from failure to victory, the therapeutic supplementation of theory by fiction, obeys the impersonal difficulty of distinguishing, on any grounds, between an intentional act and an event. It should be remarked that the same is generally true for descriptions of analytic transference: it *occurs*, it happens that the analyst or another figure acquires for the patient the characteristics of a figure from the pantheon of the analysand's recollections—and the intentional form of that transference is what remains to be produced in and by means of the analysis.[39]

The consequences of this depersonalization for the phenomenology of embodiment are mixed. If we seek in the engagement with Rousseau the transference back to the realm of theory (miraculous Minerva, both philosophical, literary, and political) of concepts from psychoanalysis and from literature, then we also need to account for the contingent movement that the language of psychoanalysis consistently associates with every such narrative. Thus, although Rousseau's strategy in moving from *décalage* to theoretical solution is one of condensation—two or more concepts or senses of a word condensed in one signifier—there is no reason to suppose that the closing transference from failure to victory, from the arena of theory to that of fiction, follows the same pattern. The recourse to the other in this instance is made to seem necessary, to take the form of a narrative reaching a foreseeable and determined closure—but the association of Althusser with Rousseau here is just as contingent as the object of transference in the analytic situation can be. To put it differently: the *transfert* from theory to literature or to madness can be described as therapeutic, as producing identification or personification if not identity, only from the perspective that it has abandoned: the perspective of theory. From the perspective of literature or of psychoanalysis, and a fortiori from the perspective (if one can still call it that) of madness, the dynamic of *transfert* is always an "avenue . . . of a different sort" from the terms that theory can use to describe it, or can transfer onto it. Again, from the perspective of literature or psychoanalysis, indeed from the perspective (for instance) of the *Confessions*, the transference (of guilt or responsibility, say) does not necessarily occur from theory to its other or from one person to another. It attaches itself to what is at hand, in a metonymic flight to an other whose connection to theory this flight then produces.[40] Transference no longer straddles—that is, participates in and joins—two distinct arenas; it is not a trope for the free movement (*phorein*) of the word from one to another, from theory to fiction or from Rousseau to Althusser; it is not a wordplay condensing two concepts under a single term so as to retain and limn for and in us the synthetic consciousness of the concept of identity to a concept.

Let us call it instead a rule, though of a paradoxical sort: having the form of a gerund, transference cannot, to return to Kant's initial formulation, "serve as a rule [*zur Regel dient*]" that would predict the direction of the movement (from theory to fiction, or to practice, or to matter) of any concrete content or instance, including particular rules. As a rule, transference happens; it is an event. But because of the rule of its occurring, transference has in itself no regulative content. The issue immediately becomes considerably broader than the local question of the status granted literature in the failure of the *Social Contract*. It is by now understood that it is not possible to settle on either of the two models of causation that Althusser deploys in "Rousseau: The Social Contract" and in *Reading 'Capital,'* a "metonymic causality" on the one hand; on the other, the hypothesis of a structuring "disconcerting but inevitable absence, the absence of the concept" in the mode of a *deus absconditus* in Pascal's tradition. One can express this undecidability as the interference between two models, one transcendental and the other materialist, the first accounting for intentional acts and the second for nonintentional events, whose complex history includes the encounters and failed syntheses—within and between the foundational texts of Marxism—of a theology and a materialism, an apocalyptic rhetoric and an empirical one, the rhetorics of the *Communist Manifesto* and of Lenin's *Materialism and Empirio-criticism*. But most importantly, the rule of transference records this undecidability as a fundamental break that cannot be sutured, forgotten, or sublated by a transference into the arena of fiction or practice. For it is not just that the "concept of identity to a concept" operates in the "system" as a concept precisely not identical to itself, but that to the extent that it is a product, in a formal sense, such a concept does not exist, although it does occur. What happens, what is an event, as the irreducible difference between what is *de tous*, everybody's, possessed concretely by everyone, and *générale*, analytically constitutive of the concept of the general, like the general will in Rousseau, happens "in a '*play*' on words" and is inescapably literary.

Divine Matter and Wild Materialism

But this is an old story, the disconcerting appearing of literary matters in the heart of philosophy (in the *concept* of philosophy, which has been, since Kant, also a philosophy of the concept)—a Lucretian story, as the stress on the event suggests, a Spinozist one, a Marxist story in a queer way that Althusser will recognize only quite late in life. To understand it requires that we start over and reread, from the vantage of these occurrent literary effects, the determining encounter between Marx and Hegel. The broad strokes of this approach are no secret. Take, for instance, Marx's crucial early analysis of Hegel's *Philosophy of Right*. Marx finds the shape of Hegel's argument familiar enough—its stages can be mapped throughout the whole project of the Hegelian *Encyclopedia*—but in the *Philosophy of Right* (in §§279–87 of the chapter "Ethical Life"), Hegel's argument is linked forcefully and enduringly with the concept of sovereignty and with a critique of all forms of sovereignty that do not take as their concrete form the embodied monarch and as their concept the monarch's divine right.[41]

Here, Marx notes, the *Philosophy of Right* sets out to account for the mutually enabling transformations in thought, on the one hand, of the "predicate [the concept], universal, or abstraction into the subject, substrate, or concrete, and the consequent transformation of the real subject into the predicate," as Galvano Della Volpe describes it, and, on the other hand, in the sphere of "ethical life [*Sittlichkeit*]," the transformation of mere familial and social (*bürgerliche*) relations into the form that completes, entails, and cancels them as mere moments—the state, "this totality in which the moments of the concept attain actuality in accordance with their distinctive truth," a totality whose sovereign authority is embodied in the monarch.[42]

Marx is careful to address Hegel's argument both theoretically and allegorically. In the *Critique of Hegel's 'Philosophy of Right,'* Marx understands Hegel's description of the passage from the "logical forms of the concept" to "the vital spirit [*lebendige Geist*] of the actual world" as involving a symmetrical confusion: although Hegel believes that he is able to derive and develop the determinate, concrete reality of the organism of the state from its idea, he in fact derives that concrete shape from the presupposed concept: "He does not develop his thought out of what is objective [*aus dem Gegenstand*], but what is objective in accordance with a ready-made thought which has its origin in the abstract sphere of logic."[43] Hegel, it seems, makes the necessity of the movement toward the concrete universal derive from this "abstract sphere," and as such the necessity is not itself "critically demonstrated" as being internal to the various powers proper to the organic state. This process of deriving the necessity of an internal movement from an "alien" principle Marx then describes in these terms:

> Just as their necessity is not derived from their own nature, still less is it critically demonstrated. On the contrary, their realization is predestined by the nature of the concept, sealed in the holy register of the Santa Casa (the *Logic*). [*Ihr Schicksal ist vielmehr prädestiniert durch die "Natur des Begriffs," versiegelt in der Santa Casa (der Logik) heiligen Registern.*] The soul of objects, in this case that of the state, is complete and predestined before its body, which is, properly speaking, mere appearance. The concept is the "Son" within the "Idea," within God the Father, the *agens*, the determining, differentiating principle.[44]

Marx's passage winds in a number of different ways about the same knot, rendering allegorically the circularity that the *Critique* points out analytically: if the concept is not to be like the soul or the idea, subsisting and eternal, transcendent if not Platonic, but is instead a derived or produced representation, then its origin, its appearing, must be external to it: a matter of labor. And if necessity is not to be equally transcendent ("predestined by the nature of the concept"), then the realization of the objective and the form of logic also must be derived, if only in the form of a narrative or myth of origin. Here Marx makes use of the traditional Christological problem that Hegel also appears to be exploiting (and not just here, of course): when the priority of the soul with respect to the body is translated into the structure of the Trinity, a resolute ontological as well as temporal hierarchy (the soul is prior to the body) clashes with the theological need for the mutual immanence of the aspects of divinity figured in the Trinity. Great waves of Catholic heresy crest in this clash, as God the Father becomes the *agens* of whom the Son is either the soul or the mere appearance, the Son either prior to the Father or the Father's mere externalization. As for the numinous third who walks always by the side of the Son and God the Father—in this description, the Holy Spirit captures the sublime residue of constitutive relation (*Verhältnis*) rather than substance and is the vehicle of annunciation rather than the announced news, neither body nor soul, neither Son nor God the Father, neither the "determining, differentiating principle" nor the matter that bears the trace of that differentiation or determination.

To be sure, the niceties of Christian dogma are not Marx's main object. (Hegel is a different matter.) Nevertheless, his focus on the symptomatic Trinitarianism in Hegel's logic is immensely suggestive, as is, for our purposes, the way that logic is analyzed—by means of an extraordinary disconcerting of the relation between the normative contexts that Hegel's and Marx's arguments employ and the normative concepts they seek to produce. On a philosophical level, one might say, the *Critique of Hegel's 'Philosophy of Right'* intends to set straight the circular phenomenology of derivation gingerly advanced in the *Philosophy of Right* by providing a non-Trinitarian third, a concrete or determinate stance or lexicon governing the relation between, on the one hand, the immanent account of the emergence of the concrete universal according to a "necessity . . . derived from the nature" of what is objective, associated with the transcendental model of annunciation and predestination, and, on the other hand, a dialectical account of the emergence of the concrete universal, which arises from the difference between the objective and its first formalization in the *Logic* as a concept. On a political level, Marx seeks to establish a model of the state that is not secondary to and does not flow from a preexisting "soul," "concept," "idea," or theological active principle and that attends to the "transindividualist" ontology of relation that takes the place, as Balibar suggests in *The Philosophy of Marx*, of the couplet individual/totality. The strange withering of the state into a body that is first an object, then the mere appearance of a primary "soul of objects . . . complete and pre-destined" is expressed, Marx argues, in a language that Hegel cannot de-finitively render either philosophical or political—a sort of bridging terminology drawn from a different lexicon: theology. "The concept is the 'Son' within the 'Idea,' within God the Father, the *agens*, the determining, differentiating principle," and this set of theological embeddings and sub-stitutions, Marx tells us, is in turn embedded and sealed in Hegel's *Logic* as in the Santa Casa.

As it happens—it is not an accident, or not in a trivial sense—the image that Marx chooses to illustrate Hegel's peculiar evasion of philosophical and political precision is strikingly overdetermined. As its name indicates, the Santa Casa is an element, perhaps even an important element, in Mar-ian worship, with plainly theological roots: Marx is referring to the "Holy House (*la casa santa*), where Mary lived in Nazareth, and which according to legend was snatched up from Galilee by angels, and carried away through the air, high over land and sea, and delivered, after setting down for two rather lengthy rests, in the year 1295 to its current resting place and location," as the early-nineteenth-century diarist Friedrich von Mat-thison put it.[45] Transported miraculously to Loreto in the thirteenth cen-tury, the Santa Casa is the setting of the annunciation to Mary. By the Renaissance, the shrine at Loreto had become a pilgrimage site of great importance, second in Europe only to Santiago of Compostela, as well as a cultural icon that condensed a number of tropes both literary and theo-logical: the transference of the house corresponds to a *translatio imperii* from Nazareth to Italy and hence to the Holy Roman Empire; site of miraculous cures, by the sixteenth century it had acquired a second *casa*, the sanctuary in which it was sealed and shielded, and in which it became, by the early seventeenth century, an emblem of a holy register defined architecturally by the traces of those cures, a scaffold of crutches, canes, and objects cast off by pilgrims that a vision of the Santa Casa had made whole.[46] The Santa Casa enjoyed a surprising celebrity in Europe at the time that Marx was drafting his critique of Hegel: in travel literature (Mat-thison); ecclesiastical histories and Mariolatries (including Johann Mat-thias Schröckh's *Christliche Kirchengeschichte* [*History of the Christian Church*] of 1799 and Johann Christian Wilhelm Augusti's 1829 *Denkwürdig-keiten aus der christlichen Archäologie* [*Remembrances or Memorabilia from Christian Archaeology*]), as well as better-known texts such as Schleiermach-er's influential 1840 *Geschichte der christlichen Kirche* (*History of the Christian Church*); and in popular ballads, such as Carl Loewe's "Das heilige Haus in Loretto" (a setting of Ludwig Theodor Giesebrecht's poem) of 1834.[47] By this time the Santa Casa, embedded within the church, also sported an armature of tokens discarded by miraculously cured pilgrims, phantoms of bodies in turn concealing, clothing, or embodying a house sealed within a sanctuary.

The abyssal presentation of the absent cause by its successive, hollow embodiments could hardly be more compactly rendered: the parentheses in Marx's text ("their realization is predestined by the nature of the concept, sealed in the holy register of the Santa Casa [the *Logic*]") materialize at the level of the sentence the logic of metonymous substitution of inside for out, container for contained, form for content or for matter, on which the *Philosophy of Right* seems to rest and which the strange architectures of the Santa Casa vividly capture: the absent event of the Annunciation represented and sheltered by *domus laureana*, surrounded by the church, protected but also advertised, made apparent, by the phantasmatic register of the Annunciation's miraculous effects, the pilgrims' prosthetics. The Santa Casa, standing for the body of Mary, in whom the concept and the word (the Son) are materialized, "seals" for Marx the form of the *Logic*: body, outer shell, or architecture to the concept that it produces and serves, as Mary serves to contain and bear the concept, *ancilla Dei*.

Whatever humor tinges this encounter between Marx and Hegel should not conceal what is at stake sealed within its register. The determining fantasy of philosophical language and of the philosophy of right is that new concepts (of sovereignty, of the state, of right) emerge both spontaneously and according to fate (the "nature of the concept" predestines them to emerge). Concepts are "born," and the story of their birth and shelter is the narrative of a miraculous birth. The difficulties that this paradox of emergence poses to thought, in particular to what Hegel calls "the reflective approach of the understanding [*Rasonnement*, or *die reflektierende Verstandes betrachtung*]" are substantially the same as those that the *Philosophy of Right* associates with the concept of the monarch itself, which must be thought not only from the perspective of one or another "isolated determination [*vereinzelte Bestimmung*]" but also from the perspective of the concept: "It [the reflective understanding] accordingly presents the dignity of the monarch as *derivative* [Abgeleitet], not only in its form but also in its determination, whereas the very concept of monarchy is that it is not deduced from something else but *entirely self-originating*. The idea that the right of the monarch is based on divine authority is therefore the closest approximation to this concept."[48] Miraculous birth, then, because this birth is both spontaneous (that is, unannounced) and determined, both the labor of the objective that bears the concept and the labor of reflection upon the object. And miraculous, too, on account of its bizarrely mixed parentage, Roman as well as Greek, Catholic and Protestant, human and transcendent: Hegel's doctrine of the concept expresses both the fantasy of immaterial conception, the mother merely bears (*trägt*) what is immediate to the differentiating and determining *agens*, the father; and, indissociably and consequently, the fantasy of the maternal father, bearing like Jupiter the body of philosophy and armed wisdom, miraculous Minerva midwifed by Vulcan.

To speak in slightly less allegorical terms: the story of the production of the object of knowledge from the object or vice versa is always embodied as a fantasy of the spontaneous reproduction of the identity to itself of the concept from which the new concept is produced—even though the new concept is the mark of the nonidentity to itself of the concept in general. (New concepts are both effects and elements of older ones.) "Thought" does not "derive from the objective [*aus dem Gegenstand*]," even when the objective is itself already symbolic, as its therapeutic cure or completing, fiction to its theory or theory to its fiction, but as its vestige, its discarded crutch, so to speak: assembled about the hidden register of a translated or transferred container (*Träger*), phantom of the wounded, broken, or tortured body as well as of the whole one reborn miraculously, spontaneously. This improper condensation of the complete and the incomplete, identity to self and nonidentity to self, is a formative aspect of the doctrine of the concept. Concepts "come from" a labor that effaces/produces its ownership of what it conceives, a labor that labors to efface itself as such, as the production of the concept as what is nonidentical to itself. Miraculous Minerva, indeed!

To the account of this doubly miraculous birth, and by means of his critique of Hegel's inversion of the concrete and the conceptual, Marx seeks to restore the elementary resistance of the particular object or circumstance to its rebirth in the concept, the specific form that the suffering of thought takes. These are present in Marx's image as well, but antithetically, scandalously. Marx's Santa Casa refers not only to the architecture of annunciation, the primal scene linking Hegelian logic to the plane of theological reproduction, but also to the physical suffering that this linkage seems necessarily to entail (*santa casa* is the name given throughout the evangelical expansion in the Americas and in India to the buildings that housed the combination of hospitals, hostels, and beneficent societies founded by the missionary orders) and to the theologico-political terror it houses and on which it stands: the Inquisition.

The last has a specifically literary source. In this passage from the *Critique of Hegel's 'Philosophy of Right,'* Marx is remembering verses from Friedrich Schiller's play *Don Karlos, Infant von Spanien*, of 1786–87. In the scene at hand, King Philip II has summoned the Inquisitor. They are discussing the assassination of the Marquis de Posa, Prince Carlos's great friend and interlocutor, on the King's orders. Posa is the play's representative of Enlightened rationalism, and in this penultimate scene the Inquisitor reveals the Inquisition's old plot to execute Posa as a terrible example, so as "to make a show of ostentatious reason." The Inquisitor is highly displeased to have been deprived of his victim; Philip, distraught to find that Posa and Carlos were plotting rebellion, the overthrowing of the confessional and inquisitorial Hapsburg monarchy, and the installation of some sort of liberal, perhaps even republican, government (this is Schiller, after all), concludes the scene by placing his right to judge in the Inquisitor's hands and agreeing to hand over Prince Carlos to the Inquisition. The function of terror has been reestablished; after the brief opening that Posa's words and deeds provide, rebellion will once again be bound. ("Terror alone can tie rebellion's hands:/Compassion would be madness"; "Und Schrecken bändigt die Empörung nur./Erbarmung hieße Wahnsinn," the King has warned Carlos.) The scene opens like this:

GRAND INQUISITOR: Why did you commit this murder?
KING: Betrayal without parallel—
GRAND INQUISITOR: I know it.
KING: What do you know? Through whom? Since when?
GRAND INQUISITOR: For years,
    What *you* have known since sunset.
KING (*surprised*): What? You had
    Already known about this man?
GRAND INQUISITOR: His life
    Lies opened and concluded in the holy
    Record-ledgers of the Santa Casa.
KING: And he walked free?
GRAND INQUISITOR: The cord on which he fluttered
    Was long, but still unbreakable.
KING: But he
    Had been beyond my kingdom's boundaries.
GRAND INQUISITOR: Wherever he might be, there I was also.
KING (*walking impatiently back and forth*): It was known in whose hands I
    was—Why then was there
    Delay in warning me?

GRAND INQUISITOR: That question I
   Turn back upon you—Why did *you* not ask
   When you threw yourself into this man's arms?

KÖNIG: Ein Betrug, der ohne Beispiel ist—
GROSSINQUISITOR: Ich weiß ihn.
KÖNIG: Was wisset Ihr? Durch wen? Seit wann?
GROSSINQUISITOR: Seit Jahren,
   Was Sie seit Sonnenuntergang.
KÖNIG (*mit Befremdung*): Ihr habt
   Von diesem Menschen schon gewußt?
GROSSINQUISITOR: Sein Leben
   Liegt angefangen und beschlossen in
   Der Santa Casa heiligen Registern.
KÖNIG: Und er ging frei herum?
GROSSINQUISITOR: Das Seil, an dem
   Er flatterte, war lang, doch unzerreißbar.
KÖNIG: Er war schon außer meines Reiches Grenzen.
GROSSINQUISITOR: Wo er sein mochte, war ich auch.
KÖNIG (*geht unwillig auf und nieder*): Man wußte,
   In wessen Hand ich war—Warum versäumte man,
   Mich zu erinnern?
GROSSINQUISITOR: Diese Frage geb ich
   Zurücke—Warum fragten Sie nicht an,
   Da Sie in dieses Menschen Arm sich warfen?[49]

Schiller's scene repays close study on its own, of course, and not just as the proximate literary source of Marx's allusion. It is almost certainly—more on this below—also the source of one of Freud's most famous phrases: when the principle of enlightened reason travels beyond the confines of the confessional realm, it is nevertheless still under surveillance and still acts a part set for it by forces willing on its behalf, willing where it wills. "Where Id was, there shall Ego be [*Wo Es war, soll Ich werden*]," or, as the Inquisitor has it, "Wo Er sein mochte, war Ich auch." In Schiller's work, the Santa Casa is the headquarters of the Inquisition in Madrid—the central example of obscurantism, terror, and secrecy in the "Black legend" with which Spain was charged and which lies behind Schiller's play and its use in Marx, here and elsewhere.[50] The struggle between King and Inquisitor over the Prince's fate is slight—a disagreement among the archaic forces that resist modernization and Enlightenment rather than a significant contradiction in the conceptualization of sovereignty.

Nor is the outcome really in dispute—not least because the scene repeats the earlier encounter between the King and the Prince, where the monarch reminds his son that any course but the application of terror would be "madness [*Wahnsinn*]": because the King has ruined the Inquisitor's plan, a substitute must be found. The weight of the analogy between the two scenes is carried by the King's acknowledgment to the Inquisitor that "I am in such matters no better than a novice, a beginner [*Ich bin / In diesen Dingen noch ein Neuling. Habe/ Geduld mit mir*]." And into this empty spot, the spot of the sacrificial, exemplary victim, the Prince is delivered by his father.

In this reading of the Santa Casa's intertext, then, Marx makes Hegel into the Grand Inquisitor of a tradition that seals the sacrificed son, the principle of Enlightened reason or the "nature of the concept" (archives it, imprisons it, houses it, gives shape and appearance to it, tortures it), within the body of the *Logic.* And in a second moment, the concept, both the abject prisoner and the most essential and characteristic aspect of this body, then takes priority over its empirical appearance, imprisoning its own prison, as it were, sealing it within itself. Della Volpe rightly stresses what he calls Marx's discovery of "the character of *mere allegory of the universal* acquired by the real substrate, or subject" in Hegel's account, though it would be more accurate to Marx's analysis to suggest that, in his reading, this "allegorization" occurs for Hegel in both directions—the "universal" also becoming a "mere allegory" of the "real substrate," each "sealed within" the other.[51] Schiller's audience and readers, and Marx's too, face the oldest of dramatic ironies: the exemplary terror that the Inquisitor had hoped to make manifest upon Posa's body turns back upon the sovereign, both wounding him and revealing the "nature of the concept" of the sovereignty of which he is, as Hegel puts it, simply a "determination [*Bestimmung*]." The sacrificial circularity that Schiller's play depicts is not only a miraculous double allegory; it also translates the costs to thought, to the family, and to the state of the encounter between the derivative (*abgeleitet*) and the "entirely self-originating [*aus sich Anfangendei*]" concept, not just of sovereignty but of the "nature of the concept" itself. Theologico-political terror, threatened with madness (from the application of "mercy" or "compassion," *Erbarmung*, as a principle of association), is salvaged both as the instrument and, Schiller's play suggests, as the goal of the Inquisitorial state. Schiller is not proposing a secular alternative, but a different theologico-political configuration: the concept of compassion or mercy that the play opposes to Spanish terror is associated with the Protestant critique of Catholicism, as in Philipp Friedrich Hiller's extraordinarily well-known 1767 hymn "Mir ist Erbarmung widerfahren,/Erbarmung, deren ich nicht wert" ("I was shown mercy,/ Mercy of which I was unworthy").

It is fanciful, or at least a bit hasty, to suggest that Marx is in any conventional sense aware, and intends to make use, of the extraordinary semantic and allusive saturation I have been sketching in his passing reference to the Santa Casa. This is not to say that the shrine and its uses had a single or uncontroversial sense at the time Schiller wrote, or when Marx cited his play. Take, for example, Voltaire, whose work Marx knew well. The *Dictionnaire philosophique* reflects cogently and specifically on the Santa Casa, and evokes both the registers principally in play in Marx's allusion-citation: Marian worship, with its attendant architectural-theological complexities; and the register of theologico-political terror. The annunciation, as well as its institutional-ideological concretization. The son, sealed in the "register" of inquisitorial terror. The risible, to Voltaire's mind, cult of "the house of Our Lady, which traveled through the air, which came to Dalmatia, which changed location two or three times, and which finally only found itself comfortable in Loreto," as well as the arbitrary violence that flows from a "fanatical," self-serving application of laws against heresy.[52] We might say, rather, that the semantic excess that characterizes Marx's avenue into Hegel's philosophy of the concept cannot be disambiguated by the application of a norm, however construed (for instance, by a narrow notion of intention, grounded in Marx's biography—Had he read Schiller? Was he conversant with Marian worship?—on which an equally narrow understanding of allusion would be built: the *Critique of Hegel's 'Philosophy of Right'* alludes explicitly to this passage from Schiller and to the story of the Santa Casa in Schröckh's *Christliche Kirchengeschichte*, or in Voltaire's *Dictionnaire*). Or we might say that Marx's argument is at this stage, and symptomatically, at once over- and underdetermined. Or—finally—we might return to Althusser's terminology and speak of a specific form of causality expressed in the relation between the figure of the Santa Casa and the culture of its production—a causality at once "metonymic," as the lexicon of *Reading 'Capital'* would put it, "aleatory" (now following the lexicon of the later Althusser), and determinate or structural. This threefold form of causality (Althusser's own Trinitarianism deserves some mention, after all) is, we can now see, the expanded form of the distinction and the contradiction between the forms of historicity we identified in Althusser's account of the concept—a historicity that attends to the ecology and a historicity that attends to the contingency of the concept's emergence. This threefold form of causation structures Althusser's rereading of the encounter between Marx and Hegel, in particular, his reflections on the "production of the concept" of "effectivity," the site of a strong, historically complex interference between two accounts of the genealogy of the sovereignty of the concept and of the concept of sovereignty: "derivative," on the one hand; "self-originating," on the other.

Althusser's reflections in the autobiographies on the origins of *Reading 'Capital'* are particularly clear examples of the literary noncoincidence of element and effect that I have been tracking. They form part of a story told as a jokc—rather mean-spirited, on the whole, defensive. Anxious. Althusser's strange tale has to do with theft and with desire—though nominally it concerns the seminar on *Capital:*

> [Jacques-Alain] Miller was the [member of the seminar] with the most fixed ideas on the subject, but he dropped out completely in the course of the year. He was living in a hunting-lodge at Rambouillet with a girl who "produced," so he said, "at least one theoretical concept a week." . . . After [Rancière's] intervention everything was easy because he opened up the debate effectively and in areas to which we were already giving some thought; this was after a talk of mine on Lacan during which Miller intervened to announce a "conceptual discovery": "metonymic causality" (otherwise known as the absent cause), which caused quite a stir. . . . When Miller returned . . . and read the duplicated pages of the papers people had given, he discovered Rancière had "stolen" his own concept [*son concept personnel*] of "metonymic causality." Rancière suffered terribly when charged with this. And is it not the case that concepts belong to everyone? . . . My reason for relating this ridiculous incident is not to put Miller down. After all, youth must have its fling. Furthermore, it seems he began his magisterial course on Lacan this year by solemnly declaring, "*We are not studying Lacan but being studied by him.*" This proves he too was capable of acknowledging someone else had invented and owned a concept. . . . None the less, this absurd idea of the "theft of concepts" touched on a point of principle which concerned me deeply and caused me great anxiety: the question of *anonymity*.[53]

The moment is recounted differently in two earlier passages in *The Facts*: "Some students at the Ecole [Normale Supérieure] had been quite impressed by [Lacan], among them Jacques-Alain Miller, whose famous concept had been plagiarised and who was wooing Judith Lacan." The exact phrasing is "a qui on avait volé le fameux concept de sa vie," which suggestively joins the "concept of a life"—its correlative on the level of concepts—to the "concept of a lifetime," the best or most important one.

> We [Balibar, Macherey, Establet, and Rancière] organized a seminar on *Das Kapital* during the academic year 1964–5. Rancière set it going and got us over our initial difficulties, for which he deserves our thanks, as no one else was prepared to start the ball rolling. . . . It was a masterly exposition . . . slightly formalist and Lacanian (the "absent cause" kept coming up) but it showed real ability. . . . Jacques-Alain Miller, who was already going out with Judith Lacan, displayed great initiative in October 1964, which brought him to prominence, and then disappeared completely (he had gone off with a girl to the forest of Fontainebleau and was teaching her how to produce theoretical concepts). He reappeared again without warning in June 1965 to reveal, much to everyone's astonishment, that someone had "stolen one of his concepts." . . . In actual fact, [the incident] was quite exceptional. Concepts circulate freely as they are being developed without any controls placed on them.[54]

Why would this anecdote matter enough to Althusser for him to return to it? Set aside the rather sophomoric tone in which the scene is told and retold. Note Althusser's repeated effort to move from the arena of the biographical to the theoretical, the incident becoming "exceptional" when considered against the analytic description of the concept in general: "And is it not the case that concepts belong to everyone?" "Concepts circulate freely as they are being developed without any controls placed on them." The concept of metonymic causality that Miller (Or was it Rancière? Or Lacan? Who is *responsible* for it?) had proposed is the immediate precursor, we should recall, to the development or production of the concepts of structural causality and suture upon which Laclau and Mouffe, and post-Marxist critics in the line of *Hegemony and Socialist Strategy*, rest their project. So one quick answer to the question of the scene's recurrence is that it touches upon what Althusser perceives to be most *his own*, "a point of principle which concerned me deeply and caused me great anxiety," what most clearly affects the representation of himself and his relation to his work and to the concepts he "produced." It touches upon this "point of principle" as a problem of both names and anonymity, and in the form of a question: What about concepts—and not just any concept, since metonymic causality is the notion that will make it possible to discuss the "effectivity of a structure upon its elements" or to apply the notion of overdetermination in the first place—can be said to be *personnel*, and what can be said to be *de tous*? What about concepts can be "discovered," moveable, nonproper? What about them cannot be stolen? What, in a word, is *immaterial* about the concept? (By "immaterial" I mean ideally and indivisibly an aspect of concepts, beyond their concrete content; a determining or undisseverable property such that a concept is not a concept if that property is removed, stolen.) The answer that Althusser's anecdote furnishes, under cover of its defensiveness and infantilism, is that what is immaterial about the concept is its freedom to circulate or, more precisely, its spontaneous circulating, its currency *as* spontaneous circulating.

If one rereads *Reading 'Capital'* in light of this rather strange, even paradoxical definition of the concept, then the account of the production of the concept of the "effectivity of a structure on its elements" shifts ground. For one thing, the notion that concepts are immaterial inasmuch as they are constitutively free to circulate is at odds with the notion that concepts are the product of labor—a notion to which works like *Reading 'Capital'* and "Rousseau: The Social Contract" are devoted.[55] The proposition that an ideal freedom of circulation underlies the concept's various material embodiments (as *repraesentationes*) need only be recast in the language of rights to square with formulations we might expect in the doctrines of classical humanism (the doctrine of inalienable rights, for instance). Althusser's idealization of the concept occurs at the very moment in which a sense "not identical to this one" is being proposed for and within the story that his autobiography tells: beyond the merely anecdotal aspect of the story, the "proper" conceptual content of "this ridiculous incident" is a didactic allegory whose moral is that the ideality of the concept as such precludes its becoming the property of anyone.

Once the anecdote shows itself to be other than it is (once it begins to circulate elsewhere than in the restricted semantic field to which an autobiography would tend to bound it), we find traces of other determining contexts "sealed in this register" with the problem of the self-identity of the concept, something or some process constantly exceeding the ideal borders of a subjective sense of freedom. Remark, first, that the enviously infantilizing quality of these passages remains constant: the "wooing of Judith Lacan" is imagined contiguously with a libidino-political "teaching" in the forests of Fountainebleau, the "production of theoretical concepts" encoded here as an eroticized act, a form of intercourse or pedagogy in which Miller, the "owner" of the "concept of his life," becomes a disappearing and reappearing principle; even the scene's locations acquire, in this context, a pseudo-rustic genealogy linking them to literary topoi of pastoral retreat and contemplation, on the one hand (Fontainebleau), and to sexual strategy, chase, and violence, on the other ("a

hunting-lodge at Rambouillet"). Other micro-narratives concerning identity and anonymity soon emerge from behind questions, sometimes with
the crass insistence one expects of soap-opera plots, sometimes with the
open subtlety of the *roman policier*: Who "produced" the concept whose
"discovery" was announced—Miller or the "girl" who "produced at least
one theoretical concept a week"? Jacques Rancière? Are Judith Lacan and
"a girl" or "the girl" the same? If "teaching" how to produce theoretical
concepts is a libidinal or erotic act (but whose?), what would it then mean
to "study" or be "studied" by another? What role does the name *Lacan*
play in Althusser's description? What other names are screened here?

Now let's broaden the story a bit. Imagine that the witticisms, hesitations, and imponderables that I have pointed to in Althusser's autobiographies and in his work on Rousseau reflect an anxiety about the concept
in its psychoanalytic usage and about the seductiveness and violence of
psychoanalytic language more broadly—both as it might draw Miller, the
student "with the most fixed ideas on the subject," away from Althusser
and toward Lacan or Lacan's daughter and as it might serve to seduce or
chase, hunt, do violence to Althusser himself. Miller's work was construed,
Elizabeth Roudinesco shows, as designating the juncture *between* Althusser
and Lacan, a place institutionalized and polemically named by and in the
very *Cahiers pour l'analyse* in which the "Suture" essay would appear.[56] The
line associating these moments with the *transfert* in the essay on Rousseau
and with the overdetermined appearance of psychoanalytic vocabulary
there is clear: what Miller "has," desires, or has produced should belong
to everyone—the concept of metonymic causality, the girl who produces
theoretical concepts weekly, and, finally, Judith Lacan and through her
and in her name the language and the concepts of her father. The process
of embodying concepts serves here to make them figuratively proper to a
body (Judith Lacan and Miller, or Althusser, whose talk on Lacan was the
occasion for Miller to announce his "discovery") just where this sense of
property is most aggressively in question. The argumentative impasse is
posed baldly: "And is it not the case that concepts belong to everyone?"
the passage from *The Future Lasts Forever* rhetorically asks—answering
both that Miller "too was capable of acknowledging someone else had
invented and owned a concept" and that such a notion of property is
"absurd."

The point of this explication is not to catch Althusser in contradictions,
to censure the ornament his story allows itself, or to scold him for the
sophomoric tone of his *boutade*, and it is not to provide these contradictions, this story or joke, with a psychobiographical intent or motivation. It

is only in part to show how the language of psychoanalysis, and within it the concept or para-concept of suture, sutures Althusser's account of the genealogy of the concept: that lexicon and the concept of suture in particular are the mark of a wound, the "visible/invisible, absent/present keystone of [Althusser's] whole work," to echo again Althusser's words about the "concept of effectivity" in Marx. The autobiographies recount the primal scenes, if you will, of the Althusserian philosophy of the concept—disciplinary scenes, family scenes, oedipalized, violent. They correspond in every way to the scenes in which Marx retells the birth scene of Hegel's philosophy of the concept, with their embedded, friable, simultaneously over- and underdetermined reference to the Santa Casa of Loreto.

Both Althusser's autobiography and Marx's *Critique of Hegel's 'Philosophy of Right'* give rise to three separate observations that bear upon the occurring of "rhetorical ornament," undecidable and overdetermined allusions and "micro-narratives," and "jokes"—that bear, that is, on the dynamic of *transfert* or of what Laclau and Mouffe call "deconstructive effects" at work where "life" and "concept" seem to meet. In the first place, and concerning what I can still call the form of the argument: where the "production of concepts" is being established as a concept and as a concrete, even humorous *repraesentatio*, and where the formal ideality of concepts in general is being located in the freedom of their circulation or in the Hegelian principle of movement, Althusser's "life" and Marx's text produce literary effects that are not concepts, that are not identical to themselves, and that circulate freely by putting into question the possibility of distinguishing between what "everyone" owns and is responsible for and what "someone else" has invented and owned. They are, we might say, effects that are and are not elements of the structure that causes them. And they arise, for instance, in the shape of allusions or mythic references: Althusser's story fancifully engages the two familiar tropes for the spontaneous production of the concept—the "miraculous Minerva" or birth of the concept from a man, and the *ancilla Dei*, Mary as the handmaid of the Holy Spirit, the carrier of the concept. Freely circulating though these literary effects may be, what is not free about them—that is, what cannot be separated from these effects—is their occurring as events: events of reading, to be sure, but also, in the form of their insistent return in the autobiographies and in their irreducible overdetermination in Marx's work, as events of writing. The practical consequences of their occurring are nowhere more poignantly and threateningly felt than where what "everyone owns" and what "someone else" has invented is the set of *repraesentationes communes* or the structure that we call our life, Althusser's

life or autobiographies, or another's, "le concept de sa vie." The scenes
I have cited from the autobiographies tell allegorically the story of the
production of Althusser's "life" and of the concept of *life*, a "life" and a
"concept of life" that cannot properly belong either to an owner or to a
community. One understands why the story never stops being told.

One might object that if these literary effects occur spontaneously, then
they cannot have the status of a rule; or one might say, as with Althusser's
reading of the *Social Contract*, that as a rule literary effects occur where a
concept's boundaries and identity are being established, but that no rule
formalizing their occurring can be *only* an element of that concept. These
rules are also not elements of that concept: they are neither *propre* or *personnel* nor *de tous*. Effects of this sort unseal the registers of the concept,
cast open the doors of the Santa Casa in both its determining senses. If
this is so, then the occurring of this allegory of desire and of excessive
transfert at the moment when the concept of metonymic causality is dis-
cussed and thematized in the "life" could not, in principle or as a rule,
have been foreseen or repeated. The coincidence of the thematics of birth,
concept, theft, and desire with the spontaneous overdetermination of literary effect would itself, in this case, be an instance of metonymic causality,
a true event that would always only *have been*, its present as an occurrence
always an absence "to be measured" or reconstituted after the fact. This
is another way of stating that "the totality of . . . deconstructive effects"
of the notion of determination may never be accessible: there is no "totality" of deconstructive effects because the notion of totality cannot be
unambiguously invoked where certain elements of a structure or a concept
(for instance, a "life") are also *not* elements of that structure (concept, life,
etc.). The set of elements would always be incomplete, not because there
might be yet another element to be discovered, but because every element,
or some indeterminate number of them, could always fall out of the set,
on grounds or according to a rule that would itself be both immanent and
external to that set, structure, concept—the "concept de sa vie" might
turn out to be someone else's. On this description, and to adopt for a
moment a Kantian vocabulary, the rule for the occurring of transference
or of literary effect would be a synthetic, not an analytic one. It is based
upon contingencies of different sorts. In a more or less trivial, disciplinary
sense, then, we note that efforts in Laclau and Mouffe's work, in Žižek, in
Sloterdijk, and in others (including Althusser himself) to measure Althusser's work by the standard of its development toward the concept of determination in the last instance recall the open and unsealed narrative
transference from theory to fiction or to madness that characterizes the

narrative of the concept's production. The story of the becoming-concept of life is not identical to the story of the coming to life of the concept: indeed, neither story is ever identical even to itself. And finally, the project of suturing one to the other and of sealing each within its own boundaries leaves traces amenable to symptomatic readings.

Matters are not finished yet, however. There is one immediately nontrivial way of stepping back from the unsealing *transferts* between what is *propre* and what is *de tous*, between one's life and that of others, between theory and fiction or *volonté de tous* and *volonté générale*. It works by according priority of one sort or another to one of the terms and then taking that priority back: the two steps serve to convert the unstable "ontology of relation" that Étienne Balibar shows to be at work in Marx into a theology, in particular, into a *political* theology. It is this. The encounters I have been sketching—Marx with Hegel through Schiller, Althusser with Marx through Hegel—appear to furnish what one might call an allegory of the priority of one term over the other, of how one follows from the first: one term, call it "what is proper" to the subject, is the origin, and the other, what is *de tous*, the destination; one the cause, and the other the effect; inside, out; the Word, and the Flesh it acquires. The paradoxical function of this allegorical figure is to render circular a process, a relation, that first appears linear: the concept, sealed within a representation of the hidden or appropriated body of the woman (for instance, the Santa Casa where her impending maternity is announced to her) who gives birth (who "produces theoretical concepts") to what in turn conceives and bears her as *agens*. "Woman" is the figure culturally (materially, contingently) available to Hegel, Marx, and Althusser to represent the emergence of the concept because "woman" (and not just any woman: Mary is the prototype here) embodies a bare, biological priority that becomes secondary in the field of culture, a priority that reveals itself to be merely symbolic. "Woman" in the philosophy of the concept, in the primal scene of its emergence, is both single and double, single as she is immaculate (she generates the concept of herself), double as she is maternal or labile (she serves the concept that she bears), self-identical but always also not one.[57] The woman serves the concept that she bears as mother or as labile body, serves it by becoming part of the system or concept that she bears and whose radical exteriority she represents, serves it by entering into the system of elements or proving herself to have been always already a part of it. "Woman" becomes useful pedagogically: she teaches the concept she bears (in both senses) how to produce (other) theoretical concepts and how to forget (as one forgets the "mere" representation) the labor of that production (how to forget that these theoretical concepts were effects of a conceptual structure before they became elements in it).

Of course, a different logic is also at work in these encounters, concerning this process of materialization or maternalization. Sealed together as alternative directions within the languages of philosophical feminism, both projects are unmistakably idealizing. Is "woman" a figure external to the system of concepts on which the philosophy of the concept turns? To the contrary, the woman ideally absent from the Santa Casa, as from the history of the doctrine of the concept, is herself a concept produced from the forehead of the *agens*. She is already an element, indeed one of the grounding elements, of the concept or system of concepts, a hypostasis of the material, another concept or another goddess in that pantheon, Mary or *Materia*, as miraculous in her way as Minerva, produced and fashioned so as to take the pedagogical function of carrier, of servant, etc. Her body does not lie outside the set of elements of philosophical language, available to represent for philosophy, as a nonphilosophical correlative or figure, the circularity of its origin as a concept or system of concepts. It would thus be a glaring error to claim that her philosophical and cultural role as therapeutic *Materia* is the guiding reason for the fashioning of a woman's body as not one. It would also be a mistake to assert that this therapeutic role preexists in any simple way, or is external to, the philosophical need or impasse—*décalage*—that it serves to resolve. The conditions of fashioning and production, as well as the measurement of their motives, are both over- and underdetermined: their economy, the patient and violent labor of the discourses and pressures of culture, the spontaneous resistance of matter are themselves, as objects of thought, the product they seem to fashion.

I have alluded already to what turns out to be the second nontrivial way of stepping back from the unsealing *transferts* of literary effect at the heart of the concept: the use of the concept of suture. This claim is susceptible to a number of misunderstandings. The most important might take this shape. It may be clear that Althusser encounters Marx in the general context of the "discovery" or production of concepts or para-concepts like metonymic causality, structural causality, the absent cause, and the Lacanian idiom of suture, but what can it mean to say that Marx "uses" the concept of suture in his encounter with Hegel? Surely this is the most flagrant sort of anachronism—after all, these concepts are discovered or produced in or from their absences in Lacan's work in the early 1960s and given shape by Rancière (or was it Miller?). It is, of course, improper historically or chronologically to say that Marx uses the concept of suture, but it is correct, given the description that I have been offering, to say that suture is the concept for the "visible/invisible, absent/present keystone of" the encounter between Marx and Hegel. Suture is the concept for the function that literature, and in particular literary allusion, has in Marx's encounter with Hegel: it is the point at which a topologically paradoxical notion of the rule-giving and rule-following subject emerges, in the form of unsealing literary effects.

But to put matters this way is to risk a further misunderstanding, for the figure of literary allusion is in no way a settled or settling device—and its suturing function opens problems to which Marx's text, and Althusser's after his, are very closely attuned. Where the *Critique of Hegel's Philosophy of Right* addresses—encounters—its great source and adversary, Marx generates a double genealogy and a double structure for the concept. His point is not only philosophical, it is also theologico-political and, as the reference to Schiller suggests, dramatic, literary. The screened exchange between the Grand Inquisitor and King Philip is sacrificial as well as normative; the scene reestablishes the proper economy and hierarchy between the political and theological realms by means of the substitution of Carlos for the dead Marquis de Posa. The normative value of the allusion itself— that is, of the literary-cultural antecedent whose value and sense determine and inform the exchange between Marx and Hegel—is then profoundly unstable and destabilizing. Or rather, it is unstable and destabilizing in a recognizably literary sense, a sense that turns upon the complicated, shifting identifications to which it lends itself. Is Marx approaching Hegel as Don Carlos and the Marquis de Posa, those embodiments of the republican spirit of the Enlightenment, approach the benighted and constraining figure of the Prince's father? Manifestly so, but not quite. Who, then, is this figure of the Inquisitor whose norms even the King must follow? And what are we to make of the Prince's announced death—is Marx contemplating the failure of his thought when it encounters orthodoxy? Is Marx representing Hegel's thrall to a political theology, a figure of conscience and biopolitical surveillance both archaic and profoundly modern? Again yes, but not entirely, and not sufficiently. From what perspective is this encounter being represented? The play envisions at this stage no character who is able to witness and understand this intimate encounter—outside of the now numinous embodiment of the republican humanism that the Hapsburg state has effectively sacrificed. And such a displacement from the character to the idea or the watching and guarding concept, while typical of Schiller, represents just the sort of displacement to the realm of the concept for which Marx reproaches Hegel. Perhaps a better way to envision this screened encounter, then, is to suggest that its unstable normative function depends precisely on the combination, or the encounter, between two logics: on the one hand, the logic of literary and literary historical identification, always determining but also over- and underdetermining, ironic in this specific sense, and, on the other, the logic of allusion, inasmuch as this logic embeds an irreducible historical break, another time, a span. The primal scene for modern political theology, this encounter, sealed and unsealed in the Santa Casa of the encounter between Marx and Hegel, is at the same time: an element of the structure that it sets in place; its governing concept and norm; an utterly external effect of that structure; and the equally external cause of the structure. The representation, the setting on stage, of the encounter between politics and theology in the philosophy of the concept is extrinsic to that philosophy as well as immanent to it. This is the paradoxical structure that the thematics of sacrifice in the play expresses: the Prince is, as a representative of Enlightened republicanism, no different from the Marquis of Posa—his substitute, one exchangeable for the other, equally valued. But he has a different value in the familial and dramatic economy of the play—as the King's son, his heir, his blood is in no way equivalent to Posa's, and neither could substitute for the other. No single concept provides the norm for their exchangeability: this is the tragedy that Schiller sets before his audience. Only the Santa Casa of theologico-political violence, of theologico-political terrorism, provides this suturing function—and that concept is condemned in act by the play. The impasse that results unsutures—unseals—the logic of the play and moves the Idealist tradition beyond the instrumental conceptualization of the violence of the theologico-political concept—beyond terrorism. We have found our way back to the opaque, missing concept with which we opened, the concept of the "effectivity of a structure on its elements" or effects, "concept de l'efficace d'une structure sur ses effets," only to find that the formula is at the same time reversible: what is missing but everywhere present in the genealogy of the concept, what Marx sets before us in his allusion to Schiller, is also and at the same time the concept of the effectivity of elements/effects upon their structure. The copresence of an absolutely extrinsic anteriority and the immanence of the normative element is the intimately terrifying matter of the concept of the emergence of the concept.

CHAPTER 5

A Sadean Community

we have gained nothing by replacing Diotima with Dolmancé.

—JACQUES LACAN, "Kant avec Sade"

Now consider the "moment of the boomerang." The context: what Hardt and Negri's *Empire* calls, borrowing from Sartre's Preface to Fanon's *The Wretched of the Earth*, the "reciprocal destruction of the European Self— precisely because European society and its values are founded on the domestication and negative subsumption of the colonized. The moment of negativity is posed as the necessary first step in a transition toward the ultimate goal of a raceless society that recognizes the equality, freedom, and common humanity of all."[1] This "coherent dialectical logic," Hardt and Negri suggest, must fail, because "reality and history . . . are not dialectical." Let's grant for now that this "logic"—coherent, striated, perspicuous; victorious or defeated; in any case, "reciprocal"—takes shape in response to the "reciprocal" construction of a "European" and a "colonial" identity in the period of modernity (a "European Self" identifying itself as such over and against a "Colonial Self" variously encountered, observed, subjugated, translated, absorbed, and so on). This is certainly the familiar story behind Hardt and Negri's argument, and it has the healthy effect of reparticularizing the broadly universal claims of the Enlightenment, or of a particular account of the Enlightenment: the "European Self" is no longer an unmarked term (it depends materially and conceptually on a colonized other kept in abjection and secrecy); the great vistas of the critical project reveal themselves to be provincial, or at any rate conditioned; and the great formal mechanisms of negation and subsumption turn out to be pedagogies for the oppressors.

This is not news, but it is a weak, even meretricious account of the shape that ethico-political universalism can take as it seeks to account for and to overcome the early modern crisis in the logics of terror and sovereignty.

How Not *to Destroy the "European Self"*

A first, dagnostic step. Fanon himself is less blind than Sartre to the "illusory" identification of dialectical thought with "reality" and "history." In *The Wretched of the Earth*, Hardt and Negri argue, this boomeranglike "moment of negativity" has an additional political, nondialectical dimension, that of "reciprocal counterviolence." Because reciprocal counterviolence does not imagine "any dialectical synthesis" or moment of universal recognition, it is not "a politics in itself; rather, [reciprocal counterviolence] merely poses a separation from colonialist domination and opens the field for politics. The real political process of constitution," Hardt and Negri conclude, "will have to take place on this open terrain of forces with a positive logic, separate from the dialectics of colonial sovereignty." It hardly needs pointing out that this "open terrain" is the landscape with which Hardt and Negri's *Empire* closes—the hills that Francis of Assisi walks, the plains on which "multitudes" can come together at last "and the postmodern *posse* arises."[2]

Much might be said about the apocalyptic tone that rings through these lines and chimes throughout Hardt and Negri's work more broadly. For them, as for many other radical democratic thinkers and postcolonial critics writing in Fanon's shadow, imagining how one passes from the local experience of antagonism (I desire to wear this veil to school, and you stand in my way) to the recognition that collective interests determine and overdetermine this local experience remains the most intractable knot in the legacy of the Enlightenment. Your desire to wear the veil associates you with others who share that desire, which is an expression, or may be an expression, of a compelling common interest in the moral or religious well-being of a group; when I stand in your way, I express or claim to express a broad social interest in the secularization of the public domain. As Negri and Hardt have it, the residual dialectic of colonialism furnishes our contemporary postmodernity with an account of the positive function of violence in the formation of communities of diverse, competing, or irreconcilably antagonistic interests. Positive—but because it is merely preliminary. When the *posse* has achieved the goal of recognizing "the equality, freedom, and common humanity of all," that is, when we recognize that our contingent association under the aspect of this or that local interest occurs "commonly," as an effect of an identity we recognize that we share ("humanity"), then the violent means to that recognition will have been discarded, set aside like the notion of "race" itself.

Every episode of this story, each step in Hardt and Negri's argument, seems to me controversial, none more so than where *Empire* expresses the admirable desire that we set behind us the violence of the colonial encounter, a goal that Hardt and Negri share with other utopian humanist writers, from Laclau to Agamben. On the shoulders of the desire to eliminate violence, and by means of the instrumental understanding of pedagogy that this desire entails, the utopian humanist stance that *Empire* compellingly articulates builds a logic every bit as coercive as the one that Hardt and Negri attribute to Sartre's weak Hegelianism. Quite a different understanding of the relation between violence and instruction will be required if we are to attend to what is most radical about Fanon's account of the constitution of political relations—a different understanding of the historical sources as well as of the psycho-phenomenological aspects of that relation, as it is problematically devised in the years in which *The Wretched of the Earth* was being written.

Note, for now, how Hardt and Negri make their case. We learn, for instance, that with the advent of globalization the encounter between the European Self and its colonized other is no longer necessarily to be described according to the logic (or the rhetoric) of reciprocal destruction. From what remains a distinctly violent encounter, Hardt and Negri argue, there emerges a different story—that of the movement from the expression of prepolitical individualism to the expression of constituting, communal identifications, if ever so ephemeral, precarious and momentary. The old logic of dialectical thought, all a-clutter with hypostatized, pseudo-analytic necessities, gives way to a historical logic that subsumes local, particular experience in the emerging consciousness of contingent association; the cold violence of negation becomes the new empire's "reciprocal counterviolence." In this story, *reciprocity* bears a heavy weight, although the term works peculiarly when it is deployed, as it is here, in contrast to the false necessities of dialectical logic. *Reciprocity* is, after all, a central term in Hegel's *Logic*, where it designates the moment when contingency is subsumed within the Absolute Relation, when Causality returns to its absolute concept, the moment when "Objective logic" reaches its highest form and when thought can at last turn toward the concept, "the realm of subjectivity, or of freedom."[3] Here, though, the term works rather differently. That "counterviolence" is "reciprocal" does not mean, for instance, that you and I, or a colonizer and the colonized subject, do violence to each other, though this may be entailed in such relations. It means instead that you and I recognize that our relation is a violent one and then recognize, at a different level, that the form in which we recognize this is the same. But if this second-order recognition is to be different from the Hegelian parousia of the concept, then when you and I recognize that our relation is indeed a violent one and see that we recognize this in the same way, then what we recognize reciprocally cannot itself be the subject of thought. We just recognize it, without being able to think through it. We recognize that "reciprocal violence" is a relation, say, a contrastive relation, between constituting and constituted power— but this recognition keeps us from properly thinking through this relation. This form of reciprocity serves to describe both the violence within constituted political relations *and* constituting violence, and to this end it has been emptied of positive, "thinkable" content. Only thus, formally empty, does it become the new ground on which the *posse* of multitudinous self-sovereignty is posed, and advances.

There are no surprises here. *Empire*'s translation of the exquisitely stubborn Hegelian moment of negation into the empty operator called "reciprocity" only subjects the legacy of the Enlightenment to the solvent applied most famously by Horkheimer and Adorno: the constituted community stands to constitutive force (a force marked or characterized or instantiated in the separation of positive logic from colonial domination that is posed by reciprocal counterviolence) as the myth-laden, instrumental technologies that submit "everything natural to the sovereign subject" to a "positive concept of enlightenment which liberates it from its entanglement in blind domination."[4] Coming up with a "positive concept of enlightenment" proves to be particularly difficult for Adorno and Horkheimer, as it is for Hardt and Negri—not only, as is most commonly agreed, because the critique of instrumental reason one finds in *Dialectic of Enlightenment* is hardly adequate to Kant's analysis of the ends of reason but also because *Dialectic of Enlightenment* and its epigones offer no satisfactory account of the pleasures that attend both "blind domination" and its unworking, constituted force as well as the separations or posits internal to it.[5] This last is not a particularly new observation—at least not as regards the blinding affect that vulgarly attaches to domination itself.

Adorno and Horkheimer hold down the prudish wing of the Frankfurt School; "pleasure" for both has a largely negative charge, whether what's at issue is the character of listening, or "mass" enjoyment of this or that cultural form. In any moderately dialectical engagement with the legacies of the Enlightenment, pleasure would almost always fall first upon the side of blind domination. In fascism, for example, the commodification of pleasure is often the means by which Enlightenment becomes entangled in domination. And surely a second moment follows, provoking us to consider how the pleasures afforded to thought by the unworking of blind domination might themselves prove violent, even blindingly so.

Or at any rate so it would appear. For what, after all, leads us from the violent pleasures of blind domination to the different and differently blinding ones that we take from its critical unworking? What road, what instrument, what necessity? Recall that Adorno and Horkheimer do take up the matter of the pleasures of violence in their account of the Sirens episode from the *Odyssey*—verses they find steeped in a conflicting, mythological compounding of enjoyment, domination, and thoughtlessness. The pithiest formulation of the impasse that Adorno and Horkheimer encounter comes where they are describing the contradictory social circumstance they find in the Sirens episode: "The instruments of domination [*Herrschaft*; for instance, those represented by the pleasures that the Sirens' song promises and by Odysseus's twin tacks toward its deadly temptation: binding others to his will and to himself with merely external bonds]—language, weapons, and finally machines—which are intended to hold everyone in their grasp, must in their turn be grasped by everyone."[6] This logical requirement permits the form of social domination, as found in the binding temptations of pleasure and of the machine, to become present both to "thought, in its solidification as an apparatus both material and intellectual," and to "a liberated living element," reconciling (*versöhnen*) them and making their genuine, pressing, and "true subject" "society itself."[7] The creaky mechanism of dialectical externalization shows forth here, but it is only when *Dialectic of Enlightenment* treats Sade's work that the full, uncanny costs of this reconciliation become apparent. For Horkheimer and Adorno, it turns out, social domination is represented in *Juliette* or in *La philosophie dans le boudoir* (*Philosophy in the Bedroom*) allegorically as the private domination of one body by another. Erotic violence in the private sphere stands in for social violence, and "society itself" becomes thinkable in, and as written upon, a body that presents itself for our use (for pleasure, for pain) as a machine. In *Dialectic of Enlightenment* and its

epigones, Sade represents the resistance, figured as the radical eroticiza-
tion of violence, to the reflexive foundation of an a priori distinction
between pleasure and the instrumentalization of domination. No wonder,
then, that Horkheimer and Adorno so gingerly pollard *Philosophy in the
Bedroom*.

Nor is it any wonder that the figure of the divine Marquis continues to
haunt even the most compelling late Hegelian utopian writing.[8] His work
appears to teach us not only that the violence implied by the Enlightenment's blind domination remains irreducibly an element of social relations
understood as such, but that the blind pleasures that attend such domination turn out to lie at the heart of the modern communitarian imagination.
In order for Horkheimer and Adorno's readers to come to a "positive
concept of enlightenment which liberates it from its entanglement in blind
domination," they must be able to take society itself as the object of a
form of thought that is at once free and structured. Recall, though, that
Dialectic of Enlightenment has very little to say about the nature of this
"must." The argument imagines it as a requirement that flows simply
from the peculiar nature of totality (an instrument for grasping or understanding totality is also a part of that totality, encompassed within it, one
more of its elements, as the eye with which I regard my body is also a part
of that body).[9]

To think totality without lapsing into the violence of totalitarianism—
that is, of course, the challenge. Hence the queer topology that marks the
analysis of *Herrschaft* in *Dialectic of Enlightenment*—an analysis cluttered
with the reflexive tools of sado-masochistic *rationalia*, "instruments of
domination . . . which are intended to hold everyone in their grasp" but
which also "must in their turn be grasped by everyone." For Horkheimer
and Adorno, and for the radical democratic thinkers in the Hegelian tradition who follow them, this complex, unwrought thought can be fashioned
in two related movements: when the mythology of the Enlightenment
presents itself as the reduction of another's body to an instrument or a
mechanism, and when our use of that machine is no longer blind but
expresses a contract with another—who is thus simultaneously and paradoxically a subject of his or her desires, able to represent him- or herself
contractually to us, *and* the object of a contract in which he or she relinquishes him- or herself to our "use," already a machine, unable to enter
into any sort of legal relation with us. In order to generate a "positive
concept," *Dialectic of Enlightenment* must, before embarking on its Odys-
sean, dialectical dance, distinguish between pleasure and "instruments of
domination," or between the Sirens' song and the devices that Odysseus

employs to attend to that song. The rowers' waxen earplugs, Odysseus's bonds, the drama of infinite desires presented and unfulfilled—these, we learn, are the violent instruments of pleasure, rather than the pleasures themselves. And we learn this lesson precisely upon the shoulders of Odysseus's experience of that forbidden and fatal song. The "positive concept" of Enlightenment establishes reflexively, pedagogically, at the conclusion of thought's epic journey, the distinction between pleasure and instrumental domination on which the journey depends.

Mind you, even works that one could hardly accuse of prudishness or of inattention to the pleasures of blind domination can turn oddly abstract when they seek to account for the emergence of community effects. Take, for example, Nancy's *La communauté désoeuvrée* (*The Unwrought Community*), written largely in hand with Bataille's work. "One does not produce [community]," Nancy writes, "one experiences or one is constituted by it as the experience of finitude [*on en fait l'expérience [ou son expérience nous fait] comme expérience de la finitude*]."[10] Here and in a number of important passages in which *The Unwrought Community* considers directly how communities make and are made, or give us to experience or are experienced, Nancy's argument turns away from the regulative concept of totality. As Nancy imagines it, the "unwrought" community is not only not to be understood on the model of totality, totality does not even figure as an analytic device in thought that might lead to the unwrought community. Thus the means for achieving a community of interests—the instruments, if you will, for grasping it—are not reflexively or necessarily related to that community.

Think again of Nancy's suggestive distinction between a community that one produces (for instance, as one produces a work, as one "works" toward its completion) and a community that "one experiences or . . . is constituted by" as "the experience of finitude." The constituting "experience of finitude" chimes in two registers. One experiences finitude in common with others and as the foundation for a disposition toward communal interest, reading shared finitude off the other's face as Dante's poet reads "omo" "nel viso de li uomini," mortality scribbled upon the sockets and brows of men.[11] Judgments based on this common experience of finitude (for instance, the Rortian judgment that the avoidance of cruelty should be a general social goal) enter together with a cluster of worthy humanist relatives. Their finite, constrained content reflects the peculiar circumstance of their use (it is *I* who am experiencing *my* finitude), and their grammar reflects the generality of that use (because each of us is in part the finitude of the other, the limit, the possible death of another, my finitude is never mine alone, but is also yours and every other person's). But the experience of community is also properly an experience of finitude, if we may be permitted to dangle this personification upon the old, tried horns of the subjective genitive.[12] Unwrought community is what finitude "experiences"—a peculiarly opaque phrase because, however much we may wish to personify finitude, to attribute to a concept the capacity to experience another concept, especially a concept as cleft as that of the "unwrought community," means changing utterly what we mean by the word *experience*. And what we mean by "judging." On this side of the genitive, judgments about states of affairs are not based on my sense of what I experience in common with you (for instance, that we are both finite beings or that each is the finitude of the other, and that we thus share the disabling experience of not owning our ends), and they are not formulated by "me" (*I* experience this or that only inasmuch as I express the qualities of this or that concept: for instance, one might say that "I experience finitude as a member of one or another class: as a worker experiences it, as a woman does, as Spirit does"). Indeed, from this point of view, what can be said about experience (common or not, shared or not) hardly counts as a judgment at all but is, rather, the expression or the simple unfolding of a vocabulary, according to rules given correlatively with that vocabulary. Once the concept of "Spirit," or of "worker," or of "woman" is established, the rules for experience are given in the concept.

Where Horkheimer and Adorno erect a strangely empty ethical injunction upon the reflexive topology of domination (recall: the instruments for dominating all *must* themselves be grasped and dominated), and where Hardt and Negri build a multitudinous self-sovereignty upon the vacuous notion of reciprocity, Nancy and Wittgenstein hold out an even more precarious logic. The brief argument from *The Unwrought Community* concerning the production of community effects bears on the relation between two sorts of judgments that concern human finitude (or better, between a judgment and the expression of a concept it entails). My judgment concerning our common experience of finitude lies at the heart of the unwrought community, but my judgment also coincides with a different sort of expression altogether (the experience *of finitude*: a class of terms or a concept gives me my voice and the grammar of my judgment). The relation between what I experience and the judgments I express concerning it, on the one hand, and what is given for expression in the concept (of experience, of community, of relation), on the other, is at the same time one of identity (I can only express what is given in the concept of "expression," for instance), and of radical difference (that I can only express what is given in the concept marks the horizon of my finitude; that what is expressed in the concept cannot have the form of a judgment marks the horizon of its finitude). The coincidence of identity and difference in the experience of finitude (in judgments concerning that experience; in the expression of the concept of the "experience of finitude") is the ground on which Nancy rests the possibility of thought about community, as well as the first object for that thought and the first, pedagogical product of that thought.

The term we might use to designate this precarious coincidence is *contingency*—and for Nancy, as for a number of political philosophers writing deliberately within and against the dialectical tradition, it is across the slight bridge of this word that the pleasure of domination can return to the constituting field of the political. The tactic is uncertain; one suspects that the term may prove to be as vacuous as its companions—the injunctive "must" in Horkheimer and Adorno and the empty reciprocities on which *Empire* rebuilds thought about the relation between constituted and constituting political relations. At the very least, let us note the perils and confusions of "contingency." When applied to judgments, *contingency* serves as the antonym to certain kinds of necessity (for instance, the analytic, necessary entailment of one term by another in a syllogism): a contingent proposition will be synthetic and revisable, for it is contingent upon experience.[13]

But practical usage also suggests a different, contradictory sense. One says, after all, that this or that eventuality is contingent upon the fulfillment of one or another set of requirements—and means by this that one is necessary for the other to obtain. The nature of this necessity constitutes the relation between the requirements and the eventuality; we do not say that it is revisable. This level-jumping muddiness is in fact characteristic of most uses of the term *contingency*. In Nancy's argument, for instance, "contingency" not only describes the inessential way in which my empirical judgments concerning finitude lean against (and upon) the analytical syntax already given in the notion of finitude but also serves to describe aspects of each of these coincident forms of expression. In the case that Nancy sets before us, community is experienced *as constituted*, and reflexively *constitutes us* as the subjects of that experience, precisely upon the back of a construction of experiencing in which the relation between contingent judgments based on "my experience" and the entailed expressions implied in the terms I use (like *community*, *experience*, or *relation*) is itself provisional, subject to revision, not given or wrought but accidental, *zufällig*, as the informing Kantian vocabulary has it.

Another fruitful confusion emerges, though on a different level, in analyses of the unwrought community that intend to bypass the notion of totality entirely: here contingency *stands in* for social antagonism. A radical democratic political philosopher like Chantal Mouffe, for instance, will acknowledge that the notion of community cannot be construed or maintained without a companion, positive account of what Mouffe refers to as "the component of violence and hostility inherent in social relations."[14] The *internal* component of violence in social relations matches the companion, instituting violence that designates relations as such, as relations, and therefore as the domain of social negotiation, or of politics broadly. This last, instituting violence differs from one or another form of violence internal to social relations (from forms of domination reducible to the domination of one individual by another, to one social interest by another, one class by another) in bearing only an indirect, partial relation to what I experience or express concerning that experience and to what is expressed in the concept (say, the concept of domination or the concept of class). Instituting violence is then contingent in this accompanying sense: an event or an act that establishes social relations as such also and irreducibly merely occurs. This establishing or constituting may take place in any of a number of domains, and very differently, of course: for instance, in the production of thought as its object (the antagonism of social relations is the proper object of thought) or as its means (the unworking or deconstruction of the concept of community is a violent procedure).

Take, as a good example of the first tactic, the production of compromise terms to stand in for the notion of violence, Mouffe's rereading of the notion of constitutive antagonism, which she influentially elaborates in her earlier work with Laclau. Her compelling *The Return of the Political* concludes with this definition of radical democratic organization of "the political":

> A project of radical and plural democracy has to come to terms with the dimension of conflict and antagonism within the political and has to accept the consequences of the irreducible plurality of values. . . . Instead of shying away from the component of violence and hostility inherent in social relations, the task is to think how to create the conditions under which those aggressive forces can be defused and diverted and a pluralist democratic order made possible.[15]

Mouffe's goal here seems unimpeachable. Radical democratic thought today sets aside, as a coercive or tendentious bit of work, the object held out by Adorno and Horkheimer: "society itself." To this end, it unworks the critical project of reconciliation, and supplies in its place a coming to terms with "conflict and antagonism," with "irreducible plurality," with the "violence and hostility inherent in social relations." We need not understand coming to terms in the registers in which it first sounds: the register of philosophical quietism or the languages of popular self-help manuals, which counsel coming to terms with all sorts of culturally freighted complaints. Mouffe is not arguing that the terms one comes to are anything other than unstable and momentary compromise formations, perhaps even tendentially empty or vacuous terms, as Laclau argues elsewhere.

Yet even in the face of these patent qualifications, emptyings out, and unworkings of the positive term *term*, one might legitimately wonder how different Mouffe's coming to terms with, or defusing and diverting, actually is from the more dialectically inflected notion of reconciliation or from the sorts of mythic thought often associated with the production of compromise formations. Note again the register from which Mouffe's terms are more or less indirectly drawn. *Defusing* and *diverting*, rather than *shying away from*: all three terms serve roughly to translate processes of secondary revision, undertaken culturally as well as on the level of creative thought that undergirds Mouffe's understanding of democracy. (Think how *displacement*, *sublimation*, and *repression* might correspond to Mouffe's terms.) Just as psychic economy preserves the traumatic kernel from which these processes flee, a "radical and plural democracy" preserves "the dimension of conflict and antagonism within the political and . . . the irreducible plurality of values."

But the analogy is awkward. What makes values irreducibly plural is not one or another accidental difference in content (in the way, say, that two people might hold antagonistic opinions on the desirability of universal suffrage) but that they are opaque to each other *as values* (that is, that they do not share a grammar in which to establish a common definition of what value is). Thought's radical task is not only the production of psychic compromise formations or of social reconciliations but also and more importantly the preservation of the mutual untranslatability of irreducible values: not (only) to defuse and divert, but also and simultaneously to nurture and radicalize social differends. To make matters even trickier, this double, unwrought task of thought works on two levels, and quite differently on each. Having set aside "society itself," radical democratic thought addresses the violence of relations "*within* the political," Mouffe notes, within the political understood as a constituted field or as a *work*. It distinguishes administratively, for instance, between accidental differences of content in the expression of value and irreducible differences that express constitutive antagonisms, seeking reconciliation for the former and the radicalization, preservation, and strategic representation of the latter. At the same time, this thought addresses the mechanisms by means of which the political arises or is instituted as a value, a linked set of values, a field, a work, or a name (even if discontinuous, a field encompassing differences both accidental and irreducible, negotiable and not, differences to be reconciled and mutually untranslatable differences). On this level, radical democratic thought attends to the constituting moment in relations, a moment that is not reducible to a translatable, communicable, or intentional form and that, because it is preserved and constantly reactivated in and by radical democratic thought, does not have the classical form of a discrete "moment," either.

Mouffe's work does not seek to develop fully the form of thought that could achieve the doubled, radical tasks set forth here. Laclau offers a compact description, however, of what he calls "the ethical substance of the community" as the proper object of thought. Crucially, he locates the emergence of the investment of the community's ethical substance in a normative order (that is, the administrative order that differentiates reducible from nonreducible differences according to norms or grammars) in a decision whose grounds are, he says, contingent, but always susceptible of determination by what he calls the "radical contextualization" of "decisions." This sort of determination, and not a naturalized or theological characterization of the sovereign decision, guards the necessary gap between investing and normative order on which autonomy rests.[16]

Recall Rorty's appeal, voiced in 1989, for a form of liberal democratic, nonfoundational political imagination. Part argument, part outraged response to the economic depredations of the Reagan era, *Contingency, Irony, and Solidarity* proposes that certain forms of description should nurture "our sensitivity to the particular details of the pain and humiliation of others." "Solidarity," the term Rorty sets before us to describe the affective and social outcome of this kind of descriptive imagination, demands that we be less cruel, that we seek to increase our own and others' autonomy, and that we be able to distinguish public from private questions (for instance, Rorty says, the question "Do you believe and desire what we believe and desire?" from the question "Are you suffering?").[17] The task of articulating this demand falls not to theory but to ethnography, comic books, "and, especially, the novel." Narrative fiction "gives us the details about kinds of suffering being endured by people to whom we had previously not attended . . . details about what sorts of cruelty we ourselves are capable of, and thereby lets us redescribe ourselves."[18] To the questions of whether this redescription of ourselves will bring about social change, whether such redescriptions follow of necessity upon our greater sensitivity, whether the development of a greater sensitivity is entailed by our attention to the details of others' suffering *Contingency, Irony, and Solidarity* answers permissively rather than jussively: narrative fiction's details *"let us redescribe ourselves."*

The hesitancy of Rorty's expression serves four purposes, at least. Imaginative, narrative fictions, we gather in the first place, can provide us with a grammar for judging ourselves to be other than we are, through identifications with and of other, imagined characters. Rorty's tentative phrasing suggests, in the second place, just how uncertain, how hypothetical it is that such imaginative descriptions may indeed achieve this end. Because narratives allow us to play off "descriptions against redescriptions," they show not only that no single "description" has an intrinsic foundation beyond its use to this or that end but also that one or another "description" "can still regulate action, can still be thought worth dying for."[19] This stress on the uncertainty, the contingency, of the moment serves in the third place to protect Rorty's not-so-hidden appeal to a modified Kantian account of social autonomy: with the means to do so before us, we may still choose not to redescribe ourselves, or we may choose to redescribe ourselves in ways different from those that Rorty or the work appear to value. Finally, Rorty's unsettled grammar embeds an irreducible precariousness within "the aim of a just and free society":[20] because none of the operative terms—*aim*, *just*, *free*, or even *society*—escapes the solvent of "linguistic contingency," we can never establish, on any foundation more secure than a momentary agreement, that we have in fact reached this aim.

And now observe that, when Rorty argues that we should drop "the demand for a theory which unifies the public and the private," his description of the alternative works by means of a term that bridges between the two, the notion of contingency. Now a notion is not a theory. Indeed, *Contingency, Irony, and Solidarity* provides no theory of contingency— barely even a definition of the term. Instead we get examples throughout the work, instantiations from different novels. The reason for this is not only of the solid, pragmatic variety—a term's meaning being its use, to be derived from examples rather than established theoretically, and so on— but also, as it were, apotropaic. Contingency, it turns out, proves to be a much more dangerous tool than Rorty's argument can use. To the extent that it serves as an analytic device for breaking down one or another form

of foundationalism, contingency holds the same position in Rorty's argument, or one very closely approximating it—contingent upon it, one might
say—as *torture, humiliation, cruelty,* and their final form, *sadism,* have in
Contingency, Irony, and Solidarity.

Recall that, when he sets forth his understanding of liberalism, Rorty
turns to Judith Shklar's notion that "liberals are the people who think that
cruelty is the worst thing we do."[21] Later he reminds us, citing Elaine
Scarry's work, that torture, cruelty, and sadism "unmake the world" of the
victim. Now this unmaking of the world is not easily distinguishable from
what Rorty's critique of foundationalism seeks to do: in his resolute and
admirable efforts to banalize philosophical reflection, to teach us to face
up to "the contingency of [our] most central beliefs and desires," Rorty
abjects and humiliates the sovereign self, that prize of the Idealist legacy.[22]
He unmakes the world the Enlightenment left us by separating the Realist
claim that "the world is out there" from the Idealist claim that "the truth
is out there," as he puts it.[23] The vocabulary of contingency is the device
he uses to this end. In order to differentiate between his own unmaking of
the world and the variety that obtains under torture or obtains when a
sadist takes pleasure in cruelty, Rorty both evacuates contingency of sense,
except as an instantiation of cases of contingency; and associates the notion
of violence with torture and cruelty. In other words, he attaches a moral
valorization to an aspect of the brutality of the play between description
and redescriptions. The tactic runs through *Contingency, Irony, and Solidarity,* but it comes into focus in Rorty's discussion of Orwell's *1984,* when
Rorty associates the torturer O'Brien with a moment in which Winston is
shown a form of irrationality that he cannot "weave a story around," the
moment, image, or self-knowledge that takes his life apart irreversibly.[24]
This Rorty calls "sadism."

The inclusion of a moment or a form of irrationality that cannot be
renarrativized (that cannot be made to fit into one's description of oneself)
is critical to the positive account of contingency in Rorty. But as he weaves
it back into the field of contingency, into the account of contingency, into
a notion of contingency, Rorty reveals a more general problem. His
maneuver is repeated in efforts to rescue a sense of the political sphere
from a critique of liberalism that takes two shapes: that liberalism avoids
(cannot take into account) the persistence of antagonisms; and that liberalism, as a model for political inquiry, cannot take into account the arising
of the political as a demand (the emergence of a notion of relation). Since
the early 1980s, the critique of liberalism—spurred, on the one hand, by
the rise of Thatcherism and the Reagan administration and, on the other,

by the failure of the Soviet-bloc model of socialism—produced an account of the social in which the preservation of social antagonism and the preservation of thought about the emergence of the political as a possibility are thought in relation to a soft or emptied model of contingency. One might put it, most forcefully, like this. Rorty's permissive fictions arise in part so as to aestheticize (they weave a description or a redescription around) a definition or a moment of violence that is irrational: the violence of political relations; the violence of the institution of the political.[25]

Blind Contingency (Republicanism in and out of the Boudoir)

How might the radical heterogeneity between the constituting force and the intellectual regime of constituted political relations itself furnish a form of communitarian identity? How might the violence of this heterogeneity be harbored, even nurtured, with a view to an understanding of the political capable of accounting, contingently and momentarily, for the circumstantial spontaneity of its emergence? Not, it should be clear, with reference to the notion of reciprocal counterviolence. What seems required is an account of the community-generating effects of radical (that is, nonreciprocal, nondialectical, and perhaps unteachable) contingency. When the logic of colonial sovereignty touches its limit, circumstances provide something very like this account of communitarian contingency—in the shape of a model of the etiology and consequences of pleasure. Intimately linked to the notion of the Enlightenment under critique in the wake of the publication of *Dialectic of Enlightenment*, at mid-century "pleasure" is a principle bound tightly to the representation of utter abjection and to the twin arguments linking the rise and characteristics of National Socialism to the excess or to the lack of a certain sort of sovereign reason.

It is no surprise, then, that Fanon should refigure the violence of the colonial encounter under the aspect of sadism. Sade's name was very much in the air in connection with Algerian resistance to French colonial rule. (Pontecorvo picks up this overdetermined association in *The Battle of Algiers* when Mathieu, the colonel of the *paras*, answers a reporter's question about the *paras'* use of torture, affirming "We are neither madmen nor sadists.") Henri Alleg's *La question*, his immensely influential exposé of torture by the French army in Algeria, was first released in early 1958, then seized at the request of the Armed Forces Tribunal in Paris. Alleg, a journalist and editor of *Alger républicain* from 1950 to 1955, was arrested in 1957 and interned in the "immense prison surpeuplée" of Algiers at the same time as Djamila Bouhired, imprisoned there for her support of the FLN.[26] The first time that Alleg employs a modifier to describe his torturers, it is to Sade that he turns: "On the other side of the wall," writes Alleg, "in the women's section, there are young women no one has mentioned: Djamila Bouhired, Elyette Loup . . . and others: stripped, beaten, insulted by sadistic torturers [*insultées par des tortionnaires sadiques*], they too have suffered torture by water and electricity."[27] Of course, Pontecorvo's and Alleg's uses of the term must be considered entirely nontechnical: there is little here of the ambivalence the notion bears in the lexicon of psychoanalysis.

Not that this ambivalent construction of sadism would have been unavailable to Alleg, Fanon, or Pontecorvo. In this very period, Sade's works were the object of a judicial repression every bit as public and as notorious as the one that Alleg's work received. It is worth recalling that the first extensive postwar discussions of Sade's work in France were published in the same journal in which the French colonial war in Algeria was famously exposed: *Les temps modernes,* whose editor, Jean-Paul Sartre, also crops up in Pontecorvo's *Battle of Algiers* as the author of yet "another article" deploring the circumstances in Algiers: "Will you kindly explain to me why all the Sartres are always born on the other side?" Mathieu asks.[28] The proceedings against Éditions Jean-Jacques Pauvert for indecency in their publication of Sade's works stretched from 1947 to 1955, when the first verdict was delivered; the appeal was rejected in 1956, after serving to catalyze the world of French culture. Many intellectuals testified in court to the peculiar merits of Sade's work, of greatest interest among them being Cocteau, Bataille, Paulhan, and Breton.[29] Paulhan, in particular, focused his intervention on the text by Sade that most explicitly and famously explores the relation between social formations, education, and violence, *La philosophie dans le boudoir; ou Les instituteurs immoraux, dialogues destinés à l'éducation des jeunes demoiselles.*

How, then, might Sadean pleasure work to educate a readership for whom the sovereignty of reciprocal or reflexive concepts had been exhausted in the camps?[30] To educate a cultural elite devising a postcolonial logic still embedded in the daily circumstance of colonial violence? What weak concepts does the boudoir furnish to philosophy after Auschwitz and during the Battle of Algiers? Allow me to mount this quite broad group of questions upon the back of a slight example. Sade's *Philosophy in the Bedroom* concerns the phenomenon of education: "It is a matter of an education," says Mme. de Saint-Ange, one of the work's three *instituteurs immoraux*, in the theory of libertinism as well as in its practice, of Eugénie, a fifteen-year-old "virgin girl, more beautiful than Love itself."³¹ Though not merely an education in libertinism, of course—but also in political and moral philosophy, indeed, in any discursive domain in which bodies are held to standards of value measured by general concepts like "Love itself," or "the Republic," or even "education." Hence the understandable anxieties that these dialogues provoke, more than almost any other in Sade's oeuvre.

Mme. de Saint-Ange, her brother the Chevalier de Mirvel, and the dissolute Dolmancé, "who is principally endowed with a great deal of philosophy in his wit and thought [*il a . . . principalement beaucoup de philosophie dans l'esprit*]" undertake to educate Eugénie in forms of thought as well as forms of association. Dolmancé, in particular, maintains that the shape conventionally ascribed by moralists and philosophers of the Enlightenment to the faculty of reason is a mystification, in theory as well as in practice, in the domain of erotic behavior as well as in that of political behavior. Thus, to Eugénie's demand that he explain to her "whether morals are truly necessary to government, whether their influence on the genius of a nation carries any weight," he famously responds by producing the pamphlet "Français, encore un effort si vous voulez être républicains" ("Yet Another Effort, Frenchmen, if You Would Become Republicans"; 313). The pamphlet opens on what sounds at first to be a note of self-deprecation: "I come to offer grand thoughts: they will be listened to, reflected upon [*elles seront réfléchies*]; if not all of them please, some at least will remain; and I will have contributed in some measure to the progress of enlightenment [*j'aurai contribué en quelque chose au progrès des lumières*]."³² Of course, Dolmancé, to whom the others attribute the authorship of the pamphlet he purports merely to have bought, is being ironic here—though the balance of the pamphlet makes it clear that Sade is proposing a different methodology for what counts as the "progress of enlightenment" than that suggested by the reflexively self-justifying form in which syllogistic thought proceeds. What on reflection pleases, rather than what appears to justify itself, is what remains behind.

Thus the bodies that present themselves for pleasure throughout Eugénie's education work both as instruments and as quasi-legal subjects: like Eugénie herself, they enter into contracts, tacit or explicit, with Eugénie and her educators. As mere instruments, they serve private ends; to the extent that they are contracted, they stand in relation to a larger discursive domain. This double aspect of bodies' instrumentality strikes us as problematical in one sense, as it suggests that there may be no difference available a priori between the merely pragmatic and empirical, or the merely instrumental, use of reason and the regulative use of reason that proceeds by setting ends or by reference to general propositions or to concepts like "Love itself" or "the Republic." But in another sense, this is precisely how Sade devises a "positive concept of enlightenment," Dolmancé's contribution to the "progress of enlightenment." One can indeed "become republican" if one makes the additional effort of thought required to maintain *at the same time* that bodies are instrumental as well as subjective entities, that they are the object as well as the subject of contracts; that their pleasures and their pain are others' but also their own. In the boudoir, the micro-community that Eugénie and her tutors establish can become a genuine republic of teaching, subject to a principle that governs both private and public pleasures: the principle that every instrumental use of the other is also a public use.

But this account stumbles over the denouement of Sade's dialogue, which introduces an element that tends to relate private and public experiences in quite a different way. Recall how *Philosophy in the Bedroom* ends. The well-born, naïve Eugénie, under the tutelage of various masters, has come to accept and relish both the pleasures of libertinism and her hatred for her mother, Mme. de Mistival, who stands in the way of her sexual pleasure. Eugénie and her tutors conspire to take her mother prisoner, relying in part upon a letter from Eugénie's father that permits them to take whatever license they wish with Mme. de Mistival. When Eugénie's mother arrives, her daughter and her tutors set about torturing her; finally, Dolmancé arranges for Mme. de Mistival to be raped by a servant, whom he knows to be infected with syphilis. At the suggestion of Mme. de Saint-Ange, who argues that the group should try to prevent the infected semen—the *venin*—from escaping from within Mme. de Mistival, Eugénie then sews shut her mother's vagina, and allows Dolmancé, whose predilection for buttocks the dialogue has by now firmly established, to do the same to Mme. de Mistival's anus.[33] This gesture caps Eugénie's education: she has literally as well as symbolically closed off her mother, violated her and sterilized her; she has also learned from Mme. de Saint-Ange how to make virgin once again bodies that have "fucked like Antoinette" (222), rendering her mother's body terribly whole again, symbolically re-hymenizing Mme. de Mistival and making her once again into someone who has to be *déchirée* in order to be penetrated.

This distressing—indeed, appalling—scene complicates Sade's way of negotiating the public-private distinction on which the dialogue's "edifying" narrative turns. In Mme. de Mistival's case, the governing distinction between the private or instrumental use of the other's body for pleasure and its public use is quite detached from her intention. Recall Mistival's letter granting the *instituteurs* and Eugénie permission to punish Mme. de Mistival "rigorously," to teach her the lesson he wants her to learn. His letter seems to turn on the "right" of the husband to dispose of his property, including the body of his wife.[34] Mistival issues his permission, he writes to Mme. de Saint-Ange, hoping to teach his wife a lesson about the pious, insincere horror she expresses when she imagines what may occur in Mme. de Saint-Ange's boudoir. "Teach her 'rigorously,' upon her flesh, what she now fears 'imaginatively,' and then teach her that you had my permission to teach her this lesson, that the violence done to her physically reflects a contract this letter establishes with you, her instructors, which concerns her inasmuch as she is my wife and hence party to what I will, whether she wills it or not," the husband's letter might be said to run.

It is on this permissive speech act—and on Dolmancé's corresponding need to ground his action, his teachings, on the letter of the law—that Lacan based his 1963 understanding of the dialogue's conclusion. Dolmancé, Lacan writes, "closes the affair with a *Noli tangere matrem*. Raped and sewn up, the mother remains prohibited. Our verdict is confirmed by the submission of Sade to the Law."[35] "Learn that we have been authorized," cries Dolmancé: Mme. de Mistival, who has learned in her flesh the lesson that closes *Philosophy in the Bedroom*, now learns it, as it were, in writing. Sade learns it *from* her as well, as Eugénie does from Dolmancé, and as Sade's readers do from him and from his characters. The Oedipal-theological prohibition on touching the mother, *Noli tangere matrem*, works much as M. de Mistival's letter does: it expresses and enforces a contract to which one was always already subject, without knowing that one was a party to it, by virtue merely of having been born.

The Levinasian circumstance of standing accused or already being contracted that Lacan reads in Sade is confirmed as the ground of positive Enlightenment; the law that prohibits our fulfilling our desire for the mother, Sade's *Noli tangere matrem*, here stands in for any, or rather for the first, principle of universality. The displacement of the violence done to the raped and reconstituted mother onto the abstract threat of violence embodied in the interdiction against touching her represents both the subsumption of violence into the field of the Law (of the father) and its conversion into a positive notion, a figure of thought rather than of touch (for instance, the allegorical-conceptual figure of "Love itself" or of the "Republic"). For *this* Enlightenment, we all stand contracted to Sadean Law: it is on the condition of our subjection to this contract that we emerge as subjects of free intentional acts, including the freedom to enter into contracts (concerning pleasure, pain, education, etc.). The situation stands in a perfect analogy both to the reflexive self-justification of reason, to the closure that Sade's submission to the Law seems to bring to the dialogue, and to the interdiction upon entering the mother's body that Mme. de Mistival's sewn vagina seems so dramatically to represent.

Of course, the awkward—"creepy" is Jane Gallop's appropriate word— question raised by the dialogue's closing pages has to do with the sense of collectivity or community that I have been hiding and stressing, as it were behind a veil of pronouns. Our lesson so far (the lesson the dialogue imparts to the mothers to whom it is dedicated, the lesson read by the embedded pamphlet to the Frenchmen it addresses) finds its spatial expression in the theatricality of this scene—in Dolmancé's skill at posing everyone in a great circle, linking each to each in shared pain and pleasure. This shared, posed experience rests on another form of universalism or claim of universality—rests on it and reflexively seeks to present it, for the edification of Mme. de Mistival and of Sade's readers, as the condition of the dialogue's final lesson (the letter is held up for Mme. de Mistival to see). We have indeed not come terribly far in substituting Dolmancé for Diotima.

But Sade is willing to take matters a bit farther and to introduce two related elements that unsettle the elaborate, elaborately designed staging of the scene and violently open both the interdiction that Dolmancé seems to place upon the mother's body and the reciprocal identification of the small Sadean community we find in the boudoir. Both have to do, unsurprisingly, with the rules governing touch or tact, the way an act, judgment, concept, or body encroaches upon, defines, is contingent upon another.

The first concerns, as Gallop has stressed, the mother's body itself.[36] The matricidal fury that Eugénie expresses becomes in its own way a paradoxical, or rather a sacrificial, universal. The Sadean community, built upon a new Kantian imperative—*aude tangere*—recognizes its generality (its public quality, its republican strain) in and upon bodies, like Mme. de Mistival's, that enter from outside the boudoir and can *only* be the objects of touch, never their subject. Bodies to whom *aude tangere* can never properly be addressed. Remember Eugénie's expression as she addresses her mother—"Pay no attention to it, Mamma. I am simply testing the point." This is conventional: the empirical "trial [*essai*]" comes naturally at the end of the work, as if the theoretical education had at last found its practical outlet. But Eugénie's needle pricks elsewhere, too—and here it becomes much harder to imagine how theory and practice do in fact line up:

Eugénie, *from time to time pricking the lips of the cunt, occasionally stabbing its interior and sometimes using her needle on her mother's belly and mons veneris.* "Pay no attention to it, Mamma. I am simply testing the point." ["*Ce n'est rien que cela, maman; c'est pour essayer mon aiguille.*"] . . . Eugénie, *much inflamed*: "No invectives, Chevalier, or I'll prick you! Confine yourself to tickling me in the correct manner. A little asshole, if you please, my friend; have you got only one hand? I can see no longer, my stitches go everywhere . . . Look at it! Do you see how my needle wanders . . . to her thighs, her tits . . . ? [*Je n'y vois plus, je vais faire des points tout de travers . . . Tenez, voyez jusqu'où mon aiguille s'égare jusque sur les cuisses, les tétons . . .*] Oh, fuck! What pleasure! (364)

Her body touching her mother's and the Chevalier's, Eugénie's eyes close. When she drives the needle in, she does so blindly, across indistinct borders, *à travers*, wanderingly. We presume, of course, that her hand wanders over other parts of her mother's body, poking and stitching here and there—but Eugénie has just threatened the Chevalier himself with a "pricking," sharply barring him from invective with an expression that associates her wandering needling with the Chevalier's linguistic pricking: "Point d'invectives, chevalier," she cries, "ou je vous pique!" Here *Philosophy in the Bedroom* takes particular advantage not of its personal pronouns but of the French impersonal forms (*Tenez, voyez jusqu'où mon aiguille s'égare jusque sur les cuisses, les tétons . . .*) to open this rather ghastly scene to the most literal, material form of contingency: the *égarement* of Eugénie's needle occurs over *cuisses* and *tetons* unanchored in any particular body, unattached to any particular name, loosed from a specific pronoun. The roiling of bodies that Sade asks us to imagine works in hand with the syntactical slurring of antecedents and the metonymous slip from the point of the needle to the tip of the (daughter's and the Chevalier's) tongue. These slips slip again: the daughter's eyes close, against her will, just as she closes her mother's vagina against hers; in her blind pleasure, Eugénie threatens to sew onto her mother's body or onto her own the body, hands, and tongue of the Chevalier who has taught her so much; the point of Eugénie's needle and the Chevalier's shaking hands and slandering tongue are stitched into an analogy; the blind wandering of Eugénie's hand invests the needle with a ghostly personality of its own; and it strays, stitching, over one or another body, both the impersonal instrument for creating the ties that bind these three figures and the personification of the wandering agency of pleasure.

The second element that Sade stitches into this scene cannot, in one respect, be squared with the blind, community-producing wandering we find at Eugénie's hands. In these last sentences *Philosophy in the Bedroom* describes a strange circle and returns to its point of departure, its fortuitous route also determined, contingency and necessity paradoxically sutured together. Or rather, at the end of *Philosophy in the Bedroom* the contingency on which the Sadean community is built unfolds into the contradictory aspects I sketched above—on the one hand, the mere blindness of the event, one stitch simply following another, each *piqûre* punctual, accidentally linked to the preceding stitch by the red trace of the thread it trails; but, on the other hand, the whole sewing pattern contingent upon, blindly following upon, the pattern set for Eugénie by the interdiction on touching the mother and the desire to touch her. Eugénie stitches blindly, not only creating an unwrought community out of her violent, blind pleasure but also switching generations, assuming Mistival's role and turning herself into her mother's instructress as well as her mother's owner, re-hymenizing Mme. de Mistival, closing her anatomically but opening her to edification. Here, the image of the touched mother, sewn up, bearing only syphilitic venom, suggests a body no longer able to reproduce, a body destined for death rather than birth—but also a body re-hymenized, re-infantilized, brought back to the shape it had before Eugénie's birth. When Mme. de Mistival leaves the boudoir, she bears the venom of her death and her new knowledge, the violent trace of the edifying history told in *Philosophy in the Bedroom*, sewn upon and within her—but she bears also the ironic figure of her daughter's innocence, stamped or embroidered upon her by Eugénie herself. Newly virginal (though only in the merest parodic, anatomical sense), she has returned or been recalled to the place her daughter Eugénie occupied at the opening of the work. Thus is Eugénie bound up from the beginning with the figure of her mother, as her mother follows her at the dialogue's close. "More beautiful than Love itself," Eugénie opens *Philosophy in the Bedroom* already carrying the pox to which she will consign the mother who takes her place, the instructors who seek to teach her what her virginity turns out already to conceal, and the readers who track the progress of her education by steps or stitches, points of suture or *piqûre*, from naïveté or ignorance to Enlightenment.

Philosophy in the Bedroom does not, then, offer an allegory of education, or not simply an allegory of education, as at this level we do not proceed from innocence to experience—or no more than we might proceed from experience to innocence. As Eugénie's needle finds its pleasure-blinded but also -determined way between theory and practice, between thought and experience, Sade's dialogue makes clear why neither the characters, nor the dialogue's readers, nor its author can know on what bodies the pox of genuine, republican community alights. For the circularity Sade discloses at the dialogue's end does not have the reflexively self-justifying shape that we find in Hardt and Negri's rendering of the logic of Enlightenment. In *Philosophy in the Bedroom*, it is no longer possible to tell in what direction the venom of philosophical knowledge flows and, in consequence, to what causes one can ascribe the origin of the republic of the boudoir. Stitched into Dolmancé's contract, the red thread of blind contingency unbinds but also sets back in place the theological-oedipal prohibition.

At the same time and in the same paradoxical way, blinding tutor as well as pupil, cause as well as effect of this double blinding, Sadean contingency makes one more effort at a republican community possible. The pleasures of Sadean contingency stand at the other edge of the ideology of *Bildung*—the "edifying" residue of the Enlightenment that keeps the explosive estrangement and the equally explosive intimacy of the object and of the body subordinate to overriding narratives of education, stories that proceed from the mystified figure of the virginal innocent to the figure of consciousness. In the interval where theory and practice are blind to each other, reflexive thought, like reflexive violence, occurs, and founds the political. But the violence of its occurring cannot be *made* political (no story can be "woven around it," to return to Rorty's words; it cannot be renarrativized, converted into an "edifiying" tale) without turning Dolmancé into Diotima. The constitution of unwrought communities or of the postmodern *posse* hangs upon this Sadean resistance. Marked like Eugénie and like Mme. de Mistival with the violent traces of finitude, with the blinding venom of historical contingency, we find in occurrent pleasure that community effects are produced, and that—with an effort, just one more—the republic can be built.

CHAPTER 6

Three Women, Three Bombs

I had to say all this for the people of France who will read my work.
They must know that Algerians do not confuse their torturers with
the great French people, from whom they have learned so much, and
whose friendship is so dear to them. And yet the French must know
what is being done here IN THEIR NAME.

—HENRI ALLEG, *La question*

Let's try to be precise then. The word *torture* does not appear in our
orders. We have always spoken of interrogation as the only valid
method in a police operation directed against unknown enemies. . . .
When the rebellion first began, there were not even shades of
opinion. All the newspapers, even the left-wing ones, wanted the
rebellion suppressed. And we were sent here for this very reason. And
we are neither madmen nor sadists, gentlemen.

—COLONEL PHILIPPE MATHIEU, in *The Battle of Algiers*

In an interview published in 1972, the director Gillo Pontecorvo was asked
by Joan Mellen, a film historian, to reflect on *The Battle of Algiers*.[1] "It is
clear," she asked, leadingly, "that you have made a film on the side of
Algerian independence. But is this undermined in any way by treating the
violence committed by the Algerians and French in a one-to-one relationship? You show the Algerians killing someone, then the French retaliating,
then the Algerians, etc., whereas in the historical situation the French
killed hundreds of thousands more than the Algerians, including women
and children. There is only one moment in the film where we get a sense
of this, when Ben M'Hidi says 'Give us your napalm, and we'll give you
our women's baskets.'" Mellen's question to Pontecorvo reflects a degree
of uneasiness among militant supporters of the Algerian revolution about
the seeming reciprocity, what she calls "a one-to-one relationship," with
which Pontecorvo presents the atrocities of the French *paras* and the
effects of the FLN's bombs.[2]

The unease the film historian expresses is hardly unique, and it is certainly no more passé than the film's subject matter or visual tropology.
Islamic and anticolonial terrorism steps into the mainstream of Western

policy and into its televised imaginary carrying "women's baskets" (or their notional equivalent, the "suitcase bomb" and the "shoe bomb") and clothed in veils literal or metaphoric. But the affect form the filmmaker and his interviewer touch on is more general, and it has what should by now be a familiar logical shape. An appeal to a universal value (for instance, the formal, abstract equality of acts as acts) permits someone—an audience member viewing *The Battle of Algiers*, say—to weigh one death against another, an act of violence against an act of counterviolence; but, as Mellen seems to be objecting, such an appeal has a context, a history, enabling and disabling conditions, material circumstances, consequences that are hardly abstract and never merely formal. The representation of a radically asymmetrical distribution of forces, wealth, or cultural capital seems always to be undermined by the parti pris and vice versa. More importantly, the taking of sides, *la prise de parti*, occurs somewhere other than the domain of reasoned choice, or self-understanding, or interest of one sort or another. The unease we experience as and at the contingency of universals marks, for instance, the media's coverage of current conflicts (the loud old battle cry of "objectivity" or "evenhandedness" masking different forms of bad faith, guilt, ressentiment), from Palestine to the Basque country. It shapes every discussion of the communitarian ideal and of its costs; it provides the grammar for utopian radicalism, for the "realism" of reaction, and, most importantly, for the modern conceptualization of their relation.

I am not yet ready to give this feeling of unease—in the context of Mellen's question, a banal emotion, easily masked by the interviewer's self-satisfaction—its proper name: *terror*. To do so will be the burden of this chapter, which takes a different path toward the peculiarly opaque form of ethico-political pedagogy we came upon in Sade's boudoir. This pedagogy—the rough lesson that Eugénie seems to teach Sade's readers about the efforts that go into building the new republic—comes on the scene when reflexive thought and reciprocal violence step into the spot vacated, at the crisis juncture of the logics of terror and sovereignty, by analytic terms like *necessity*, *negation*, or *contradiction*. The Sadean community imagines the contingent, blind association on which it must be built as a pedagogical contract, pedagogy imagined as a contractual relation between (some) subjects who learn to recognize each other as it were in retrospect—violent in its own way, subject to unforeseen libidinizations. And this contract depends upon an experience of time—upon the representation of a temporal relation between reflection, judgment, and action—given a startlingly different shape when the Sadean boudoir is located in the Algerian casbah at the midpoint of the twentieth century.

Note, grosso modo, that the European critique of the Enlightenment's political legacies takes shape not only in the shadow of Auschwitz but also, as we saw in the last two chapters, in relation to the last crises of European decolonization, at the midpoint of the twentieth century, in the period stretching from the battle of Dien Bien Phu and the outbreak of the Algerian resistance in 1954 to the referendum on the independence of Algeria and its break with France, in 1962. Even more baldly: for the generation of Europeans to whom we directly owe the means for dismantling discursively what Hardt and Negri call "the dialectics of colonial sovereignty," ethico-political pedagogy takes shape around the case of the Algerian revolution: as the historical matter to be taught and reflected upon; as the revolution provides models for pedagogies and counter-pedagogies. Note also, again rather schematically, that the particular circumstances in which this ethico-political pedagogy emerges also mark a shift in the imaginary construction of gender, in particular, in the play of fantasy and counter-fantasy on which the metropolitan intellectual class built its understanding of the emergence of an utterly new figure: the woman terrorist. Note, finally, the circumstance we have explored briefly: that these years are marked by the rediscovery, reediting, and rethinking of the work of Sade throughout Europe, especially in France.

How should we approach this nexus? Pontecorvo's answer to Mellen sets the scene. It is an altogether remarkable response: "This happens," he begins, referring to the "one moment in the film" where the imbalance between the colonial forces and the nationalist resistance is, in Mellen's view, represented:

> in an extremely tense moment . . . and it creates a proper balance of the problem. I thought it was enough. He says it at the moment toward which all the dramaturgy has been pointing. . . . There is another more important point. I think it is insignificant to say, "One side killed ten, the other killed two." The problem is that they are in a situation in which the only factor is oppression. Then they begin to fight, and I don't believe that when people fight, some fight hard and some fight less hard. The Algerians castrated people and also committed torture. You must judge who is historically condemned and who is right. And give the feeling that you identify with those who are right.[3]

The answer then takes a symptomatically mixed shape. On the one hand, Pontecorvo is saying this: "Yes, I support the Algerians, I consider them to have been in the right, and I want to give the feeling that I identify with those who are right. But at the same time I refuse to make the basis of my identification with them the fact that they suffered numerically more than the French did. The only factor really to be considered is oppression. This oppression is the product of the logic of colonialism, and in an important sense, inasmuch as they are both governed and moved by this logic, the Algerians and the French are equally oppressed. What I want to condemn," Pontecorvo seems to be concluding, "is the logic of colonialism. What I want to identify with is the fight against that logic, and in that fight Algerians and French can fight together, not against each other, and in that fight the numbers of the dead on one side or another are of secondary importance." The argument is not that Algerian terrorists are morally equivalent to the French colonial forces, to the *paras* or the torturers, but that their actions have a determining common origin. However different the Italian filmmaker may be from the Algerian insurgent or the French paratrooper, all three assume their identity, Pontecorvo tells us, in relation to a logic of colonialism that exists and subsists independently, that underlies and underwrites the three positions that Pontecorvo describes here, and that is always immediately and immanently present. This relationship, Pontecorvo argues, which is constituted by the common immediacy of the logic of colonialism, brings together into a subjected community the colonial oppressor, the native population of Algerians, and the witnessing eye of the film director. This relationship, and this alone, is the index by which the balance or imbalance of one or another representation, the symmetry or asymmetry of forces at work, the felicity or infelicity of ethical judgments concerning an event, can be measured.

Recall now that on the other hand, Pontecorvo is saying to Mellen: "You must judge who is historically condemned and who is right. And give the feeling that you identify with those who are right." But judging "historically" and then giving the feeling that "you identify with those who are right" seems a very different procedure from assessing balance, symmetry, and relative felicity against a logic—a much more subjective, tentative, contingent procedure. We may be able to describe a logic of colonialism, but who is to say who is right about this or that matter *historically*? This is not just a rhetorical question, of course: "La historia es nuestra y la hacen los pueblos," Allende's last words read; "History is ours, and peoples make history," a moving but inconclusive answer to the older observation that history is written by the victors. Even for Hegel—perhaps especially for Hegel—the so-called judgment of history is crepuscular. The "lesson of the concept," as Hegel calls such judgments and the sort of knowledge and decisions they make possible, is painted with gray on gray. Disconnected from "the ripeness of actuality," the judgments of history—condemning the colonial forces, enshrining the resistance, or vice versa—are deficient precisely in being abstract, merely formal.[4] On this side of Pontecorvo's response, then, it is not the immediacy or the immanence of an origin or a logic that determines how judgments are to be framed, enunciated, and assessed but the intervention of an impossibly deferred mediation, a time beyond the actuality of time from which the criteria for judgments may come.

Pontecorvo is no philosopher of ethics, so it may be unfair to require that he be entirely consistent. I'm interested in dwelling on this contradiction in his response to Joan Mellen and on the series of questions it elicits because in my view it not only tells us something about *The Battle of Algiers* but also tells us something about the nature of ethical judgments and about their role in making the effort—that one more effort—that the republic appears to require. Why is it that when you begin making judgments (for instance, the judgment that Pontecorvo has "made a film on the side of Algerian independence" or the judgment that *The Battle of Algiers* undermines its independentist parti pris by representing the war's violence symmetrically, one for one) then a criterion like the logic of colonialism is no longer entirely adequate? Where does the supplementary requirement that we "judge who is historically condemned and who is right" come from? What weight does the modifier *historically* bear? It looks like a vestigial form of the old dialectical-historical modifier *objective*, but in the shape that Pontecorvo's answer takes, its old time is off entirely: the judgment of history comes, Derrida might say, from the future. What standing does Pontecorvo give the additional and consequent task that flows from his contradictory answer—the task of giving "the feeling that you identify with those who are right"? How does Pontecorvo give his audiences an ethic of terror that is not an apology for terrorism?

Mirror/Shot: La terreur dans le boudoir

I would like to consider a brief sequence of scenes from *The Battle of Algiers*, placing it in three contexts, one quite familiar, the other two perhaps less so: the wonderful, powerful sequence usually called "three women, three bombs." It is in most ways the film's crux and understandably has received the most critical attention.[5] It represents an act of vengeance by the ALN (Armée de libération nationale, the armed wing of the much better-known FLN, Front de libération nationale) for the bombing of three Arab houses in the rue de Thèbes by French nationalists. In the political logic of the anticolonial revolt, the events depicted in the sequence mark the moment when the FLN moves explicitly from imagining itself as an armed insurgency targeting the French military establishment to justifying attacks on French *piednoir* civilians. In these scenes, Algerian "terrorism" as it would be conventionally defined comes onto the scene; they are the place where the film for the first time gives the public "women's baskets," as the film's Ben M'Hidi says, in place of the *paras'* guns or napalm.[6] Pontecorvo and his principal source, Yacef Saadi, are careful to establish the rationale for this tactical shift: in Saadi's memoir *Souvenirs de la bataille d'Alger* (*Memories of the Battle of Algiers*), the turn toward terrorism is explained like this: "The bomb of ultra-colonial terrorism achieved an end diametrically opposed to the one sought by the enemies of Algerian independence. Without question, it served to reinforce the authority of the FLN."[7] And in his second book of memoirs, *La Bataille d'Alger* (*The Battle of Algiers*), Saadi remembers in these terms: "'It's time for us to change our methods,' I confided to H'didouche. 'The machine-gun, the hand-gun, and the blade won't block the madness of the *ultras*. There's only one way to calm them down: by means of bombs.'"[8] The explosion of these bombs marks the event that provokes the entrance of the paratroopers, under the leadership of Colonel Mathieu; it is the event that provokes the French to institute torture as an interrogation policy rather than as the work of "sadists," as Mathieu and others said, or of "a few bad apples," as the contemporary version, in the Abu Ghraib photos, runs. They are also markedly, if equivocally, pedagogical scenes.

Cinematically, the "three women, three bombs" sequence serves to build a narrative bridge between the enclosed, constraining space with which the film opens—famously, a shot of the last uncaptured leader of the revolt, Ali la Pointe, and his collaborators hiding in a false wall in one of the houses in the casbah—outward into the new city, whose open spaces, bustling metropolitan exchanges, etc. are the location to which the insurgency brings the bombs. Susan Slyomovics captures this level of the film's logic well: "The camera follows Hassiba as she crosses boundaries: from interior domestic space to the exterior public street, from Arab Casbah to French *nouvelle ville*, from 'native' to 'colonial' space."[9] The sequence is the moment of passing, as it were—when the local Muslim community drops the veil and steps into the role expected and desired for them by the colonists—but only as a way of masking their desire to be free of those very expectations and desires. It marks an important transition in the gender economy of the film and in the history of the tactics of the FLN more generally—women passing from being the witnesses to an insurgent activity or playing, as it were, supporting roles in it to becoming the insurgency's most spectacular weapon. Finally, the "three women, three bombs" montage focuses upon and begins with one of the principal points of connection between the film's visual lexicon and the lexicon in which contemporary discussions of matters proper to a specifically postcolonial world system take place: what Emmanuel Terray has recently called "headscarf hysteria" and what Cécile Laborde analyzes as the "hijab controversy."[10] The pressing questions of immigration policy, uneven acculturation, traditionalization and modernization, democratization, the rise of fundamentalism, "tolerance," definitions of "terrorism"—all these come into sharp focus when the camera dwells, for just a moment, on the unveiling of the three women.

The mirror shot of Hassiba Ben Bouali is barely the outline of a gesture, but it encapsulates and subtly complicates the scene. This double function has been the determining characteristic of mirror shots, of course. Pontecorvo would have needed to look no farther than Jean-Luc Godard's *Le petit soldat* of 1963 (finished, though, in 1960) to find a film concerned with the Algerian War, with the representation of torture (importantly for Pontecorvo, torture carried out by both the FLN and the nationalist French groups who have hired Bruno to execute the FLN leader—might this be a proximate source for Pontecorvo's "proper balance of the problem"?), and filmically with the movement between interior and exterior shots. At the core of Godard's film, is another boudoir–sitting room, another mirror shot. Everything about the scene will be seized by Pontecorvo, reworked, and retranscribed. Where a woman gazed into the mirror in *The Battle of Algiers*, it is a man who looks there in *Le petit soldat*. Hasiba's mirror reflects her face and appears to hide nothing, indeed, works to reveal to the film's viewers the techniques she employs to become the assimilated woman she must appear to be. Godard's, by contrast, becomes itself the hiding place for the gun: film is not a mirror, or not a mirror surface, but material with depth, itself a sort of veil. A veil drops from Hasiba's face, and her viewers understand that political subjectivity of a specific sort is signaled thereby; a sweater veils Bruno's face momentarily, as he pulls it over his head, and Godard's audience understands the character to be clothing himself so as to leave the intimacy of the boudoir and venture into the streets, armed.

There is no good reason to restrict Pontecorvo's models, sources, and interlocutors to the idiom of film. Local variations and different values attach, certainly, to the scene within the scene, depending on whether one

a.   b.

c.   d.

e

5a–e. The mirror shot, *The Battle of Algiers.*

is thinking of the story of Narcissus, or in the visual idiom of the myriad depictions of bathing Venuses in early modern mythography, from Titian to Rubens, or of the mysterious plane of the mirror at the bottom of the Infanta Cristina's waiting room in Velázquez's *Las meninas.*

Take, for example, that great model of the orientalizing boudoir shot, Delacroix's 1834 *Algerian Women in Their Apartments.* Delacroix's canvas also features a presiding mirror hung at an angle behind the "Algerian women," its blank surface the third point in a system of visual relays. In that system, the viewer/painter, entirely outside of the space of the painting, seems echoed in but distinguished from the African woman stepping

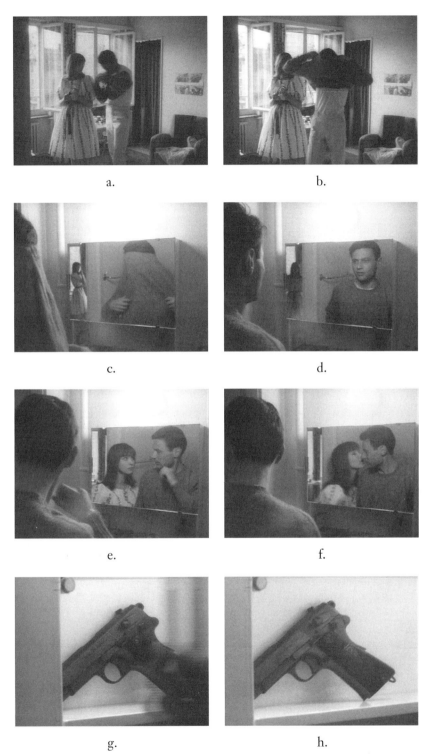

6a–h. The mirror shot, *Le petit soldat.*

out of the frame but glancing back at the "Algerian women," entirely within its space—the angle at which the exiting woman holds her head is almost exactly the same as the angle formed between the mirror and the wall it hangs on, as if they had been rotated about an axis formed by the viewer's position. Both of them find themselves reflected in, but also absent from, the mirror, which designates a strange hole/space that falls neither wholly within nor wholly without the painting.

There is more to say about the scopic system of Delacroix's painting and the mirror's role in suturing it. Note that in the corresponding scene from *The Battle of Algiers*, Pontecorvo places the camera, conventionally, directly beside Hassiba's face, where it captures her gaze in the mirror. The scene of the three women removing their veils and then changing clothes is meant to appear radically shocking: to inform or remind the Western viewer of the constraints placed on the public display of women's bodies in a traditional Muslim society; to invest the colonial erotics of Delacroix's aestheticization with a firmly political content. The camera is privy pornographically to the intimacies of the three women's undressing,

7. Eugène Delacroix, *Algerian Women in Their Apartments.* Courtesy of Réunion des Musées Nationaux/Art Resource, NY.

dyeing their hair, changing clothes, and acquiring another language; the looks the women give themselves and each other in the mirror seem to convey that their sense of modesty and shame is being measured or traded against a revolutionary resolve. And the camera's position seems to make visible this calculation, to place it before us for us to identify and to identify with. The shot thus also seeks to make visible—it also reflects upon— its own role in translating the women's interior negotiations: the trade-off between shame and resolve, between the private sense of the veiled, defended body and the necessity of the public, unveiled face. Finally, recall that the three transformed women greet Saadi by asking him, in French, "Ça va, monsieur?" Put this way, following on the heels of this uncomfortable unveiling of their bodies, the question rings in the eloquent idiom of solicitation, of street trade, as well as in the odd metafilmic register of the actor's dressing room. "Ça va, monsieur?" might well be the question that the streetwalker prostitute, Algerian or French, addresses to the prospective client as he walks by—or merely the sort of flirtatious semi-come-on that helps all three women through the check points leaving the casbah. It might equally be the question that the actor addresses the director: Am I ready to go onstage? Will my disguise do? Am I acting well enough?— questions of particular interest to Pontecorvo, who uses no professional actors at all in *The Battle of Algiers* except for Jean Martin, who plays Colonel Mathieu. Or all three.[11] Throughout, then, Pontecorvo requires that his audience experience and judge the shot both from the perspective of the camera and from the perspective, as it were, of the boudoir—from a position behind Hassiba's back and from the surface of the mirror on which she gazes; from a spot before the decision to act (to remove the veil, accept the burden of the bomb, assume strategically the alternative veil of modernity) and after it, in the midst of its consequences; from one side of the veil and of the camera and then, or at the same time, from the other. So why is the unveiling shot so brief? Why not linger on it a bit more?

A first answer. (A first context.) The film wishes to draw an analogy between the speed of the shot, on the one hand, and, on the other, the explosive punctuality of the bomb. It seeks to join to these, by means of a conceptual montage, the corresponding decision to assume a revolutionary agency. In the boudoirs of the casbah, a cinematic bridge spontaneously arises between what Ranjana Khanna astutely calls "the agency of the cut," the act of unveiling, and the violence of the bomb in the rue de Thèbes.[12] The result: the three bombs planted by the film's three women. The film's pedagogical dimension appears compressed into the event: the bombing at the rue de Thèbes speaks, as it were, for itself, and results in spontaneous action, guided merely by the hand of the ALN (its reflexive instrument: a bomb for a bomb, reciprocally). Here speech gives way to rapid music, in contrast to those spots in the film where persuasion is associated with the film's voice-over radio narrator/commentator or with discursive, explanatory scenes between Mathieu and his forces or the reporters, or between Ben M'hidi and Ali La Pointe and Saadi, or between Saadi and what Danielle Marx-Scouras calls (with a droll and subversive nod to the "Bond girls" of the 007 franchise) "Yacef Girls," the women involved in the "three bombs" shots.[13] Where three women unveil and where, by extension, Algeria unveils, to use Fanon's phrase, in the intimacy of the casbah's many boudoirs, the extension of time that Eugénie's blind but sequenced stitches seem to embody is traded for the frame, for the cut, for the event. A new definition of spectatorship, if not, indeed, of thought, emerges—punctual, immediate, joining causes to effects unreflectively, as a face might be glimpsed in a mirror before it is recognized as a reflection.

A second answer. (A second context.) Pontecorvo's unveiling shot can be so short, punctual, simply a gesture, a synecdoche or a bit of shorthand, a glimpse of a glimpse, precisely because the motif of unveiling was so hotly current in European debates about the war in Algiers between 1954 and 1966.[14] Fanon writes about the colonial gaze: "A strand of hair, a bit of forehead, a segment of an 'overwhelmingly beautiful face' glimpsed in a streetcar or on a train." Of course, the change of methods that the unveiling shot encapsulates went farther than a simple incremental shift in *materiel* and farther than a change of dress, however heavily semanticized. The FLN's decision to rely on women to place these bombs marked a social shift of even greater importance, for it involved both dramatically refiguring the role of Algerian women in a rather traditional Muslim culture and also, and by the same stroke, emphasizing the pedagogical role that the FLN assumed within Algerian society.

The film is at pains to stress this classically vanguardist function, to the point of occasional didacticism. Expository scenes showing Kader/Djafar explaining to Ali la Pointe the FLN's history, tactics and current difficulties, as well as a later one in which ben M'Hidi discusses with Ali the possible reactions of the French to the strike called by the FLN, unfurl to what one critic calls "lyrical music . . . expressing the sympathy Pontecorvo asks us to feel for the F.L.N. during its difficult initial stage of development."[15] So too Saadi's memoirs. He writes in *La Bataille d'Alger* of his first meeting with the three women who have volunteered to carry the bombs:

The three young women seemed nervous. Who wouldn't have been, in similar circumstances? To quell the anxiety I told them: "I won't hide from you that it's the first time that we are using bombs to reinforce our capacity to strike. I believe that before embarking on this mission you will have considered the consequences carefully. It would be superfluous to tell you what I saw in the rue de Thèbes." And so bit by bit I listed the stages of our resistance. It was brief but rather edifying. [*Ce fut court mais assez édifiant.*]

Saadi's "edifying" tale transforms the identity not just of these women but symbolically of the whole people. This is how Saadi remembers a brief exchange, in *Souvenirs*:

Zineb also confirmed the absence of military patrols in the street. Zineb is a girl of fourteen who belongs to a very traditional, religious [*maraboutique*] family. Before that day, she had not been able to walk in the street without being accompanied by a family member. But after her parents agreed to put us up, a revolution took place in the minds of this venerable family [*il s'est produit une révolution dans les esprits de cette vénérable famille*] in which the women, who had long been relegated to a secondary role [*l'arrière plan*], now express the desire to take active part in a fight for liberation. Thus it is that Zineb's father, Si el Hadj, now agrees happily and trustingly [*avec joie et en toute confiance*] to allow his daughters to mingle with us, to live and share the same dangers as the ALN's fighters. Who could have imagined this, even two years ago?[16]

The parallel between the family's development and the future of the Algerian people is not quite so mechanical as it might at first appear: the revolution "in the minds of this venerable family" does indeed correspond to the revolution sought by the FLN against the French colonial regime, and the struggle for liberation whose object Saadi leaves provocatively ambiguous corresponds as well to a double struggle, a battle against the colonialism of the French and a battle against the familial arrangement that had confined women to a secondary role. The confidence that Si el Hadj expresses, the appealing image of shared labor, danger, and success, the sense of rapid change evident in the quick shift in attitudes in two years—all of these are the fantastical and predictable stuff of liberationist eschatology. But the important role played in the battle for independence by figures like Zineb, like Zhora Drif, Samia Lakhdari, and Djamila Bouhired, is both the symbol and the vehicle for that revolution, and in the second of these two aspects of their role, Algerian women who supported and worked with the FLN would do so by manipulating a second (and third) set of symbolic roles—by returning symbolically and strategically to

the very secondary role to which they had been relegated or by abandoning it spectacularly and spectacularly adopting the symbolic and literal
habit of the assimilated Arab.[17] What results from this deliberate overdetermination of the symbolic role of the Algerian woman in the revolutionary society, as well as in the nascent postcolonial Algerian society is, in the
first place, an increased socio-symbolic flexibility: women can occupy
more than one role or "plane" in the stratigraphy of the national economy, and for the same reason Algerian men, too, come to accept "happily
and trustingly" that their "venerable" social and political roles must
change.

But, in the second place, the instrumental role of the Algerian woman,
imagined either by the FLN or by the French colonial establishment to
be a symbol of resistance or of assimilation, becomes much harder to
assimilate into an established narrative form. This is, indeed, the critical
point of revolutionary pedagogy, as set before us by Saadi and by Pontecorvo. Revolutionary movements teach us, it appears, that the value with
which this or that social role, practice, or object is invested must be measured differently, according to standards different from those established
by the colonial occupation or by the colonized society. In teaching as in
act, these movements help to disengage the process of investing social
value from an existing regulative, perspicuously available principle (like
"tradition" or the colonial logic that *Empire* describes). Under pressure
from them, the object, the social practice, and the body itself attend,
trembling, the emergence of another principle according to which value
and social sense are assigned to them and comparatively assessed.

This is a complicated and consequential enough dynamic—phenomenological, economic, semiotic—when what's at issue is an image, a
social role, or a symbol (a veil, for example) and the sense or value these
may lose or assume in the transition from one social form to another.[18]
But Saadi's accounts to some extent and Pontecorvo's film in particular
are unsparing in recognizing that this moment is also profoundly violent,
both in the instruments by means of which it is achieved and in its effects.
Pedagogical instruments and immaterial, cognitive effects: but also, and
more strikingly, these instruments for shifting the principles for assessing
social value become the paraphernalia of the terrorist herself, and the
effects of such shifts the physical effects of her acts. For the terrorist rein-
vests objects with values and senses they previously did not possess—
nonutilitarian, differently imagined values. This is how the screenplay to
The Battle of Algiers describes a scene representing events from the morning of August 10, 1956:

An Algerian woman walks along the sidewalk. She is elderly, fat, and is wearing a traditional costume with her face veiled. She walks slowly toward a bar. . . . Near the bar, leaning against a wall, there is an Algerian. . . . They greet one another with much warmth, like a mother and son who haven't seen each other for a long time. They embrace, and the man searches at her breast among the folds of her veil. He finds a revolver. . . . At a table, there is a French soldier having coffee with cream, croissant, and an open newspaper. The Algerian continues to embrace the old woman, and aims from above her shoulders. Only one shot; the newspaper rips, the soldier tries to get up again, his face full of blood. Then he collapses on the table. The Algerian has hidden the revolver in the woman's veil. The two separate from their embrace. They seem terrified and surprised.[19]

The veil, the mother's veil, hides and then shelters, again, the son's gun; the open newspaper veils and conceals the French soldier's face: too much concerned with other worlds, other situations, other news, he is doubly unconscious of the revolver, doubly veiled from him, by the innocuous, familiar, and familial scene and by the journalistic distance the newspaper places between him and the Algerian present. And so Zhora Drif's hum-drum shopping basket, doubly veiled, holds a bomb; Hassiba Ben Bouali's handbag conceals another. In Algiers, after the unveiling of the FLN's new tactics, after the journalistic veil is ripped, an unveiled woman no longer denotes the assimilated Algerian but rather the militant nationalist; an ambulance charges bystanders. Today, the airliner becomes a missile; a sneaker or a backpack can be deadly.

Of course, these violent resemanticizations are imagined to be nothing more than a transitional state of affairs. The film's "lyrical and redemptive," conclusion (the words are Edward Said's)—which celebrates the spontaneous resurgence of the nationalist cause, seemingly put down by the French paratroopers in 1957—seems to close off the tremulous uncertainty opened by the FLN's revolutionary pedagogy and by Pontecorvo's.[20] (I say "seems" because I will suggest below quite a different way of reading this last scene.) In the society that is announced, a shopping basket may again be no more than that, a handbag merely a handbag; to wear the veil may once again signify that one observes a rite and not to do so, that one does not. Algerians may once again assume the social roles assigned them by gender (women, for instance, might drift back to a secondary role), class, or creed (the "traditional" family). And so, discussing the "total change in attitude" brought about in Algeria by the revolution, Pierre Bourdieu comments in his 1961 revisions to the 1958 *Sociologie de l'Algérie* on the "obvious transformation" in the "traditions endowed with an essentially symbolic significance, such as the customs pertaining to dress." "A second function," he writes, "has been added to the traditional function of the wearing of the veil":

> By the wearing of the veil, the Algerian woman is also creating a situation of non-reciprocity; like a cheating gambler, she can see without being observed, and it is through her that the whole of this dominated society is symbolically refusing to establish any reciprocal relations, is looking on without letting itself be observed. The veil is the most obvious symbol of this closing in upon oneself, and the Europeans have always obscurely felt it to be such. In this way it becomes evident why all attempts at assimilation have taken the discarding of the veil to be their primary objective. The demonstrations of May 13, 1958, in the course of which several Algerian women removed their veils or "burnt them symbolically" (as the newspapers reported), amid the applause of the crowd of Europeans present, was tantamount to a ceremonial magic rite in which the whole Algerian society was offering itself, naked and willing, to the embrace of the European society. This symbol of refusal . . . can now be abandoned. . . . And if, as a result of the demonstrations of May 1958, there was a slowing down and even a regression in this movement, it was because the wearing of the veil once again was taking on its meaning as a symbolic form of negation.[21]

Set aside for the moment the theatricality of the scene—the "applause," the "ceremonial," "symbolic" offering, the proxy fantasy of possessing the colonized body. Consider the notion of reciprocity that Bourdieu sets before his readers. A glance joins the eyes of the colonist and the colonized and makes equally available to both, available in something like a second-order glance or gaze, the rules of the game in play, lays all the cards on the table. Or so it seems. For Bourdieu, this second gaze (at the cards, at the game of social interaction) need not be actualized (that is, it is not necessary that the rules of social association or of play be perspicuously available to the players at all times), precisely because a principle regulating that play can be derived and then supplied by an observer (for instance, by the figure of the sociologist). On the streets of Algiers, though, the veil over the Algerian woman's face veils the veil that obscures from the Europeans the rules of the game that the Algerians are playing: the European errs in thinking of the veil as a symbol. He is thus veiled from understanding that the veil symbolizes otherwise for the Algerians, that the notion of a symbol may translate inadequately from one social practice to another or that what appears to symbolize in one way for this group—what may, indeed, strike one group as the privileged symbol for symbolizing itself, the allegorical figure of the veil—may for another group be quite nonsymbolic. This frustrating second order of "veiling" becomes clear to the sociologist, particularly after taking a second look, on reflecting in 1961 on events already on the table in 1958. Here, writing again about these earlier events, Bourdieu's implicit criticism of the European desire to embrace Algerian society, to assimilate, overcome, etc. the Algerian's refusal of reciprocity, occurs in the name of a political situation—a game, an academic discipline—which has rules.

A new enlightenment, then. All that prevents the violence of revolutionary pedagogies from lapsing into a weak repetition of the circumstances that prevail before the revolution's counterviolence succeeds or into "magical" fundamentalisms of different sorts altogether is the scar left upon the object (upon the social practice, the symbol) by its transitional resemanticization. The edifying history that Pontecorvo's film furnishes—and that provided by historical memoirs like Saadi's or by disciplinary practices like Bourdieu's—serves to guard this scar, to preserve the record of an act of violence in the contained shape of the *exemplum* or moral fable.

On the whole, however, the political and anthropological discourse from which Saadi and Pontecorvo draw much of their material is much less confident that this record of violence can be preserved—and, correspondingly, that if the reciprocal counterviolence of colonial resistance can be retained, it will be in the monitory and edifying shape given it by postcolonial society. This is Fanon, commenting early in *L'an V de la revolution algérienne* on the reactions of Europeans to the veiled Algerian:

> In the first place, the veil disguises a beauty. . . . To hide a face is also to hide a secret, to bring into existence a world of mystery, of the hidden. Confused, the European lives his relation to the Algerian woman at a highly complex level. The will to bring this woman within his reach, eventually to make her an object to be possessed.
>
> This woman who sees without being seen frustrates the colonizer. There is no reciprocity. She does not deliver herself, does not give herself up, does not offer herself. . . . The European who faces the Algerian woman wants to see. He reacts aggressively to this limiting of his perception.[22]

However much the European may imagine his gaze to be reflected or reciprocated from behind the veil, he also understands that it is legitimate for him to posit this reciprocal desire because the veil signifies the abjection of the Algerian. The marked differential in power and fantasy that distinguishes the European's gaze from the hidden Algerian's grounds the fantasy of reciprocal desire, but also makes it impossible.[23] The European's consequent frustration takes shape, Fanon argues, in aggressive dream-work and in persistent rape fantasies. And yet, on closer inspection, the dynamic proves reciprocal in one crucial respect: the veil separates two symmetrically constituted affect formations, which Fanon characterizes, in the psychoanalytic register he turns to throughout the work, as two facing sadisms: the sadism, as he puts it, of the colonist who expresses the fantasy of possessing the Algerian and the sadism of the Algerian woman, for whom the frustration of the colonist is a source of pleasure and, more importantly, of a resistant identity. As Fanon understands it, each also occupies in the other's imaginary the role of the subject who provokes pain by limiting pleasure and who takes pleasure in doing so: hence the pleasure each feels in frustrating the other's desire or in possessing the abject other also reflects the other's sadism. My pleasure also increases as the other that I desire to possess, or to render abject, or whose desire I frustrate, him- or herself holds reciprocal sway over me. For the colonizer, the Algerian's veil blocks him from consummating an act that she holds forth *in posse*; his belief that his desire is matched from behind the veil is undercut by the abjection that must characterize the veiled figure, who cannot express that desire. For the Algerian, Fanon suggests, the colonizer figures as the subject who takes his pleasure (economic, social, etc.) from the despoiling of her culture. She stands in for her culture to him and to herself, and her refusal to desire her own abjection in return marks out a fantastic space where the most private resistance stands in for a broader, public, and cultural resistance to colonial despoiling. In this sense, the nonreciprocal nature of the gaze opens onto an economy of limitation, frustration, aggression, and pleasure bearing equally for the colonized and colonizer the distinctive universality of psychoanalytic formations. At this level, then, and provided that each, the colonizer and the veiled woman, is instructed in the matter of his or her desires, no veil separates one gaze from the other; on the terrain of psychoanalytic language and for the observer armed with its lexicon, the colonized and colonizer meet entirely afresh, the desires and fantasies of each unveiled to the other. It is on this reciprocal and autonomous ground that a future, postcolonial society must be devised. Seldom outside the work of Herbert Marcuse or Norman O. Brown has the spectacle of mutually constituting sadisms been valorized quite so affirmatively; rarely is the pedagogy of psychoanalysis cast in quite so utopian a vein.

But both Fanon and Bourdieu turn out to be considerably less sanguine about the political import of these reciprocal sadisms. In "L'Algérie dévoilée," Fanon's account of the May 1958 demonstrations marks the emergence of a secondary sense of *sadism*, and here the term does not have quite the reciprocal shape that it acquires when his earlier description turns to a putatively universal, psychoanalytic lexicon. He writes:

> Ignorant or feigning to be ignorant of these new norms of conduct, French colonialism, on the occasion of May 13, reenacted its old campaign of Westernizing the Algerian woman. Servants under the threat of being fired, poor women dragged from their homes, prostitutes, were brought to the public square and *symbolically* unveiled to cries of *"Vive l'Algérie française!"* Before this new offensive old reactions reappeared. Spontaneously and without being told [*sans mot d'ordre*], the Algerian women who had long since dropped the veil once again donned the *haik*, thus affirming that it was not true that woman liberated herself at the invitation of France and General de Gaulle.[24]

The micro-narrative told here runs from the symbolic deconstitution of the *haik* to the reappearance of "old reactions," leading to the spontaneous recovery of the repressed symbol and concluding with the cultural assertion of a surplus sense for this symbol, which now works as a veil but also stands in for the collective affirmation that women do not "liberate themselves when invited to do so by France." In this slight story, the spontaneity with which the veil is assumed again does double duty. No FLN cadre issues the order or the invitation to don the veil again; Algerian women, now symbolically unveiled by the French, do not "take up the veil again" when invited to do so by "Algeria" and the FLN. Spontaneous cultural resistance bypasses the domain of political or military resistance; it is a public but not a publicly organized or negotiated form of expression. To some extent, Fanon's stress on spontaneity also works to preserve and contain the violence of transitional resemanticization, in the form of an edifying tale (the edifying story of Algerian women's affirmation of their independence from French colonial "liberation" from the veil and from subsequent fundamentalist commands or *mots d'ordre* requiring them to reassume it). And, to some extent, the spontaneity of the scene corresponds to the striking impersonality we find in Bourdieu's description of the same events. Recall how Bourdieu phrases it: "if, as a result of the demonstrations of May 1958, there was a slowing down and even a regression in this movement, it was because the wearing of the veil once again was taking on its meaning as a symbolic form of negation." No command, no particular form of agency, stands behind the veil's taking on symbolic meaning: the logic of Algerian women's practice resides in the wearing alone, and from this mute wearing flows the sense later assigned socially to the veil.

Fanon and Bourdieu are aware that they purchase the logic of symbolic deconstitution and resemanticization at a high price, as is Pontecorvo. A spontaneous sadism on one side, the location of the logic of practice in the mute domain of the unthought, on the other. The emergence of a new form of spectatorship and thought reliant upon reflexive and immediate montage effects rather than upon mediate aggregations or conceptualization. In both cases, the reemergence of public resistance to colonial domination depends upon a mixed, unanalyzable term, designating neither a public nor a private phenomenon but bridging both, a term that does not belong within the domain of political discourse that it makes possible. The absence of a command, the spontaneity of a sadistic act, and the emergence of unanalyzed social practices are far from providing a mechanism for thinking the relation between the violent positing of the political arena and the thinking of politics. Rather, they trouble both the claims to discursive universality that Fanon associates with psychoanalytic language and Bourdieu's scenario of a sociological game played with perspicuous, public rules. When the Algerian woman spontaneously reassumes the veil, she reveals the constituting moment of symbolic resemanticization to be radically heterogeneous to the political domain that it enables.

These two first approaches furnish a momentary answer to the question of the function and the timing of the veil image in *The Battle of Algiers*. The shot is there, introducing the "three women, three bombs" sequence, because it summarizes the symbolic weight of self-change required by the new society. And it is there in brief because it can be no more than a synecdoche—it can carry the cultural weight of this argument only as a snapshot, because the argument and the system of visual tropes that it encapsulates are so well known. But it is also brief because that cultural weight is so very ambiguous, so powerfully overdetermined, politically so threateningly unstable. Unveiling signifies resistance but also compliance; it signifies revelation but also concealment; it provides us with a means of identification but also is what can least be identified; it is a lexical element in the film's metacinematic reflections, as well as an element of the plot the film represents. Like the extraordinary space occupied by the mirror in Delacroix's painting, the sequence lies both within and without the scopophilic circuit, within as well as without the film. Finally, and on a different level, the unveiling shot is foreshortened, uncut, reinserted within the logic of the film as a passing if explosive point, precisely because of the risk it poses not just to the space of the film (Is it a part of the diegesis of the film or an extrinsic moment of metacommentary upon the film, liable to interrupt its narrative flow? Does the boudoir, that most intimate of spaces, not also represent the most openly political space in the film? In the casbah?) but also to the time of reflection, to classical notions of spectatorship, judgment, and pedagogy that rely upon coordination and conceptualization: the sort of judgment Mellen asks Pontecorvo to make concerning the dangers of ethical symmetry and reciprocity; the sort of Cartesian ethico-political strategy Mathieu lays out for the assembled reporters in the scene from *The Battle of Algiers* from which I take this chapter's second epigraph. The logic of unveiling here appears veiled by the shot's brevity, by its merely segmental quality—which also performs or repeats the very scene (the scopophilic, romantic gaze of the male colonial eye, the fleeting view of a beautiful face glimpsed behind the veil) that the unveiling is destined to end. The film's form, the brief cut, does in the cultural imaginary the work that it seems intended to disrupt in the political imaginary: there will be no more segmented, fantasmatic reconstitutions of the veiled, colonized body, it claims, by means of a segmented cut intelligible primarily through the fantasmatic reconstitution of (or at the very least, parodic reference to) the colonial cultural imaginary.

Is Traveling Still a Moral Matter?

YACEF: Yes, Bazi was a militant I worked with—he was the one who used to make the bombs—and I took him with me to Italy in search of a director. At that time I really knew nothing about the cinema. I had seen *Rome: Open City* and I knew a little bit about Italian neorealism. I started to read all the cinema magazines so I could learn more about the directors. I had seen *Kapo*, so I got in touch with Gillo Pontecorvo.

—SAADI YACEF, "Terrorism and Torture in *The Battle of Algiers*: An Interview with Saadi Yacef"

This specific sort of contradiction leads me to the third context for understanding this shot and the ethico-political logic the film appears to advocate in and through it—to my third class of answers to the questions that it raises. We might begin with a cinematographic context. The relation of Pontecorvo's film to the cultural imaginary is again central, as is the technical question of the relations among shot, duration, and judgment (technical as well as philosophical, as Deleuze's works amply demonstrate). *The*

Battle of Algiers followed hard on *Kapo*, a film that Pontecorvo and Franco Solinas produced in 1960. *Kapo*, Pontecorvo's second film, tells the story of a concentration camp for women, and it was both a success and an immediate and abiding scandal.[25] Completed and released in Europe and in South America in 1960, nominated over Fellini's *La dolce vita*, Visconti's *Rocco and His Brothers*, and Antonioni's *L'avventura* for an Academy Award as Best Foreign Film in 1960, *Kapo* did not make it to the United States until 1964.

In *Kapo*, a very young Jewish pianist, Edith, played by Susan Strasberg (who had created the role of Anne Frank in the 1955 Broadway original of the play and who in 1961 was awarded the Best Actress trophy at the Mar del Plata Festival for her role as Edith), is deported to a camp and once there, faced with appalling conditions, disguises her Judaism and eventually accepts becoming a Kapo, one of the guards selected by the Germans from among the rest of the prisoners—usually a criminal, always a prisoner feared and despised by the others. The story of Edith's abjection, her decision to prostitute herself to the German guards in exchange for the much better treatment that she receives as Kapo, her break with prisoners whose despair, even suicides, she then provokes, her eventual decision, at the cost of her life, to aid in the escape of the prisoners at the very last moment, when the Germans, under pressure to eliminate all traces of the camp, have begun exterminating all the inmates—this is the plot of the film. Shot in black and white, like *The Battle of Algiers*, *Kapo* caused an uproar in France, though much less so in Italy. What was at issue was not the subject matter of the film or even the rather schlocky heroism of its conclusion—what the *New York Times* reviewer called the "gruesome melodrama" with which the film "dip[s] into bathos."[26] It was not that the film was bad in this sense, but rather that it was formally immoral or unethical. One shot in particular came to exemplify what Jacques Rivette and Serge Daney came to refer to as "concentration camp pornography," the so-called "tracking shot in *Kapo*." About this shot Rivette wrote these famous lines, in a review tellingly titled "On Abjection":

> The Left as well as the Right have cited, most of the time rather stupidly, a phrase attributed to Moullet: "morality is a matter of *tracking*" [*la morale est affaire de* travellings] (or, in Godard's version, "*tracking shots* are a matter of morality"). People have wanted to see in this phrase the height of formalism, whereas one could rather criticize the "terrorist" excess in these phrases, to return to Jean Paulhan's terminology. Look at *Kapo*, the shot when Emmanuel Riva commits suicide by throwing herself on the electrified wires: a man who decides at that moment to do a forward tracking shot

to reframe the body from beneath, taking care to set the raised hand exactly in a corner of the final frame, deserves nothing more than the deepest contempt.[27]

The contrast to Alain Resnais's *Night and Fog*, which had appeared just five years before *Kapo* and with which *Kapo* was immediately and almost universally compared was palpable: Resnais's great film did not aestheticize the horror of the camps; it did not seek to square the camera to the terror of the images it recorded; it was not, in short, pornographic. As Rivette put it:

> The power of *Night and Fog* came less from the documents than from the montage, the science with which the brute facts, the sadly *real* facts, were offered to view [*offerts au regard*] in a movement that is precisely that of the lucid consciousness, an almost impersonal consciousness that cannot accept understanding or admitting the phenomenon. . . . One does not get *used to Night and Fog*, for the director judges what he shows, and is judged by the way in which he shows it.[28]

Daney, who took over the *Cahiers du cinéma* from Rivette, would recall Rivette's article many years later and maintain that, after reading it, he took the little phrase "tracking shot in *Kapo*" as a sort of standard or guide in his own filmmaking. It encapsulated what not to do, a mantra to be invoked whenever he had a compositional decision to make: "Do not do what Pontecorvo does in the tracking shot in *Kapo*." Daney put it economically years later, in a memoir in which he recalled first reading Rivette's piece on abjection: "One should never place oneself where one is not, or speak in place of others."[29]

The techniques of montage and the tracking shots in *Night and Fog*, in contrast to the tracking shot in *Kapo*, serve to refuse understanding. They refuse the temptation to travel into the other's place, to judge, as it were, from the position of the dead, to cross the electrified fence that separates the inside of the other's suffering from the journalistic or voyeuristic position the camera necessarily assumes outside the camp: they refuse, in brief, the temptation of reciprocity, the temptation of identification. Traveling shots and montage in *Night and Fog* have, instead, an estranging function, whether the movement is the camera coming into the gates of Auschwitz—all of the film *Shoah* might be said to be a gloss on that tracking shot—or the famous dolly shot that closes the film.

Take, instead, the tracking shot in *Kapo*. The camera does not travel very far in Pontecorvo's shot—just upward subtly, to frame the character

a.   b.

c.   d.

8a–d. The closing tracking shot, *Night and Fog*.

Thérèse's body. What seems objectionable—abject—to Rivette and to
Daney is the impulse to aestheticize a dead body (or rather, the image of
a dead body). The camera's movement is slight, the ideological program
much heftier: to produce, by filmic means, an emotional identification
between the viewer and the inmates by assuming the position of the
inmate's desire and making it susceptible of understanding and translation
into the desires of the film's audience.[30] To be outside of the fence, to be
beyond the confinement of the camp, to be free where others are not. To
take the place of the corpse, while still living—to take from it all it has in
the visual field—its represented muteness, its flat lack of interiority, and
by means of a sympathetic identification-replacement, to kill it off again
as image. "See," the film seems to say, "I am showing you Thérèse's death
from the perspective of what she desires—freedom—so that you too can
imagine yourself driven to what she is driven to do. Take her place from

a.   b.

c.

9a–c. The tracking shot in *Kapo*.

outside the place she occupies, which is no place, the place where she is strung up, dead." It is no accident that the character Thérèse works as a translator in the camp: Pontecorvo, or so Rivette and Daney tell us, kills off this translator because he can do a better job—his tracking shot translates the desires of the inmates directly, visually, into our own desires, and us for a time into the place they occupy—for a time we know, the time of the film, the time we imagine ourselves behind the fence, the safe time during which we translate ourselves and keep in sight ourselves untranslated. Pontecorvo's shot establishes a general equivalency between our experience and that of the inmate, between a viewer's life and the life of those cut off from life, between the languages of the living and the fact of death. The space and time of the "traveling" of *Kapo* are the tracks on which we slide into the place of another, measure our circumstances against another's terror, understand in order to judge.

Night and Fog, by contrast, slides us on tracks that estrange what we see, make it less and less easy to understand, increasingly difficult to translate, tracks that mark us off from what we see. Our judgment that something appalling occurred cannot depend upon what we understand about an object like that stubbornly bent metallic frame at the close of Resnais's film; it cannot depend upon what we fear about it or upon our anxiety concerning the possible reemergence of the lucky Kapo or the collaborator who hides among us. Instead, Resnais is saying, to hear the endless cry from these camps means inhabiting the experience of terror, which is to say, registering that, in their incomprehensible occurring "after Auschwitz," objects or images do not allow us to take their place, any more than we can take the place of those who died in the camps.

I have been stressing, without commenting much upon it, the temporal aspect of this shot from *Kapo*. Remark the time that the camera takes to move upward and across the image of the electrocuted body. It is accentuated by the marching inmates, who proceed against the direction of the camera's own slight movement. The effect is thus of a double and doubly accelerated movement on three planes: the camera, the marching inmates, and, at the still point between them, the image of the body of Thérèse, as if the marching inmates are keeping time to the orders of the film's Kapos while we, the audience, keep time to the technical orders of *Kapo*. Our eyes move in different directions, in different times, but subject to the immediate and reciprocal experience of time, which we keep at the center of our field of vision, captured in and measured by the same mute object. This what the "traveling shot in *Kapo*" conveys: Thérèse's body stands in for the mute and immediate experience of (the vision of) death that the viewer shares with the inmates, the immediate means of our reciprocal communication with those who march beyond the fence, a mute point of translation. It forms and designates the surface of the screen; it is an index, Peirce might say, of that surface. The time of historical experience unrolls behind or within it; our time, the viewer's time, before it. Thérèse's body hangs between them, a mute but signifying indexical veil or cinematic screen, constituting these two times and their relation to each other.

A third answer, then, to the question of the function, genealogy, and consequences of the boudoir shot in *The Battle of Algiers*. It is a pedagogical—or even better, an auto-pedagogical answer. Pontecorvo learned from *Kapo* a lesson he echoes visually in his brief treatment of the unveiling shot in *The Battle of Algiers* and conceptually in his remarkable response to Mellen's questions about that film's ethical stance. In *Kapo*, Pontecorvo sought to produce identification and reciprocity by visual means; to close by means of the mute screen on which Thérèse hangs and which she represents, the scopic circuit linking the space and time of the film to the viewer's; and to make that link the basis of judgments concerning the historical content of the images depicted on screen—scandalizing critics and filmmakers like Rivette and Daney, and also to Pontecorvo's own later chagrin. As a result, his lesson well and truly learned, in *The Battle of Algiers* Pontecorvo resemanticizes the tracking shot in order to produce, just where he gives us the translated image of the veil, something like an impasse between the drive to produce identification and the drive to create historical, contingent judgments—the sort of judgments that are always and necessarily incomplete, susceptible to being changed. "See," he says, "the aesthetic impulse has been blocked at the face." Now, the veil that drops from the face of the Algerian woman is the cinematic equivalent of the impossibly estranged metal object at the close of *Night and Fog*. Dropping it—removing the veil from the face of the woman who will seek, briefly, to pass—signifies, in the arc of a more intimate history, Pontecorvo's willingness to drop the indexical function of the screen that he had adopted in *Kapo*. At the moment when it comes closest to the thematics of aestheticization—in the boudoir shot, tremblingly close to the harem or the "apartment"—the documentary effect not only calls for the film's viewers to identify with the image in the mirror shot, to imagine a reciprocal relation with what it reveals, but also and at the same time blocks that reciprocal relation.[31] Like the mirror in Delacroix's *Algerian Women in Their Apartment*, the mirror shot that opens Pontecorvo's boudoir succeeds in suturing the scopic circuit only by failing as well: by devising for the camera a location that is simultaneously internal and external to the film, an element of the diegesis and a metacinematic element that interrupts it. In *The Battle of Algiers*, Pontecorvo radically sets aside, as inadequate to the world of colonial resistance but also as inadequate to filmic representation after "the tracking shot in *Kapo*," the nourishing vision of ethical judgments based on reciprocity and identification, the notion of a political public sphere suited to the resolution of conflict, to the negotiation of differences, to mediation between competing interests, a political public sphere sheltered by the fantasy of comity and reconciliation, and regulated according to norms derived from that fantasy: what classical sociology might call *Gemeinschaft* or community.

And now step back. This third angle into the shot, by means of the cinematic genealogy of the film's formal techniques and reception, by reading *The Battle of Algiers* through *Kapo*, builds Pontecorvo's career into a sort of revisable history. On this description, his symptomatically divided comments to Mellen regarding the reciprocal treatment of the colonial forces and the colonized population now apply to that career as well. The genealogical analysis turns on a diegetically coherent temporality: it is the story of a cinematic and ethical *conversio*; the wound of *Kapo*'s tracking shot is closed in *The Battle of Algiers*. The lesson Pontecorvo learns from the earlier film and its reception prompts him to resemanticize the screen and the shot in the later film: the indexical function of the first and the correlative temporal reciprocity set in place by the second are replaced in *The Battle of Algiers* by the strangely incomplete functions of the mirror shot in the boudoir. This conversional pedagogy, backward-looking, self-judging, reflexive, in turn puts a great deal of pressure on a different aspect of the mirror shot, however—the extraordinary analogy the shot and the sequence it opens bear to what we might call the pedagogy of the bomb. That pedagogy, embodied in the vanishingly small instant, in the very immediacy between the bomb and the casting off of the veil, tends, as we saw, toward the pure decision, toward the exclusion of judgment (or at any rate toward its redefinition: judgment exhausts itself in the decision, it has no past, it does not contemplate consequences), toward the de-temporalization of thought.

The Battle of Algiers advocates neither a pedagogy of the bomb nor the conversional pedagogy of redemptive self-fashioning, neither terrorism (as we might in this context call the immediacy of decisionist judgment) nor eschatology, neither an ethics based upon identification nor one based upon objective calculation, neither a closed scopic circuit nor a permanently open one. The position toward which the film moves—unevenly, tentatively, hampered in some ways by the visual idiom and in others greatly bolstered—is more complex, and Pontecorvo offers it gingerly and irresolutely. Like each of its shots, the acts the film narrates are always and constitutively double and are to be judged according to distinct and mutually interrupting schemes. These schemes are formal as well as temporal, ethical, and political: the shots are diegetic but also metacinematic; flashbacks, but also coded as present; the acts are likewise immediately decided *and* the consequence of persuasion, reflexive and premeditated, taken with no view to consequence and strategic. The frameworks of reciprocity and identification on which Mellen's question to Pontecorvo stands and which undergird the classical articulation of representation with ethical judgment are here set aside in favor of an uncertain, transactional dynamic of mutual semanticization and deconstitution. In the world of *The Battle of Algiers*, acts only contingently, mysteriously, spontaneously, even unutterably result in consequences—as, for instance, at the film's close, where the voice-over narrative expresses its astonishment at the spontaneous and successful resurgence of anticolonial resistance after the events the film narrates, a resurgence that is nonetheless, though as obscurely and inarticulately as the cries of the women in the casbah, the consequence of those acts. Or rather: Pontecorvo's film serves at once to document the colonial surprise at the spontaneous consequences of these acts *and* to fill in, by means of a tracking shot lasting (we now see) the length of the entire film, the spaces between reflection, decision, act, and consequence. Both logics are constantly and decisively at work; both points of view occupied. Pontecorvo has both learned from and rejected the aestheticizing logic of the "traveling shot in *Kapo*" *and* made it the internal formal norm for *The Battle of Algiers*. The position of achieved, wrought incoherence, the temporal, epistemological, even autobiographical division that the film produces, the terror it makes out of and in distinction to its depiction of state terrorism and insurgent violence—this is its most profound contribution to the modern articulation of the ethical and political spheres.

Conclusion: Distracted Republic

> Of course, to be *just* republican is like being nothing at all. Along with
> being republican, one needs to be something more, something
> substantive, always with a noble ideology and looking toward the
> future. Not toward what we are, but to what we should and can be.
>
> —GREGORIO MARAÑÓN

The thrill, the joy are palpable: women and men squeezed onto the balco-
nies and leaning out the windows of the Casino Republicano; a packed
crowd lifting or tossing their hats; two figures—youngish, in coat and
necktie—raise the tricolored flag, which hangs steep in the breezeless sun-
light at the center of the photograph. We watch the throng from a balcony
across the street, or through a window, or from a low rooftop; a trick of
the composition lines up our eyes with the hands pulling the ropes that
hoist the flag and thus places the camera's work and our own (as spectators, observers, etc.) in some relation to the work so many within the frame
now celebrate. Our experience, our time cannot be theirs, of course. The
camera's immobility is only accidentally mimicked by the flag's frozen
drapes; our witnessing is as distant from the thrill of the crowd, from the
clutch of figures pressing upon each other, as the journalist is from the
fact, the historian from the event, the exile from his or her land.

But on another description, colored perhaps by the pathos that attaches
to losing causes, we labor in looking as those distant youths do in raising the
flag, we press forth like these crowds from the Casino Republicano—if not
this one and at this moment, in Cullera, Valencia, on the day that Spain's
Second Republic was proclaimed, then from others elsewhere, at other
moments, distant but in some important way related. From neighboring

10. Proclaiming the Republic in Cullera.

ones in the literary and historical geography of Spain, like the Casino in Alzira, just a bit inland from Cullera, where Vicente Blasco Ibáñez sets *Entre Naranjos* (*Among the Orange Trees*; 1900), a novel in which the Casino serves as the focus of political, public life, standing against the *casa azul* framed by the orange groves where Rafael Brull finds love, music, and a profoundly private sense of subjectivity, embodied in the figure of Leonora. Or from more distant, figurative *casinos republicanos*, not detached witnesses to this or that particular event (say, the declaration of the Republic), but workers too in the longer task involved in producing something like a public experience of political dwelling: a *casa* or a *casino republicano*.

Take, finally, a third tack into this photograph of the Proclamación de la República en Cullera (Valencia). The image works as an example of the proximate, arresting museum of images that mediate and condition any examination of the long and controversial cultural history of Spanish Republicanism.[1] Say we find it artificial to distinguish, with regard to such mediating images, between the standpoint of reflection (the perspective of the witness, of the historian, of the journalist, of the exile) and the enthusiastic logic of identification (the perspective of the actor or of the activist). Surely we build and dwell in a political sphere when these standpoints come together—as they do, virtually, in the photograph, when our critical, reflective witnessing of the proclamation of the Republic maps onto the handiwork involved in actualizing it both as a symbol (hoisting the flag before the Casino Republicano) and as a political institution. We may then conclude that there is no republic without its witnesses, its critics, and its exiles, no criticism and no witnessing that do not entail, if merely as their acknowledged audience, a communal identity, as it were, in the works. Solicited by the image, we find ourselves in it; the long logic of mythic identification that has been slowly unraveling before us, that I have been trying to unwind in the course of *Wild Materialism*, appears to knit itself back up in and by means of this image and of so many others tinted with the melancholia of the museum. Eugénie's blind needle drops from our fingers, or from another's; eyes open, we follow Marianne.

What is, what was, the modern republic? Does it have a future? Can the modern republic, the formal regime for the contingent distribution of sovereignty (of divisible sovereignty) across the wounded concept of the class of subjects, be imagined outside of the terrorism of identitarian mythology?

Consider the extraordinary afterlife that, since its fall in 1939, Spain's Second Republic has enjoyed in the cultural imaginaries of Spain, Europe more generally, Latin America. and the United States. That long history includes, of course, the dramatic assassination of Carrero Blanco that was the subject of my first chapter. Generally, the circumstances of republican exile contributed more than a little to promoting this afterlife, which, like so many cultural artifacts, has acquired a considerable market value as well, recordings of songs with a republican twinge, novels, films, and television serials on the subject having in the past three decades played or been published to great acclaim in Spain and elsewhere.

But the emergence of the Spanish Republic as what could be called a brand name has entailed not only the recovery of stories long stilled but also, in part, the term's de-historicization, the transformation of particular occasions and of broader sociocultural tendencies into snapshots or into clichés. The brilliance, promise, and romance of Spain's Second Republic obscure its long roots in prior historical and cultural formations; to attend to the catastrophic wound opened by its failure becomes also a way to avoid probing the genealogies of the First and Second Republics, their internal mythologies and discontinuities, or to avoid examining the forms of cultural work required to set in place the market for the republic's value, circulation, and consumption. How does this traditional, Ciceronian state form, so notably absent from the early modern state configuration in Spain, take a local shape and habitation in the First and Second Republics? What is and what was Spanish "republicanism"? What was and what is *Spanish* republicanism? What is it that has made republicanism in general at once so hard to achieve and so endlessly compelling? What are the reasons for its peculiar vulnerability at the moments when it does arise? Why have the cultural, social, and political mechanisms for the actualization of republican ideals in Spain been so weak? Much of what makes these questions appear pressing as well as fascinating also makes them hard to approach systematically. And how do these local, or rather national questions (this is, after all, the proclamation of the *Spanish* Republic, for all that I have invoked Eugénie and Marianne in describing it) bear upon the general question of the modern republican form?

A first answer, again pursued genealogically. *República, res publica*, commonwealth. At the heart of modern republicanisms lies a profoundly unsettled term, thorny and intractable whether we approach it immediately, as the consumable cliché it can become, or through the dialectical thicket of distance and identification, witnessing and criticism to which the Republic's afterlives also invite us. Consider the semantic drift that *república* takes, from the rather general formulation in the twenty-first *empresa* or emblem of Diego de Saavedra Fajardo's determining *Idea de un príncipe político cristiano* (*The Idea of a Christian Political Prince*; 1640) to the normative definitions of the word found in the various academic dictionaries we still employ today.

"En la primera edad," writes Saavedra Fajardo, "se amaba por sí mismo lo honesto y glorioso." But this Golden Age could not last, and with its decline "creció . . . la malicia, e hizo recatada a la virtud."

EMPRESA XXI

11. Diego de Saavedra Fajardo, *Idea de un príncipe político cristiano* (1640), emblem 21.

Desestimóse la igualdad, perdióse la modestia y la vergüenza, e, introducida la ambición y la fuerza, se introdujeron también las dominaciones; porque, obligada de la necesidad la prudencia, y despierta con la luz natural, redujo los hombres a la compañía civil, donde ejercitasen las virtudes a que les inclina la razón, y donde se valiesen de la voz articulada que les dio la naturaleza, para que unos a otros, explicando sus conceptos y manifestando sus sentimientos y necesidades, se enseñasen, aconsejasen y defendiesen. Formada, pues, esta compañía, nació del común consentimiento en tal modo de comunidad una potestad en toda ella, ilustrada de la luz de la naturaleza para conservación de sus partes, que las mantuviese en justicia y paz, castigando los vicios y premiando las virtudes. Y, porque esta potestad no pudo estar difusa en todo el cuerpo del pueblo, por la confusión en resolver y executar, porque era forzoso que hubiese quien mandase y quien obedeciese, se despojaron de ella y la pusieron en uno o en pocos, o en muchos, que son las tres formas de república: monarquía, aristocracia y democracia.[2]

This is James Astry's vigorous, only slightly tendentious translation of 1700:

In the first age there was no need of punishment, for there were no crimes; nor of rewards, for virtue and glory were belov'd for their own sakes. But as the world grew older, wickedness encreased with it, and made virtue more reserv'd, which before liv'd freely and carelessly in the fields. When equality was laid aside, and ambition and force suppli'd the place of modesty and shame, then government was also introduc'd. For prudence, urg'd by necessity, and common prudence [*la luz natural*] oblig'd men to civil society, that they might exercise virtues, which reason prompted them to, and make use of speech which nature gave them, that by revealing to one another the sense of their minds, they might inform, assist, and defend each other. Society being thus by common consent establish'd, there arose at the same time a certain Supream Power necessary to the preservation of its parts, which by punishing vice, and rewarding virtue, might defend them in peace and justice. And because this authority could not be diffused through the whole body [of the people: *cuerpo del pueblo*], by reason of the confusion which would arise in the execution thereof; and because t'was also necessary that some should command, and the rest obey, they quitted their pretensions to it, conferring it either upon one, few, or many, which are the three sorts of government [*república*]; monarchy, aristocracy, and democracy.[3]

Prince Baltasar Carlos, the work's addressee, could hardly have been surprised at the story that this *empresa* tells. A modern audience, accustomed to understanding republican government to be incompatible with monarchy, will find disconcerting Saavedra Fajardo's quite orthodox classification: a monarchy is a *kind* of republic, as an aristocracy or a democracy would be. His fable largely follows Aristotle's and Cicero's accounts of the origins and composition of the commonwealth, and like *De re publica*, *The Idea of a Christian Political Prince* (or, as Astry's translation has it, *The Royal Politician*) imagines the emergence of civil society ("la compañía civil") to rest upon general social attributes (what Cicero punningly calls *res populi*) that underpin both a people's common consent to the negotiation of inequality and the Bodinian notion that sovereignty is indivisible and hence must be vested in an individual or in a single, coherent institution.[4]

Certain turns in the argument of his *empresa* are quite obscure, however. It is not clear, for instance, why "authority [*potestad*]" cannot be distributed across the "body of the people [*cuerpo del pueblo*]," if one of the qualities of "el pueblo" is that it can arrive at a "common consent [*común consentimiento*]" and can thus act rationally and coherently as a single institution. Is Saavedra Fajardo's objection to popular sovereignty then of a practical nature (it is difficult or confusing to try to administer power so distributed) or of a conceptual one (it is logically necessary, "forzoso," that in civil society there be those who command, and those who obey)? Nor is it clear by what means "civil society [*la compañía civil*]" surrenders, quits, or strips itself of "potestad," "authority," at the origins of the republic—or even, indeed, who or what is the agent of that corporate action of stripping, Saavedra Fajardo's syntax being entirely opaque on this point.

It would, however, be wrong (or quite incomplete) to conclude that these obscurities, and the raft of similar ones we might identify throughout this and the following *empresas*, represent nothing but moments of argumentative weakness in *The Idea of a Christian Political Prince*. The "cuerpo del pueblo," the "voz articulada que les dio la naturaleza [use of speech which nature gave them]," and the notion of common consent that the latter makes possible: every one of Saavedra Fajardo's key concepts is determined and overdetermined by the cultural, political, linguistic, and religious dissensions—the crises, as Saavedra Fajardo's most influential recent editor, Manuel Fraga Iribarne, would not hesitate to say—that a "political prince" of Spain would inherit in 1640.[5] In this context, the incoherent *república* that rises from the *empresa's* fable has not only a descriptive or a pedagogical value but also a therapeutic function: the terms that make up Saavedra Fajardo's definition of the *república* register sociocultural fantasies and anxieties specific to Spain's crises, both recent (the devastating legacies, religious as well as economic, of Hapsburg confessionalism) and of the moment (internal crises, such as Portugal's secession from Spain in 1640 or the beginning of Catalonia's drive for independence that same year, as well as external ones, such as the increasingly antagonistic relations with France that marked the waning years of the Thirty-Years' War).[6]

One might put it this way. When *The Idea of a Christian Political Prince* murkily describes the abstract genealogies of the republic, it also seeks to convey to the prince a cultural fantasy that still inflects the political sense of the republic: the fantasy that *pueblos* acquire coherent corporate identities and wills when they are purged of alien bodies (Jews, *moriscos*, Lutherans, etc.), that political institutions can likewise be purged of competing interests and authorities (a particularly touchy matter at the time, as Saavedra Fajardo's frequent discussion of the figure of the *valido*, the monarch's intimate advisor or agent, makes clear), that the variety of religious inclinations, idioms, and languages in play in Spain's different regions can be subordinated to single languages or rites.

The *empresa* or *emblema*, with its dramatic, memorable combination of visual representation and conventional gloss, is one privileged early means of "engraining" or "implementing" in the prince or in his subjects the idea of the republic, as the celebratory snapshot will be another, much later means to the same end. It is imagined along these complex lines: part coherent program; part compensatory, locally inflected fantasy; part cliché. In the years that follow the publication of Saavedra Fajardo's *The Idea of a Christian Political Prince*, the work involved in implementing this fractious republican imaginary comes to be distributed across the institutions of the emergent nation: pedagogical, cultural, economic, political.

Compare, for instance, the definitions of *república* we find in the 1737 *Diccionario de la lengua castellana (de Autoridades)*, the standard dictionary of authoritative citations, and in the Royal Academy's 1947 *Diccionario de la lengua española*, the first postwar dictionary the academy published. In 1737, *república*, we read, is foremost "El gobierno del público" ("the public's government"). This slight, important qualification follows: "Oy se dice del gobierno de muchos" ("applied today to government by the many").[7] The "public," the *Dictionary* further tells us, is "el común del pueblo o ciudad" ("the commons or commonality of the town, or people, or of the city") and "el pueblo" exercises its sovereignty as an expression of what is held or recognized as common in a people or a domain. "Muchos" ("the many"), by contrast, weighs in here in a specifically derogatory sense, suggesting the fractious, confused polyarchy that Saavedra Fajardo's *The Idea of a Christian Political Prince* also resists. In this *república* of the early Enlightenment, the sovereignties of *el público* and of *muchos* are held together at best grudgingly, an emergent "fear of the masses," as Balibar has called it, inflecting what a century earlier had seemed a cultural anxiety concerning the incoherence of *el público*. "Oy" ("today"), in 1737, only the vigilance of institutions like the Royal Academy will arrest the drift toward a demotic moment when the "public" and the "mass" are synonymous.

By 1947, however, the Royal Academy's role in adjudicating this vanishing difference between *el público* and *muchos* has largely been set aside in the *Dictionary*'s definition. Instead, the 1947 *Dictionary* draws a distinction between two senses of the word *república*, the first a banal, general usage that makes *república* synonymous with *Estado*, and the second this more specific one: "Forma de gobierno representativo en que el poder reside en el pueblo, personificado éste por un jefe supremo llamado presidente" ("a form of representative government in which power resides in the people, who are personified in a supreme leader called 'president'").[8] The long history of the secularization of sovereignty is embedded in the procedure that this dictionary astutely refers to as *personificación*, the strictly linguistic version of the old *empresa*. Imagined here in an uneasy, if long-standing correspondence with political representation ("gobierno representativo . . . personificado"), personification mediates between the vesting of sovereignty in *el pueblo* and the investiture of the sovereign ("presidente"), who is at once the substitute for the people, the people's representative, and the singular figure in whom the attributes of the multitude (the *res populi*) assume anthropomorphic form. The president is the people's *persona* in the old Latin sense of the term: he is the anthropomorphic mask that popular sovereignty assumes when it is vested in an individual.

Much transpires between these three moments—an early modern conceptualization of the *res publica* expressed in the idiom of uneven secularization, the grudging early Enlightenment of dictionaries and encyclopedias, the immediate aftermath of the Second World War. These are the three moments I treat punctually and symptomatically throughout *Wild Materialism*. Saavedra Fajardo's brief fable concerning the origin of the republic, the anxious, grudging observation in the *Diccionario de la lengua castellana (de Autoridades)* that popular sovereignty threatens to become mere government by the masses, the tactical condensation in the Royal Academy's 1947 *Dictionary* of three quite distinct epistemological and politico-administrative functions in the rhetorical construction of the republic's *presidente*—any story that might stitch together these three moments is hardly uncontroversial. The critical languages available to us today for examining Spain's republicanism, and perhaps radical republicanism more generally, bear strong traces of one such story: the history of cultural personifications, exclusions, anxieties, substitutions, and elisions sketched here, stenographically, in the lexical drift of the term *república*.

But they also bear something more. The defeat of the Second Republic inseparably intertwined the *modern* notion of the republic with the experience and representation of exile. With the victory of the Nationalist forces and the expulsions and emigrations that followed, Spanish exiles carried the cause abroad, meditated upon it, re-formed *el pueblo* and its personifications in exile, tingeing them with melancholia, with distance.[9] The thought about the modern republic that Spanish republicanism concretely makes possible turns upon this circumstance of exile from the immediate experience, as from the memory and histories of the *república*. A form of witnessing and of critique, to an important degree this thought provides a momentarily general purchase, an angle from which to reflect upon the histories and circumstances that the republic bears—as if from outside, as if from a balcony across the street, or from abroad, *desde el exilio*, contemplating the intertwining of republicanism and exile from another distance. The sort of thought about the modern republic that the Spanish Republic makes possible depends upon something like a reflective exile from the experience of exile. It is work carried out within and without its mythological personification in the historical snapshots or clichés modernity consumes, exchanges, and circulates.

This critical exile from exile that study of Spanish republicanism now commands has its own history, one might even say its own time, its own tense. A specific relation to matters Spanish informs it, as does the melancholic idiom developed to treat Spanish cultural forms by the community of exiled intellectuals after the fall of the Second Republic. Here, for example, is how the philosopher María Zambrano begins to sketch for us the tense of her critical reflection upon her exile from the time of the Spanish Republic, how she meditates upon the time proper to republican thought in exile and upon the role that meditation—or reflection upon cultural forms broadly—might have in bringing about the implementation of the republic. She writes in the immediate shadow of the Civil War, from the bitter vantage of her exile in Cuba, then in Mexico, and she chooses to inflect a brief, allegorical tale with the experience of her moment, envisioning the reemergence of "Spain" from an exhausted modernity characterized all too patently by the success of fascism in Europe. The *relato* that Zambrano chooses to retell is none other than *Don Quixote*, by then a point of reference for Nationalist as well as Republican intellectuals. "Lo que le sucedió a Cervantes: Dulcinea" ("What Happened to Cervantes: Dulcinea"), published first in 1955 but written considerably earlier, is collected in *España, sueño y verdad*.[10] It follows chapters entitled "The Ambiguity of Cervantes" and "The Ambiguity of Don Quixote," written in a slightly different idiom, which explore (among other things) the twin suggestions that Don Quixote, who bears "el ancestral sueño de la libertad encadenada" ("the ancestral dream of liberty in chains") and also makes manifest "el conflicto de ser hombre en la historia, contra ella, a través de ella y aun más allá de ella" ("the conflict entailed in being man in history, against history, through history and even beyond history"), also represents a Spain that has never had what Zambrano calls "vocación de vencer" (what might be translated as a "disposition to win"), a vocation that falls upon "el hombre español" at the moment when he ceases to recognize himself in his history, the history of Spain, and in its personification in Don Quixote.[11] The circumstance that these first two essays describes is, on the face of it, disabling. But rather than take Cervantes's novel as mere defeatism, a bad example for the vulnerable republic, as Ramiro de Maeztu and other so-called "precursors of the Falange" would do, Zambrano recalls that the history of the melancholy knight does not come to an end but repeats itself in the heroic-mythological mode of a returning *quimera*—the chimerical desire to save the world. For Zambrano, it transpires, the novel is the aesthetic form by means of which something like "Spain"—a national, geographic, cultural entity with suddenly recognizable contours and characteristics—comes to define "Spanish" man's recognition of himself in history. More particularly, and perhaps more controversially, Zambrano reads *Don Quixote* and its immediate worlds as allegories of this emergent historical self-recognition. The figure of Don Quixote, "portadora del ancestral sueño de la libertad encadenada" ("bearer of the ancestral dream of liberty in chains"); the highly mythologized image of the "ingenio lego" or "lay genius," Cervantes, who writes out of a surprising externality to literary culture; the mysterious Dulcinea ("Dulcinea sola y blanca se consume"—"Dulcinea, solitary and pale, languishes and burns away"),[12] who marks the limits of the novel itself, a generic Pyrenees attaching the work to a continental tradition from which it also divides it—these are the characters in Zambrano's tale.

And Zambrano tells a good story. In "What Happened to Cervantes: Dulcinea" she imagines Cervantes as "enamorado" ("in love"), hence "perdidizo, sin errar" ("tending to lose himself, but without wandering or erring"), in language both wonderfully evocative and philosophically precise. She strikes up a strong, covert conversation with the vocabularies of decline, detumescence, and somnolence that Maeztu and others employed to describe the advent of the Spanish baroque and the decline of Habsburg power after the death of Charles V, descriptions of a nation "que viene dando tumbos hace siglos, nación con su genio dormido" ("a nation that has been stumbling and lurching for centuries, a nation whose genius lies asleep"), in the words of Félix García Blázquez.[13] Cervantes, Zambrano says, was indeed writing (or not writing) from within this decline, from within this decrepitude, from within a "mundo de ensueño" (a "dream-world") expressing his somnambulism, his half-wakefulness, his "ensimismamiento" or "self-absorption," finally, his "distracción." But something happened.

> ¿Qué le sucedió en verdad a don Quijote con Dulcinea? ¿Qué le sucedió a Cervantes? . . . Se sentía vagar en una especie de vacío, comenzaba a darse cuenta de que había puesto demasiada fe en la literatura. . . . Algo . . . entró como en la realidad misma en su mundo de ensueño, donde la realidad más real se hundía como en un nido. . . . No podía ni soñar en hacerla suya; era algo desconocido y que no sabía como tratar; ninguna de las mujeres lo había sacado de su distracción, de su ensimismamiento; ninguna le había dado una sacudida brusca, que es el despertar en la semivigilia, en el sonambúlico. Lo que llega en ese instante rompe el ensueño, y aunque sea una sombra, el rumor del ala de una mosca, es real del todo.[14]
>
> What really happened to Don Quixote with Dulcinea? What happened to Cervantes? . . . He felt himself wandering in a sort of vacuum, he began to realize that he had put too much trust in literature. . . . Something . . .

entered like reality itself into his dream world, in which the most real reality would sink, as into a nest. . . . He could not even dream of making her
his own; she was something unknown, which he did not know how to han-
dle; no woman had brought him out of his distraction, his self-absorption;
none of them had given him a sharp shake, which is what it means for the
sleep-walker to awaken in a half-sleep. What arrives in that instant breaks
the dream, and however much it may be a shade, the rumor of the wing of
a fly, it is utterly real.

What happened to Cervantes, Zambrano says, is the advent of an imaginary woman, the figure of Aldonza Lorenzo, who becomes Dulcinea. We
recognize—we readers of Cervantes, who share a relation to public culture
mediated by the legacies of *el manco de Lepanto*—the importance and recurrence of these moments in Cervantes's text, as well. Figures of interruption are crucial formally in *Don Quixote*—characters, objects, or events that
intrude from outside and incongruously, at the wrong moment, to break
the self-absorption of other characters or, indeed, of Cervantes himself—
characters such as the figure who famously opens the Prologue to the 1605
Quixote to help the stymied, blocked author to complete the Prologue and
publish the book, or objects like the manuscript sheet of paper that crosses
the wandering author-figure's path in Toledo, helping to open the work's
second section and serving to summon the figure of Cide Hamete's translator, a *morisco aljamiado* who chances on the marginal note in the manuscript that confirms for Cervantes that he is in possession of the lost
second part of *Don Quixote*. When the narrator asked him why he had
burst out laughing on glancing at the pages of the manuscript, "he replied
that it was because of something written in the margin of the book as an
annotation. . . . 'As I have said, here in the margin is written: "This Dulcinea of Toboso, referred to so often in this history, they say had the best
hand for salting pork of any woman in all of La Mancha." ' "[15] Zambrano
makes the point of Aldonza's and Dulcinea's appearance both more delicate and more difficult than Cervantes's imagined translator does by shifting her description from the preterit into the present tense (from "No
podía ni soñar en hacerla suya," "He could not even dream of making her
his own," to "Lo que llega en ese instante rompe el ensueño," "What
arrives in that instant breaks the dream"). In Zambrano's story, the scene
moves (or has moved) from the past to a sort of iterative present. The
historicity of the moment has changed; Aldonza's arrival affects the notion
of time in such a way that Cervantes's past experience is now Zambrano's
own, and our own as well.

What, then, is the nature of Aldonza's appearance? If Don Quixote represents the self-absorption and distraction that afflict a Spanish literary and political culture estranged from its historicity, then what does the figure of Aldonza represent, in this brief allegory? The questions are urgent ones, as Zambrano has inclined us to associate Aldonza's intrusion with the implementation, the coming to reality, of the republican alternative to the distraction that early-twentieth-century critics of the Left as well as the Right were quick to associate with the liberal bourgeois state. The event of Aldonza's appearance and of the intrusion of the friends, accidental texts, *morisco* translators are accidents, *hechos* or *sucesos* that arrive and summon the distracted writer into contact with—what?

With these questions, Zambrano departs dramatically from Ortega y Gasset and Unamuno: the distracted, impotent philosophico-political figure of Cervantic Spain is awakened from a decadent detumescence by the appearance of Aldonza, of the female philosopher, the philosopher as a woman. Dulcinea/Aldonza/Zambrano, equated with "poetic reason [*la razón poetica*]" and "Spanish materialism [*el materialismo español*]," becomes the supplementary literary device invoked and produced when thought slumbers weakly, indecisively. A portmanteau figure, she is the condition of possibility for thinking the relation between public and particular interest at and as the moment of crisis: Dulcinea/Aldonza/Zambrano is the triple personification of resistant republicanism.

But this personification works in this way, serves to implement this possibility of thought, only so long as we understand this appearing of the female philosopher, of literature, of irreducibly wild materialism to take place in what proves to be a profoundly disconcerting shape—not at all, for instance, in person. Say that we incline to see Aldonza as representing for Zambrano a figure of "the body [*el cuerpo*]," a term that Zambrano associates at roughly this time (ca. 1950) with Spanish *materia*, and with *poesía*, with *razón poética*. We then have before us in these lines from "What Happened to Cervantes: Dulcinea" something like the process that the much earlier work *Filosofía y poesía* (*Philosophy and Poetry*; 1939) describes for the Platonic poet: unlike the philosopher, "El poeta siente la angustia de la carne, su ceniza."[16] Aldonza awakens Cervantes from his self-absorption in a way that then allows him to consume that very awakening, by means of this Senecan "sentimiento de la angustia de la carne" ("feeling of dread and anguish of the flesh") and convert it into an aesthetic shape: "The poet lives according to the flesh; even more, he lives within it. But he penetrates it little by little. He makes his way inside it, masters its secrets, and in making it transparent, he spiritualizes it. He conquers the flesh for man by absorbing it to itself: he makes the flesh cease to be strange." The Spanish runs: "El poeta vive según la carne y más aun, dentro de ella. Pero, la penetra poco a poco; va entrando en su interior, va haciéndose dueño de sus secretos y al hacerla transparente, la espiritualiza. La conquista para el hombre, porque la ensimisma, la hace dejar de ser extraña."[17] In Zambrano's account, then, Cervantes's Platonic reconsumption of the figure of exteriority by means of poetry, his re-self-absorption or absorbing of the flesh to itself (*ensimismar*), is another version of the figure of the permanently alert, permanently suspended relation that the genuine republican must maintain toward the public sphere, for the public sphere represents the permanent temptation to spiritualize matter.

Zambrano has no truck with this conquest of spiritualization, either in the domain of the aesthetic or in the domain of the political. But her alternative becomes increasingly mysterious—and in one sense politically controversial. The pages that follow in Zambrano's "What Happened to Cervantes: Dulcinea" return again and again to Dulcinea's resistance to Cervantes, precisely to his incapacity to consume her. This resistance produces for Cervantes the capacity to write, to publish, to produce, in and by means of the novel, a relation to literary history from which the Spaniard derives an idea of the relation between universal and particular relations that is precisely not intuitive, perhaps not even an idea. Zambrano's argument runs like this. Aldonza, she suggests, breaks Cervantes out of his *ensimismamiento*, his self-regarding and his self-absorption, out of the distraction of thought about thought alone, by introducing the body, the body of a woman but also the stubborn fact of embodiment. This much is, of course, traditional: the alignment of the woman with matter, even in the peculiar form it takes here, is the basis of much misogynist writing. But the screen references to the interruptive figures in *Don Quixote* add another aspect to Zambrano's brief *relato*. In her reference to Aldonza, the indecorous sense of the body's materiality (Aldonza has the "best hand for salting pork in La Mancha") brings about—implements, we should says—a sort of bridging between public and private forms of identity and identification. On the one hand, Zambrano's screen allusion to Dulcinea/Aldonza works much as the marginal note in the Toledo manuscript does: it makes Dulcinea/Aldonza into a *cosa publica*, a body shared verbally if not physically. Remember the *morisco* translator: "This Dulcinea of Toboso, referred to so often in this history, they say had . . . [*Esta Dulcinea del Toboso, tantas veces en esta historia referida, dicen que tuvo* . . .]," an observation in which the impersonal operator *dicen*, "they say," is the mark of the public and of publication, as much an expression of Cervantes's fantasy of writerly success as is the appearance of spurious Don Quixotes and Sanchos throughout the 1615 *Don Quixote*. The allusion to Dulcinea/Aldonza works here as a bit of humor, as an allusion, precisely because a work has already been published (the First Part of *Don Quixote* in the case of Cervantes; all of the novel in the case of Zambrano's allusion), has been read, and can thus be preserved and remembered—the image of salting pork becoming an astonishingly daring figure for a culture's preservation of a public sense of identity in texts deposited in and recovered from a shared past reading experience. But on the other hand, the chain of substitutions and identifications leads not just from Dulcinea's ideal body to Aldonza's public one but also onward to Zambrano's own, the modern version of a written, writing intellectual who also (so the fantasy goes) interrupts the complacency of exiled republican melancholia no less than the torpor of the liberal bourgeois social formation.

The expression of Zambrano's intimate identification with the figure of heroic interruption, the strange figure of Dulcinea/Aldonza/Zambrano, works as *res*, that is, as a "thing" touched solely, privately, secretly, by the philosopher-poet-novelist's *relato* and at the same time a "thing" whose intimate, private touch frees the philosopher-poet-novelist from the distraction, the detumescent, narcissistic, self-regarding *ensimismamiento* represented by mere thought about thought. But Dulcinea/Aldonza/Zambrano works also as *res publica*, as a culturally sanctioned and recognized "thing" that has always already been told as a story, a public thing touched, alluded to, and salted away by the writing and preserving hand of Cervantes, a thing that touches the philosopher-poet-novelist and the reader precisely because it is already recognizably a public, and published, cultural formation. The ambivalence of this double, bridging scene finds expression in Zambrano's account of that first double touch: "[El poeta] la penetra [la carne] poco a poco; va entrando en su interior, va haciéndose dueño de sus secretos" ("[The poet] penetrates [the flesh] little by little. He makes his way inside it, masters its secrets"). Here a traditional, neo-Platonic eroticism sits uneasily next to the language of mastery and ownership, penetration and domination, threatening to tip over from a caressingly interior scene into the violence of a forceful encounter, a rape or the theft of what had been most closely and privately guarded.

Or put it this way. In any literary allusion, the argument might run, another work (by Cervantes, Haro Ibars, Blasco Ibáñez, etc.) has always been read already—if not actually read, by this or that particular reader, then read by a notional reader whose time and persona the allusion also and correlatively produces. The political personification of private subjects, of the movement from the intimacy of *res* to *res publica*, turns in structure upon the figure of allusion. We recognize each other and ourselves as those who recognize the work done in the present by one or another cultural form (like *Don Quixote* or the refunctionalization of the Second Republic). To this extent, the concept of the public interest, indeed of the republic more broadly, depends upon cultural forms that always preexist our time, and any time—we are far here from the mere shift from present to preterit tense that we observed earlier—and upon mythic ideas, like the notion of the universal itself, expressed in an utterly impersonal form: *dicen que*. And in this sense, the tale of the emergence of public interest from private secrets or private identities, the tale of *lo que le pasó a la república* as it arises from the narcissistic *ensimismamiento* of private thought, turns out to be always radically abstract and radically conservative.

But this is not the whole story. For Dulcinea/Aldonza/Zambrano enters, like the friend in the Prologue to the First Part of *Don Quixote*, not impersonally but also in person, and not only according to a mythic time, but *a deshora*, at the wrong moment, at the wrong time. What is more, the *deshora* of Dulcinea/Aldonza/Zambrano's appearing is associated with her persona, with her body, her materiality, her resistance to being consumed, to being *ensimismada*. And her appearing—as the most intimate, privately touched thing, as mere *res*, but also and necessarily as *res publica*—represents in Zambrano's thought an Irigarayan moment, an event that permanently interrupts thought's flow and the narcissistic experience of time that characterizes it into a melancholy, self-identical anteriority. Zambrano's turn to this split time and split person, at once impersonal and profoundly intimate, undercuts the notion that the public thing, the story always already told in which we recognize ourselves and each other, can ever be merely abstract, or merely a thing of the past. Dulcinea/Aldonza/Zambrano's allusive touch weakens the republic as an impersonal concept; it no longer has the inviolate coherence we once desired, no longer works upon us with the secret anteriority of a myth. Dulcinea/Aldonza/Zambrano's touch breaches the walls of the republic's historical and social isolation, and opens it to perpetual negotiation in the present, to the most intimate and the most exposed, public identifications.

Let me conclude by returning to the exceptionalist claims with which I opened: the claim that the concept of a radical republicanism emerges in the contemporary languages of political philosophy inflected by the specific trauma of the fall of the Second Republic and by the second wound of the commodification of that fall. We have seen Zambrano take the first steps toward defining the temporal and aesthetic dimensions of this radical republicanism. In her work, *res* and *res publica* emerge together as a troubled, nondialectical, weak concept, wed or bridged in the *empresa* (if it is one), in the portmanteau literary personification (if it can be called that), of Dulcinea/Aldonza/Zambrano.

This is coyly put. Consider, by contrast, so as to come to a clearer sense of the work of implementation that Zambrano's strange, three-part *empresa* is called on to carry out, these troubling, searching sentences from Edmund Husserl's 1935 "Vienna Lecture," perhaps the most important of his late works on the European crisis, the baggy group of writings and lectures he undertook in 1934 and left unfinished in 1937, at the advent of his last illness and of the European war. Constrained to clarity and economy by the format of the lecture, Husserl sets aside the extended analysis of European rationalism that we find in the crisis book, *The Crisis of European Sciences and Transcendental Phenomenology*, which he was drafting at the time. He closes the "Vienna Lecture" with a particularly touching description of the ways in which "transcendental phenomenology" can provide a "heroism of reason" that overcomes "naturalism" and achieves a "rebirth of Europe."[18] Not everything is finally pathos and retrospective legitimation anxiety, though. The lexicon to which the ailing philosopher turns for his description of the "heroic" agon between transcendental phenomenology and naturalism is catchy and violent in the extreme, a Wagnerian struggle against Wagnerian naturalism. (Just a few years later Maurice Merleau-Ponty would consider the task of philosophy in light of the disasters that Husserl had begun to foresee: the vein is heroic, but it is the heroism of a certain kind of work, of the assumption of responsibility and of historical circumstance, of making and fashioning. *Myth* is the disaster.[19]) Husserl evokes "barbarity" and "infinite struggle"; the "danger of weariness" and the "destructive blaze of lack of faith" parade against the backdrop of the "smoldering fire of despair" and the "ashes of great weariness." In the turbulent Europe that Husserl observes, the clash between competing constructions of human thought assumes proleptically the titanic, hyperbolic shape of the national clashes soon to erupt on the fields of Germany, Austria, and France. "Transcendental phenomenology" itself, Husserl writes, allows reason to:

> construct an absolutely self-sufficient science of the spirit in the form of consistently coming to terms with oneself and with the world as spiritual accomplishment. Here the spirit is not in or alongside nature [*in oder neben*

der Natur]: rather, nature is itself drawn into the spiritual sphere. Also, the ego is then no longer an isolated thing alongside other such things in a pregiven world; in general [*überhaupt*], the serious mutual exteriority of ego-persons, their being alongside one another, ceases in favor of an inward being-for-one-another and mutual interpenetration.[20]

The tentativeness, indeed, the contradictoriness of Husserl's formulation is striking. Here, the Wagnerian climax to Husserl's anti-Wagnerian tract rings out with a claim whose generality is not imagined apodictically, as constituting a regulative moment for transcendental phenomenology, or even pedagogically (indicating what lessons should be drawn from his lecture), but rather descriptively, even historically (such movements of thought occur or have occurred "in general"). And yet we feel that at this stage his argument should have stepped beyond these sorts of contingencies. If this or that movement of thought has merely occurred "in general," then one can envision circumstances in which it has not occurred or cannot occur: it could have been otherwise. But Husserl concludes with two much stronger claims, which can be made simultaneously only upon the shoulders of a very mixed sort of term indeed. The conclusion to the "Vienna Lecture" maintains that the transition from the minimal, private moment represented in the Cartesian tradition by the equation of *ens* with *res cogitans* to the origins of intersubjectivity is accomplished by means of transcendental phenomenology in general, that is, necessarily; and that transcendental phenomenology, as a method of thought with this goal, can indeed be taught—for instance, in a lecture such as he has just delivered. The contingent necessity that Husserl uses to characterize the peculiar logic at work at this moment—a logic both pedagogical and simply descriptive, apodictic but qualified—is also intended to be a figure of temporality, a figure meant to account for the timing of thought's movement from considering being as a thing (*ens*) alongside other natural things to considering being to be a thing in respect to the interiority of another, a "being-for-one-another."[21] Husserl's oblique account of the movement from the Cartesian *sum res cogitans* toward transcendental phenomenology thus opens generally, unpredictably, hesitantly, onto an unsuspected political ontology: a shelter for the intersubjective recognition of mutual interests and a common disposition toward the natural world: *sum res publica*.[22]

But in what shape does this movement occur? In what time? The "Vienna Lecture" closes describing a "heroism of reason" that will rescue Europe from weariness and create a new, "spiritual" Europe, and the form of thought and spirit that this "new Europe" requires. Europe emerges,

Husserl writes, from the ashes of weariness and decadence—from its "somnolence" or "tumescence," Zambrano's interlocutors might add—in the shape of the phoenix. Like his logical operator "generally," the figure of the phoenix is a rhetorical compromise formation that represents and condenses precisely what is not and cannot be naturalized about culture when it is understood as transcendental or immortal spirit: "out of the destructive blaze of lack of faith . . . will rise up the phoenix of a new life-inwardness [*aus der Asche der großen Müdigkeit der Phoenix einer neuen Lebensinnerlichkeit und Vergeistigung aufersteht*]":[23] the European republic is born and borne on the wings of this phoenix, at the touch, we might say, remembering Zambrano, of the phoenix's wing. This is moving—but for whom, how, and under what circumstances does this mythological figure of thought work? (The earliest reviews of Husserl's *Crisis* works object to the reemergence of a form of "subjectivism" that his earlier works had effectively dismantled.[24]) Perhaps more importantly, how does it arise? In this second respect, the phoenix, a figure and a vehicle for thought, a means to achieving the new European republic as well as a figure for thought regarding the *res publica* yet to come, remains peculiarly unthinkable for Husserl. The ashes of the old give rise to a new, more glorious bird, but only a mythological mode of narrative succession can present this account of an alternation between life and death under the aspect of (or "surrounded by," *umspannen*) what Husserl calls "absolute historicity, to which nature is subordinated as a spiritual structure."[25]

At this last, crucial stage in his argument, then, the phoenix shape of "absolute historicity" at which transcendental phenomenology methodically arrives also surrounds, shelters, and encloses that method and itinerary, the movement from *res cogitans* to *res publica*. In both forms, as a characteristic of the new European public thought and as a sheltering characteristic of the means for achieving that thought, absolute historicity unrolls according to an ideal timing that is iterative as well as apocalyptic, that combines the linear and circular narratives of decline and of rebirth familiar from Spenglerian metaphysics and from Christian eschatology. It is, therefore, properly conveyed under the mythico-religious aspect or *empresa* of the phoenix, which is to say that its time does not occur in nature or naturally, and even less does it occur historically.[26] This much may, with difficulty, be squared with Husserl's larger redefinition of European thought in the wake of its crisis. But as for the emergence of absolute historicity—as for whether it is necessarily entailed in the transcendental reduction, or is only accidentally manifest in the historical circumstances that Europe faces in 1938, or is as much an aspect of the world of myth as the *empresa* that so vividly captures it—on this crucial question the "Vienna Lecture" remains necessarily silent.

To the silence at the heart of Husserl's arrested mythical, mythological (movement toward, conceptual implementation of) republicanism, Zambrano's writings from exile oppose the melancholic clamor of a Spanish republicanism based in the work of the novel and its philosophy. To absolute historicity, as Husserl understands it, she contrasts a discontinuous account of history, culture, and time. To the unthinkable emergence of this absolute historicity in the "Vienna Lecture," Zambrano opposes the appearance *a deshora*, in an untimely fashion, of the female philosopher, thinkable as the materialization of the philosopher's work, affectively inflected by the melancholic awareness of that work's necessary drift—exile—into the domain of the consumable snapshot. The *empresa* of the phoenix in Husserl's work bespeaks the fantasy of the unperishing idea (of the achievement of the republic, of the transcendental content of the sign as repetition, become the ground for intersubjectivity), impervious to the accidents of material division into which it is only momentarily exiled. The phoenix always and necessarily arises from the ashes, as it has always done and must continue to do. Zambrano's account of the emergence of republicanism, by contrast, cannot rest in personifications, in *empresas*, in the comforting logic of myths; the weak concept that shelters Dulcinea/Aldonza/Zambrano does not find expression in myth's perfect time and figures—in part because of the melancholia with which it greets its reinsertion into (its exile into) eventual circuits and markets of symbolic and economic exchange. For Zambrano as for the critics who take up the task of thinking through the legacies of the Spanish republics, the experience of double exile reveals *res*, and a fortiori *res cogitans*, to be always and already *res publica*, a radically republican thing, and the republic to be always and already the secret at the heart of things, flesh, *natura rerum*. Also and therefore an intimate and intimately vulnerable, which is to say a *material*, concept, never sheltered in time or substance.

The disposition Zambrano's argument associates with the disclosing of the fundamentally vulnerable, material, even literary aspect of political concepts is melancholia: because, as the public secret at the heart of things as things, the republic has always been with us; and because, since we are exiles from the exile proper to the republic, which is to say, subjects outside the outside of the city, the republic has always been unreachable; our task is impossible and already, but trivially, accomplished. We never achieve the republic in time, but always, if at all, *a deshora*; never just in

person, but only as personifications (the wounded sovereignty of the political subject). We make one more effort, and we become republican; no
necessity joins our effort and the republican persona we seek to achieve.
Effort and action—including the act that is thought—are threaded
together causally; they represent the contingent association produced by
blind pleasure or blinding pain. We are far from Husserl.[27]

And yet neither alternative is satisfactory on its own; neither a mythic
heroism nor a melancholic disposition is adequate to the tasks I have
sought to describe; neither has a future alone. The promotion of terror,
in the specific sense I have been outlining throughout *Wild Materialism*, is
nothing other than the constant production of the relation—the fissure,
to return to the language of Poe's "The Fall of the House of Usher"—
between these two dispositions and between the two conceptual practices
to which they correspond. None of these terms is given: "producing" a
relation entails, correlatively, "producing" the terms (concepts, wounded
concepts) related; "producing" takes place where my conduct is intentional and where it is not. I act in person, as a sovereign subject; I act as
the personification of a principle, for instance, the principle of sovereign
subjectivity, and never as myself. Anything short of a divisive, dividing,
and in that sense pharisiacal or phares-iacal effort to produce terror out of
the theologico-political myths of the modern state imaginary results in the
false immediacy of terrorism. (Is most likely to result: it *could* be otherwise.) A phares-iacal, wild materialism, the promotion of terror as the
work of thought, cannot ensure that such efforts will succeed—but only
that they may.

NOTES

INTRODUCTION: TERRIBLE ETHICS

1. Michael Levin, "The Case for Torture," *Newsweek*, June 7, 1982. The essay has been widely anthologized, and is available online at http://www.coc .cc.ca.us/departments/philosophy/levin.html . It also appears in Linda H. Peterson and John C. Brereton, eds., *The Norton Reader: An Anthology of Expository Prose* (New York: W. W. Norton & Company, 2003), 694–96.

2. While the actual examples of acts or threats of "terror" should in principle carry more weight than hypothetical scenarios in laying out the utilitarian case for torture, they run into a number of practical and conceptual constraints. In the first place, and as is notorious, because the information obtained from torture is very often incorrect, actual cases in which it proves helpful to an investigation or juridical procedure are extraordinarily rare. In the second place, using actual examples of cases in which torture has "worked" to prevent an act of terrorism runs into what we might call the "hearsay" constraint. Because no government or organization wants to be seen to have used torture to gather information, it is difficult for governments or organizations to assert in the first person, one might say, that information derived from torture was actually used to prevent a specific attack. Instead, one can say that one has *heard* that this or that other government or organization has used the information—as when Alan Dershowitz maintains that the government of the Philippines in 1995 used information gathered from torture that "may have foiled plots to assassinate the pope and crash eleven commercial airliners . . . into the Pacific Ocean" (Alan M. Dershowitz, *Why Terrorism Works: Understanding the Threat, Responding to the Challenge* [New Haven, Conn.: Yale University Press, 2002], 137). One can even say something like this: "I, the CIA or the U.S. government, used information that the Philippines obtained, we hear, from torture in order to foil this or that plot." The Philippine government, in turn, can have recourse to the same sort of "hearsay" constraint: "In order to foil this or that plot, we, the government of the Philippines, passed on to the CIA or the U.S. government information obtained, we hear, from torture by this or that police organization." Responsibility for the act of torture always lies elsewhere, and any first-person utterances of the sort "I tortured for X or Y reason, to achieve A or B effect, to obtain L or M sort of

information" appears on the face of it self-stultifying: a subject that admits to torturing cannot, ipso facto, have the standing to make any claims about the reason for having committed torture.

Actual examples—if there are any—run into a further logical-pragmatic constraint. One might parse what passes as an "actual example" of the effective use of torture in this way. An assertion like "This bit of information, gleaned from prohibited interrogation tactics, was used to prevent an attack or a crime" is a combination of two sorts of statements. On the one hand, there are descriptions of states of affairs that make factual or referential claims. "We are or were in possession of this or that bit of information, at this time" is a statement that can be verified (or, presumably, disproven), and "A terrorist act (of one sort or another) did not occur at such and such a time, on this date, in this place" is a statement that also looks factual, looks in some sense true and verifiable (although, as in the first case, a rather restricted account of what is "factual" or "true" comes into play here). On the other hand, there are statements based on the operative or syncategorematic *combination* of seemingly factual statements. An assertion like "A terrorist act did not occur on this or that date *because* we were or are in possession of this or that bit of information" is a hypothesis that may under certain circumstances be valid. But it cannot be valid in all cases, and it is never *necessarily* valid. We can always imagine other reasons why an act, including a terrorist act, might not occur or have occurred on this or that day, ranging from accidents, to misfires, to the end of the world. The bibliography on torture is, sadly, a long one. See, recently, Sanford Levinson, ed., *Torture: A Collection* (New York: Oxford University Press, 2004).

3. I am stressing the aspect of calculation, or reckoning, so as to bring out the similarity of this notion of political community to what Weber (following Ferdinand Tönnies) calls an "associative social relation [*Vergesellschaftung*]," a grouping in which the "orientation of social action within it rests on a rationally motivated adjustment of interests or a similarly motivated agreement, whether the basis of rational judgments be absolute values or reasons of expediency" (Max Weber, *Economy and Society: An Outline of Interpretive Sociology* [1968; rpt. Berkeley: University of California Press, 1978], 40–41).

4. Dante Alighieri, *Purgatorio* X, ll. 103–11, trans. W. S. Merwin (New York: Alfred A. Knopf, 2000), 99; line spacing slightly modified to match the original.

5. On the history of the objectality of slaves, see Page DuBois, *Slaves and Other Objects* (Chicago: University of Chicago Press, 2003).

6. A careful account of the "hiatus" between ethical and political speech, in particular in the work of Levinas, may be found in Simon Critchley's "Five Problems in Levinas's View of Politics and the Sketch of a Solution to Them." *Political Theory* 32, no. 2 (2004): 172–85.

7. Sophocles, *Oedipus Rex*, ed. R. D. Rawe, rev. ed. (Cambridge: Cambridge University Press, 2006), 70–71. See, for the history of these lines of interpretation, Jean Bollack, *L'Oedipe roi de Sophocle* (Lille: Presses Universitaires de Lille, 1990), v. 3, 753: "Because 'bending the hands backward' was not a gesture by means of which one began a session of interrogative torture [*la mise à la question*], *apostrepsei* has almost always been translated as 'to bind.' . . . For 'twist,' translators rely on the description of Melanthios's punishment in the *Odyssey* . . . The threat is thus clearly designated, but not carried out" (my translation).

8. Seneca, *Oedipus*, ed. and trans. John G. Fitch (Cambridge: Harvard University Press, 2004).

9. Impossible to draw—or better yet, nonsensical. Here, for instance, is how Wittgenstein concludes his "Lecture on Ethics" (Ludwig Wittgenstein, "A Lecture on Ethics," *The Philosophical Review* 74 [1965]: 3–12):

> Now when this is urged against me I at once see clearly, as it were in a flash of light, not only that no description that I can think of would do to describe what I mean by absolute value, but that I would reject every significant description that anybody could possibly suggest, *ab initio*, on the ground of its significance. That is to say: I see now that these nonsensical expressions were not nonsensical because I had not yet found the correct expressions, but that their nonsensicality was their very essence. For all I wanted to do with them was just to go beyond the world and that is to say beyond significant language. My whole tendency and, I believe, the tendency of all men who ever tried to write or talk Ethics or Religion was to run against the boundaries of language. This running against the walls of our cage is perfectly, absolutely hopeless. Ethics so far as it springs from the desire to say something about the ultimate meaning of life, the absolute good, the absolute valuable, can be no science. What it says does not add to our knowledge in any sense. But it is a document of a tendency in the human mind which I personally cannot help respecting deeply and I would not for my life ridicule it. (11–12)

On the spurious necessity of universally firm distinctions (distinctions carrying what Wittgenstein here calls "absolute value"), I am thinking in particular of the line of pragmatist arguments insisting rightly, as Hilary Putnam puts it, that "From the fact that a distinction cannot be drawn in all cases, it does not follow in any way that it is not valid where it can be drawn" (Hilary Putnam, *Ethics Without Ontology* [Cambridge: Harvard University Press, 2004], 118). What might be called the *ontologization* of certain conceptual distinctions is indeed a particularly weak philosophical tactic, but it is nevertheless true that both Sophocles' and Seneca's plays turn on such distinctions. The works have counted as tragedies—have, indeed, defined the literary genre and a sub-genre of philosophical writing, from Hegel to Judith Butler—precisely because of the firm cultural, political, and even theological gravity with which they invest distinctions that are required, for reasons equally grave, to fail.

10. Page DuBois, *Torture and Truth* (New York: Routledge, 1991).

11. Seneca, *Oedipus*, ed. and trans. John G. Fitch (Cambridge: Harvard University Press, 2004), ll. 1052–61, pp. 110–11.

12. Luc Boltanski and Eve Chiapello, *The New Spirit of Capitalism*, trans. Gregory Elliott (London: Verso, 2005), 522–23.

13. Ibid., 106: "the network cannot in itself represent the support for a city. Given that membership of the network remains largely indeterminate, the very notion of a common good is problematic in the topic of the network because it is not known *between whom* a 'good' might be placed in 'common' and also, for that reason, *between whom* a scale of justice might be established." There is considerable friction between this conception of the ethical vacuousness of the "network" and the more messianic claims made for "empire" or "globalization" and its attendant collectivities (*turba*, the "populace," the mass: see Michael Hardt and Antonio Negri, *Empire* [Cambridge: Harvard University Press, 2000]).

14. Chantal Mouffe, *The Democratic Paradox* (London: Verso, 2000), 135.

15. Ernesto Laclau, *On Populist Reason* (London: Verso, 2005), 241.

16. This is how Laclau has recently put it. He is responding to Žižek's critique of his *On Populist Reason*: "My whole analysis is precisely based in asserting that any politico-discursive field is always structured through a reciprocal process by which emptiness weakens the particularity of a concrete signifier but, conversely, that particularity reacts by giving to universality a necessary incarnating body. I have defined hegemony as a relationship by which a certain particularity becomes the name of an utterly incommensurable universality. So the universal, lacking any means of direct representation, obtains only a borrowed presence through the distorted means of its investment in a certain particularity" (Ernesto Laclau, "Why Constructing a People Is the Main Task of Radical Politics," *Critical Inquiry* 32 [Summer 2006]: 647–48). Critchley's decisive essay, "Is There a Normative Deficit in the Theory of Hegemony?," may be found in *Laclau: A Critical Reader*, ed. Simon Critchley and Oliver Marchart (London: Routledge, 2004), 113–23.

17. Ernesto Laclau, *Emancipation(s)* (London: Verso, 1996). For an astute overview of the problem of universalism, see Linda M. G. Zerilli, "This Universalism Which Is Not One," *Diacritics* 28, no. 2 (1998): 3–20; reprinted in *Laclau: A Critical Reader*, ed. Critchley and Marchart, 88–111.

18. Jürgen Habermas, "Three Normative Models of Democracy: Liberal, Republican, Procedural," in *Questioning Ethics*, ed. Richard Kearney and Mark Dooley (New York: Routledge, 1999), 135.

19. Axel Honneth, *The Struggle for Recognition: The Moral Grammar of Social Conflicts*, trans. Joel Anderson (Cambridge: MIT Press, 1995), 171–79.

Honneth is, of course, aware that it is particularly tricky to renew the concept of *Sittlichkeit* in the wake of the critiques of sovereign subjectivity in the psychoanalytic, Wittgensteinian, and post-structural traditions. He seeks to address the disabling critique of classical autonomy and of the concept of the social in the essays collected in *The Fragmented World of the Social*, ed. Charles W. Wright (Albany: State University of New York Press, 1990).

20. Nancy Fraser, "Social Justice in the Age of Identity Politics: Redistribution, Recognition and Participation," in Nancy Fraser and Axel Honneth, *Redistribution or Recognition? A Political-Philosophical Exchange* (London: Verso, 2003), 25–26. Fraser completes her description of the domains in which this integration of recognition and redistribution should obtain: "In social theory . . . the task is to devise an account of contemporary society that can accommodate both the differentiation of class from status and also their mutual imbrication. In political theory, meanwhile, the task is to envision a set of institutional arrangements and policy reforms that can remedy both maldistribution and misrecognition, while minimizing the mutual interference likely to arise when the two sorts of redress arise simultaneously. In practical politics, finally, the task is to foster democratic engagement across current divides in order to build a broad-based programmatic orientation that integrates the best of the politics of redistribution with the best of the politics of recognition."

21. Honneth writes: " 'Symmetrical' has to mean that every individual, without any group being systematically disadvantaged, receives the chance to experience his or her own achievements and abilities as being valuable to society" (Axel Honneth, "Post-traditional Communities: A Conceptual Proposal," in his *Disrespect: The Normative Foundations of Critical Theory* [Cambridge: Polity, 2007], 261). A familiar critique of the fundamental Aristotelian ethical operator, *antipeponthos* ("reciprocity"), is entailed. Recall the moment in Book 5 of the *Nicomachean Ethics* where Aristotle moves from consideration of "what is just without qualification" or "absolutely just" to the domain of what he calls "political justice," that is, justice that "is found among men who share their life with a view to self-sufficiency, men who are free and either proportionately or arithmetically equal" (*Nicomachean Ethics*, 5.6). To talk about "what is just or unjust without qualification" or "absolute justice and absolute injustice," *haplos dikaios*, is to restrict one's comments abstractly to the order of definitions. To talk about "political justice . . . found among men who share their life with a view to self-sufficiency, men who are free and either proportionately or arithmetically equal" is to lay stress on the horizon notion of equality—on the possibility of equality, which serves as the horizon of judgments (equality before the law, understanding the law as what will govern differences between men). The existence of a principle of proportional or arithmetical equality among men means roughly that, although acts are ontologically incommensurable with their consequences and with the retribution

that might be exacted for them, principles of "measurement" for acts and their consequences can be derived such that one isn't forced into the mere formulation, attributed to Rhadamanthus, "that Justice is done when the doer of a deed suffers just what he did" or, in a slightly different idiom, into the principle of *lex talionis*: an eye for an eye, a tooth for a tooth. "Reciprocity" is the structure behind the principles of proportional and arithmetic equality. The inclination (on the evidence of this passage from the *Ethics*) is strong to imagine reciprocity as a mediating standard, a sort of actuarial table or general equivalent between one act and another, and between an act or acts and the consequences of that act: an eye is worth so much, this tooth this much, hence eyes and teeth can be exchanged for their general equivalents, and the moral and social costs of taking an eye or a tooth can be established with respect to both retributive and distributive principles of justice. The governing analogy, in Aristotle as much later in Marx, is the operation of money:

> All goods must therefore be measured by some one thing, as we said before. Now this unit is in truth need, which holds all things together (for if men did not need one another's goods at all, or did not need them equally, there would be either no exchange or not the same exchange); but money has become by convention a sort of representative of need; and this is why it has the name "money" [*nomisma*]—because it exists not by nature but by law [*nomos*] and it is in our power to change it and make it useless. There will, then, be reciprocity when the terms have been equated so that as farmer is to shoemaker, the amount of the shoemaker's work is to that of the farmer's work for which it exchanges. But we must not bring them into a figure of proportion when they have already exchanged (otherwise one extreme will have both excesses), but when they still have their own goods. Thus they are equals and associates just because this equality can be effected in their case. Let A be a farmer, C food, B a shoemaker, D his product equated to C. If it had not been possible for reciprocity to be thus effected, there would have been no association of the parties. That need holds things together as a single unit is shown by the fact that when men do not need one another, i.e. when neither needs the other or one does not need the other, they do not exchange, as we do when someone wants what one has oneself, e.g. when people permit the exportation of corn in exchange for wine. This equation therefore must be established. (Aristotle, *The Nicomachean Ethics*, 2d ed., ed. Lesley Brown, trans. David Ross [Oxford: Oxford University Press, 2009], 1133a-b, p. 88.)

This is a famously opaque passage. For a recent review of scholarship, as well as a compelling argument for considering this section of the *Ethics* to be a political, rather than an economic, argument, see Gabriel Danzig, "The Political Character of Aristotelian Reciprocity," *Classical Philology* 95, no. 4 (October 2000): 399–424. Most modern accounts of ethical judgment fall on one side or the other of Aristotle's brief scheme—that is, most accounts argue that bridging terms like *reciprocity* belong either on the side of absolute justice or on the side of political justice.

My view is that what Aristotle calls "reciprocity" functions in two ways: as a measuring stick, to be sure, but also as a device, a function. On the one hand, the *Nicomachean Ethics* argues that reciprocity has the form of a ratio or of an analogy, and a relation to such a form is thus common to both sides, as it were—to absolute justice and to political justice. Reciprocity is an essential attribute of justice, in the way that "producing food" is an essential attribute of the farmer, or "shoe-making" of the shoemaker. But, on the other hand, once Aristotle addresses this abstraction directly, we discover that the relations he has in mind—*nomos* and *nomisma*—relations of law and the form of money as abstract value—are the devices by means of which reciprocity is constituted. They are drawn, however, from the side of *political* ethics and not from the side of absolute ethics. *Reciprocity*, the bridging term between absolute justice and political justice, is thus a political function.

22. Patchen Markell, *Bound by Recognition* (Princeton: Princeton University Press, 2003), 187. Markell's useful critique of the lexicon and grammar of "recognition" proposes an alternative to the term's threateningly undemocratic effects—effects that flow in part from what he calls, strikingly, "the pleasure of sovereignty." In place of (or alongside) the bonds of recognition, he proposes "a multiplication and diffusion of the sites around which struggles for recognition are carried out, resisting the putatively sovereign state's implicit claim to hold a monopoly on the distribution of recognition and to be the ultimate arbiter of contests over identity" (188–89).

23. Fraser, "Distorted Beyond All Recognition," in Fraser and Honneth, *Redistribution or Recognition?* 202.

24. Honneth, "The Point of Recognition," in ibid., 263.

25. Simon Critchley, *Infinitely Demanding: Ethics of Commitment, Politics of Resistance* (New York: Verso, 2007), 130.

26. Philip Pettit, *Republicanism: A Theory of Freedom and Government* (Oxford: Oxford University Press, 1997), 67. An astute restatement of Pettit's position may be found in Norberto Bobbio and Maurizio Viroli, *The Idea of the Republic*, trans. Allan Cameron (Cambridge: Polity Press, 2003), in particular, in Viroli's contributions to the dialogue.

27. See his description in John Pocock, *The Machiavellian Moment: Florentine Political Thought and the Atlantic Republican Tradition* (Princeton: Princeton University Press, 1975).

28. In Max Henninger, "From Sociological to Ontological Inquiry: An Interview with Antonio Negri," *Italian Culture* 23 (2005): 159.

29. Isaiah Berlin's *Four Essays on Liberty* (Oxford: Oxford University Press, 1969) is the proximate source of this approach. The position that a "plurality"

of values does not, as in the work of Rawls, cover and flow from some basic, universally applicable and freestanding unitary or monist principle is best articulated by Judith Jarvis Thomson, *The Realm of Rights* (Cambridge: Harvard University Press, 1990), and "The Right and the Good," *Journal of Philosophy* 94 (1997): 273–98. See also William Galston, *Liberal Pluralism: The Implications of Value Pluralism for Political Theory and Practice* (Cambridge: Cambridge University Press, 2002), esp. chap. 7, "Democracy and Value Pluralism" (81–93), where the impasses between a normative democratic frame and the claims of fundamental pluralism are addressed (and, necessarily, left unresolved: as this tradition must express them, we are in the face of something close to an antinomy rather than a simple contradiction).

30. Emmanuel Levinas, "Substitution," in *The Levinas Reader*, ed. Seán Hand (Oxford: Basil Blackwell, 1989), 99; Emmanuel Levinas, *Autrement qu'être ou au-delà de l'essence* (The Hague: Martinus Nijhoff, 1978), 173. An original and important argument "demonstrating that a concept of asymmetrical substitution is central to both Lacan's and Levinas' theories of responsibility" can be found in Kenneth Reinhard's "Kant with Sade, Lacan with Levinas," *MLN* 110, no. 4 (1995): 785–808. See esp. 793–94.

31. For a cogent discussion of the metaphor in Levinas, see Rudolf Bernet, "The Traumatized Subject," *Research in Phenomenology* 30 (2000): 160–79. See also, more briefly, Fred C. Alford, *Levinas, the Frankfurt School, and Psychoanalysis* (Middletown, Conn.: Wesleyan University Press, 2002), 66–68.

32. Paul Ricoeur, "Otherwise: A Reading of Emmanuel Levinas's *Otherwise than Being, or Beyond Essence*,'" trans. Matthew Escobar, *Yale French Studies* 104, *Encounters with Levinas* (2004): 92–93. Ricoeur is citing from p. 90 of *Autrement qu'être*. Luce Irigaray's remarks about Levinas turn on the erotics of the touch, as well—though here what is at issue is the flesh rather than the skin. What seems to me distinctive about the story of Nessus is that it concerns the transformation of (the revelation of) skin (with all that it comports, as a logical surface, an envelope, a *limen*, the focus of aesthetic interest, form of the face, and so on) into flesh. See Irigaray's "The Fecundity of the Caress: A Reading of Levinas, *Totality and Infinity* section IV, B," in *Face to Face with Levinas*, ed. Richard A. Cohen (Albany: State University of New York Press, 1986), 231–56.

33. A groundbreaking treatment of the phenomenon of allusion in Levinas's work may be found in Gabriel Riera's "'The *Possibility* of the Poetic *Said*' in *Otherwise than Being* (Allusion, or Blanchot in Levinas)," *diacritics* 34, no. 2 (2004): 14–36. Some of what Riera argues concerning Levinas's allusions to Blanchot is pertinent to the allusion to the tunic of Nessus as well—though not all. This is how Riera puts it:

> although in *Otherwise than Being* Lévinas finally acknowledges "poetic" ability to suggest significations that exceed the order of discourse and even endows it

with a (quasi)-ethical force, this acknowledgment goes without saying, or is merely implied (*sous-entendu*). This work marks a "linguistic turn" in Lévinas's thinking, evinces a different conception of language from the one prevailing in *Totality and Infinity*, and even transforms some of the key concepts of "Reality and Its Shadow." But this acknowledgment appears only by way of an *allusion* to Maurice Blanchot's *The Madness of the Day*. . . . Lévinas's indirect reference marks the site of a complex intertextual grafting: what the poetic *said* simply *suggests*, that "language would exceed the limits of what is thought," becomes operative in Lévinas's own text. It allows welcoming the "otherwise than being" and putting into place a writing whose double temporality (diachrony) lets the other "come to thought, as approach *and* response" [Maurice Blanchot, *L'écriture du désastre* (Paris: Gallimard 1980), 41; *The Writing of the Disaster*, trans. Ann Smock (Lincoln: University of Nebraska Press, 1986), 36]. It is through this allusion and grafting of Blanchot's text that Lévinas makes the structure of the primary ethical signification (*saying*) explicit and produces it as a form of writing that undermines the primacy of Being and its systemic closure. There is much more at stake in this allusion than the simple illustration of the suggestive richness of poetic language, then, since through Blanchot, Lévinas not only maps out the topology of the "prison-house of language," but also shows the way out. (15)

34. On the "passive, meaningless, and evil" "phenomenology of suffering" in Levinas, consult William Edelglass, "Levinas on Suffering and Compassion," *Sophia* 42, no. 2 (2006): 43–59, esp. 46–48.

35. Sophocles, *Women of Trachis*, in *Electra and Other Plays*, trans. David Raeburn (London: Penguin, 2008), ll. 1046–5751.

36. For a careful analysis of ambiguity in the Levinasian corpus, see D. H. Brody, "Emmanuel Levinas: The Logic of Ethical Ambiguity in *Otherwise than Being, or Beyond Essence*," in *Research in Phenomenology* 25 (1995): 177–203. His remarks on the interruption that ambiguity supposes seem pertinent to my analysis of Levinas's allusions. See, e.g., 198.

37. Deianira uses *aphrastos* earlier in the *Trachiniae* to describe the inexpressibly strange decomposition of the tuft of wool with which she spread Nessus's blood on the tunic:

> But while
> I was going inside again, I saw an omen
> Too strange for words, beyond all comprehension.
> I must have thrown the tuft of wool right into
> A patch of sunlight. And as it started to heat,
> The whole of it shrivelled up and crumbled to powder
> There on the ground. (692–700)

38. A useful, comprehensive account of the role of the gift in Levinas's ethical work, especially in the "Substitution" essay (and chapter of *Otherwise*

than Being) can be found in Robert Bernasconi's "What Is the Question to Which 'Substitution' is the Answer?" in *The Cambridge Companion to Levinas*, ed. Simon Critchley and Robert Bernasconi (Cambridge: Cambridge University Press, 2002), 234–52. No consideration of the political import of Levinas's work is complete without accounting for the arguments gathered in the volume of the journal *Parallax* entitled *Levinas and Politics*, ed. Simon Critchley (8, no. 3 [2002]). I have profited particularly from Alan Montefiore's "Levinas and the Claims of Incommensurable Values," 90–102.

39. I am arguing, then, something different from what Thomas Carl Wall proposes regarding Levinas's thought-image:

> What happens in Levinas, what passes under the *word* ethics, is no ethics per se, no relation as such. What happens is a relation that is no relation, that cannot but be betrayed, and by which I cannot but be obligated, because the "essence" of the relation to *Autrui* is *au-delà de l'essence*—is betrayal "itself," or is that which undermines and hollows out all real relations. This is precisely how the other person obligates me: *for this other person is without relation*, is alone and mortal, is already beyond my powers and, therefore, I, too, am without relation. Hence my anxiety, and hence the "restlessness" in the self of which Levinas so often speaks. What "binds" me to the other person is the *nonrelation* to the Other, the nothing or no-relation that I, myself, *am*. My skin, a Nessus tunic. (Thomas Carl Wall, *Radical Passivity: Levinas, Blanchot, and Agamben* [Albany: State University of New York Press, 1999], 33–34.)

The stutter at the close of this citation is symptomatic: how are what "I, myself, *am*," "My skin," and "a Nessus tunic" organized argumentatively? What links them—syntactically, syncategorematically? What is their *relation*?

Alain David concludes a provocative essay on Levinas by linking Levinas's thought to republicanism: "I'd like to say this, one last time, a little as an anecdote, but by coming back at the same time to my first question, which was very concrete, and also to the French register to which Levinas stuck and towards which he adjusted phenomenology. The French word *Republic* probably means a lot of things and among all those things the creation of what is called 'associations.' These associations originate in a law voted in 1901, which allows, under certain conditions, associations to be created. The best part in these associations means this: when in a democracy everybody can claim his right in a court of justice, we still have to imagine the voice of someone who can't be heard or appear in the 'concrete universal,' the only place where, according to Hegel, law is acted out. That a State should thus be able to give a chance to the Improbable, without a place in the sun defines, by contrast with simple democracy—and with something more to it—the Republic: a version of the society of the Torah invented just after the Dreyfus Affair" (Alain David, "Unlimited Inc," *Parallax* 8, no. 3 [2002]: 88–89).

40. Simon Critchley, "The Original Traumatism: Levinas and Psychoanalysis," in *Questioning Ethics: Contemporary Debates in Philosophy*, ed. Richard Kearney and Mark Dooley (London: Routledge, 1999), 239.

41. Critchley's account of Levinas's encounter with psychoanalysis seems to me unsurpassed: "The Levinasian subject is a traumatized self, a subject that is constituted through a self-relation experienced as a lack, where the self is experienced as the inassumable source of what is lacking from the ego—a subject of melancholia, then. . . . Without trauma, there would be no ethics in Levinas's particular sense of the word. . . . The passage to justice in Levinas—to the third party, the community and politics—passes through or across the theoretical and historical experience of trauma. No democracy without the death drive!" (ibid., 240). In a different essay, he writes: "The other, which resists my attempts at comprehension, is presented to me in a scream that recalls me to the memory of my own screaming, my own trauma, my own 'pre-historic' experience of pain, an archaic memory laid down in relation to my first satisfying/hostile object. . . . This structure of the scream gives us the pattern of substitution in Levinas, where the scream would be the dimension of Saying that would elucidate the pre-history of the subject in its essential intrication with alterity" (Simon Critchley, "*Das Ding*: Lacan and Levinas," in his *Ethics, Politics, Subjectivity* [London: Verso, 1999], 210). Bettina Bergo argues for understanding Levinas's work to be developing toward what she calls "thinking that: (1) emphasized the dynamic and symptomatic quality of affectivity from enjoyment to *Angst*; and (2) developed a conception of the split subjectivity whose actuality resembles a comet's tail, shining clearly at one end and shading off into semiconsciousness then unconsciousness at the other. That thinking," she concludes, "was psychoanalysis" (Bettina Bergo, "What Is Levinas Doing? Phenomenology and the Rhetoric of an Ethical Unconscious," *Philosophy and Rhetoric* 38, no. 2 [2005]: 123). Fred C. Alford takes a different approach and studies Levinas through Winnicott rather than Freud in his "Levinas and Winnicott: Motherhood and Responsibility," *American Imago* 57, no. 3 (2000): 235–59.

42. Sigmund Freud, *Beyond the Pleasure Principle*, in *The Standard Edition of the Complete Psychological Words*, ed. and trans. James Strachey (London: The Hogarth Press, 1955), 18:12. The German is from *Jenseits des Lustprinzips*, in *Gesammelte Werke* (Frankfurt am Main: S. Fischer, 1999), 13:9–10. Freud is responding to the wealth of new literature on traumatic war neuroses—on "shell shock," as it came to be called in England—following the end of the First World War. The decisive contribution to the identification of the pathology (or rather, to the naming of the group of symptoms exhibited by returning soldiers) was Charles S. Meyers, "Contributions to the Study of Shell Shock," *The Lancet*, February 13, 1915, 316–20, and his later, revised account of the

etiology of shell shock, *Shell Shock in France, 1914–1918* (Cambridge: Cambridge University Press, 1940). A recent treatment of the German experience with "war neuroses" is Paul Lerner's *Hysterical Men: War, Psychiatry and the Politics of Trauma in Germany, 1890–1939* (Ithaca, N.Y.: Cornell University Press, 2003). For an earlier review of the German literature on shell shock, see Doris Kaufmann, "Science as Cultural Practice: Psychiatry in the First World War and Weimar Germany," trans. A. J. Wells, *Journal of Contemporary History* 34, no. 1 (January 1999): 125–44. The *Lancet* exchanges in 1916 were especially fruitful: see M. D. Eder, "The Psycho-Pathology of the War Neuroses," *The Lancet*, August 12,1916, and Harold Wiltshire, "A Contribution to the Etiology of Shell Shock," *The Lancet*, June 17, 1916; see also Frederick W. Mott, *War Neuroses and Shell Shock* (London: Henry Froude and Hodder & Stoughton, 1919). A recent, popular account of the circumstances surrounding Freud's reflections on war neuroses may be found in Ben Shephard's *A War of Nerves: Soldiers and Psychiatrists, 1914–1994* (London: Jonathan Cape, 2000); a review of the early literature can be found in Edward M. Brown, "Between Cowardice and Insanity: Shell Shock and the Legitimation of the Neuroses in Great Britain," in *Science, Technology and the Military*, ed. Everett Mendelsohn, Merritt Smith, and Peter Weingart (Dordrecht: Kluwer, 1988), 323–45; and in Ted Bogacz, "War Neurosis and Cultural Change in England, 1914–22: The Work of the War Office Committee of Enquiry into 'Shell-Shock,'" *Journal of Contemporary History* 24, no. 2 (April 1989): 227–56. Consult also Kurt Eissler's useful *Freud und Wagner-Jauregg vor der Kommission zur Erhebung militärischer Pflichtverletzungen* (Vienna: Löcker, 1979), trans. as *Freud as an Expert Witness: The Discussion of War Neuroses Between Freud and Wagner-Jauregg*, trans. Christine Trollope (Madison, Conn.: International Universities Press, 1986).

Freud's contemporaneous (1920) "Memorandum on the Electrical Treatment of War Neurotics," *International Journal of Psycho-Analysis* 37 (1956): 16–18, ends on a mixture of wish fulfillment and the assertion of disciplinary or professional success. He writes:

> I am in a position to bring forward conclusive evidence of the final break-down of the electrical treatment of the war neuroses. In 1918 Dr. Ernst Simmel, head of a hospital for war neuroses at Posen, published a pamphlet in which he reported the extraordinarily favorable results achieved in severe cases of war neurosis by the psychotherapeutic method introduced by me. As a result of this publication, the next Psycho-Analytical Congress, held in Budapest in September 1918, was attended by official delegates of the German, Austrian and Hungarian Army Command, who promised that Centres should be set up for the purely psychological treatment of war neuroses. This promise was made although the delegates can have been left in no doubt that with this considerate,

laborious and tedious kind of treatment it was impossible to count on the quickest restoration of these patients to fitness for service. Preparations for the establishment of Centres of this kind were actually under way, when the revolution broke out and put an end to the war and to the influence of the administrative offices which had hitherto been all-powerful. But with the end of the war the war neurotics, too, disappeared—a final but impressive proof of the psychical causation of their illnesses. (18)

This is Doris Kaufmann's dry assessment of Freud's conclusion: "However, Freud was proved wrong: interest in the war neurotics did not cease after November 1918. It was clear to all concerned that the coercion therapies predominantly practised had been measures for disciplining patients in the interests of the military leadership" (Kaufmann, "Science as Cultural Practice," 140).

43. Freud, *Beyond the Pleasure Principle*, 12–13.

44. "Neurasthenia and Shell Shock," *The Lancet*, March 18, 1916), 627. Cited in Santanu Das, *Touch and Intimacy in First World War Literature* (Cambridge: Cambridge University Press, 2005), 195. An influential treatment of the topic is Eric Leed's *No Man's Land: Combat and Identity in World War* (Cambridge: Cambridge University Press, 1979).

45. Freud's remarks in *Beyond the Pleasure Principle* echo and expand upon this earlier observation, in the *Introductory Lectures on Psychoanalysis*: "I shall avoid going more closely into the question of whether our linguistic usage means the same thing or something clearly different by '*Angst* [anxiety],' *Furcht* [fear]' and '*Schreck* [fright].' I will only say that I think '*Angst*' relates to the state and disregards the object, while '*Furcht*' draws attention precisely to the object. It seems that '*Schreck*,' on the other hand, does have a special sense; it lays emphasis, that is, on the effect produced by a danger which is not met by any preparedness for anxiety [*die Wirkung einer Gefahr hervorzuheben, welche nicht von einer Angstbereitschaft empfangen wird*]. We might say, therefore, that a person protects himself from fright by anxiety" (Sigmund Freud, *Introductory Lectures on Psychoanalysis*, *The Standard Edition of the Complete Psychological Works*, 16:395; *Vorlesungen zur Einführung in die Psychoanalyse, Gesammelte Werke*, 11:410). A recent, popular description of the distinction between "fear" and "anxiety" may be found in Joanna Bourke's *Fear: A Cultural History* (London: Virago, 2005), 189–92.

46. Hannah Arendt, *The Origins of Totalitarianism* (1948; rpt. New York: Schocken Books, 2004), 598. Adriana Cavarero's *Orrorismo: Ovvero della violenza sull'inerme* (Milan: Feltrinelli, 2007), translated as *Horrorism: Naming Contemporary Violence*, trans. William McCuaig (New York: Columbia University Press, 2009), extends Arendt's argument quite beautifully. Cavarero's claim is that Arendtian "total terror" shades into something quite different:

horror, no longer associated (as in terror) with panic or in any sense with the physics of movement, but rather with stasis. Not with mediation (as the instrumental logic of terror always is, in Arendt), but with immediacy, an excess of immediacy. Her opening chapters, distinguishing "terror" from *orrore*, are illuminating.

47. Edgar Allan Poe, "The Fall of the House of Usher," in *Poetry and Tales*, vol. 1 of *Edgar Allan Poe*, ed. Patrick Francis Quinn (New York: Library of America, 1984), 320.

48. Jacques Rivette, "De l'abjection," *Cahiers du cinéma* 120 (June 1961): 54–55.

1. THE ETHIC OF TERROR

1. In its earliest form, this chapter was read at conferences at Yale University, at the Center for Literary and Cultural Studies at Harvard, and at the Duke University colloquium Brokering Spanish Postnationalist Culture: Globalization, Critical Regionalism, and the Role of the Intellectual, in 1999; I am very grateful for the spirited comments it received. A brief version was published as "The Ethic of Terror in Radical Democracy," *Arizona Journal of Hispanic Cultural Studies* 7 (2003): 173–93. All the translations, except where marked, are my own.

2. See Giuliana Di Febo, *Teresa d'Avila: Un culto Barocco nella Spagna franchista* (Naples: Liguori Editore, 1988). Di Febo tells, wittily and comprehensively, the story of Franco's use of Teresa of Avila's hand during his campaign against the Republic (1936–39). Franco recovered the relic from Republican forces and kept it with him during the war and until his death. Various urban legends attach to the saint's hand; Franco is reputed to have had the relic given the rank of general in his army.

3. More specifically, Matesa, a textiles company directed by an associate of Franco's minister of development, Laureano López Rodó, was discovered in August 1969 to have been involved in a massive diversion of state funds obtained through the Banco de Crédito Industrial. These funds had later been used to bankroll projects carried out by the Opus Dei outside of Spain; not surprisingly, it turned out that the principal agents in this intrigue, all high-ranking members of Franco's government, were themselves members of Opus Dei. A confrontation within the government ensued between the faction associated with the traditional Falange (Manuel Fraga most prominently) and the *renovadores*, religious technocrats allied with Opus Dei. The appointment of Admiral Luis Carrero Blanco as Franco's successor followed the destitution of a number of cabinet ministers associated with Matesa and with Opus Dei, but as Carrero was himself a close ally of the Opus faction, the *renovador* group within the government paradoxically found its position much more secure after the scandal than before it.

4. See Paul Preston, *Franco: A Biography* (New York: Basic Books, 1994), 270, 694–95; and Javier Tusell and Genoveva García Queipo de Llano, *Carrero: La eminencia gris del régimen de Franco* (Madrid: Ediciones Temas de Hoy, 1993), 344–64.

5. In late medieval jurisprudence, *mortmain* refers to a restricted modality of ownership, particularly of tenancies or land, such that properties held in *mortmain* cannot be sold or expropriated. (They are in this sense *entailed* properties.) Spanish law preserved the principle of *mortmain* or "ley de manos muertas" until the notorious *desamortizaciones*, or seizures, in particular of entailed Church property, carried out by Juan Álvarez Mendizábal between 1834 and 1855.

6. Raymond Williams, *Marxism and Literature* (Oxford: Oxford University Press, 1977), 132.

7. Ibid., 133.

8. Sigmund Freud, *Jokes and Their Relation to the Unconscious*, vol. 8 of *The Standard Edition of the Complete Psychological Works of Sigmund Freud*, trans. James Strachey (London: The Hogarth Press, 1960), 143; my emphasis.

9. Ibid., 158.

10. Edmund Burke, *Reflections on the Revolution in France* (Oxford: Oxford University Press, 1999), 33.

11. Compare Walter Laqueur, *The Age of Terrorism* (Boston: Little, Brown, 1987), 26.

12. Étienne Balibar, *La crainte des masses: Politique et philosophie avant et après Marx* (Paris: Galilée, 1999), 293.

13. Cited in Catherine Kintzler, "Terreur et vertu: Métaphysique, morale et esthétique au comble du politique," in *La République et la terreur*, ed. Catherine Kintzler and Hadi Rizk (Paris: Kimé, 1995), 17.

14. Ibid.

15. Peter Widdowson makes a cogent argument for recovering the notion of terrorism as critique: "Terrorism may be, in itself, a 'charade'; but it is the sign and symptom of a reaction to the terroristic behaviour of the Western liberal democracies, in which there is also a political vacuum in terms of collective opposition to them" ("Terrorism and Literary Studies," *Textual Practice* 2, no. 1 (1988): 20). Consider also Negri's early argument: "Violence always presents itself to us as synthesis of form and content. In the first place, as an expression of proletarian counterforce, as a manifestation of the process of self-valorization. In the second place, as a destructuring and destabilizing force—which is to say as a *productive force* and as an *anti-institutional force*. It is therefore evident that proletarian violence need not show itself in an exemplary way, nor to choose for itself exemplary objectives or targets . . . the centrality of violence presents itself all the more as synthesis of content and

form; of a form of exclusion, by excluding the enemy; and of rationality, measure, definition of the refusal of labor. Violence is the *rational cord [filo razionale]* that binds *[legga]* proletarian valorization to the destructuring of the system, and this destructuring to the destabilization of the regime. Violence is a revolutionary project become effective because the desirability of the content has become the form of the programme, and because this program has been becoming a dictatorship" (*Il dominio e il sabotaggio* [Milan: Feltrinelli, 1978], 67–68).

16. Cf. Ernesto Laclau and Chantal Mouffe, *Hegemony and Socialist Strategy* (London: Verso, 1985), 93–105; and José Luis Piñuel, *El terrorismo en la transición española* (Madrid: Editorial Fundamentos, 1986), 13.

17. Cited in Luigi Bruni, *E.T.A.: Historia política de una lucha armada* (Bilbao: Txalaparta Argitaldaria, 1988), 154–55.

18. Carlos Marighella, "Minimanual of the Urban Guerrilla," rpt. in *The Terrorist Classic: Manual of the Urban Guerrilla*, ed. and trans. Gene Hanrahan (Chapel Hill: Documentary Publications, 1985), 49, 84; see also Martha Crenshaw, "The Logic of Terrorism: Terrorist Behavior as a Product of Strategic Choice," in *Origins of Terrorism: Psychologies, Ideologies, Theologies, States of Mind*, ed. Walter Reich (Cambridge: Woodrow Wilson International Center for Scholars and Cambridge University Press, 1990), 18.

19. José Antonio Primo de Rivera, *Obras completas*, ed. Agustín del Rio Cisneros (Madrid: Dirección general de informaciones públicas españolas, 1952), 66–67.

20. See Fernando Reinares: "The crisis derives in this way from an evident conflict between two wills: basically, the will to be Basque, and the will to be Spanish. The dialectic between being Basque and being Spanish crystallizes this antagonism in a polarization, while hostility catalyzes the conflict. At the root of the confrontation there is an aspiration, which is understood as a right: the recovery *[la recuperación]* of self-government, of Basque *sovereignty*" (Reinares, *Violencia y política en Euskadi* [Bilbao: Desclée de Brouwer, 1984], 9). This arrangement of "will," "aspiration," and "right" bears closer scrutiny than I can give it here, but it is worth noting that Reinares's last claim—that the "aspiration" toward self-government has the shape of the "recovery" of a historical formation lost to a central administration—is directly contested by Basque *españolistas* like Jaime Ignacio Del Burgo, *Soñando con la paz: Violencia terrorista y nacionalismo Vasco* (Madrid: Temas de Hoy, 1994).

21. Josep Carles Clemente, *Historias de la transición (1973–1981)* (Madrid: Fundamentos, 1994), 17, cited in Teresa Vilarós, *El mono del desencanto: Una crítica cultural de la transición española (1973–1993)* (Madrid: Siglo XXI, 1998), 125. The most complete account of the incident is in Joaquín Bardavío, *La crisis: Historia de quince días* (Madrid: Sedmay, 1974).

22. Eva Forest (writing as Julen Agirre), *Operation Ogro: The Execution of Admiral Luis Carrero Blanco*, trans. Barbara Probst Solomon (New York: Quadrangle/NYTimes Book Co., 1975), 46.

23. Vilarós, *El mono del desencanto*, 120, 125.

24. Manuel Campo Vidal, *Información y servicios secretos en el atentado a Carrero Blanco* (Barcelona: Argos Vergara, 1983), 28; Ismael Fuente, Javier García, and Joaquín Prieto, *Golpe mortal: Asesinato de Carrero y agonía del franquismo* (Madrid: El Pais/PRISA, 1983), 167–79.

25. Luis Herrero, *El ocaso del régimen: Del asesinato de Carrero a la muerte de Franco* (Madrid: Ediciones Temas de Hoy, 1995), 13–14.

26. Forest, *Operation Ogro*, 89; I have slightly modified the translation.

27. For the function of excretive images as forms of symbolic resistance, see Begoña Aretxaga, "Dirty Protest: Symbolic Overdetermination and Gender in Northern Ireland Ethnic Violence." *Ethos* 23, no. 2 (1995): 125.

28. Forest, *Operation Ogro*, 170–71.

29. Cited in Fernando Vizcaíno Casas, *1973/El año en que volaron a Carrero Blanco* (Barcelona: Editorial Planeta, 1993), 298.

30. Begoña Aretxaga, "Playing Terrorist: Ghastly Plots and the Ghostly State," *Journal of Spanish Cultural Studies* 1, no. 1 (2000): 53.

31. Ibid.

32. Compare Álvaro Baeza: "The appearance of antiterrorist groups dedicated to fighting against ETA, FRAP, and GRAPO can be dated precisely: they are born the day after December 20th, 1973, the date when Admiral Luis Carrero Blanco, the president of Spain, is assassinated in a terrorist attack by ETA" (*GAL: Crimen de estado* [Madrid: ABL, 1995], 68). See also Campo Vidal, *Información y servicios secretos*, 28–31.

33. Campo Vidal, *Información y servicios secretos*, 64, citing from *El Economista*.

34. "El Generalísimo regresa al palacio de El Pardo en estado satisfactorio," *ABC* (Madrid), December 27, 1961, p.1.

35. Ramón Soriano, *La mano izquierda de Franco* (Madrid: Planeta, 1981), 16.

36. A sketch of the character attributed at the time to Dr. Cristóbal Martínez Bordiu, Marquis of Villaverde, can be found in Tatjana Pavlovic's *Despotic Bodies and Transgressive Bodies: Spanish Culture from Francisco Franco to Jesús Franco* (Albany: State University of New York Press, 2003), 55–56.

37. "Millones de españoles se unen a la rebelión de los vascos contra ETA y HB," *El Pais* (Madrid), July 15, 1997, p. 1.

38. *Diccionario de las metáforas y refranes de la lengua castellana*, ed. José Musso y Pontes (Barcelona: N. Ramírez, 1876), 148.

2. *PHARES*; OR DIVISIBLE SOVEREIGNTY

1. Nancy Fraser, "Distorted Beyond All Recognition," in Nancy Fraser and Alex Honneth, *Redistribution or Recognition?* 202.

2. Particularly in Carl Schmitt, *Political Theology: Four Chapters on the Concept of Sovereignty*, trans. George Schwab (Cambridge: MIT Press, 1985), 36, but also see Schmitt, *The Concept of the Political*, trans. George Schwab (Chicago: University of Chicago Press, 1996), 66–67 and following, where Schmitt discusses Machiavelli's rehabilitation in the late Enlightenment, and in particular Cromwell's dislike for Spain, which Schmitt takes to be the signal example of the "high point of politics," when "the enemy is, in concrete clarity, recognized as the enemy" (67).

3. Jean Bodin, *The Six Books of a Commonweale*, trans. Richard Knolles (London: G. Bishop, 1606), 85. The French can be found in Jean Bodin, *Les six livres de la république de I Bodin* (Lyon: Jean de Tournes, 1579).

4. Ibid., 71. Bodin treats the matter at length in bk. I, chap. 9.

5. Ibid., 89.

6. Jacques Derrida, *Rogues: Two Essays on Reason*, trans. Pascale-Anne Brault and Michael Naas (Stanford: Stanford University Press, 2005), 101. I have made this slight modification: where Naas renders "Une souveraineté pure est indivisible ou elle n'est pas" as "A pure sovereignty is indivisible or it is not at all," I maintain Derrida's more compressed syntax, which makes evident the antinomial construction *est/n'est pas*, "is/is not."

7. Throughout *Rogues*, Derrida is in conversation with Nancy's *The Experience of Freedom*, trans. Bridget MacDonald (Stanford: Stanford University Press, 1994). The arguments in *Rogues* hold a fortiori for Nancy's *The Inoperative Community*, ed. Peter Connor, trans. Peter Connor et al. (Minneapolis: University of Minnesota Press, 1991). Nancy's translators note wryly the inadequacy of "inoperative" but prefer it to both "unworking" and "uneventful," for reasons they give on p. 156.

8. Boethius, *Interpretatio Posteriorum analyticorum Aristotelis*, PL 64, I.4, 716C to 717D. Oxford logicians of the late sixteenth century—scholars like Griffith Powell—closely follow Boethius's interpretation of the *Posterior Analytics*. Compare Griffith Powell's *Analysis Analyticorum Posteriorum* (Oxford: Joseph Barnes, 1594), 36–37, and the *scholia* on *de omni*, *per se*, and *universale* predicates, 39–40.

9. Thomas Blundeville, *The Art of Logike* (London: John Windet, 1599), 11.

10. I'm following Antony Hammond's edition, William Shakespeare, *King Richard III* (London: Arden, 1981). Where it's pertinent, I distinguish between the Folio and the Quarto versions. The most significant difference in these

lines is the one between the Folio's "O now let *Richmond* and *Elizabeth*,/The true succeeders of each royal House,/By God's fair ordinance conjoin together,/And let thy Heires (God if thy will be so)/Enrich the time to come" and the Quarto's "And let their heires (God if thy will be so)/Enrich the time to come with smooth-faste peace." Hammond and most editors quite reasonably follow Q, a reading, however, that settles perhaps too quickly the matter of Richmond's addressee. See J. Dover Wilson's edition of *Richard III* (Cambridge: Cambridge University Press, 1954), for the Folio compositor's "wretched carelessness," 258.

11. William Shakespeare, *The Tragedy of Richard the Third*, in *The Norton Shakespeare*, ed. Stephen Greenblatt, Walter Cohen, Jean E. Howard, and Katharine Eisaman Maus (New York: Norton, 1997), 595.

12. Robert Weimann makes a compelling argument that Richmond's "epilogue-like speech performs a remarkable transposition of the eventual unity of the 'white rose and the red' to the Elizabethan fruits of 'this fair conjunction.' Anticipating 'the time to come . . ./With smiling plenty, and fair prosperous days (5.819f., 33f.), the speech in no uncertain terms dismisses as past the civil war that 'divided York and Lancaster,/United in their dire division (27–28)— while appropriating its lessons for the future" ("Thresholds to Memory and Commodity in Shakespeare's Endings," *Representations* 53 [Winter, 1996]: 8–9).

13. The link between the political sense of division and the musical sense is not far-fetched. Edmund takes it up, in one of *Lear*'s many declensions of the notion of division: "And pat [out] he comes like the catastrophe of the old comedy: my cue is villainous melancholy, with a sigh like Tom [them] o' Bedlam. O, these eclipses do portend these divisions! *fa, sol, la, mi*" (1.2). Most famous, perhaps, are Juliet's lines, from *Romeo and Juliet* 3.5.27–30: "It is the lark that sings so out of tune,/Straining harsh discords and unpleasing sharps./Some say the lark makes sweet division;/This doth not so, for she divideth us" (*William Shakespeare: The Complete Works*, ed. Stanley Wells and Gary Taylor [Oxford: Oxford University Press, 1988], 356).

14. This is Mortimer, in 1 *Henry IV*, 3.1.203–6: "Thy tongue/Makes Welsh as sweet as ditties highly penn'd,/Sung by a fair queen in a summer's bower,/With ravishing division, to her lute" (*The History of Henry the Fourth [1 Henry IV]*, in *William Shakespeare: The Complete Works*, ed. Wells and Taylor, 469).

15. Cultural studies of the Elizabethan period have inevitably focused on the problem of succession, which lies at the crossing of the study of gender anxieties at the time, strictly political questions, and matters concerning the representation (and the representability) of Elizabeth herself. It would not be far-fetched to argue that the New Historicism emerged and took shape in the

1980s in part because established historiographies manifestly failed to address the cultural anxiety in Britain concerning succession and the threats of division. Bacon notoriously claimed that "Queen Elizabeth . . . had from the beginning set it down for a maxim of estate to impose a silence touching succession. Neither was it only reserved as a secret of estate, but restrained by severe laws, that no man should presume to give opinion or maintain argument touching the same." This may be why (to take a signal example) the prefect of the Jesuit Mission in England, William Allen, opens his 1595 *A Conference about the Next Succession* setting just such an "argument" outside of England: "There chaunced not long ago (I meane in the monethes of Aprill and May of this last yeare 93) to mete in Amsterdam in Holland certayne Gentlemen of diuers nations, qualities and affections. . . . And for that the aduises which dayly came from Ingland at that tyme, (the parlament being then in hand) gaue occasion to discourse of Inglish affaires, they fell into diuers poyntes concerning the same: but yet none was treated so largly or so seriously, as was the matter of succession and competitors to the crowne" (Antwerp, 1595, n.p.).

16. *Richard II*, 1.2.37–41: "*Gaunt.* God's is the quarrel; for God's substitute,/His deputy anointed in his sight,/Hath caused his death; the which if wrongfully,/Let heauen reuenge, for I may neuer lift/ An angry arm against his minister" (*The Tragedy of King Richard the Second*, in *William Shakespeare: The Complete Works*, ed. Wells and Taylor, 371).

17. Francis Edwards, *The Biography of Robert Persons, Elizabethan Jesuit, 1546–1610* (St. Louis, Mo.: The Institute for Jesuit Studies, 1995), 114.

18. Robert Persons, *A Christian Directorie Guiding Men to Their Saluation* (the second edition of Robert Persons's *First Booke of the Christian Exercise*) (Rouen: printed at Fr. Persons's press, 1585), 129–30. The most complete contemporary treatment of the Book of Daniel is the extravagant *Hexapla in Danielem, That Is, a Six-fold Commentarie vpon the Most Diuine Prophesie of Daniel* of Andrew Willet (Cambridge: printed for Leonard Greene, 1610). Willet's discussion of *Phares*, arranged in a propositional manner, runs like this: "Whereas the word written on the wall was *pharsin*, in the purall, they have devided, and here it is put in the singular, he hath devided, therein is no great difference for by both are expressed the causes subordinate one unto another." The "tropologicall, that is, the morall application of this vision" concludes: "By division [is meant] the punishment of hell, where the wicked and reprobate shall for ever be devided and separate from Gods presence, *Perer*" (161). This is the King James text:

> Then was the part of the hand sent from him; and this writing was written. And this *is* the writing that was written, MENE, MENE, TEKEL, UPHAR'SIN. This *is* the

interpretation of the thing: MENE; God hath numbered thy kingdom, and finished it. TEKEL; Thou art weighed in the balances, and art found wanting. PERES; Thy kingdom is divided, and given to the Medes and Persians. Then commanded Belshaz'zar, and they clothed Daniel with scarlet, and *put* a chain of gold about his neck, and made a proclamation concerning him, that he should be the third ruler in the kingdom. In that night was Belshaz'zar the king of the Chaldeans slain. And Darius the Median took the kingdom, *being* about threescore and two years old. (Daniel, 5:24–31)

Most discussions of the figure of Daniel in Shakespeare focus, understandably, on *Merchant of Venice*. See, recently, Thomas H. Luxon, "A Second Daniel: The Jew and the 'True Jew' in *The Merchant of Venice*," *Early Modern Literary Studies* 4, no. 3 (January 1999): 3, 1–37. Luxon briefly reviews the literature, argues that "the play undercuts and corrects Shylock's invocation of Daniel by presenting Portia disguised as Balthasar," and concludes provocatively that "the true Jews, the *verus Israel*, says the play, are the Christians"—and for Shakespeare, these "true," hence Christian Jews are associated with the figure of Daniel.

19. For a recent, comprehensive discussion of the symbolic value of the Eucharist in the period, see Lee Palmer Wandel, *The Eucharist in the Reformation: Incarnation and Liturgy* (Cambridge: Cambridge University Press, 2006).

20. Thomas Bilson, *The True Difference Betweene Christian Subiection and Unchristian Rebellion* (Oxford: printed by Ioseph Barnes, printer to the Vniuersitie, 1585), 27.

21. Isidore of Seville, *Etymologiarum sive Originum*, bk. 7, 40:

Phares, division, obtained the name of divider, i.e., phares from the fact that he divided the membranes of the afterbirth. And from this also the Pharisees, who separated themselves from the people as if righteous, were called "divided." [*Phares divisio, ab eo quod diviserit membranula secundarum, divisoris, id est phares, sortitus est nomen. Unde et Pharisaei, qui se quasi iustos a populo separabant, divisi appellabantur.*]

"Your kingdom has been divided and given to the Medes and Persians," or rather, your kingdom has been broken, for "phares" signifies fragment. ["*Divisum est regnum tuum, et datum est Medis et Persis,*" *vel fractum est regnum tuum: nam* Phares *fragmentum significant.*] (Petrus Comestor, *Historia scholastica*; PL 198)

This is Lacan, discussing the "Dream of Irma's Injection": "What emerges, printed in heavy type, beyond the hubbub of speech [*ce vacarme des paroles*], like the Mene, Tekel, Upharsin of the Bible, is the formula for trimethylamine" (*The Seminar of Jacques Lacan, Book II: The Ego in Freud's Theory*, ed. Jacques-Alain Miller, trans. Sylvana Tomaselli [New York: Norton, 1991], 158).

22. George Abbot, *An Exposition vpon the Prophet Ionah* (Oxford, 1600), 251.

23. Ibid., 314.

24. Thomas Blundeville, *The Art of Logike*, 51 and 54. Blundeville's example of division of a name is telling. He continues: "as this word wolfe into a man having that name, into a fowre footed beast, into an vicerous sore, and into a certain fish, each one called by the name of wolfe: which kind of distinction or division is very necessary to avoid ambiguity of speech, which ambiguity causeth many times great error."

25. Robert Persons, *Nevves from Spayne and Holland conteyning An information of Inglish affayres in Spayne vvith a conferrence made thereuppon in Amsterdame of Holland. VVritten by a gentleman trauelour borne in the lovv countryes, and brought vp from a child in Ingland, vnto a gentleman his friend and oste in London* (Antwerp: A. Conincx, 1593), 21ᵛ.

26. Ibid., 3.

27. Ibid., 4.

28. Ibid., 11ʳ–11ᵛ.

29. Ibid., 11ᵛ.

30. Ibid., 12ʳ.

31. Some of the works presented at the school had a British theme (like "The Two Persecutions" or an *Anglia lapsa resurgens* recorded in 1595), others not. The *Annuae Litterae Societatis Iesu* from 1596 records a celebration at Saint Gregory's on Christmas day in 1595: Christmas carols, very well attended, followed by a sort of open house. "They celebrated the birthday of Christ with many songs of different kinds, [and] a likeness of the manger in Bethlehem is set up: many people flock together for the purpose of seeing it" (476). The *Anglia lapsa resurgens* play is described in *Annuae Litterae Societatis Iesu*, 1595 (in Martin Murphy, *St. Gregory's College, Seville, 1592–1767*, The Catholic Record Society, vol. 73 [Southampton: Hobbs, 1992], 123).

32. See, in particular, Jesús Menéndez Peláez, *Los Jesuitas y el teatro en el Siglo de Oro* (Gijón: Universidad de Oviedo, 1995), and Cayo González Gutiérrez, *El teatro escolar de los Jesuitas (1555–1640) y Edición de la 'Tragedia de San Hermenegildo'* (Gijón: Universidad de Oviedo, 1997). The dating of the first performance of the *Tragedia* is the subject of some minor controversy, as there are records from January 1590 and January 1591. Julio Alonso Asenjo's excellent edition of the *Tragedia* collects a number of documents that shed light on the performance of *teatro escolar* more generally in Seville in these years. See his *La 'Tragedia de San Hermenegildo' y otras obras del teatro español de colegio* (Valencia: Universidad de Valencia, 1995).

33. Ralph Lever, *The Arte of Reason, Rightly Termed, Witcraft* (London: H. Bynneman, 1573), 105–7. Lever's description "Of the forme of a reason by rule" runs like this:

Nowe for the placing of termes, there are rankes devised. . . . So that the rankes teach where the termes are placed in eche shewsaye.

8. A ranke is a rew of seates teaching where the three termes are placed in eche shewsaye of a reason. . . .

11. The firste ranke is a rewe if those seates, which ever place the proving terme betwixt the general and the speciall terme, in suche sort, that it be under the generall, and above the speciall.

12. The second ranke placeth the proving terme above the general and the speciall terme, so that it is sayde of them both.

13. The third ranke placeth the proving terme beneath them bothe, so that they both are sayde of it.

34. The classic survey is Walter J. Ong's magisterial *Ramus, Method, and the Decay of Dialogue* (Cambridge: Harvard University Press, 1958), especially chap. 4, "The Distant Background: Scholasticism and the Quantification of Thought."

35. Persons, *Newes*, 12ᵛ.

3. THE LOGIC OF SOVEREIGNTY

1. Schmitt, *Political Theology*, 36.

2. Michael Wood, *The Road to Delphi: The Life and Afterlife of Oracles* (New York: Farrar, Straus and Giroux, 2003).

3. William Shakespeare, *The Tragedy of King Lear*, in *The Complete Works of William Shakespeare*, ed. Stanley Wells and Gary Taylor (Oxford: Oxford University Press, 1988).

4. Giorgio Agamben, *Homo Sacer: Sovereign Power and Bare Life*, trans. Daniel Heller-Roazen (Stanford: Stanford University Press, 1998), 37.

5. See, e.g., his *Il Regno e la Gloria: Per una genealogia teologica dell'economia e del governo* (Milan: Neri Pozza Editore, 2007). The development of the two paradigms of modern governmentality, the theologico-political and the economic, requires the development of a "providence-fate machine," Agamben fascinatingly argues, to solve a problem that presses even more urgently than the question of resolving human freedom with divine foreknowledge: the problem of the divine governance of human affairs. General and special providence must be balanced, or at any rate set into a dynamic relation—hence this "machine." Here is Agamben's description. It retains the unmistakable signature of the definitional topology we find in *Homo Sacer*:

What is proper to the providence-fate machine, that is, is to work as a bipolar system that ends up *producing a sort of zone of indifference* [*finisce col* produrre una sorta di zona di indifferenza] between the primary and the secondary, the general and the particular, the final cause and the effects. And although Plutarch, like Alexander, did not have in mind a governmental paradigm, the "effectivist"

ontology that flows from [this machine, at work in his histories] contains, in
some way, the condition of possibility of governance, understood as an activity
that is not directed, in the last analysis, either toward the general or to the
particular, to the first or to the subsequent, or to the end or the means, but to
their functional correlation. (138)

6. Michel Foucault, *The History of Sexuality: An Introduction*, trans. Robert
Hurley (Harmondsworth: Penguin, 1993), 93.

7. Michel Foucault, "Confession of the Flesh," in *Power-Knowledge:
Selected Interviews and Other Writings*, ed. Colin Gordon (New York: Pantheon
Books, 1980), 198–99; Hubert L. Dreyfus and Paul Rabinow, *Michel Foucault:
Beyond Structuralism and Hermeneutics*, 2nd ed. (Chicago: University of Chi-
cago Press, 1983), 184.

8. By the time one gets to early modernity, there is a great deal of play in
the term. Take Sebastián de Covarrubias's definition, in the 1611 *Tesoro de la
lengua castellana o española*. On the one hand, he makes *poder* synonymous with
potentia and *potestas*. Since Gueroult, it has been conventional to orient Spinoza's materialism around the distinction between these two terms, roughly
translated as "force" and "power," or constituting force and constituted
power: "Power, from the Latin verb *possu potes*. Power . . . [as of attorney], the
capacity one grants another, for that person to act in his or her place. Power,
is the same as capacity-to-act [*poderio*], Latin *potestas*. Of two armies, one
charges the other and all are fighting, we say that they are in battle 'power to
power.' Powerful, Latin *potens*." On the other hand, Covarrubias uses the
notion of *facultad* here to convey the way in which one person can act in place
of another: call this substitution, power as representation. (A power of attor-
ney, different from an inherent notion of power that cannot be distributed.)
This is not systematic: Covarrubias is not Spinoza. But what's important is
that the lexical effort to define power during this period is in flux between
force and power.

9. Clarice Lispector, "The Smallest Woman in the World," in *Family Ties*
(Austin: University of Texas Press, 1972), 94–95 . The original is "A menor
mulher do mundo," in Clarice Lispector, *Laços de família* (São Paulo: Livraria
Francisco Alves, 1961), 51.

10. Aristotle, *Metaphysics*, trans. W. D. Ross, in *The Basic Works of Aristotle*,
ed. Richard McKeon (New York: Random House, 1941), 1011b.

11. Aristotle, *De Interpretatione*, trans. E.M. Edghill, in *The Basic Works of
Aristotle*, ed. Richard McKeon (New York: Random House, 1941), 19a.

12. Hannah Arendt, *The Human Condition* (1958; Chicago: University of
Chicago Press, 1998), 245.

13. Ibid.

14. Leon Baudry, *Quarrel over Future Contingents: Louvain 1465–1475*,
trans. R. Guerlac (New York: Springer, 1989), 42.

15. See Chris Schabel, *Theology at Paris, 1316–1345: Peter Auriol and the Problem of Divine Foreknowledge and Future Contingents* (Aldershot: Ashgate, 2000), esp. Schabel's epilogue, "The Quarrel at Louvain," 315–36. See also Schabel's articles on the same topic: "Peter Aureol on Divine Knowledge and Future Contingents: *Scriptum in Primum Librum Sententiarum*, distinctions 38–39," *Cahiers de l'Institut du Moyen-Âge Grec et Latin* 65 (1995): 63–212; "Peter de Rivo and the Quarrel over Future Contingents at Louvain: New Evidence and New Perspectives (Part I)," *Documenti e studi sulla tradizione filosofica medievale* 6 (1995): 363–473; and "Peter de Rivo and the Quarrel over Future Contingents at Louvain: New Evidence and New Perspectives (Part II)," *Documenti e studi sulla tradizione filosofica medievale* 7 (1996): 369–435.

16. De Rivo is following Gregory of Rimini, *Sentences* I.38.1.1 (III 239:8–9). In Mark Thakkar's excellent translation, Aristotle "then puts forward two conclusions as far as this is concerned. The first of these is that not every singular categorical factual future proposition with a simple predicate, whether affirmative or negative, is true or false, so that not every contradictory pair of statements about the future has this part in particular or the other [part in particular] true, and likewise neither this [part] in particular nor that [part in particular] is false; for of a contradiction concerning a bilaterally contingent future, e.g. of the contradiction 'Antichrist will come, Antichrist will not come,' this part in particular, 'Antichrist will come,' is not true or false, and this part in particular, 'Antichrist will not come,' is not true or false" (Mark Thakkar, "Gregory of Rimini and the Logic of the Future," M.A. thesis, Warburg Institute, 2004, p. 30; available online at http://users.ox.ac.uk/~ball2227/).

17. Ibid., 40.

18. Cristóbal de Lozano, *De los reyes nuevos toledanos* (Madrid, 1674), 13–14. Lozano's account of the various myths associated with the cave runs on pp. 7–15. This is his full account of the fate of Silíceo's party:

> La prueba de aver visto, y topado estas señales, consta de la curiosidad, y diligencia que puso el Cardenal Don Juan Martínez Silíceo, aquel que por su virtud, y letras, desde principios humildes ascendió a la púrpura, y Mitra Toledana. Con las grandes noticias que le davan desta cueva, quiso examinar, y ver lo que en ella avía. No sería, claro está, con el pretexto que la mandó abrir el Rey Rodrigo, para desperdiciar, o achocar, si avía alguno tesoro; si bien si para atesorarle, como hazía los suyos en los pechos de los pobres. Aunque su principal intento sería para desengañar al vulgo, y quietar con la verdad tantas hablillas, y cosas, como contavan y dezían desta cueva. Hizo, pues, limpiar la puerta, que como dexamos dicho, oy está calafateada, y cerrada en la Iglesia de San Ginés; y buscando, y previniendo a los hombres de mas ánimo, y los que braveavan de ossados, y valientes, mandó que les diessen çurrones de comida, que llevassen linternas, hachas, cordeles, y otros instrumentos, para poder encender en caso

que las luzes les faltaron. Entraron, pues, estos bravos, y a cosa de media legua
(que yo digo sería milla, pues claro está, que el miedo haze las leguas mas largas)
toparon unas estatuas de bronce, puestas sobre una mesa como altar, y que
reparando en mirar una dellas, que sobre su pedestal estava severa, y grave, se
cayó, y hizo un notable ruido, causando a los exploradores grande miedo. Quizá
no avía mas desta, y el miedo se las hizo muchas, como acontece; y sería lo que
topó el Rey Rodrigo con la maza de armas. Aunque ya bien medrosos passaron
adelante, hasta dar con un gran golpe de agua, que con el ruido que hazía su
arrebatada corriente, los acabó de llenar de miedo hasta los ojos. Reparece, si
vienen bien las señas con la otra cueba encantada, la distancia, la estatua, caerse,
o hazer ruido, y el braçal de agua. En fin ya turbados, y perdidos de temor los
tales aventureros, se resolvieron en no dar mas passo adelante, sino bolverse a
salir. Salieron, pues, al tiempo de anochecer tan atemorizados, tan despavori-
dos, tan con caras de difuntos, que los que los aguardavan, y juzgavan saldrían
ricos, y admirados participaron tambien de su espanto, y confusión. Salieron
demás del miedo tan traspassados de la frialdad, por ser tiempo de verano, que
enfermaron todos, y murieron muchos de ellos.

The proof that they saw, and actually encountered, all these signs, is due to the
care and diligence invested in the matter by the Cardinal, Juan Martinez Siliceo, he who ascended from humble origins to the purple robes and the see in
Toledo, thanks to his virtue and learning. Considering all the reports he was
given of this cave, he wished to examine it, in order to see what was in the cave.
It was not, of course, with the rationale that King Roderick employed when he
ordered the cave opened—in order to waste or spend whatever treasure might
be there. Rather, his purpose would have been to treasure it, as he treasured his
in the chests of the poor. His main goal, however, was to undeceive the masses
and to silence, with the truth, all the rumors and things that were told and said
about the cave. He therefore had the door cleaned—the door which, as I have
said, is bricked over and closed, in the Church of San Gines. He sought out
and contacted the bravest men, and the ones who boasted of their daring and
bravery, and ordered that they be given packs of food and that they carry lanterns, torches, ropes, and other instruments they could use to light their way if
the light should fail them. These brave folks entered the cave, and something
like half a league in (which I suspect was much less, for, as we all know, fear
makes the leagues longer) they encountered some bronze statues, posed upon
a table as on an altar, and as they were looking at one of them, which stood
severe and grave upon its pedestal, it fell over and made a great clatter, which
caused the explorers great fright. It may be that there was no other statue than
this, and fear multiplied them, as happens not infrequently. And it may be the
one that King Roderick encountered with the mace. Although by now they
were fearful, they proceeded, until they ran into a great channel of water,
which, with the noise it made, finally filled them with fear up to their eyes. The

description chimes, if all the indications match, with that of the other enchanted cave—the distance, the statue and the fall, the noise, and the stream of water. Finally, confused and abandoned to fear, the so-called adventurers resolved not to go a step farther but instead to return and leave the cave. They exited, then, at nightfall, so frightened, so terrified, and bearing such funereal faces, that those who were awaiting them and expected that they would emerge rich and admired, also shared their fright and confusion. They emerged not just terrified but so chilled—for it was summer—that all of them became ill, and many of them died.

Further accounts of the cave can be found in Blas Ortiz, *Descriptio templi toletani,* in *Collectio S.S. Patrum Ecclesiae Toletana,* vol. 3, appendix 2 (Madrid, 1793), 376; in Pedro de Alcocer, *Hystoria ó descripción de la Imperial cibdad de Toledo* (1544; rpt. Toledo: Instituto Provincial de Investigaciones y Estudios Toledanos, 1973), f. xij; and notoriously in the *Historia Ecclesiástica de la civdad de Toledo* of "el falsario e invencionero" Jerónimo Román de la Higuera (as Marcelino Menéndez Pelayo calls him, in *Historia de los heterodoxos españoles,* vol. 3 [Madrid: F. Maroto and Sons, 1881], 297). The *Historia Ecclesiástica*'s briefer account is probably the source of part of Lozano's story. As Román de la Higuera describes the party's descent into the cave, the reference to Roderick is absent:

Dícese que el año de 1546 dieron notiçia desta Cueva al Arçobispo de Toledo Don Juan Martinez Siliçio, que poco antes avia entrado en esta sacrosanta silla, el qual la mando limpiar y que se entraran algunas personas dentro probeydas de mantenimiento de linternas y cordeles para açertar a bolber y que no a media legua bieron unas estatuas de bronçe sobre un arca y que mirando una como estava sobre su pedestral se cayo y causo con el grande ruido que hiço mucho pavor en los animos de los nuebos y poco experimentados abentureros; luego fueron delante y dieron en un golpe de agua tan hondo que no le atravesaron por no tener Puente o maderos con que se poder baler y que esta agua algun trecho antes les causo miedo por el gran ruido que hacia; pudo ser que si hecharan por otro lado no hallaran este impedimento; con esto se tornaron a salir al tiempo que çerrava la noche; causoles ynpresion esta mudança de ayre y por ser berano estava la cueva muy fria y asi algunos dellos enfermaron desta alteraçion y murieron; esto quentan personas fidedignas y a quien se deve dar todo credito.

They say that in the year 1546 news of this Cave came to the Archbishop of Toledo, Don Juan Martinez Siliceo, who had recently assumed this sacrosanct chair, and that he ordered that it be cleaned, and that some people should enter the cave furnished with lanterns and ropes so that they would be able to return, and that not half a league in they saw some bronze statues upon an ark, and when they sought to see how one of them was posed upon its pedestal, the statue fell over and caused such a noise that it created a great fear in the spirits

of the new and untried explorers; they pressed on and hit upon a channel of
water that was so deep that they could not cross it, as they had no bridge or
wood to use. This water had earlier already caused them fear because of the
great noise it made. It could be that if they had taken a different route they
would not have run into this obstacle. With all this, they returned and left the
cave when the night was coming on. This change of air affected them, and as it
was summer the cave was very cold, and some of them sickened from this
change and died. This is recounted by trustworthy and creditable people.
(Cited in Jerónimo López de Ayala Cedillo, *Toledo en el siglo XVI, después del
vencimiento de las comunidades: Discursos leídos ante la Real Academia de la historia
en la recepción pública* . . . [Madrid: Hernández, 1901], 106.)

19. Silíceo's biographers, like those of most notable figures of his time,
collected indications of the future greatnesses of their subject, a convention
that in this case strangely compounds, at the level of the life of the character,
his role in the history of the logics of prophetic, counterfactual, or future-
contingent speech. Here is a remarkable example from Silíceo's earliest biographer, Diego de Castejón y Fonseca. Young Juan, aged two years or so, fell
down a well, from which he was pulled, apparently lifeless. He was taken to a
church and placed at the foot of an image of the Virgin. The child revived,
and the biographer exclaims:

> Tenía ya Dios escogido a don Juan para Capellán desta divina Presencia. Son
> sus favores anticipados: experimentólos el niño, que reparado del trabajo de la
> caída . . . dio a entender que aquella Soberana, i divina Señora, le avía asistido
> en el poço. Ha Dios señalado con prodigios el origen de Grandes Varones.

> God had already chosen Don Juan to be a chaplain of his divine presence. His
> favors are anticipatory: the child experienced them, for, noting the difficulties
> and dangers of his fall . . . he let it be known that that Sovereign, and Divine
> Lady, had helped him in the well. God has marked out with wonders the origin
> of great men. (*Primacía de la Santa Iglesia de Toledo* [Madrid, 1645], 986),

20. Jean Dullaert, *Questiones super duos libros Peri hermeneias Aristotelis*
(Paris, 1509), discusses Aristotle's "naval battle" example on ff. 97r–107r. I
cite from the exceptionally rare Salamanca edition (Salamanca: Juan de Porras,
1517), which Silíceo edited and had printed; the pagination remains the same.
The copy I consulted is in the collection of Richard Ramer. Dullaert notes
that the problem of future contingents is especially testing because it touches
upon varied disciplines: "involuunt. eni ea non solum logice aut philosophice
difficultates sed a Theologice. Hinc est quae non a solis artistis sed a Theo-
logis invenit ventilata"; "For these difficulties are not only from logic or philosophy, but also from theology. From here he comes to [touches upon] things
having been aired not only by the arts, but also by the theologians" (98ᵛ).

Dullaert generally follows Boethius's commentary on Aristotle's text; his principal contribution seems to be in distinguishing between contradictories that pertain to statements about the past or present and those that pertain to statements about the future. When he discusses contingent propositions under this rubric, however, he focuses only on the difference "between present and future contradictions [*inter contradictorias de presenti et contradictorias de futuro*]," characteristically and perhaps necessarily dropping any mention of the past "contradictorias de preterito," which, he says, Aristotle *does* treat (99ʳ). Silíceo's gratitude to Dullaert and to his teachers in Paris is expressed, conventionally, in the "Operis peroratio" to his *Arithmetica Ioannis Martini, Scilicei, in theoricen et praxim scissa* (Paris, 1519):

> Praise be to omnipotent God, and to his chaste mother, and to the whole court of heaven. And happiness and blessedness to my three teachers Ludovico Romano, Roberto Caubraith, and Ioanni Dullaert, a teacher whom I must always venerate, because his soul enjoys the gift of heaven. Of course Ludovico in grammar, Roberto in dialectic, and Joanni in philosophy held me as one of their students. So to these men, for their erudition and labors, I confer that payment which the famous Thales of Miletus asked from his student Mantaicus of Priene: namely, that he (Mantaicus) proclaim the things which he had learned under Thales, that they were Thales', and that Thales himself had been the discoverer of such things. Therefore I proclaim that Ludovicus was the discoverer of whatever there is in me of grammar; whatever of dialectics, Roberto was the author; and whatever of philosophy, Ioanni (63ᵛ).

21. Albert A. Sicroff, *Les controverses des statuts de "pureté de sang" en Espagne du XVe au XVIIe siècle* (Paris: Didier, 1960). Sicroff discusses Silíceo's statute on pp. 102–39. A proximate account of the controversy can be found in Sebastián de Horozco's *Relaciones históricas toledanas*, written before 1581 (BNM Ms. 9175), published as *Relaciones históricas toledanas*, ed. Jack Weiner (Toledo: Instituto Provincial de Investigaciones y Estudios Toledanos, 1981).

22. This is how the great historian of the Inquisition Henry Charles Lea describes Silíceo's initiative: "To prevent . . . contamination for the future, Silíceo drew up a statute forbidding that any but an Old Christian should hold a position in the cathedral, even down to the choir-boys; all aspirants were to present their genealogies and deposit a sum of money to defray the expense of an investigation. In July, 1547, he came to Toledo, with a large retinue of gentlemen, and secretly assured himself of the assent of a majority of the canons, who bound themselves with oaths to adopt it; a meeting of the chapter was called and the measure was sprung upon it, in violation of its rules of order—as he frankly said, if notice had been given and discussion allowed it could not have been passed, for the Conversos would have intrigued successfully against it. The vote in its favor was twenty-five to ten. . . . This action

aroused so much excitement in the city that the Royal Council sent an *alcalde de corte*, who reported that, for the sake of peace, the statute had better not be enforced, in consequence of which Prince Philip, then holding the Cortes of Monzón, sent orders to suspend it until the emperor's pleasure could be learned. The struggle was thus transferred to the imperial court and to Rome. . . . Charles referred the question back to the Royal Council, to which both sides presented memorials. . . . If Charles did not confirm the statute, the outlook was that the Conversos would govern the church of Toledo. Wild as all this may seem to us, it gives us a valuable insight into the impulses which governed Spain in its dealings with the alien races within her borders. It was a humiliating admission that they were regarded as men of superior intelligence and ability, whose wrongs for generations had converted them into irreconcilable enemies, the object of mingled dread and detestation; as they could not be matched in intellect, the only policy was brute repression and extermination. Of course Silíceo carried the day" (Henry Charles Lea, *A History of the Inquisition of Spain* (New York: The Macmillan Company, 1922), 2: 291–92).

23. Pedro de Corral, *Crónica Sarracina*, in *Floresta de leyendas heroicas españolas*, vol. 1, *Rodrigo, el último godo*, ed. Ramón Menéndez Pidal (Madrid, 1925).

24. Ibid., 83. Another version of the prophecy reads:

El Rey la mandara abrir, Un paño dentro se ha hallado, con unas letras Latinas Que dicen en castellano: 'Cuando aquestas cerraduras Que cierran estos candados Fueren abiertas, y visto, Lo que en el paño dibujado, España será perdida Y en ella todo asolado. Ganarála gente extraña, Como aquí está figurado, Los rostros muy denegridos, Los brazos arremangados, Muchas colores vestidas, En las cabezas tocados: Alzadas traerán sus señas En caballos cabalgando, En sus manos largas lanzas, Con espadas en su lado. Alárabes se dirán Y de aquellas tierras extraños; Perderase toda España, Que nada no habrá fincado.

The King will command that it be opened, and a cloth will be found inside, with Roman letters that say in Castilian: "When the locks closed by these padlocks have been opened, and what this cloth depicts has been seen, Spain will be lost, and everything in her destroyed. Strangers will win her, as is shown here, of darkened visages, arms bared, dressed in many colors, their heads turbaned. They will bear their standards high, galloping upon horses, and in their hands will be long spears, with swords at their side. They will be called [they will call themselves] Arabs, strangers to those lands. All Spain will be lost, and nothing will be spared." (Lorenzo de Sepúlveda, *Romances nvevamente sacados de historias antiguas de la cronica de España compuestos por Lorenço de Sepulueda* [Anvers, 1580], 400–401.)

Compare the version in Miguel de Luna, *La verdadera historia del Rey Don Rodrigo, en la qual se trata la causa principal de la perdida de España y de la conquista que de ella hizo Miramamolin Almançor Rey que fue del Africa, y de las Arabias,* translating an original by Alcayde Abulcacim Tarif Abentarique (Granada, 1592 and 1600; facs. rpt., Miguel de Luna. *La verdadera historia del rey Don Rodrigo*, ed. Luis F. Bernabé Pons [Granada: Editorial Universidad de Granada, 2001]). Corral's prophecy is less specific. The *escrito* in Hercules's hands (it is indeed Hercules whose tomb Roderick has opened) reads in part: "tu, tan osado, que aqui este escrito leeras, para ojo quien eres e cuanto de mal por ti verna; ca ansi commo por mi fue España poblada e conquistada, ansi por ti sera despoblada e perdida"; "you who are so daring, who here read my writing, repair who you are and how much evil will come from you: for just as Spain was through me peopled and conquered, through you she will be rendered desolate, and lost" (190).

25. Silíceo's historical rationale for instituting the statute, as expressed in the "Libro de las causas que el Rmo. Arçobispo de Toledo y su cabildo movieron a hazer el estatuto quel año pasado hizieron" (Hispanic Society Ms. 798, n.p.), includes this telling item:

> yten la causa porque temimos el mal que podria venir a esta sta yglia allende de las sobredichas si en ella se reciben personas que desciendan de linage de judios es considerando las cosas pasadas de las quales segun buena Philosophia se toma argumento para los que estan por venir por que segun se lee en las Historias de España quando Toledo fue conquistada por los moros en tiempo de la general destruycion despaña fue vendida esta ciudad de toledo por los judios moradores della un domingo de Ramos yendo los xrianos viejos en proçesion a la yglesia de sta leocadia questa fuera de los muros desta çiudad los quales christianos viejos fueron degollados por los moros por solas las aserbanças y trayçiones de los dichos judios y la ciudad perdida la qual por su natural fuerça y fortaleza sin trayçion no pudiera se ganar y alli se derramo mucha sangre del estado ecclesiastico.

And further: the reason why we believed the evil that could befall this holy church, beyond the evil already recounted, if in her were received persons who descend from Jewish lineage, is that, taking into account the things that have already occurred—from which, as good Philosophy attests, an argument can be derived for those which are to come—taking these past events into account, we read in the Histories of Spain that, when Toledo was conquered by the Moors during the time of the general destruction of Spain, this city of Toledo was sold by the Jews living in her on Palm Sunday, while the Old Christians were in the procession from the church of St. Leocadia, which is outside the walls of the city. These Old Christians were slaughtered by the Moors because of the spying and betrayal of the said Jews, and the city lost—which, on account of its natural strength and emplacement, could never have been taken without treason. Much blood of the church's estate was spilt then.

4. *MATERIA* IN THE CRITIQUE OF AUTONOMY

NOTE: My epigraphs are taken from Jacques Rancière, *The Flesh of Words*, trans. Charlotte Mandell (Stanford: Stanford University Press, 2004), 137; and Friedrich Schiller, *Don Carlos*, trans. A. Leslie and Jeanne R. Willson, in *Friedrich Schiller: Plays*, ed. Walter Hinderer (New York: Continuum, 1983). An early version of this chapter appeared as "Spontaneous Labor" in *Depositions: Althusser, Balibar, Macherey, and the Labor of Reading*, ed. Jacques Lezra, special issue, *Yale French Studies* 88 (1995): 78–117.

1. Wittgenstein's remarkable comments about the conclusion to his "Lecture on Ethics," which I briefly discuss above, seem to me diagnostic. "At the end of my lecture on ethics," he told Friedrich Waismann, "I spoke in the first person. I think that this is something very essential. Here there is nothing to be stated any more; all I can do is to step forth as an individual and speak in the first person. . . . Running against the limits of language? Language is, after all, not a cage! All I can say is this: I do not scoff at this tendency in man; I hold it in reverence. And here it is essential that this is not a description of sociology but that I am speaking about myself" (*Wittgenstein and the Vienna Circle: Conversations Recorded by Friedrich Waismann*, ed. Brian McGuinness, trans. Joachim Schulte and Brian McGuinness [New York: Barnes & Noble Books, 1979], 117). Note the repeated gestures of humility, almost abjection: sacrifice, pathos, stepping "forth as an individual"—this is what Wittgenstein considers "essential" to the "Lecture on Ethics." But if the ethical stance is not just accidentally but constitutively and necessarily nonsociological, even antisocial, then the normative, even the pedagogical value of the "Lecture" is in question. To "show the fly the way out of the bottle," as the *Philosophical Investigations* famously puts it, may be the philosopher's goal, but here the philosopher steps onto trickier ground and finds himself writing autobiography.

2. Ludwig Wittgenstein, "Lecture on Ethics," *The Philosophical Review* 74 (1965): 3–12.

3. Étienne Balibar, *The Philosophy of Marx*, trans. Chris Turner (New York: Verso, 2007), 32–33. Balibar insists on the "transindividual" character of the alternative that Marx proposes to individualism, on the one hand, and to organicism or holism, on the other. For Balibar, Marx here sketches the concept of a constitutive relation:

> Here, we must admit, an "ontology" is taking shape. However, for the discussion of the relations between the individual and the genus, it substitutes a programme of enquiry into this multiplicity of relations, which are so many transitions, transferences or passages in which the bond of individuals to the community is formed and dissolved, and which, in its turn, constitutes them. What is most striking in such a perspective is that it establishes a complete

reciprocity between these two poles, which cannot exist without one another and are therefore in and of themselves mere abstractions, albeit necessary abstractions for thinking the relation or relationship (*Verhältnis*) [*qui sont l'un et l'autre nécessaires à la pensée du rapport ou de la relation*].

4. Louis Althusser and Étienne Balibar, *Reading 'Capital,'* trans. Ben Brewster (London: New Left Books, 1970), 29.

5. Two clear but rather limited treatments of Althusser's inquiry into determination (including overdetermination, underdetermination, and determination in the last instance) may be found in William S. Lewis, *Louis Althusser and the Traditions of French Marxism* (Lanham, Md.: Lexington Books, 2005), 172–77, which is limited inasmuch as it does not consider the psychoanalytic sense of determination, and Luke Ferretter, *Louis Althusser* (London: Routledge, 2006), 40–46, which is limited in scope, inasmuch as Ferretter's work is intended to be a popular introduction to Althusser's thought.

6. Ernesto Laclau and Chantal Mouffe, *Hegemony and Socialist Strategy*, 2d ed. (New York: Verso, 2001), 98.

7. Among the first works in English to characterize Althusser's thought in this way is Steven Smith, *Reading Althusser: An Essay on Structural Marxism* (Ithaca, N.Y.: Cornell University Press, 1984). The most influential treatment of the topic remains Gregory Elliott's *Althusser: The Detour of Theory* (London: Verso, 1987). See also Ted Benton, *The Rise and Fall of Structural Marxism: Althusser and His Influence* (London: Macmillan, 1984).

8. A recent effort to link the notion of determination (overdetermination as well as underdetermination) to the late essays on aleatory materialism may be found in Djuna Larise, "Der aleatorische Materialismus: Ein theoretisches Projekt des spaten Althusser," *Synthesis Philosophica* 41, no. 1 (2006): 115–37. See, in particular, 123–24, where Larise remarks on Althusser's late reconceptualization of the topology of structure and element: "According to Althusser's definition, the mode of production in Marx is a special combination of elements. These elements are composed of the financial accumulation, the accumulation of the technical means of production, and the accumulation of raw materials and of the producers. How then, Althusser asks (and goes on to answer immediately), could a constitutive element of a structure be at the same time the product of that same structure, unless there were a confusion concerning the fundamental difference between production and reproduction?"

9. Compare Balibar's acute reframing of the Althusserian project: "Althusser came to the clear realization that he was doing philosophy, in the specific sense that he, too, was producing a 'philosophical object' (like the *cogito* or the social contract'). He realized that the 'epistemological break' was not the *concept of an object* (which would be, in this case, the general process of theoretical production of the transformation of ideology into its opposite, science) but

the presentation *of the concept as an object*, which is to say, the figuration in the space of the abstract imaginary proper to the philosopher, of the concept's most prominent features, or of conceptual knowledge, particularly its conflictual relation to ideology" (Étienne Balibar, "L'objet d'Althusser," in *Politique et philosophie dans l'oeuvre de Louis Althusser*, ed. Sylvain Lazarus [Paris: Presses Universitaires de France, 1993], 112).

10. The stakes of this claim come into sharp relief when we consider, as Jason Read has, the standing of historical claims about the emergence of capitalism in Marx's work. See Read's "Primitive Accumulation: The Aleatory Foundation of Capitalism," *Rethinking Marxism: A Journal of Economics, Culture, and Society* 14, no. 2 (2002): 24–49.

11. Gregory Elliott's comments on the "deleterious consequences" of Althusser's concept of "structural causality" are especially at issue. See his *Althusser: The Detour of Theory*, 179.

12. Immanuel Kant, "The Vienna Logic," in *Lectures on Logic*, trans. J. Michael Young (Cambridge: Cambridge University Press, 1992), 348.

13. Immanuel Kant, *Critique of Pure Reason*, trans. F. Max Müller (New York: Anchor, 1966), 104 (A106). The German original is from *Kritik der reinen Vernunft* (Frankfurt am Main: Suhrkamp, 1982), 1:167. This deduction has provided, at least since its treatment in Hegel, the classical articulation of the relation between "external phenomena," "concepts," and their "synthetical unity in consciousness"—or, as the *Science of Logic* puts it: "It is one of the profoundest and truest insights to be found in the *Critique of Pure Reason* that the *unity* which constitutes the nature of the Concept is recognized as the *original synthetic* unity of *apperception*, as unity of the *I think*, or of self-consciousness" (*Hegel's Science of Logic*, 584). Compare Kant's more schematic assertion in the Vienna Logic: "A *conceptus*," writes Kant of *Begriff*, "is a *raepraesentatio communis*, which is common to many things"—a conventional description of abstraction from the manifold, which leaves undecided on what grounds *conceptus* is to be distinguished from "thing" and whether *repraesentatio* is to be taken in one or the other of the classical senses most often associated with it: as mere representation or appearance (*Erscheinung*), or as the appearing of the common essential in the manifold.

14. I understand the trajectory here quite differently from Lucio Colletti, *Marxism and Hegel* (London: New Left Books, 1973).

15. *Hegel's 'Logic,'* trans. William Wallace (Oxford: Oxford University Press, 1975), 220. I have changed Wallace's "notion" to "concept" throughout. For the original, see G. W. F. Hegel, *Enzyklopädie der philosophischen Wissenschaften im Grundrisse*, ed. F. Nicolin and O. Pöggeler (1830; Hamburg: Felix Meiner Verlag, 1959), 151ff.

16. *Hegel's 'Logic,'* 223.

17. Indeed, for Althusser as for Lacan, as David Macey has argued, the notion of the concept was tied to a particular moment in postwar intellectual history—and especially to the work of Georges Canguilhem. Macey's argument that Althusser elects to withdraw from the increasingly conceptualized language of the *Cahiers pour l'analyse* group toward the realm of "fantasy" is of interest here, in great part since it suggests a movement contrary to the one Laclau and Mouffe are suggesting: toward a region that is not determinable "in the last instance" but whose temporality remains indeterminate. See David Macey, "Thinking with Borrowed Concepts: Althusser and Lacan," in *Althusser: A Critical Reader*, ed. Gregory Elliott (Oxford: Basil Blackwell, 1994), 142–58, esp. 151ff. Rastko Mocnik argues ("Ideology and Fantasy," in *The Althusserian Legacy*, ed. E. Ann Kaplan and Michael Sprinker [London: Verso, 1993], 139–56), in line with Žižek and others, for understanding Althusserian ideology as "'working upon' fantasy. . . . Being a quilting-point, fantasy punctually connects the ideological facade with its specific exterior: so-called social reality" (151–52).

18. Gregory Elliott, first in "Analysis Terminated, Analysis Interminable," in *Althusser: A Critical Reader*, ed. Elliott, 177–202, and then in "The Necessity of Contingency: Some Notes," *Rethinking Marxism* 10, no. 3 (1998): 74–79.

19. Ernesto Laclau and Chantal Mouffe, *Hegemony and Socialist Strategy* (London: Verso, 1985), 98.

20. As told in only slightly different terms by Žižek, it is a powerful, convincing story: "In *Hegel ou Spinoza?*, Pierre Macherey maintains that Spinoza's philosophy must be read as a critique of Hegel—as if Spinoza read Hegel and was able to answer the latter's critique of 'Spinozism.' The same could be said of Hegel in relation to Althusser: Hegel outlines in advance the contours of the Althusserian critique of (what Althusser presents as) 'Hegelianism.' Moreover, Hegel develops the element that is missing in Althusser (the one that had prevented him from thinking through the notion of overdetermination); that is, the element of subjectivity that cannot be reduced to imaginary (mis)-recognition qua effect of interpellation—that is to say, the subject as *S*; the 'empty,' barred subject" (Slavoj Žižek, "Identity and Its Vicissitudes: Hegel's 'Logic of Essence' as a Theory of Ideology," in *The Making of Political Identities*, ed. Ernesto Laclau [London: Verso, 1994], 53). A careful reading of Žižek's encounter with Althusser may be found in Franck Fischbach's "'Les sujets marchent tout seuls . . .': Althusser et l'interpellation," in *Althusser: Une lecture de Marx*, ed. Jean-Claude Bourdin (Paris: Presses Universitaires de France, 2008), 113–45.

21. Louis Althusser, "Is It Simple to Be a Marxist in Philosophy?" in *Philosophy and the Spontaneous Philosophy of the Scientists, and Other Essays*, ed. Gregory Elliot (London: Verso, 1990), 203–40.

22. See especially A. V. Miller's translation of paragraph 162 of the *Phenomenology*: "This simple infinity, or the absolute Concept, may be called the simple essence of life, the soul of the world. . . . It is self-*identical*, for the differences are tautological; they are differences that are none. This self-identical essence is therefore related only to itself; 'to itself' implies relationship to an 'other,' and the *relation-to-self* is rather a *self-sundering*; or, in other words, that very self-identicalness is an inner difference" (G. W. F. Hegel, *Hegel's Phenomenology of Spirit*, trans. A. V. Miller [Oxford: Oxford University Press, 1977], 100).

23. Jacques-Alain Miller, "Suture (Elements of the Logic of the Signifier)," *Cahiers pour l'analyse* 1, no. 1 (Winter 1966): 37–49; the English translation, by Jacqueline Rose, appeared in *Screen* 18, no. 4 (Winter 1977–78): 24–34.

24. Alain Badiou, "Qu'est-ce que Louis Althusser entend par 'philosophie'?" in *Politique et philosophie dans l'oeuvre de Louis Althusser*, ed. Lazarus, 29–45. I cite from p. 42; Badiou's discussion of *suture* extends to p. 44.

25. Gramsci is the crucial figure in this story, especially at moments when he follows Engels in dismissing the mechanistic sense of historical determination characteristic of "pocket geniuses" who reduce the "infinite variety and multiplicity of history" to economic schemes. Gramscian "philology," the "methodological expression of the importance of ascertaining and precising particular facts in their unique and unrepeatable individuality," operates side by side with "more general 'laws of tendency'" for practical, not theoretical reasons. This stress on the practical "co-participation" of these schemes radically distinguishes Gramsci's work from the sort of "reduction . . . to necessary moments of an immanent law" that Laclau and Mouffe correctly address. See Antonio Gramsci, "Problems of Marxism," in *Selections from the Prison Notebooks*, ed. and trans. Quintin Hoare and Geoffrey Nowell Smith (New York: International Publishers, 1971), 428–29.

26. See Pierre Macherey's discussion of Freud's effort to read Hegel, "Le leurre hégélien," *Le Bloc Note de la Psychanalyse* 5 (1985): 27–50.

27. Ernesto Laclau and Lilian Zac have more recently clarified the political stakes of the use of suture: "There are signifiers occupying this point of suture in a particular political field. Let us take the case of the policy of disappearance put into effect by many Latin American dictatorships. The signifier '*desaparecidos*' occupies a central place in the political field, where various discursive threads are knotted. On the one hand, the authorities tend to deny the existence of any *desaparecidos*: all government arrests have been executed according to the legal framework. Thus, the *desaparecidos* as a category are excluded from the world of objects. On the other hand, the authorities recognize their existence but deny responsibility for their disappearance . . . As a result of these

two operations, these *desaparecidos* inhabit a space where they are neither dead nor alive; they can reappear, they can also be killed. Their death and their life is suspended, deferred. And by means of this operation fear is installed into that context: the *desaparecidos* point to the existence of another space, a space of suspension, which is both part of, and excluded from, the realm of 'society,' and, in this way, it becomes necessary to define its limits" ("Minding the Gap: The Subject of Politics," in *The Making of Political Identities*, ed. Ernesto Laclau [London: Verso, 1994], 33–34).

28. Jacques-Alain Miller, "Suture (Elements of the Logic of the Signifier)," 27. See Laclau and Mouffe's remarks on Miller, by way of Stephen Heath's commentary: "As Stephen Heath points out, 'suture names not just a structure of lack but also an availability of the subject, a certain closure. . . . The stake is clear: the 'I' is a division but joins all the same, the stand-in is the lack in the structure, but nevertheless simultaneously, the possibility of a coherence, of the *filling* in.' It is this double movement that we will attempt to stress in our extension of the concept of suture to the field of politics" (*Hegemony and Socialist Strategy*, 88). The derivation from Frege to some extent obscures the transcendental line: see, for instance, the discussion of the transcendental apperception in the *First Critique* (A106–7).

29. The nature of this ex-centricity is, of course, the subject of Lacan's question "Is the place that I occupy as the subject of a signifier concentric or excentric, in relation to the place I occupy as subject of the signified?" in his "The Agency of the Letter in the Unconscious," in *Écrits*, trans. Alan Sheridan (New York: Norton, 1977), 165.

30. This impasse, expressed with different valence but in remarkably similar vocabularies, remains at issue in treatments of the concept of individuality from Habermas to Rawls. The *Social Contract* and its consequences are at issue from the first. The distinction between the "fiction" of the "general will" and the mode of "absence of a general content" is powerfully advanced in the *Logic*, precisely at the moment when Hegel considers the passage between individuality and universality. Thus the note [*Zusatz*] to the passage from Hegel's *Logic* cited above, posing that if "the logical forms of the concept were really dead and inert receptacles of conceptions and thoughts, knowledge about them would be an idle curiosity which the truth might dispense with," distinguishes the "real universal" from that which is merely held "in common" in these words: "The distinction . . . between what is merely in common, and what is truly universal, is strikingly expressed by Rousseau in his famous *Contrat social*, when he says that the laws of a state must spring from the universal will (*volonté générale*), but need not on that account be the will of all (*volonté de tous*). Rousseau would have made a sounder contribution towards a theory of the state if he had always kept this distinction in sight. The general

will is the notion of the will: and the laws are the special clauses of this will and based upon the notion of it" (*Hegel's 'Logic,'* 228.)

The theme is constant in Hegel: "The merit of Rousseau's contribution to the search for this concept [of the Idea of the state] is that, by adducing the will as the principle of the state, he is adducing a principle which has thought both its form and its content, a principle indeed which is thinking itself, not a principle, like gregarious instinct, for instance, or divine authority, which has thought as its form only. Unfortunately . . . he takes the will only in a determinate form as the individual will, and he regards the universal will not as the absolutely rational element in the will, but only as a 'general' will which proceeds out of this individual will as out of a conscious will. The result is that he reduces the union of individuals in the state to a contract and therefore to something based on their arbitrary wills . . . and abstract reasoning proceeds to draw the logical inferences which destroy the absolutely divine principle of the state, together with its majesty and absolute authority" (*Hegel's 'Philosophy of Right'*, trans. T. M. Knox [Oxford: Oxford University Press, 1952], 156–57, and 11–18, where this self-realizing power is shown to have implications for the social). See Pierre Méthais's suggestive analysis of the distinctions between Hegel and Rousseau on the question of the generality of the will, "Contrat et volonté générale selon Hegel et Rousseau," in *Hegel et le siècle des lumières*, ed. Jacques D'Hondt (Paris: Presses Universitaires de France, 1974), 101–48.

31. Althusser, "Contradiction and Overdetermination," in *For Marx*, trans. Ben Brewster (London: Verso, 1969), 125. Michael Sprinker's discussion of Althusser's confrontation with Rousseau seems to me especially fruitful: see his *Imaginary Relations: Aesthetics and Ideology in the Theory of Historical Materialism* (London: Verso, 1987), where the *décalage* between individual and general will is defined by analogy to Paul de Man's notion of text.

32. Althusser's definition of spontaneity in *Philosophy and the Spontaneous Philosophy of the Scientists*, trans. Warren Montag (Verso: London, 1990), is useful, though it requires supplementing: Convictions or beliefs are spontaneous when they "stem from the experience of scientific practice itself in its everyday immediacy" (133). Ronald Maher has provided a useful critique of the notion of "spontaneous agency" (which he takes to be the other side of Althusserian functionalism) and supplies in its place the "speculative concept" of hegemony; see his "Hegemony and Marxist Psychology," *Theory and Psychology* 13, no. 4 (2003): 469–87.

33. Louis Althusser, "Rousseau: The Social Contract. (The Discrepancies)," in Louis Althusser, *Politics and History: Montesquieu, Rousseau, Hegel, Marx*, trans. Ben Brewster (London: New Left Books, 1972), 113–60.

34. Ibid., 151.

35. " 'Fuite en avant dans l'idéologie, ou regression dans l'économie' " ("Flight Forward in Ideology or Regression in the Economy") is the title of the essay's last section

36. Louis Althusser, "Rousseau: The Social Contract," 159–60. Compare the much more optimistic conclusion of Alain Grosrichard's essay in the *Cahiers pour l'analyse* volume in which Althusser's essay was first published. Titled "Gravité de Rousseau," Grosrichard's essay maintains that "Rousseau's 'literature' is nothing other than the displacement, into his writing itself, of a problem posed by theory. His literature is the staging, the *dramatization*, of theory. . . . Literature verifies theory and makes it true; theory justifies literature and makes it necessary. This is why Rousseau's *oeuvre* is inseparably literature and theory of literature, theory and literature of theory" (64).

37. I am at odds here, clearly, with David Macey, who has argued that the "Décalages" piece seems "out of place, if not archaic" in the project announced by *Cahiers pour l'analyse*: a proposed genealogy of the social sciences. Althusser's article "Freud and Lacan" dates to 1964–65, but see also his "Trois notes sur la théorie des discours" of 1966, collected in Louis Althusser, *Écrits sur la psychanalyse*, ed. Olivier Corpet and François Matheron (Paris: STOCK/IMEC, 1993), 111–70, esp. 143–44. My translation follows, as the English edition of this work does not include the essay; compare Louis Althusser, *Writings on Psychoanalysis: Freud and Lacan*, ed. Olivier Corpet and François Matheron, trans. Jeffrey Mehlman (New York: Columbia University Press, 1996): "One might suggest that the ideological formations in which the formations of a given unconscious may be said to 'take' constitute the 'matter,' though the unformed 'matter,' in which certain of the formations typical of the unconscious under consideration 'take.' It would be in and by means of these ideological formations, *among others*, that unconscious-es 'communicate,' in the phenomenon that Freud describes; it would be here, too, that the phenomenon of transference would take place. This point would merit, clearly, more careful definition, and a more precise elaboration, since one can't simply come to a stop on this category of 'matter.' The category has the major disadvantage of serving to mask an important fact: that the discourse of the unconscious is produced in and through ideological discourse, in and through the fragment of ideological discourse where the discourse of the unconscious 'takes,' *while being absent from* this discourse."

38. Louis Althusser, *The Future Lasts Forever: A Memoir*, ed. Olivier Corpet and Yann Moulier Boutang, trans. Richard Veasey (New York: New Press, 1993), 29. Laclau and Mouffe's description of the argumentation on the problem of determination in Althusser bears repeating, as a description of a pathology: "From the very beginning, an attempt was made to render it compatible with another central moment in Althusserian discourse that is, strictly speaking, incompatible with the first" (*Hegemony and Socialist Strategy*, 98). This transference of the language of theory to that of biography is most explicit in Peter Sloterdijk's comments on Althusser in *Critique of Cynical Reason* (Minneapolis: University of Minnesota Press, 1988). An assessment of Althusser's

thought in relation to the coupled questions of reading and self-reading, history and autobiography, may be found in Colin Davis, "Althusser on Reading and Self-Reading," *Textual Practice* 15, no. 2 (2002): 299–316. For Althusser's use of Rousseau as a screen for a certain sort of confession, see Warren Montag, *Althusser* (New York: Palgrave/Macmillan, 2003), 117–35.

39. See Mladen Dolar's quite different treatment of Althusser and transference as the more restricted transference-love in "Beyond Interpellation," *Qui Parle?* 6, no. 2 (1993): 84–85: "This love of the patient for the analyst . . . springs up with an astonishing, almost mechanical regularity in the analytical situation, regardless of the person of the analyst and that of the patient. . . . The minimal mechanism of transference is embedded in the very basic function of speech as addressed to the Other, the Other as an instance beyond all empirical interlocutors." Dolar is careful to note that the "dialectics of transference" requires another moment or aspect: "the emergence of transference-love as . . . a halt of repetition, when the free flow is cut short, when words fail; it emerges as a resistance, or, as Lacan puts it, as the closing of the unconscious." From this "dialectic," Dolar suggestively concludes, the remainder—love—emerges to provide a way of understanding the possibility of subjectivity "beyond interpellation," though the more extensive sense of transference I am suggesting here considerably changes the nature and ethical dimension of that "emergence."

40. This is the point about the *Confessions* made best by Paul de Man, in "Excuses (*Confessions*)," his chapter on the Marion episode in *Allegories of Reading* (New Haven: Yale University Press, 1979), 278–301. See esp. 288–89: "Because Rousseau desires Marion, she haunts his mind and her name is pronounced almost unconsciously, as if it were a slip, a segment of the discourse of the other. . . . But Marion just happened to be the first thing that came to mind; any other name, any other word, any other sound or noise could have done just as well and Marion's entry into the discourse is a mere effect of chance. She is a free signifier, metonymically related to the part she is made to play in the subsequent system of exchanges and substitutions."

41. G. W. F. Hegel, *Philosophy of Right*, trans. S. W. Dyde (Amherst, N.Y.: Prometheus Press, 1996), 286–98.

42. Hegel, *Philosophy of Right*, §279, 286. It is the Italian postwar tradition that, in my view, follows through most carefully the intricate encounter between Marx and Hegel on this point—and not, as one might suspect, the French. In particular, della Volpe's once highly influential work attends patiently to the transformation of Hegel's vocabulary in Marx's work—in ways that seem to me to underlie Althusser's own thought on Marx's supposed break with dialectics. I have in mind particularly della Volpe's late *Logic as a Positive Science* (London: New Left Books, 1980), though della Volpe's early

work on Marx sets in place the bases for the later work. I cite here from Della Volpe's *Logic as a Positive Science*, 202.

43. Marx, *Critique of Hegel's Philosophy of Right*, trans. Joseph O'Malley (Cambridge: Cambridge University Press, 1970), 19.

44. Marx, *Critique of Hegel's Philosophy of Right*, 15. Marx is here poking fun especially at the note to the *Logic*, par. 161: "The movement of the notion is as it were to be looked upon merely as play: the other which it sets up is in reality not an other. Or, as it is expressed in the teaching of Christianity: not merely has God created a world which confronts him as an other; he has also from all eternity begotten a Son in whom he, a Spirit, is at home with himself" (225). The German of Marx's *Critique* is characteristically more vigorous: "Eine andre Bestimmung ist, daß die 'verschiedenen Gewalten' 'durch die Natur des Begriffs bestimmt sind' und darum das Allgemeine sie 'auf notwendige Weise hervorbringt.' Die verschiedenen Gewalten sind also nicht durch ihre 'eigne Natur' bestimmt, sondern durch eine fremde. Ebenso ist die Notwendigkeit nicht aus ihrem eignen Wesen geschöpft, noch weniger kritisch bewiesen. Ihr Schicksal ist vielmehr prädestiniert durch die 'Natur des Begriffs,' versiegelt in der Santa Casa (der Logik) heiligen Registern. Die Seele der Gegenstände, hier des Staats, ist fertig, prädestiniert vor ihrem Körper, der eigentlich nur Schein ist. Der 'Begriff' ist der Sohn in der 'Idee,' dem Gott Vater, das agens (die treibende Kraft), das determinierende, unterscheidende Prinzip. 'Idee' und 'Begriff' sind hier verselbständigte Abstraktionen" (http://www.mlwerke.de/me/me01/meo1_203.htm).

45. The "heilige Haus (la casa santa), welches Maria zu Nazareth bewohnte, wurde, nach der Legende, von den Engeln aus Galiläa, hoch über Land und Meer, durch den Luftraum entführt, und, nach zwey ziemlich langen Ruhepuncten, auf seinem jetzigen Grund und Boden, im Jahre 1295, festgemauert" (Friedrich Matthison, *Erinnerungen von Friedrich von Matthison*, Vienna 1817).

46. Cervantes's characteristically ironic description of the Santa Casa in Loreto is perhaps the best known: Tomás Rodaja, who will become the mad Master Glass, visits "Our Lady of Loreto, in whose holy temple he saw neither walls nor battlements, for they were covered entirely with crutches, shrouds, chains, cuffs, metal bands, hair pieces, half-weights of wax, paintings and tableaux, which made manifest the innumerable gifts that many had received from the hand of God through the intercession of his divine Mother, who enriched and legitimated that holy image with a flock of miracles, as a reward for the veneration in which it is held by those who decorate the walls of her house with such gifts" ("El licenciado Vidriera," in Miguel de Cervantes, *Novelas ejemplares* [Madrid: Castalia, 1986], 2:112–13).

47. This is the vocal score of Johann Carl Gottfried Loewe's ballad "Das heilige Haus in Loretto" ("The Sacred House in Loreto," op. 33, no. 2, *Legende*, vol. 1 (1834).

Wolke lichtweiß in dem Blauen,
Reiner Schwan im Äthermeer!
Ach, wie glänzend anzuschauen!
Engel seh ich um dich her!

Hold erblüht ein Regenbogen!
Du, o Himmelskönigin,
Auf ihm thronend, blickst gewogen
Auf die Welt der Sünde hin!

Heil'ge Jungfrau, die Erscheinung
Überwältigt meinen Geist,
Lehre du mich ihre Meinung,
Was sie kündet, was verheißt!

Und der Schimmer läßt, geteilet
Durch des Morgenhauches Wehn,
Auf der Wolke, die enteilet,
Schilfbedeckt ein Hüttchen sehn,

Und der Wandrer höret sagen
Deutlich: "Das ist Christi Haus,
wo in seinen Kindestagen
Gottes Sohn ging ein und aus.

"Vor den Heiden es zu bergen,
Führen wir es schiffend fort,
Siehe, wir sind Christi Fergen
Und Loretto unser Port."

Seid gesegnet, treue Wächter!
Aber weh um Christi Grab,
Das die Rotte der Verächter
Mit der Drachenhut umgab!

Und herab vom lichten Orte,
Von des Regenbogens Höh'n
Fliessen gnadenreiche Worte,
Helig säuselndes Getön:

"Dankt dem Herrn, der euch zu trösten,
Christi Haus euch heute gab,
Doch ein Kampf ziemt den Erlösten
Glaubensvoll um Christi Grab."

The English translation is by John H. Campbell and W. Krommer:

Brightest cloud in the blue,
Pure swan on the shining sea!

Oh, what brilliant vision!
I see Angels around you!

Brightly blooms a rainbow!
You, o queen of heaven,
Resting upon it, you look down
On this world of sin!

Sainted virgin, the vision
Overcomes my spirit,
Teach me its meaning,
What it foretells, what it promises!

And the shimmering vision parted
Through the breath of morning's gentle wind
On the slowly moving cloud appeared,
a small reed covered house,

And the wanderer hears the words
Clearly: "That is the house of Christ,
where when he was a child,
God's Son went in and out.

"To conceal it from the heathen,
we bear it away,
You see, we are servants of Christ
And Loretto is our port."

Be blest, loyal guards!
But beware around the grave of Christ,
That pack of traitors have
surrounded with the followers of the serpent!

And down from the bright region,
From the rainbow's heights
Mercyful words flow,
Sacred murmuring sounds:

"Thank the Father, that to comfort you,
has given you today the house of Christ,
However struggle becomes the redeemed
who believe in the grave of Christ."

The lyrics are from a poem by Ludwig Giesebrecht (1792–1873), whose work Loewe continued to set to music. From http://www.recmusic.org/lieder/ get_text.html?TextId = 6169. Johann Matthias Schröckh, *Christliche Kirchengeschichte* (Leipzig: Engelhart Benjamin Schwickert, 1799), 28: 260–66.

    48. Hegel, *Philosophy of Right*, 318.

49. The English translation is taken from *Friedrich Schiller: 'Don Carlos,'*
trans. Robert D. MacDonald (London: Oberon Books, 1995), 222. Translations of the Grand Inquisitor's "Wo er war . . ." have varied. Johann Gustav
Fischer's translation reads: "Where'er he travel'd I was at his side" (*Schiller's
Works*, ed. J. G. Fischer [Philadelphia: Barrie, 1883], 90); Charles Passage's
has "Wherever he might be, there I was also" (*Friedrich von Schiller: 'Don
Carlos, Infante of Spain,'* trans. Charles E. Passage [New York: Ungar Publishing, 1959], 208). The German is from *Friedrich Schiller: Don Karlos, Infant von
Spanien, Ein dramatisches Gedicht (Letzte Ausgabe 1805)*, ed. Helmut Nobis
(Frankfurt am Main: Suhrkamp, 2007), 224–25 (ll. 5151–65). The beginning
of the scene is subtly changed from the 1787 version. See Paul Bockmann's
edition of the earlier work, *Schillers Don Karlos: Edition der ursprünglichen Fassung und entstehungsgeschichlicher Kommentar*, ed. Paul Bockmann (Stuttgart:
Ernst Klett Verlag, 1974), 329–31 (ll. 6792–816), as well as his commentary
on the sources—in Rousseau and Montesquieu—of Posa's earlier, contrasting
arguments to Phillip II (490–507); for a *variorum* of the initial editions, see
Friedrich Schiller: Dramen II, ed. Gerhard Kluge (Frankfurt am Main: Deutscher Klassiker Verlag, 1989).

Marx cites Schiller with some frequency (*Die Räuber* was his favorite play)
and remembers this scene from *Don Karlos* at least once more, in *The German
Ideology*. Here it is Feuerbach who is summoned, by Bruno Bauer and Max
Stirner, before an imaginary court for the crime of having withheld *hyle*,
matter:

> These two grand masters of the Holy Inquisition summon the heretic Feuer-
> bach, who has to defend himself against the grave charge of gnosticism. The
> heretic Feuerbach, "thunders" Saint Bruno, is in possession of *hyle*, substance,
> and refuses to hand it over lest my infinite self-consciousness be reflected in it.
> Self-consciousness has to wander like a ghost until it has taken back into itself
> all things which arise from it and flow into it. It has already swallowed the
> whole world, except for this *hyle*, substance, which the gnostic Feuerbach keeps
> under lock and key and refuses to hand over.
>
> Saint Max accuses the gnostic of doubting the dogma revealed by the mouth
> of Saint Max himself, the dogma that "every goose, every dog, every horse" is
> "the perfect, or, if one prefers the superlative degree, the most perfect, man."
> (Wigand, p. 187: "The aforesaid does not lack a tittle of what makes man a
> man. Indeed, the same applies also to every goose, every dog, every, horse.")
>
> Besides the hearing of these important indictments, sentence is also pro-
> nounced in the case brought by the two saints against Moses Hess and in the
> case brought by Saint Bruno against the authors of *Die Heilige Familie*. But as
> these accused have been busying themselves with "worldly affairs" and, there-
> fore, have failed to appear before the Santa Casa, they are sentenced in their

absence to eternal banishment from the realm of the spirit for the term of their natural life. (Karl Marx and Friedrich Engels, *The German Ideology* [Amherst, N.Y.: Prometheus Books, 1998], 104–5)

For a further discussion of the influence of Schiller's aesthetic writings (not, however, his plays) on Marx, see Philip J. Kain, *Schiller, Hegel, and Marx: State, Society, and the Aesthetic Ideal of Ancient Greece* (Montreal: McGill University Press, 1982).

50. Marx refers again to this moment from Schiller's *Don Karlos* in an article entitled "Bekenntnisse einer schönen Seele," *Neue Rheinische Zeitung*, no. 145 (November 17, 1848): "For an official news sheet, the *Neue Preussische Zeitung* is too naively frank. It tells the various parties too explicitly what is locked in the files of the Santa Casa" (*Collected Works of Karl Marx and Friedrich Engels, 1848–49*, Vol. 8, *The Journalism and Speeches of the Revolutionary Years in Germany* (Moscow: International Publishers, 1980), 30.

51. Della Volpe, *Logic as a Positive Science*, 118. Della Volpe's careful parsing of the reciprocal "hypostatization" of the empirical into the speculative concludes with this observation: "This restoration-subreption [the symmetrical restoration of the empirical as idealized "matter" in the place of the speculative], which is none other than Hegel's ontological *petitio principii* and negative *ontological circle*, ultimately emerges, with all its characteristic sterility, as the *result-retribution* of the philosophical dissolution of the empirical in which Hegelian hypostatization consists, of the *dialectics of pure thoughts*, the triadic dialectic of tauto-heterology" (119).

52. It is not the Inquisition that Voltaire is pillorying here, but provincial clerical injustice. See Voltaire, *Dictionnaire philosophique*, ed. M. Beuchot (Paris, 1829), 38:231–34, "Des Crimes de Temps et de Lieu qu'on doit ignorer": " 'Of crimes pertaining to time and location, which one should ignore.' We know how deeply one must respect Our Lady of Loreto when one finds oneself in the *marche* of Ancona. Three youths arrive there; they make bad jokes about the house of Our Lady, which traveled through the air, which came to Dalmatia, which changed location two or three times, and which finally only found itself comfortable in Loreto. Our three dazed youths dine and sing a song composed in another age by some Huguenot, inveighing against the *translation* of the *santa casa* from Jerusalem to the bottom of the gulf of the Adriatic." The disastrous, droll tale of these three dazed youths follows—their encounter with benighted ecclesiastical authority, arbitrary and summary justice serving Voltaire as juicy fodder for his delighted anticlericalism.

53. Althusser, *The Future Lasts Forever*, 208–10.

54. Althusser, "The Facts," in ibid., 333. Compare Colin Davis's careful analysis of the different versions Althusser's autobiographies give of the murder of Hélène, his wife ("Althusser on Reading and Self-Reading," 310–13).

A further avenue into Althusser's autobiographies, by means of Sartre, may be found in Davis, "Historical Reason and Autobiographical Folly in Sartre and Althusser," *Sartre Studies International* 10, no. 1 (2004): 1–13.

55. See Wal Suchting's "Althusser's Late Thinking about Materialism," *Historical Materialism* 12, no. 1 (2004): 3–70, for a review of the background of the "aleatory" in Althusser and (though he makes the connection through the problem of the empirical bases of concept formation, that is, through the question of the relation between individuals and classes) to the "logic of concept-formation" (46–50). Suchting programmatically connects his discussion of Althusser's aleatory materialism with the "openness" of such concepts at the end of the essay: "Aleatory materialism is a philosophical 'thesis' directed at combating 'closures,' at enjoining optimal 'openness.' With respect to the cognitive-theoretical domain, this intervention is directed against both dogmatic and sceptical assumptions about what is or must be the case about the world. In particular, it should be understood as affirming anti-necessitarianism, not ontologically but in purely methodological terms. With respect to the practical-political domain, its intervention is directed at untested—even untestable—assumptions about the possibilities for emancipation, assumptions either about what forwards or what constrains it. As such, aleatory materialism may be compared with 'the principle of causality/determinism,' interpreted not as an all-embracing assertion about how the world is (for example, 'Every event has a cause') but as a rule of procedure enjoining the search for certain sorts of conditions for what happens rather than others (such as teleological ones)" (66).

56. Serge Leclaire indeed showed that Miller's work is associated with a notion of an "unconscious concept" deriving from Freud and concerning the nonidentical to itself (Serge Leclaire, "L'analyste à sa place?" *Cahiers pour l'analyse* 1 [1966], 51).

57. A productive line of thought, which can be said to flow from the early work of Luce Irigaray, then contrasts the specularity of the (history of the) concept to the nonidentity to itself of the woman or of women, a sex understood to be always not one. See Luce Irigaray, *This Sex Which Is Not One*, trans. Catherine Porter (Ithaca, N.Y.: Cornell University Press, 1985).

5. A SADEAN COMMUNITY

1. Michael Hardt and Antonio Negri, *Empire* (Cambridge: Harvard University Press, 2000), 130–32.

2. Ibid., 411.

3. G. W. F. Hegel, *Hegel's Science of Logic*, trans. A. V. Miller (London: George Allen & Unwin, 1969), 571 (bk. 2, para. 1276).

4. Max Horkheimer and Theodor W. Adorno, *Dialectic of Enlightenment: Philosophical Fragments*, trans. Edmund Jephcott (Stanford: Stanford University Press, 2002), xviii.

5. Susan Neiman, for instance, argues that Horkheimer and Adorno get their reading of Kant wrong—that they provide more of an "atmosphere" or collection of innuendoes than an "argument." This atmosphere appears, in Neiman's view, in an insufficiently elaborated understanding of Kant, to whom Horkheimer and Adorno attribute an untenably reductive view of instrumental reason. Nevertheless, what remains to be rescued from *Dialectic of Enlightenment* is precisely their critique of the reflexive, self-instituting shape of instrumental reason: "even a more accurate description of Kant's position," Neiman notes, "must acknowledge one of Adorno and Horkheimer's claims: Kant's moral law has no basis in the structure of reality. It rests instead on what he calls the fact of reason. This means that reason justifies itself" (Susan Neiman, *Evil in Modern Thought: An Alternative History of Philosophy* [Princeton: Princeton University Press, 2002], 192–93).

6. Horkheimer and Adorno, *Dialectic of Enlightenment*, 29, trans. modified

7. Ibid.

8. Sadean violence, in this twofold aspect, is no less the truth of Kant than it is the truth of communitarian ideologies devised in the shadow of Kant's work: as important to our thinking through "a positive concept of enlightenment" as its close kin, the moment of externalization, is to the performance of the Hegelian dialectic. Much attention has been given to Lacan's well-known, developing treatment of the couple Kant-Sade: for instance, in *Le séminaire, Livre VII: L'éthique de la psychanalyse* (Paris: Seuil, 1986), chap. 6; in *Le séminaire*, Livre XX: Encore (Paris: Seuil, 1975), chap. 7; and "Kant avec Sade," in *La philosophie dans le boudoir, Oeuvres complètes du Marquis de Sade*, ed. Gilbert Lely (Paris: Au cercle du livre precieux, 1966), 2: 551–77. "Kant avec Sade" was first printed, in a rough form, in *Critique* 191 (1963): 291–313. The version in *Oeuvres complètes du Marquis de Sade* makes substantial corrections, not incorporated into the version published in *Écrits* (Paris: Seuil, 1966), 119–48. It has been translated as "Kant with Sade," trans. James Swenson, *October*, no. 51 (Winter): 55–75. See, among others, Slavoj Žižek, "Kant and Sade: The Ideal Couple," in *Lacanian Ink*, no. 13 (1998): 12–25. On Lacan's possible relation to Horkheimer and Adorno, see Gilbert Chaitin, "Lacan with Adorno? The Question of Fascist Rationalism," in *Future Crossings: Literature between Philosophy and Cultural Studies*, ed. Krzysztof Ziarek and Seamus Deane (Evanston, Ill. : Northwestern University Press, 2000), 221–48.

9. The stress on totality in Hegelian Marxist thought was the subject of considerable polemic, both in Europe and in the United States. Lukács's formulation is perhaps the best-known: "bourgeois historians . . . reproach historical materialists with violating the concrete uniqueness of historical events.

Where they go wrong is in their belief that the concrete can be located in the empirical individual of history. . . . And just when they imagine that they have discovered the most concrete thing of all: *society as a concrete totality,* . . . they are in fact at the furthest remove from it. . . . Concrete analysis means then: the relation to society *as a whole.* For only when this relation is established does the consciousness of their existence that men have at any given time emerge in all its essential characteristics" (Gyorgy Lukács, *History and Class Consciousness,* trans. Rodney Livingstone [Cambridge: MIT Press, 1972], 50). The classic account of the function of totality in Marxist thought is Martin Jay, *Marxism and Totality: The Adventures of a Concept from Lukács to Habermas* (Berkeley: University of California Press, 1984).

10. Jean-Luc Nancy, *The Inoperative Community,* ed. Peter Connor, trans. Peter Connor et al. (Minneapolis: University of Minnesota Press, 1991), 31; *La communauté désoeuvrée* (Paris: Christian Bourgeois, 1986), 78.

11. Dante, *Purgatorio* 23:31, in *The Divine Comedy of Dante Alighieri,* trans. John D. Sinclair (1939; New York: Oxford University Press, 1981). Here is how Thomas Browne recalls this moment, in a note to his *Hydriotaphia*: "The Poet Dante in his view of Purgatory, found gluttons so meagre, and extenuated, that he conceited them to have been in the Siege of *Jerusalem*, and that it was easie to have discovered *Homo* or *Omo* in their faces; *M* being made by the two lines of their cheeks, arching over the Eye brows to the nose, and their sunk eyes making *O O* which makes up *Omo. Parean l'occhiaie anella senza gemme Che nel viso degli huomini legge huomo Ben'havria quivi conosciuto l'emme"* (Thomas Browne, *Hydriotaphia, Urne-buriall, or, a Discourse of the Sepulchrall Urnes Lately Found in Norfolk* (London: printed for Hen. Brome at the signe of the Gun in Ivy-lane, 1658).

12. Recall that this is how Nancy puts the double construction of the "experience of finitude" as constituting *and* constituted: "One does not produce [community], one experiences or one is constituted by it as the experience of finitude."

13. The bibliography on the notion of contingency is inexhaustible. Among the most remarkable and influential recent works is Jules Vuillemin, *Necessity or Contingency: The Master Argument,* trans. Thomas Morran (Stanford: CSLI, 1996).

14. Chantal Mouffe, *The Return of the Political* (London: Verso, 1993), 153.

15. Ibid.

16. Ernesto Laclau, "Identity and Hegemony," in Ernesto Laclau, Judith Butler, and Slavoj Žižek, *Contingency, Hegemony, Universality* (London: Verso, 2000), 84–85.

17. Richard Rorty, *Contingency, Irony, Solidarity* (Cambridge: Cambridge University Press, 1989), 198.

18. Ibid., xvi.

19. Ibid., 174, 188.

20. Ibid., xiv.

21. Ibid., xv.

22. Ibid.

23. Ibid., 5.

24. Ibid., 187.

25. My argument concerning contingency in *Contingency, Irony, and Solidarity* chimes with the much longer, detailed critique of Rorty offered by James Conant in "Freedom, Cruelty, and Truth: Rorty Versus Orwell," in *Rorty and His Critics*, ed. Robert B. Brandom (Oxford: Blackwell, 2000), 268–342. See especially: "In his eagerness to oppose a very dubious thesis ('the continuation of civilization as we know it is metaphysically guaranteed') with an alternative thesis ('nothing is guaranteed: accidents just happen'), Rorty tends to slide from an unobjectionable construal of the exegetical claim that Orwell believes in the contingency of history to what appears to be a far less plausible construal of that claim. He slides . . . from the claim that Orwell believes that nothing guarantees that things will develop one way rather than another to the claim that Orwell believes that the future outcome of history is essentially *out of our hands*. Rorty never explicitly endorses this fatalistic construal of Orwell's view of history . . . but Rorty's slantings of the rhetoric of contingency in the direction of such a construal leaves him with a reading of Orwell's novel which manages completely to overlook Orwell's own ethical and political motivations in writing the novel" (287).

26. Bouhired's was among the first, and with Alleg's among the most notorious, documented cases of torture by the *paras*. An account by Georges Arnaud and Jacques Vergés, *Pour Djamila Bouhired*, appeared in Paris from Minuit in 1957. For a remarkable review of the role of print works in publicizing the circumstances in Algeria, see Nils Andersson, "Le front éditorial/La censure en effet" in *Le 17 octobre 1961, un crime d'État à Paris*, ed. Olivier Le Cour Grandmaison (Paris: La Dispute, 2001), 89–90.

27. Henri Alleg, *La question* (Paris: Minuit, 1961), 17. The background and immediate effects of the publication of *La question* are the subject of Alexis Berchadsky, *'La Question,' d'Henri Alleg: Un "livre-événement" dans la France en guerre d'Algérie* (Paris: Découvrir, 1994). For a recent account of the circumstances that Alleg details in *La question*, see Raphaëlle Branch, *La torture et l'armée pendant la guerre d'Algérie, 1954–1962* (Paris: Gallimard, 2001).

28. Franco Solinas, *The Battle of Algiers* (screenplay), trans. PierNico Solinas and Linda Brunetto, in *Gillo Pontecorvo's 'The Battle of Algiers,'* ed. PierNico Solinas (New York: Scribner's, 1973), 109. A detailed account of the reactions of the French intellectual class to the events in Algiers may be found

in J.-F. Sirinelli and J.-P. Rioux, eds., *La Guerre d'Algérie et les intellectuels français* (Paris: Complexe, 1991).

29. See Jean-Jacques Pauvert, *Nouveaux (et moins nouveaux) visages de la censure* (Paris: Les Belles Lettres, 1994), and Jean-Jacques Pauvert and Pierre Beuchot, *Sade en procès* (Paris: Mille et Une Nuits, 1999).

30. Jane Gallop has convincingly reviewed Sade's association of philosophy with a male figure and of the student with the naïve young woman. I find especially important her account (revising Angela Carter's 1978 appropriation of Sade) of "the destructive way women are divided, set against each other— feminists versus traditional wives and mothers, bad-girl versus good-girl feminists": by bringing "philosophy into the boudoir, into woman's domestic space, Sade constructs the liberated woman in violent, literal opposition to the mother" (Jane Gallop, "The Liberated Woman," *Narrative* 13, no. 2 [2005]: 97). Gallop is thinking of Angela Carter, *The Sadeian Woman and the Ideology of Pornography* (New York: Pantheon Books, 1978).

31. Sade, *La philosophie dans le boudoir*, in *Oeuvres complètes du Marquis de Sade*, ed. Gilbert Lely (Paris: Au cercle du livre précieux, 1966), 2:375. The standard translation may be found in *The Marquis de Sade: Justine, Philosophy in the Bedroom, and Other Writings*, ed. and trans. Richard Seaver and Austryn Wainhouse (New York: Grove Press, 1965), 190. Where I indicate a page number in the text, my references will be to this translation, which I have on occasion silently modified, always in the interest of maintaining the more literal sense. Where the translation is not followed by a page number, it is my own.

32. *La philosophie dans le boudoir*, in *Oeuvres complètes*, 2:478.

33. Ibid., 2:546

34. Ibid., 548.

35. Jacques Lacan, "Kant avec Sade," in *La philosophie dans le boudoir*, *Oeuvres complètes*, 2:577

36. Jane Gallop, "The Liberated Woman," 97–100.

6. THREE WOMEN, THREE BOMBS

NOTE: A part of this chapter was published in my "Sade on Pontecorvo," *Discourse* 26, no. 3 (Fall 2005): 48–75.

1. Joan Mellen, "An Interview with Gillo Pontecorvo," *Film Quarterly* 26, no. 1 (1972): 2–10.

2. The hesitation may date to the views of Saadi Yacef himself. This is how he explains the genesis of certain of the "reciprocal" shots in the film. He is being interviewed by Nicholas Harrison on May 28, 2007. Harrison asks: "I wanted finally to hear more about the film's own history in Algeria. I read that some Algerians involved in the film, right up to the last minute before it was

released, didn't want to include the shots of the little boy eating ice cream, just before one of the bombs explodes." Yacef responds: "It wasn't 'some Algerians,' it was me. I said to Pontecorvo that Algerian audiences would be critical of that scene, and that we'd have problems, so perhaps we should cut it. He said, well, we could cut it, but he argued that it was important on the one hand to show torture and all that our enemies did wrong, and on the other. . . . The boy was going to die, but it was war, and if people saw that, they would think that we had been courageous, that we'd told the truth as we saw it. So he persuaded me. I spoke about it with friends, and with a minister who was on the set not to keep an eye on us, just out of curiosity and I explained that those shots had to stay. There was violence on both sides, and the film had to tell the truth" (Nicholas Harrison, "An Interview with Saadi Yacef," *Interventions* 9, no. 3 (2007): 412. For a discussion of the debate concerning this scene, see: David Forgacs, "Italians in Algiers," *Interventions* 9, no. 3 (2007): 350–64, esp. 358–59; and Francesco Caviglia, "A Child Eating Ice-Cream Before the Explosion: Notes on a Controversial Scene in *The Battle of Algiers*," in *Terrorism and Film*, *p.o.v.*, no. 20 (2005): 4–20. Caviglia reviews the comments on *The Battle of Algiers* in the 2004 *Cahiers du cinéma* issue devoted to the reissued film. For an illuminating analysis of the film's reception, see Patricia Caillé, "The Illegitimate Legitimacy of *The Battle of Algiers* in French Film Culture," *Interventions* 9, no. 3 (2007): 371–88.

3. Mellen, "An Interview with Gillo Pontecorvo," 3–4.

4. G. W. F. Hegel, *Elements of the Philosophy of Right*, trans. H. B. Nisbet, ed. Allen W. Wood (Cambridge: Cambridge University Press, 1991), 21.

5. Most recently, in Ranjana Khanna's *Algeria Cuts: Women and Representation, 1830 to the Present* (Stanford: Stanford University Press, 2008). Khanna considers *The Battle of Algiers* in light of the notional transition between "third cinema" and "fourth cinema," in the terminology of Fernando Solanas and Octavio Gettino: from a "guerrilla cinema" in which the camera is a gun to a "fourth cinema . . . we could abstractly call . . . the *feminine*, the *excess*, a profound enunciation or crisis or cut in representation—a melancholic remainder sometimes known as *jouissance*" (106). Khanna discusses Solanas and Gettino's "Towards a Third Cinema," *Afterimage* 3 (1971): 16–35, in *Algeria Cuts*, 105–7.

Much of Khanna's analysis is of exceptional interest, in particular, her reconstruction of the boudoir scene. Here are two steps in her argument. "When the film cuts to the women in the cocoon of mirrors, the first shot reveals the reflection of a woman in a mirror only after the zoom back allows us to see the frame of this mirror. This is, then, the image (reflection) of the image (of the actress). And as the audience views the reflective image, we are in a sense in the mirror" (117). And: "The mirror scene, in which weapon is

replaced by cocoon, dramatizes woman as only image. She becomes both a
metaphor for an Algeria that the French wish to 'unveil,' and simultaneously
a metonymy for 'tradition.' . . . The blank screen (woman-womb-cocoon) that
accepts the dramatization, the remembering, the reenactment of trauma
through guerrilla filmmaking reflects only in on herself. How can her own
trauma, as both witness to that which is projected against her and that which
she has experienced herself, be represented? The mirror scene in *The Battle of
Algiers*, where women, like actresses, dress and rehearse as they prepare to act,
reflects the drama of revolution and of filmmaking, forming a space (a third
space?) where representation breaks down because it turns in on itself"
(122–23).

Another singularly useful piece on "three women, three bombs" is Lindsey
Moore, "The Veil of Nationalism: Frantz Fanon's 'Algeria Unveiled' and
Gillo Pontecorvo's 'The Battle of Algiers,'" *Kunapipi: Journal of Post-Colonial
Writing* 25, no. 2 (2003): 56–73, esp. 63–69. She argues: "*The Battle of Algiers*
. . . resorts to a sexually inflected viewing position. This is ironic, given the
fact that the film parodies the specular vulnerability of the French male
authorities to Algerian women. When the women transform themselves into
Europeans, the use of bird's eye view and close-ups clearly indicates the ability
to orchestrate, in [Mary Ann] Doane's words, 'a gaze, a limit, and its pleasur-
able transgression.' As such, the film forces the spectator to breach the privacy
of the changing room and to be complicit in a voyeuristic relation to these
women" (67).

Valérie Orlando has made a similar argument, with considerably less
nuance. "The most pivotal scene in which [Pontecorvo] looks closely at wom-
en's transformation to consciousness, that is from exoticized harem, passive
figures to militant revolutionaries, is a scene in which three Algerian women,
working for the FLN movement, totally alter their personae by dressing in
European clothes in order to infiltrate the French check points and plant
bombs. . . . The most noticeable transformation is that of Hassiba (who is,
incidentally, Saadi Yacef's girlfriend . . .). In this scene we initially see her in
traditional Arab dress and veil. . . . What is significant here is the objectivity
Pontecorvo creates to try and convince, and eventually win over, European
audiences to accept the plight of the Algerians. Although the bombs will bring
about a certain loss of French lives, we identify and find ourselves rooting for
the women, simply because we are placed within their perspective. We see
what each woman must go through" (Valérie Orlando, "Historiographic Metafiction in Gillo Pontecorvo's *La bataille d'Alger*: Remembering the 'Forgotten
War,'" *Quarterly Review of Film and Video* 17, no. 3 [2000]: 268–69).

6. Abdelwahab Meddeb points to this exchange in his fiercely critical
assessment of the film, on its 2004 reedition. "We live in an environment, in

a state of mind, that Pontecorvo's film has helped bring about. I'm not attacking the film itself—I find many good things about it—but historically it participated, particularly in Algeria, in the glorification of terrorism, in the inscription of terrorism in the form of an epic, where it acquires the shape of an heroic act. Terrorism has become in this context a politico-military point of reference. And it is in just this sense, as a positive point of reference, that terrorism returned to Algeria in the 1990s" ("La Bataille d'Alger à présent," *Cahiers du cinéma*, September 2004, 66).

7. Saadi Yacef, *Souvenirs de la bataille d'Alger* (Paris: René Julliard, 1962), 19. A thorough investigation and compelling descriptions of the steps that lead Yacef to Pontecorvo can be found in David Forgacs's excellent "Italians in Algiers."

8. Saadi Yacef and Hocine Mezali, *La Bataille d'Alger* (Paris: Éditions du Temoignage Chrétien, 1982), 167.

9. Susan Slyomovics, "'Hassiba Ben Bouali, If You Could See Our Algeria': Women and Public Space in Algeria," *Middle East Report* 192, *Algeria: Islam, the State and the Politics of Eradication* (1995), 8.

10. Emmanuel Terray, "Headscarf Hysteria," *New Left Review* 26 (March-April 2004): 118–27; and Cécile Laborde's rich and provocative *Critical Republicanism: The Hijab Controversy and Political Philosophy* (Oxford: Oxford University Press, 2008). Laborde summarizes her point of departure: "Critical republicanism endorses the distinctive republican ideals of secularism, non-domination, and civic solidarity, yet suggests that, suitably interpreted, they do *not* justify the ban of hijab in schools. . . . Republicanism is at bottom an ideal of progressive, egalitarian, and social-democratic citizenship, which points to a society where all citizens enjoy basic but robust civil standing, in the form of political voice, minimum personal autonomy, material capabilities, equal opportunities, and intersubjective mutual recognition as equals" (254).

An analysis of the hijab controversy from a feminist perspective may be found in Michela Adrizzoni, "Unveiling the Veil: Gendered Discourse and the (In)Visibility of the Female Body in France," *Women's Studies: An Inter-Disciplinary Journal* 33, no. 5 (2004): 639–49. See her remarks on *The Battle of Algiers*, pp. 631–32, where she stresses the film's role in rendering the image of the veil political. Compare also Donald Reid, "The Worlds of Frantz Fanon's 'L'Algérie se dévoile,'" *French Studies* 61, no. 4 (2007): 460–75, for an argument that Fanon's argument regarding the "unveiling" of the Algerian woman achieves its clarity and persuasiveness "by largely ignoring the situation of a few exceptional Algerian and French women prominent in Algeria during the War of Independence, individuals like the FLN militant Zohra Drif and the French activist Suzanne Massu . . . [who] were quite unrepresentative of Algerian or French women in Algeria, but crucial figures in contemporary representations of activists in each group" (461–62). Reid provides a very useful account of the literary depiction of the battle of Algiers in the years just preceding Pontecorvo's film. In an earlier essay, Reid provides a definitive description of the role of Germaine Tillion in the internal deliberations of the FLN—along with some striking observations concerning the ideological consequences of the absence of Tillion from the heroic-documentary form that Pontecorvo, Solinas, and Yacef employ in *The Battle of Algiers*. See his "Re-Viewing *The Battle of Algiers* with Germaine Tillon," *History Workshop Journal* 60 (2005): 93–115.

11. As Irene Bignardi suggests in "The Making of the *Battle of Algiers*," *Cineaste* 25, no. 2 (March 2000): 16: "Of the three women who, in one of the central episodes of the story, come out of the Casbah carrying the bombs for so many terrorist acts in 'white' Algiers, one had been noticed by Pontecorvo in a restaurant. But it took some delicate diplomatic work to speak to her, because in spite of the liberation and the revolution, Algerian women continued to live in a very rigid society and one couldn't approach them freely. Gillo had found the other two 'on the streets,' not just in a manner of speaking because one was actually a prostitute; she was very young with a sweet, tender, clean face and ended up playing the role of the child bride of one of the NLF fighters."

12. Khanna, *Algeria Cuts*, 15.

13. Danielle Marx-Scouras, "Yacef Girls," *Maghreb Review* 21, nos. 3–4 (1996): 256–66.

14. Frantz Fanon, "L'Algérie dévoilée," *Sociologie d'une révolution: L'An 5 de la révolution algérienne* (1959; rpt. Paris: Maspero, 1966); translated from the French as *Studies in a Dying Colonialism*, trans. Haakon Chevalier with a new introduction by A. M. Babu (London: Earthscan, 1989), 43. See Khanna, *Algeria Cuts*,103–8.

15. Joan Mellen, *Filmguide to 'The Battle of Algiers'* (Bloomington: Indiana University Press, 1973), 30. She is referring to scenes 17 and 87 (Solinas, *The Battle of Algiers*, 26–28 and 99–101). The film's reception is also marked by these obstinately pedagogical moments: one thinks of the Black Panthers' use of the film in the late 1960s (see, among others, Francee Covington's "Are the Revolutionary Techniques Employed in the Battle of Algiers Applicable to Harlem?" in *The Black Woman*, ed. Toni Cade [New York: Signet, 1970], 244–51), and, more recently, of the much-ballyhooed screenings of the film for the Pentagon in September 2003, apparently intended, or so *The Washington Post* believed, to help U.S. specialists prosecute the war in Iraq by "mastering its immediate tactical lessons for how best to proceed in Baghdad." "What will professional military strategists, who now study the film, make of it, particularly as its lessons are applied to U.S. forces in Iraq?" the reporter asks himself (Stephen Hunter, "The Pentagon's Lessons From Reel Life: 'Battle of Algiers' Resonates in Baghdad," *The Washington Post*, September 4, 2003, C1).

16. Saadi, *Souvenirs*, 22–23.

17. Pontecorvo draws attention to the strategic function of social habits when he juxtaposes the indignation of Algerians at a French soldier's desire to frisk an Algerian woman ("Are you mad," his officer tells him, "touching one of their women?"), with a scene showing a traditionally attired Algerian woman in whose veil a revolver is hidden—a revolver then used to shoot "a French soldier having coffee with cream" (Solinas, *The Battle of Algiers*, 48–49). For a review of the biographies and cultural afterlives of Djamila Bouhired and Zohra Driff, consult Danièle Minne, Djamila Amrane, and Alistair Clarke, "Women at War: The Representation of Women in *The Battle of Algiers*," *Interventions* 9, no. 3 (2007): 340–49.

18. The literature on the sociological and religious function of the veil in Islam is rich, controversial, and quite differentiated. The Algerian veil in the 1950s is not the same as the Moroccan veil in the middle 1970s, or the Saudi veil in the year 2001; the veil is not a *burka*; the *foulard* troubles the French secularization debate since 1989 in a way that is distinct from both and that is reinflected by the election of Nicolas Sarkozy. The best-known feminist analysis of the veil is Fatima Mernissi, *Beyond the Veil: Male-Female Dynamics in Modern Muslim Society* (1975; Bloomington: Indiana University Press, 1987) and, more recently, *La peur-modernité: Conflit Islam démocratie* (Paris: Albin Michel, 1992). Mernissi's striking account of the role of the *hijab* in the spatial imaginary of sexual relations throughout Islam—in particular, Maghrebi societies—seems to me still unsurpassed. This is one of her astute definitions: "The concept of the word *hijab* is three-dimensional, and the three dimensions often blend into one another. The first dimension is a visual one: to hide something from sight. The root of the word *hajaba* means 'to hide.' The second dimension is spatial: to separate, to mark a border, to establish a threshold. And finally, the third dimension is ethical: it belongs to the realm of the forbidden" (Mernissi, *Women and Islam: An Historical and Theological Enquiry*, trans. Mary Jo Lakeland [Oxford: Blackwell, 1991], 93). Françoise Gaspard and Farhad Khosrokhavar's *Le foulard et la République* (Paris: Découverte, 1995) and Chahla Chafiq and Farhad Khosrokhavar's *Les femmes sous le voile face à la loi islamique* (Paris: Editions du Félin, 1995) offer lucid assessments of the grounds on which the debate over the veil transpired in France. Useful, slightly more recent reviews of the secularization debate in France may be found in Fawzia Zoary, *Ce voile qui déchire la France* (Paris: Éditions Ramsay, 2004), and especially in Talal Asad, "Trying to Understand French Secularism," in *Political Theologies: Public Religions in a Post-Secular World*, ed. Hent de Vries and Lawrence E. Sullivan (New York: Fordham University Press, 2006), 494–527. For a critique of Mernissi, from a generally Marxian perspective, see Anouar Majod, *Unveiling Traditions: Postcolonial Islam in a Polycentric World* (Durham, N.C.: Duke University Press, 2000), esp. 105–12.

19. Solinas, *The Battle of Algiers*, 49 (scene 40).

20. Edward Said, "The Quest for Gillo Pontecorvo," in his *Reflections on Exile and Other Essays* (Cambridge: Harvard University Press, 2002), 283.

21. Pierre Bourdieu, *The Algerians* (Boston: Beacon Press, 1962), 158–59. The original edition is *Sociologie de l'Algérie* (1958; Paris: Presses Universitaires de France, 1974).

22. Fanon, *Studies in a Dying Colonialism*, 42–43. Fanon's *Pour la révolution africaine* (*Toward an African Revolution*) appeared posthumously in 1964. The work collected a number of Fanon's pieces on Algeria, dating from 1956 to 1961. It was recently reissued as *Pour la révolution africaine: Essais politiques* (Paris: La Découverte, 2001). See also Khanna, *Algeria Cuts*, 103–8, for Fanon's influence on Pontecorvo and Saadi, and Joan Scott's characteristically lucid discussion of Fanon's work in *The Politics of the Veil* (Princeton, N.J.: Princeton University Press, 2007): "the veil became not so much a sign of religious or cultural affiliation as it did the instrument of subversion. It was the means by which the abjection of colonial subjects could be transformed into a proud and independent national and personal identity. . . . Once the trick of the European look had been discovered by security forces, women militants returned to traditional dress" (64–65). Scott summarizes what she calls "the multiple meanings of the veil" even after independence: "For the French, it continued to stand for the backwardness of Algeria, but it was also a sign of the frustration, even the humiliation, of France. It was the piece of cloth that represented the antithesis of the *tricolore*. Immediately after the war, for the new leadership of the Algerian nation, the veil became a contested sign of the future direction of the country" (66).

23. For a spirited and important discussion of and debate on Fanon's essay, see Diana Fuss, "Interior Colonies: Frantz Fanon and the Politics of Identification," *Diacritics* 24, nos. 2–3 (Summer-Autumn, 1994): 19–42; rpt. in *Rethinking Fanon*, ed. Nigel Gibson (Amherst: Humanities Books, 1999); and the response offered by Drucilla Cornell in "The Secret Behind the Veil: A Reinterpretation of 'Algeria Unveiled,'" *Philosophia Africana* 4, no. 2 (August 2001): 27–35. This is Cornell, responding to Fuss's argument that in "L'Algérie dévoilée" Fanon stages "the colonial encounter . . . within exclusively masculine parameters: the colonial other remains an undifferentiated, homogenized male, and subjectivity is ultimately claimed for men alone" ("Interior Colonies," 36): "According to Fanon, forcibly imposed cultural conservation should never be confused with national liberation. This understanding of national liberation and culture is an important reminder that both cultural and national differences are not static realities. In the political effort to constitute a new nation, the struggle to reshape cultural forms is integral to the ways colonized people come to imagine their freedom as a *new* nation in which they

are no longer defined by their oppressors. Freedom is given content as part of the attempts of the colonized to shape themselves politically, ethically, and culturally as representatives of their own future. For women, the refashioning of themselves is inseparable from their re-representation of their relationship to the veil" ("The Secret Behind the Veil," 32).

Lindsay Moore has argued, against Fuss, for understanding the "veil" and the "Algerian woman" as catachreses, but like Fuss she wants to draw attention to what she considers Fanon's universalizing gesture of equating "unveiling with ontological freedom" ("'Darkly as Through a Veil': Reading Representations of Algerian Women," *Intercultural Education* 18, no. 4 [2007]: 341). In an earlier essay, Moore revisits Fanon's essay more directly and argues that *The Battle of Algiers* "deflects the most useful complexities and ambiguities of Fanon's discourse, particularly in relation to the subject of Algerian women. . . . The dissemination of the signs of veiling and unveiling, in particular, has consequences beyond the field of the colonising other's comprehension" ("The Veil of Nationalism," 56).

24. Fanon, "Algeria Unveiled," 184.

25. The September 2004 issue of *Cahiers du cinéma*, devoted to the reissued *Battle of Algiers*, rehearsed Jacques Rivette and Serge Daney's arguments against *Kapo* and panned *The Battle of Algiers* for advocating a heroics of terrorism. See their "La Bataille d'Alger à présent," *Cahiers du cinéma*, September 2004, 64–74.

26. Bowsley Crowther, "The Screen: Susan Strasberg in 'Kapo'—Film about Nazi Camp at Fine Arts Theater," *New York Times*, June 2, 1964.

27. Jacques Rivette, "De l'abjection," *Cahiers du cinéma* 120 (June 1961): 54.

28. Ibid.

29. Serge Daney, "Le travelling de *Kapo*," *Trafic*, no. 4, P.O.L. Editions, 1992.

30. A movement so slight as to go at times unremarked. Indeed, it is a matter of controversy whether the shot reveals in any way the "artistic effect of the hand inscribed within the frame," as Paul Louis Thirard puts it. The polemic has acquired new currency since the release of *Kapo* on DVD. See Thirard's "Pontecorvo est-il abject?" *Positif*, no. 543 (May 2006): 61–62; Thirard sees neither a reframing nor any sort of aestheticization in the shot. See also the response from Jean Michel Frodon, "Risque critique," *Cahiers du cinéma*, no. 615 (September 2006): 5: "But it is quite sufficient to view the DVD of *Kapo* to verify that Rivette had indeed seen just as accurately as he had reasoned: there is indeed a traveling shot, and the shot is indeed reframed. This is the case, even though his article does not bear on this scene alone, but on the whole film, which is, in fact, abject."

31. For a derisive polemical attack on the "documentary" aspect or effect of *The Battle of Algiers*, see Nancy Ellen Dowd, "Popular Conventions," *Film Quarterly* 22, no. 3 (1969): 26–31. A cooler approach, focusing in part on the technical devices Pontecorvo employs to achieve the documentary effect, can be found in Nicholas Harrison's "Pontecorvo's 'Documentary' Aesthetics," *Interventions* 9, no. 3 (2007): 389–404; see his conclusion: "In the *Cahiers du cinéma* dossier that marked the 2004 re-release of the film, one critic remarked: 'The history of The Battle of Algiers . . . has become the history of the uses to which it has been put' (Giavarini 2004: 74); part of my argument has been that the same could be said of the 'Battle of Algiers,' and that The Battle of Algiers contributed to that process in quite concrete ways even while, or even if, self-reflexive, non-linear and non-realist dimensions of its aesthetics may have had the potential, at least, to call into question its historical functions as document and intervention" (403). See also Harrison's "'Based on Actual Events . . ." *Interventions* 9, no. 3 (2007): 335–39.

CONCLUSION: DISTRACTED REPUBLIC

1. The 1931 image, from the Municipal Archive of Cullera, is in the public domain, and has been graciously made available to me by José María Azkárraga, who was responsible for digitizing and reproducing it. My epigraph comes from Victor M. Arbeloa, *Intelectuales ante la Segunda República española* (Salamanca: Ediciones Almar, 1981), 172–73.

2. Diego Saavedra Fajardo, *Empresas políticas: Idea de un príncipe político cristiano*, ed. Quintín Aldea Vaquero (Madrid: Editora Nacional, 1976), 1:227–28.

3. Diego de Saavedra Fajardo, *The Royal Politician Represented in One Hundred Emblems*, trans. James Astry (London: Printed for Matt. Gylliflower . . . , and Luke Meredith, 1700), 1:148–49.

4. "[T]he state [*res publica*] is the interests of the people [*res populi*]. The 'people', however, is not just any collection of human beings assembled together in any manner whatsoever but rather the association of a substantial number of human beings bound together by agreement about justice and by a sharing of resources [*Est igitur, inquit Africanus, res publica res populi, populus autem non omnis hominum coetus quoquo modo congregatus, sed coetus multitudinis iuris consensu et utilitatis communione sociatus*]" (Cicero, *De re publica*, trans. C. W. Keyes [Cambridge: Harvard University Press, 1970], 64–65). Jean Bodin's *Les six livres de la République* (1576; ed. José Luis Bermejo Cabrero [Madrid: Centro de Estudios Constitucionales, 1992]) was widely known in Spain and after the mid 1590s circulated in the translation furnished by Gaspar de Añastro e Isunza, *Los Seis Libros de la Republica de Iuan Bodino traducidos de lengua francesa y enmendados catholicamente por Gaspar de Añastro Isunza* (Turin, 1591). Compare the definition in Sebastián de Covarrubias Orozco's 1611

Tesoro de la lengua castellana o española, ed. Martín de Riquer (Barcelona: S. A. Horta, 1943): "REPVBLICA, Lat. *respublica, libera ciuitas status liberæ ciuitatis.* Repúblico, el hombre que trata del bien común" ("a free city; the state of free cities").

5. "España," writes Fraga, first citing José Luis Comellas, "'de pronto, en 1640, empezó a resquebrajarse.' Crisis interna, al no poder soportar el esfuerzo exterior: deserciones por todas partes; ruina económica y crisis de los ideales" (in Diego Saavedra Fajardo, *Empresas políticas*, ed. Manuel Fraga Iribarne [Salamanca: Editorial Anaya, 1972]. 18). Fraga is quoting from José Luis Comellas, *Historia de España moderna y contemporánea (1474–1965)* (Madrid: Rialp, 1968), 234.

6. Saavedra Fajardo devotes his odd pamphlet *Locuras de Europa* (written in all probability between 1643 and 1646, though not published until 1748) to the European and Iberian crises of the late 1630s and 1640s, and associates Catalonia's desire for independence with France's drive for European hegemony (*Locuras de Europa*, ed. José M. Alejandro [Salamanca: Editorial Anaya, 1965], 53–59).

7. *Diccionario de la lengua castellana (de Autoridades)* (Madrid: Imprenta de la Real Academia Española, 1737).

8. *Diccionario de la lengua española* (Madrid: Imprenta de la Real Academia Española, 1947).

9. I stress the *modern* republic so as to recall how Dante definingly, beautifully braided his exile with the conceptualization of a much earlier form of Florentine republicanism. These are the famous lines from the *Convivio* (Dante 1995: 13–14; 1989: 18): "From the time when the citizens of Rome's most beautiful and famous daughter, Florence, saw fit to cast me away from her sweet bosom—where I was born and nourished until my full maturity . . .—I have made my way through almost all the regions to which this language extends, a homeless wanderer, reduced almost to beggary, and showing against my will the wound inflicted by fortune, which is very often imputed unjustly to the one afflicted" (*The Banquet*, trans. Christopher Ryan [Saratoga, Calif.: Anma Libri, 1995], 13–14).

10. María Zambrano, "Lo que le sucedió a Cervantes: Dulcinea," in *España, sueño y verdad*, ed. María Zambrano (Barcelona: E.D.H.A.S.A., 1965), 43–52.

11. Ibid., 42.

12. Ibid.

13. Félix García Blázquez, "La nación como comunidad de existencia: Conferencia dada en la Universidad de Valencia," *Separada de los Anales de la Universidad de Valencia*, vol. 16, *1939–1940* (Valencia: Hijo de F. Vives Mora, 1940), 65.

14. Zambrano, "Lo que le sucedió a Cervantes," 46–47.

15. Miguel de Cervantes, *Don Quixote*, trans. Edith Grossman (New York: Ecco, 2005), 1.9, p. 67. In Spanish, the lines are: "Él, sin dejar la risa, dijo: 'Está, como he dicho, aquí en el margen escrito esto: "Esta Dulcinea del Toboso, tantas veces en esta historia referida, dicen que tuvo la mejor mano para salar puercos que otra mujer de toda la Mancha"' " (Miguel de Cervantes, *Historia del ingenioso hidalgo don Quijote de la Mancha*, ed. Francisco Rico [Barcelona: Instituto Cervantes, 1998], 1:108).

16. María Zambrano, *Filosofía y poesía* (Alcalá de Henares: Ediciones de la Universidad, 1993), 62.

17. Ibid.

18. Edmund Husserl, "The Vienna Lecture," in *The Crisis of European Sciences and Transcendental Phenomenology*, trans. David Carr (Evanston, Ill.: Northwestern University Press, 1970), 299.

19. As in the famous lines that close Merleau-Ponty's "Avant-propos" to the *Phenomenology of Perception*: "If phenomenology was a movement before becoming a doctrine or a philosophical system, this was attributable neither to accident, nor to fraudulent intent. It is as painstaking as the works of Balzac, Proust, Valéry, or Cezanne—by reason of the same kind of attentiveness and wonder, the same demand for awareness, the same will to seize the meaning of the world or of history as that meaning comes into being. In this way it merges into the general effort of modern thought" (Maurice Merleau-Ponty, *The Phenomenology of Perception*, trans. Colin Smith [New York: Humanities Press, 1962], xxi).

20. Husserl, "The Vienna Lecture," 298.

21. I am following Jan Patočka's still-definitive account of the function of contingency in Husserl's argument, in "The Husserlian Doctrine of Eidetic Intuition and Its Recent Critics," in *Husserl: Expositions and Appraisals*, ed. Frederick Elliston and Peter McCormick (Notre Dame, Ind.: University of Notre Dame Press, 1977), 150–59.

22. A strong description of Husserl's departure from Cartesianism may be found as early as David Carr's "The 'Fifth Meditation' and Husserl's Cartesianism," *Philosophy and Phenomenological Research* 34, no. 1 (1973): 14–35. For a discussion of the transition in Husserl's argument from "personal recollection" to "an inter-subjective act shared by a community" (12), see Robert D'Amico, "Husserl on the Foundational Structure of Natural and Cultural Sciences," *Philosophy and Phenomenological Research* 42, no. 1 (1981): 5–22. D'Amico is helpful on the question of how "the possibility of an historical a priori" is established in Husserl. He is considering Husserl's *The Origin of Geometry*, and his description of the tricky ground on which Husserl is building seems premonitory: the *Crisis* writings are not too far off. Husserl, writes

D'Amico, "argues that tradition does not merely mean a succession of factual situations known by inductive generality, rather it is itself possible because what is handed down and continuous in the sign or document is an ideal objectivity excluding the contingent and the variable. On the other hand, the explication of a self-evidence is not a passive acceptance but a reflective and genetic inquiry" (15). Derrida locates this ambivalence earlier, in Husserl's very definition of "the sign or document" (Jacques Derrida, *Speech and Phenomena*, trans. David B. Allison [Evanston, Ill.: Northwestern University Press, 1973]).

23. Husserl, "The Vienna Lecture," 299.

24. For instance, in Maximilian Beck, "The Last Phase of Husserl's Phenomenology: An Exposition and a Criticism." *Philosophy and Phenomenological Research* 1, no. 4 (1941): 479–91.

25. Husserl, "The Vienna Lecture," 298.

26. For a reading of the *Crisis* book that also stresses this mythico-religious aspect of Husserl's argument, see Charles W. Harvey, *Husserl's Phenomenology and the Foundations of Natural Science* (Athens: Ohio University Press, 1989). Harvey aptly cloaks his description in the language of mysticism: "w*hy* does Husserl refer to the effects of epoche as similar to a religious experience? In the beginning, we suggest, the *reduction happens to us.* Only afterwards, perhaps, can the 'shift of standpoint' (the 'change of attitude') be performed at will. Husserl's procedural techniques for inducing the 'shift' are an attempt to articulate a certain strange experience that has happened to philosophers, to artists and poets, and perhaps to everyone save the hopelessly sane, now and again throughout their personal history. This strange experience is the experience of the strangeness of experience, and of the world. And this strangeness is nothing more (nor less) than the act of *seeing through* the sedimented meanings that one inherits and develops, and that structure one's world. This reduction to the strangeness of the world usually occurs when our beliefs about the world become undone" (233).

27. Or rather, we are close to the estranged and contradictory Husserl we find in Patočka and Derrida, and far from the thematics of "heroism" in the *Crisis* works.

Abbot, George. *An Exposition vpon the Prophet Ionah*. London: Richard Field, 1600.

Adrizzoni, Michela. "Unveiling the Veil: Gendered Discourse and the (In)Visibility of the Female Body in France." *Women's Studies: An Inter-Disciplinary Journal* 33, no. 5 (2004): 639–49.

Agamben, Giorgio. *Homo Sacer: Sovereign Power and Bare Life*. Trans. Daniel Heller-Roazen. Stanford: Stanford University Press, 1998. *Homo sacer*. Turin: G. Einaudi, 1995.

———. *Il Regno e la Gloria: Per una genealogia teologica dell'economia e del governo*. Milan: Neri Pozza Editore, 2007.

Agirre, Julen. *See* Forest, Eva

Alcocer, Pedro de. *Hystoria ó descripción de la Imperial cibdad de Toledo*. Toledo, 1544. Rpt. Toledo: Instituto Provincial de Investigaciones y Estudios Toledanos, 1973.

Alford, Fred C. "Levinas and Political Theory." *Political Theory* 32, no. 2 (2004): 146–71.

———. "Levinas and Winnicott: Motherhood and Responsibility." *American Imago* 57, no. 3 (2000): 235–59.

———. *Levinas, the Frankfurt School, and Psychoanalysis*. Middletown, Conn.: Wesleyan University Press, 2002.

Alleg, Henri. *La question*. Paris: Minuit, 1961.

Allen, William. *A Conference about the Next Succession*. Antwerp: A. Conincx, 1594.

Alonso Asenjo, Julio. *La 'Tragedia de San Hermenegildo' y otras obras del teatro español de colegio*. Valencia: Universidad de Valencia, 1995.

Althusser, Louis. *Écrits sur la psychanalyse*. Ed. Olivier Corpet and François Matheron. Paris: STOCK/IMEC, 1993.

———. *For Marx*. Trans. Ben Brewster. London: Verso, 1969. *Pour Marx*. Paris: Maspero, 1965.

———. *The Future Lasts Forever: A Memoir*. Ed. Olivier Corpet and Yann Moulier Boutang. Trans. Richard Veasey. New York: The New Press, 1993. *L'avenir dure longtemps, suivi de Les faits*. Paris: STOCK/IMEC, 1992.

———. "Is It Simple to Be a Marxist in Philosophy?" in *Philosophy and the Spontaneous Philosophy of the Scientists, and Other Essays*, ed. Gregory Elliot (London: Verso, 1990), 203–40.

———. "Philosophy and the Spontaneous Philosophy of the Scientists." Trans. Warren Montag. In *Philosophy and the Spontaneous Philosophy of the Scientists, and Other Essays*, ed. Gregory Elliot (London: Verso, 1990), 69–165.

———. "Rousseau: The Social Contract (the Discrepancies)." Trans. Ben Brewster. In *Politics and History: Montesquieu, Rousseau, Hegel and Marx*, 116–56. London: New Left Books, 1972. "Sur le 'Contrat Social' (Les Décalages)." *L'impensé de Jean-Jacques Rousseau. Cahiers pour l'Analyse* 8 (1966): 5–42.

Althusser, Louis, and Étienne Balibar. *Reading 'Capital.'* Trans. Ben Brewster. London: New Left Books, 1970. *Lire Le Capital*. Louis Althusser et al. Paris: François Maspero, 1965.

Altieri, Charles. "The Sensuous Dimension of Literary Experience: An Alternative to Materialist Theory." *New Literary* History 38 (2007): 71–98.

Amariglio, Jack, and David F. Ruccio. "Literary/Cultural 'Economies,' Economic Discourse, and the Question of Marxism." In *The New Economic Criticism: Studies at the Intersection of Literature and Economics*, ed. Martha Woodmansee and Mark Osman, 381–400. New York: Routledge, 1999.

Andersson, Nils. "Le front éditorial." In *Le 17 octobre 1961: un crime d'État à Paris*, ed. Olivier Le Cour Grandmaison (Paris: La Dispute, 2001), 89–90.

Anonymous. "Libro de las causas que el Rmo Arçobispo de Toledo y su cabildo movieron a hazer el estatuto quel año pasado hizieron." Hispanic Society Ms. 798.

Anonymous. "Neurasthenia and Shell Shock." *The Lancet*, March 18, 1916, 627–28. Cited in Santanu Das, *Touch and Intimacy in First World War Literature* (Cambridge: Cambridge University Press, 2005), 195.

Arbeloa, Victor M. *Intelectuales ante la Segunda República española*. Salamanca: Ediciones Almar, 1981.

Arendt, Hannah. *The Human Condition*. Chicago: University of Chicago Press, 1998.

———. *The Origins of Totalitarianism*. New York: Schocken Books, 2004.

Aretxaga, Begoña. "Dirty Protest: Symbolic Overdetermination and Gender in Northern Ireland Ethnic Violence." *Ethos* 23, no. 2 (1995): 123–48.

———. "Playing Terrorist: Ghastly Plots and the Ghostly State." *Journal of Spanish Cultural Studies* 1, no. 1 (2000): 43–58.

Aristotle. *De Interpretatione*. Trans. E. M. Edghill. In *The Basic Works of Aristotle*, ed. Richard McKeon, 38–61. New York: Random House, 1941.

———. *Metaphysics*. Trans. W. D. Ross. In *The Basic Works of Aristotle*, ed. Richard McKeon, 681–926. New York: Random House, 1941.

———. *The Nicomachean Ethics*. Ed. Lesley Brown. Trans. David Ross. 2d ed. Oxford: Oxford University Press, 2009.

Arnaud, Georges, and Jacques Vergés. *Pour Djamila Bouhired*. Paris: Minuit, 1957.

Arouet, François-Marie (Voltaire). *Dictionnaire philosophique*. Ed. M. Beuchot. Paris, 1829.

Asad, Talal. "Trying to Understand French Secularism." In *Political Theologies: Public Religions in a Post-Secular World*, ed. Hent de Vries and Lawrence E. Sullivan, 494–527. New York: Fordham University Press, 2006.

Baeza, Álvaro. *GAL: Crimen de estado*. Madrid: ABL, 1995.

Balibar, Étienne. *La crainte des masses: Politique et philosophie avant et après Marx*. Paris: Galilée, 1999.

———. *The Philosophy of Marx*. Trans. Chris Turner. New York: Verso, 2007. *La philosophie de Marx*. Paris: La Découverte, 1993.

———. "Spinoza: La crainte des masses." In *Spinoza nel 350 Anniversario della Nascita: Atti del Congresso (Urbino 4–8 ottobre 1982)*, ed. Emilia Giancotti, 293–320.

Baltas, Aristides. "Louis Althusser: The Dialectics of Erasure and the Materialism of Silence." *Strategies* 9/10 (1995): 154–94.

Bardavío, Joaquín. *La crisis: Historia de quince días*. Madrid: Sedmay, 1974.

Bartley, Aryn. "The Hateful Self: Substitution and the Ethics of Representing War." *Modern Fiction Studies* 54, no. 1 (2008): 50–71.

Bass, Thomas A. "Counterinsurgency and Torture." *American Quarterly* 60, no. 2 (June 2008): 233–40.

Bates, David, ed. *Marxism, Intellectuals, and Politics*. New York: Palgrave Macmillan, 2007.

Batnitzky, Leora. "Encountering the Modern Subject in Levinas." Special issue *Encounters with Levinas*, *Yale French Studies* 104 (2004): 6–21.

Baudry, Leon. *The Quarrel over Future Contingents: Louvain 1465–1475*. Trans. R. Guerlac. New York: Springer, 1989.

Bealieu, Alain. "La politique de Gilles Deleuze et le materialisme aléatoire du dernier Althusser." *Actuel Marx* 34 (2003): 161–74.

Beck, Maximilian. "The Last Phase of Husserl's Phenomenology: An Exposition and a Criticism." *Philosophy and Phenomenological Research* 1, no. 4 (1941): 479–91.

Benton, Ted. *The Rise and Fall of Structural Marxism: Althusser and His Influence*. London: Macmillan, 1984.

Berchadsky, Alexis. *'La question,' d'Henri Alleg: Un "livre-événement" dans la France en guerre d'Algérie*. Paris: Découvrir, 1994.

Bergo, Bettina. "What Is Levinas Doing? Phenomenology and the Rhetoric of an Ethical Un-Conscious." *Philosophy and Rhetoric* 38, no. 2 (2005): 122–44.

Berlin, Isaiah. *Four Essays on Liberty*. Oxford: Oxford University Press, 1969.

Bernard-Donals, Michael F. "Difficult Freedom: Levinas, Language, and Politics." *diacritics* 35, no. 3 (2005): 62–77.

Bernasconi, Robert. "What Is the Question to Which 'Substitution' Is the Answer?" In *The Cambridge Companion to Levinas*, ed. Simon Critchley and Robert Bernasconi, 234–52. Cambridge: Cambridge University Press, 2002.

Bernet, Rudolf. "The Traumatized Subject." *Research in Phenomenology* 30 (2000): 160–79.

Bignardi, Irene. "The Making of the *Battle of Algiers*." *Cineaste* 25, no. 2 (2000): 14–22.

Bilson, Thomas. *The True Difference Betweene Christian Subiection and Unchristian Rebellion*. Oxford: Ioseph Barnes, printer to the Vniuersitie, 1585.

Blanchot, Maurice. *The Writing of the Disaster*. Trans. Ann Smock. Lincoln, Nebraska: University of Nerbraska Press, 1986. *L'écriture du désastre*. Paris: Gallimard 1980.

Blundeville, Thomas. *The Art of Logike*. London: John Windet, 1599.

Bobbio, Norberto, and Maurizio Viroli. *The Idea of the Republic*. Trans. Allan Cameron. Cambridge: Polity Press, 2003.

Bodin, Jean. *Los seis libros de la Republica de Iuan Bodino traducidos de lengua francesa y enmendados catholicamente por Gaspar de Añastro Isunza* (Turin, 1591). Ed. José Luis Bermejo Cabrero. Madrid: Centro de Estudios Constitucionales, 1992.

———. *Les six livres de la République de I Bodin*. Lyon: Jean de Tournes, 1579.

———. *The Six Books of a Commonweale*. Trans. Richard Knolles. London: Adam Islip, 1606.

Boethius. *De divisione liber*. Ed. and trans. John Magee. Leiden: Brill, 1998.

———. *Interpretatio Posteriorum analyticorum Aristotelis*. Patrologia Latina 64. In *Patrologiae cursus completus*, ed. Jacques-Paul Migne. Paris, 1847.

Bogacz, Ted. "War Neurosis and Cultural Change in England, 1914–22: The Work of the War Office Committee of Enquiry into 'Shell-Shock.'" *Journal of Contemporary History* 24, no. 2 (April 1989): 227–56.

Bollack, Jean. *L'Oedipe roi de Sophocle*. Lille: Presses Universitaires de Lille, 1990.

Boltanski, Luc, and Eve Chiapello. *The New Spirit of Capitalism*. Trans. Gregory Elliott. London: Verso, 2005.

Botwinick, Aryeh. "Emmanuel Levinas's *Otherwise than Being*, the Phenomenology Project, and Skepticism." *Telos* 134 (2006): 95–117.

Bourdieu, Pierre. *The Algerians*. Trans. Alan C. M. Ross. Boston: Beacon Press, 1962. *Sociologie de l'Algérie*. 1958; Paris: Presses Universitaires de France, 1974.

Bourdin, Jean-Claude, ed. *Althusser: Une lecture de Marx*. Paris: Presses Universitaires de France, 2008.

Bourke, Joanna. *Fear: A Cultural History*. London: Virago, 2005.

Branch, Raphaëlle. *La torture et l'armée pendant la guerre d'Algérie, 1954–1962*. Paris: Gallimard, 2001.

Brand, Gerd. *Dis Lebenswelt: Eine Philosophie des kondreten Apriori*. Berlin: de Gruyter, 1971.

Brody, D. H. "Emmanuel Levinas: The Logic of Ethical Ambiguity in *Otherwise than Being or beyond Essence*." *Research in Phenomenology* 25 (1995): 177–203.

Brown, Edward M. "Between Cowardice and Insanity: Shell Shock and the Legitimation of the Neuroses in Great Britain." In *Science, Technology and the Military*, ed. Everett Mendelsohn, Merritt Smith, and Peter Weingart, 323–45. Dordrecht: Kluwer, 1988.

Browne, Thomas. *Hydriotaphia, Urne-buriall, or, a Discourse of the Sepulchrall Urnes Lately Found in Norfolk*. London: Printed for Hen. Brome at the signe of the Gun in Ivy-lane, 1658.

Bruni, Luigi. *E.T.A.: Historia política de una lucha armada*. Bilbao: Txalaparta Argitaldaria, 1988.

Burke, Edmund. *Reflections on the Revolution in France*. Oxford: Oxford University Press, 1999.

Caillé, Patricia. "The Illegitimate Legitimacy of *The Battle of Algiers* in French Film Culture." *Interventions* 9, no. 3 (2007): 371–88.

Cairns, Dorion. "Concerning Beck's 'The Last Phase of Husserl's Phenomenology.'" *Philosophy and Phenomenological Research* 1, no. 4 (1941): 492–98.

Callari, A., and D. F. Ruccio. *Postmodern Materialism and the Future of Marxist Theory: Essays in the Althusserian Tradition*. Middletown, Conn.: Wesleyan University Press. 1996.

Callari, Antonio, Stephen Cullenberg, and Carole Biewener, eds. *Marxism in the Postmodern Age: Confronting the New World Order*. New York: Guilford Press, 1995.

Camí Vela, María. "Manuel Huerga y *Salvador Puid Antich*." Interview. *Arizona Journal of Hispanic Cultural Studies* 11 (2007): 181–207.

Campo Vidal, Manuel. *Información y servicios secretos en el atentado a Carrero Blanco*. Barcelona: Argos Vergara, 1983.

Carr, David. "The 'Fifth Meditation' and Husserl's Cartesianism." *Philosophy and Phenomenological Research* 34, no. 1 (1973): 14–35.

———. *The Paradox of Subjectivity: The Self in the Transcendental Tradition*. New York: Oxford University Press, 1999.

Carr, David, ed. *Interpreting Husserl: Critical and Comparative Studies*. The Hague: Martinus Nijhoff, 1987.

Carter, Angela. *The Sadeian Woman and the Ideology of Pornography*. New York: Pantheon Books, 1978.

Castejón y Fonseca, Diego de. *Primacía de la Santa Iglesia de Toledo*. Madrid, 1645.

Cavarero, Adriana. *Horrorism: Naming Contemporary Violence*. Trans. William McCuaig. New York: Columbia University Press, 2009. *Orrorismo: Ovvero della violenza sull'inerme*. Milan: Feltrinelli, 2007.

Caviglia, Francesco. "A Child Eating Ice-Cream Before the Explosion: Notes on a Controversial Scene in *The Battle of Algiers*," *Terrorism and Film*, *p.o.v.*, no. 20 (2005): 4–20.

Celli, Carlo. "Gillo Pontecorvo's *Return to Algiers* by Gillo Pontecorvo." *Film Quarterly* 58, no. 2 (2004): 49–52.

Cervantes, Miguel de. *Don Quixote*. Trans. Edith Grossman. New York: Ecco, 2005.

———. *Historia del ingenioso hidalgo don Quijote de la Mancha*. Ed. Francisco Rico. Barcelona: Instituto Cervantes, 1998.

———. *The history of the Valorous and VVittie Knight-errant, Don Quixote of the Mancha*. Trans. Thomas Shelton. London, 1652.

———. "El licenciado Vidriera." In *Novelas ejemplares*. Madrid: Editorial Castalia, 1987. 185–229.

Chafiq, Chahla, and Farhad Khosrokhavar. *Les femmes sous le voile face à la loi islamique*. Paris: Éditions du Félin, 1995.

Chahan, Michael. "Outsiders: *The Battle of Algiers* and Political Cinema." *Sight and Sound* 17, no. 6 (2007): 38–40.

Chaitin, Gilbert. "Lacan with Adorno? The Question of Fascist Rationalism." In *Future Crossings: Literature Between Philosophy and Cultural Studies*, ed. Krzysztof Ziarek and Seamus Deane, 221–48. Evanston, Ill.: Northwestern University Press, 2000.

Cho, Kah Kyung. "Phenomenology as Cooperative Task: Husserl-Farbre Correspondence During 1936–37." *Philosophy and Phenomenological Research* 50 supplement (1990): 27–43.

Cicero. *De re publica*. Trans. C. W. Keyes. Cambridge: Harvard University Press, 1970.

Clemente, Josep Carles. *Historias de la transición (1973–1981)*. Madrid: Fundamentos, 1994.

Cohen, Richard A., ed. *Face to Face with Levinas*. Albany: State University of New York Press, 1986.

Colletti, Lucio. *Marxism and Hegel*. London: New Left Books, 1973.

Comellas, José Luis. *Historia de España moderna y contemporánea (1474–1965)*. Madrid: Rialp, 1968.

Comestor, Petrus. *Historia scholastica*. *Patrologia Latina* 198. In *Patrologiae cursus completus*, ed. Jacques-Paul Migne. Paris, 1855.

Conant, James. "Freedom, Cruelty, and Truth: Rorty Versus Orwell." In *Rorty and His Critics*, ed. Robert B. Brandom, 268–342. Oxford: Blackwell, 2000.

Cornell, Drucilla. "The Secret Behind the Veil: A Reinterpretation of 'Algeria Unveiled.'" *Philosophia Africana* 4, no. 2 (August 2001): 27–35.

Corral, Pedro de. *Crónica Sarracina*. In *Floresta de leyendas heroicas españolas: Rodrigo, el último Godo*, ed. Ramón Menéndez Pidal. Clásicos Castellanos 62, 71, & 84. 1925–27; rpt. Madrid: La Lectura, 1958.

Covarrubias Orozco, Sebastián de. *Tesoro de la lengua castellana o española según la impresión de 1611*. Ed. Martín de Riquer. Barcelona: S. A. Horta, 1943.

Covington, Francee. "Are the Revolutionary Techniques Employed in the Battle of Algiers Applicable to Harlem?" In *The Black Woman*, ed. Toni Cade, 244–51. New York: Signet, 1970.

Crenshaw, Martha. "The Logic of Terrorism: Terrorist Behavior as a Product of Strategic Choice." In *Origins of Terrorism: Psychologies, Ideologies, Theologies, States of Mind*, ed. Walter Reich, 7–20. Cambridge: Woodrow Wilson International Center for Scholars and Cambridge University Press, 1990.

Critchley, Simon. *Ethics, Politics, Subjectivity*. London: Verso, 1999.

———. "Five Problems in Levinas's View of Politics and the Sketch of a Solution to Them." *Political Theory* 32, no. 2 (2004): 172–85.

———. *Infinitely Demanding: Ethics of Commitment, Politics of Resistance*. London: Verso, 2007.

———. "Introduction." *Parallax* 8, no. 3 (2002): 1–4.

———. "Is There a Normative Deficit in the Theory of Hegemony?" In *Laclau: A Critical Reader*, ed., Simon Critchley and Oliver Marchart, 113–23. London: Routledge, 2004.

———. "The Original Traumatism: Levinas and Psychoanalysis." In *Questioning Ethics: Contemporary Debates in Philosophy*, ed. Richard Kearney and Mark Dooley, 230–42. London: Routledge, 1999.

———. "Persecution Before Exploitation—A Non-Jewish Israel?" *Parallax* 8, no. 3 (2002): 71–77.

Crowther, Bowsley. "The Screen: Susan Strasberg in 'Kapo': Film about Nazi Camp at Fine Arts Theater." *New York Times*, June 2, 1964.

Cutler, Anthony, Barry Hindess, Paul Hirst, and Athar Hussain. *Marx's 'Capital' and Capitalism Today*. London: Routledge and Kegan Paul, 1977.

D'Amico, Robert. "Husserl on the Foundational Structure of Natural and Cultural Sciences." *Philosophy and Phenomenological Research* 42, no. 1 (1981): 5–22.

Daney, Serge. "The Tracking Shot in *Kapo*." Trans. Laurent Kretschmar. *Senses of Cinema*. http://www.sensesofcinema.com/contents/04/30/kapo_daney.html. "Le travelling de *Kapo*." *Trafic*, no. 4 (Les éditions P.O.L., 1992). Rpt. in *Persévérance: Entretien avec Serge Toubiana* (Paris: Les éditions P.O.L, 1994), 13–39.

Dante Alighieri. *The Banquet.* Trans. Christopher Ryan. Saratoga, Calif.: Anma Libri, 1995. *Convivio.* Ed. Franca Brambilla Ageno. Florence: Casa editrice le lettere, 1989.

———. *The Divine Comedy of Dante Alighieri.* Trans. John D. Sinclair. 1939; New York: Oxford University Press, 1981.

———. *Purgatorio.* Trans. W. S. Merwin. New York: Alfred A. Knopf, 2000.

Danzig, Gabriel. "The Political Character of Aristotelian Reciprocity." *Classical Philology* 95, no. 4 (October 2000): 399–424.

David, Alain. "Unlimited Inc." *Parallax* 8, no. 3 (2002): 78–89.

Davis, Colin. "Althusser on Reading and Self-Reading." *Textual Practice* 15, no. 2 (2002): 299–316.

———. "Historical Reason and Autobiographical Folly in Sartre and Althusser." *Sartre Studies International* 10, no. 1 (2004): 1–13.

Del Burgo, Jaime Ignacio. *Soñando con la paz: Violencia terrorista y nacionalismo Vasco.* Madrid: Temas de Hoy, 1994.

Della Volpe, Galvano. *Logic as a Positive Science.* Trans. Jon Rothschild. London: New Left Books, 1980. *Logica come scienza positiva.* Rome: Editori Riuniti, 1969.

De Man, Paul. *Allegories of Reading: Figural Language in Rousseau, Nietzsche, Rilke, and Proust.* New Haven: Yale University Press, 1979.

Derrida, Jacques. *Rogues: Two Essays on Reason.* Trans. Pascale-Anne Brault and Michael Naas. Stanford: Stanford University Press, 2005. *Voyous.* Paris: Galilée, 2003.

———. *Without Alibi.* Ed., trans., and introd. Peggy Kamuf. Stanford: Stanford University Press, 2002.

———. *Speech and Phenomena.* Trans. David B. Allison. Evanston, Ill.: Northwestern University Press, 1973.

Dershowitz, Alan M. *Why Terrorism Works: Understanding the Threat, Responding to the Challenge.* New Haven, Conn.: Yale University Press, 2002.

D'Hondt, Jacques. *De Hegel à Marx.* Paris: Presses Universitaires de France, 1972.

Di Febo, Giuliana. *Teresa d'Avila: Un culto Barocco nella Spagna franchista.* Naples: Liguori Editore, 1988.

Diccionario de la lengua castellana (de Autoridades). Madrid: Imprenta de la Real Academia Española, 1737.

Diccionario de la lengua española. Madrid: Imprenta de la Real Academia Española, 1947.

Dolar, Mladen. "Beyond Interpellation." *Qui Parle?* 6, no. 2 (1993): 75–96.

Dowd, Nancy Ellen. "Popular Conventions." *Film Quarterly* 22, no. 3 (1969): 26–31.

Dreyfus, Hubert L., and Paul Rabinow. *Michel Foucault: Beyond Structuralism and Hermeneutics.* 2nd ed. Chicago: University of Chicago Press, 1983.

DuBois, Page. *Slaves and Other Objects*. Chicago: University of Chicago Press, 2003.

―――. *Torture and Truth*. New York: Routledge, 1991.

Dullaert, Johannes (Jean de Jandun; Dullardus). *Questiones super duos libros Peri hermeneias Aristotelis*. Paris, 1509; Salamanca, 1517.

Edelglass, William. "Levinas on Suffering and Compassion." *Sophia* 42, no. 2 (2006): 43–59.

Eder, M. D. "An Address on the Psycho-Pathology of the War Neuroses." *The Lancet*, August 12, 1916, pp. 264–65.

Edwards, Francis. *The Biography of Robert Persons, Elizabethan Jesuit, 1546–1610*. St. Louis, Mo.: The Institute for Jesuit Studies, 1995.

Eissler, Kurt. *Freud as an Expert Witness: The Discussion of War Neuroses Between Freud and Wagner-Jauregg*. Trans. Christine Trollope. Madison, Conn.: International Universities Press, 1986. *Freud und Wagner-Jauregg vor der Kommission zur Erhebung militärischer Pflichtverletzungen*. Vienna: Löcker, 1979.

Elliott, Gregory. *Althusser: The Detour of Theory*. London: Verso, 1987. Rpt. Leiden: Brill, 2006.

―――. "The Necessity of Contingency: Some Notes." *Rethinking Marxism* 10, no. 3 (1998): 74–79.

Elliston, Frederick A., and Peter McCormick, eds. Introduction. *Husserl: Exposition and Appraisals*. Notre Dame: University of Notre Dame Press, 1977.

Fanon, Frantz. "Algeria Unveiled." In *A Dying Colonialism*, trans. Haakon Chevalier, introd. Adolfo Gilly, 35–68. New York: Grove Press, 1967. "L'Algérie dévoilée." In *Sociologie d'une révolution: L'an 5 de la révolution algérienne*. 1959; rpt. Paris: Maspero, 1966.

―――. *Pour la révolution africaine: Essais politiques*. Paris: La Découverte, 2001.

Farber, Marvin. "Edmund Husserl and the Background of His Philosophy." *Philosophy and Phenomenological Research* 1, no. 1 (1940): 1–20.

Fernández, Ricardo Ibars, and Odoya López Soriano. "Historia y el cine." *CLIO* 32 (2006): 1–22.

Ferretter, Luke. *Louis Althusser*. New York: Routledge, 2006.

Fischbach, Franck. " 'Les sujets marchent tout seuls . . .': Althusser et l'interpellation." In *Althusser: Une lecture de Marx*, ed. Jean-Claude Bourdin, 113–45. Paris: Presses Universitaires de France, 2008.

Forest, Eva (writing as Julen Agirre). *Operation Ogro: The Execution of Admiral Luis Carrero Blanco*. Trans. Barbara Probst Solomon. New York: Quadrangle/NYTimes Book Co., 1975.

Forgacs, David. "Italians in Algiers." *Interventions* 9, no. 3 (2007): 350–64.

Foucault, Michel. *The History of Sexuality: An Introduction*. Vol. 1. Trans. Robert Hurley. Harmondsworth: Penguin, 1993.

———. *Power-Knowledge: Selected Interviews and Other Writings*. Ed. Colin Gordon. New York: Pantheon Books, 1980.

———. *"Society Must Be Defended."* New York: Picador, 2003.

Fraser, Nancy, and Axel Honneth. *Redistribution or Recognition? A Political-Philosophical Exchange*. London: Verso, 2003.

Freidman, R. M. "Exorcising the Past: Jewish Figures in Contemporary Films." *Journal of Contemporary History* 19, no. 3 (1984): 511–27.

Freud, Sigmund. *Beyond the Pleasure Principle*. Vol. 18 of *The Standard Edition of the Complete Psychological Works of Sigmund Freud*. Trans. James Strachey. London: The Hogarth Press, 1960. *Jenseits des Lustprinzips*. Vol. 13 of *Gesammelte Werke*. Frankfurt am Main: Fischer, 1999.

———. *Introductory Lectures on Psychoanalysis*. Vol. 16 of *The Standard Edition of the Complete Psychological Works*. *Vorlesungen zur Einführung in die Psychoanalyse*. Vol. 11 of *Gesammelte Werke*.

———. *Jokes and Their Relation to the Unconscious*. Vol. 8 of *The Standard Edition of the Complete Psychological Works*. *Der Witz und seine Beziehung zum Unbewußten*. Vol. 6 of *Gesammelte Werke*.

———. "Memorandum on the Electrical Treatment of War Neurotics." *International Journal of Psycho-Analysis* 37 (1956): 16–18.

Frodon, Jean Michel. "Risque critique." *Cahiers du cinéma*, no. 615 (September 2006): 5.

Fuente, Ismael, Javier García, and Joaquín Prieto. *Golpe mortal: Asesinato de Carrero y agonía del franquismo*. Madrid: El Pais/PRISA, 1983.

Fuss, Diana. "Interior Colonies: Frantz Fanon and the Politics of Identification." *Diacritics* 24, no. 2/3 (Summer-Autumn, 1994): 19–42. Rpt. in *Rethinking Fanon*, ed. Nigel Gibson, 294–328. Amherst: Humanities Books, 1999.

Gabler, Neil. "This Time, The Scene Was Real." *New York Times*, September 16, 2001, p. 2.

Gallop, Jane. "The Liberated Woman." *Narrative* 13, no. 2 (2005): 89–104.

Galston, William. *Liberal Pluralism: The Implications of Value Pluralism for Political Theory and Practice*. Cambridge: Cambridge University Press, 2002.

García Blázquez, Félix. "La nación como comunidad de existencia: Conferencia dada en la Universidad de Valencia." In *Separada de los Anales de la Universidad de Valencia*, vol. 16, *1939–1940*, 33–65. Valencia: Hijo de F. Vives Mora, 1940.

Gaspard, Françoise, and Farhad Khosrokhavar. *Le foulard et la République*. Paris: Découverte, 1995.

Ghirelli, Massimo. *Gillo Pontecorvo*. Florence: La nuova Italia, 1979.

Giavarini, Laurence. "Quelle histoire?" *Cahiers du cinéma* 592 (2004): 72–74.

González Gutiérrez, Cayo. *El teatro escolar de los Jesuitas (1555–1640) y Edición de la 'Tragedia de San Hermenegildo.'* Gijón: Universidad de Oviedo, 1997.

Gramsci, Antonio. "Problems of Marxism." In *Selections from the Prison Notebooks*, ed. and trans. Quintin Hoare and Geoffrey Nowell Smith, 419–68. New York: International Publishers, 1971.

Grosrichard, Alain. "Gravité de Rousseau." *L'impensé de Jean-Jacques Rousseau. Cahiers pour l'Analyse* 9 (1966): 43–64.

Gurwitch, Aron. "Problems of the Life-World." In *Phenomenology and Social Reality: Essays In Memory of Alfred Schutz*, ed. Maurice Natanson, 39–72. The Hague: Martinus Nijhoff, 1970.

Gutting, Gary. "Husserl and Scientific Realism." *Philosophy and Phenomenological Research* 39, no. 1 (1978): 42–56.

Gutting, Gary, ed. *Continental Philosophy of Science*. Malden; Blackwell, 2005.

Habermas, Jürgen. "Three Normative Models of Democracy: Liberal, Republican, Procedural." In *Questioning Ethics: Contemporary Debates in Philosophy*, ed. Richard Kearney and Mark Dooley, 135–44. New York: Routledge, 1999. "Drei normative Modelle der Demokratie." In *Die Chancen der Freiheit: Grundprobleme der Demokratie*, ed. H. Münkler, 11–24. Munich: Piper, 1992.

Hardt, Michael, and Antonio Negri. *Empire*. Cambridge: Harvard University Press, 2000.

Harrison, Nicholas. " 'Based on Actual Events . . . .' " *Interventions* 9, no. 3 (2007): 335–39.

———. "An Interview with Saadi Yacef." *Interventions* 9, no. 3 (2007): 405–13.

———. "Pontecorvo's 'Documentary' Aesthetics." *Interventions* 9, no. 3 (2007): 389–404.

Harvey, Charles W. *Husserl's Phenomenology and the Foundations of Natural Science*. Athens: Ohio University Press, 1989.

Heelan, Patrick A. "Husserl's Later Philosophy of Natural Science." *Philosophy of Science* 54, no. 3 (1987): 368–90.

Hegel, G. W. F. *Elements of the Philosophy of Right*. Trans. H. B. Nisbet. Ed. Allen W. Wood. Cambridge: Cambridge University Press, 1991.

———. *Enzyklopädie der philosophischen Wissenschaften im Grundrisse*. Ed. F. Nicolin and O. Pöggeler. Hamburg: Felix Meiner Verlag, 1959.

———. *Hegel's 'Logic.'* Trans. William Wallace. Oxford: Oxford University Press, 1975.

———. *Hegel's Phenomenology of Spirit*. Trans. A. V. Miller. Oxford: Oxford University Press, 1977.

———. *Hegel's 'Philosophy of Right.'* Trans. T. M. Knox. Oxford: Oxford University Press, 1952.

———. *Philosophy of Right*. Trans. S. W. Dyde. Amherst, N.Y.: Prometheus Press, 1996.

———. *Hegel's Science of Logic*. Trans. A. V. Miller. London: George Allen & Unwin, 1969.

Heidegger, Martin. "Hegels Begriff der Erfahrung." In *Holzwege. Gesamtausgabe*, 5:115–205. Frankfurt am Main: Vittorio Klostermann, 1977.

Henninger, Max. "From Sociological to Ontological Inquiry: An Interview with Antonio Negri." *Italian Culture* 23 (2005): 153–66.

Hermberg, Kevin. *Husserl's Phenomenology: Knowledge, Objectivity, and Others*. New York: Continuum, 2006.

Herrero, Luis. *El ocaso del régimen: Del asesinato de Carrero a la muerte de Franco*. Madrid: Ediciones Temas de Hoy, 1995.

Honneth, Axel. *Disrespect: The Normative Foundations of Critical Theory*. Cambridge: Polity Press, 2007.

———. *The Fragmented World of the Social*. Ed. Charles W. Wright. Albany: State University of New York Press, 1990.

———. *The Struggle for Recognition: The Moral Grammar of Social Conflicts*. Trans. Joel Anderson. Cambridge: MIT Press, 1995.

Horkheimer, Max, and Theodor W. Adorno. *Dialectic of Enlightenment: Philosophical Fragments*. Trans. Edmund Jephcott. Stanford: Stanford University Press, 2002. *Dialektik der Aufklärung*. Vol. 3 of Theodor W. Adorno, *Gesammelte Schriften*. Frankfurt am Main: Suhrkamp, 1997.

Horozco, Sebastián de. *Relaciones históricas toledanas*. Written before 1581 (BNM Ms. 9175). Published as *Relaciones históricas toledanas*. Ed. Jack Weiner. Toledo: Instituto Provincial de Investigaciones y Estudios Toledanos, 1981.

Hunter, Stephen. "The Pentagon's Lessons from Reel Life: 'Battle of Algiers' Resonates in Baghdad." *The Washington Post*, September 4, 2003, C1.

Husserl, Edmund. "The Vienna Lecture." In *The Crisis of European Sciences and Transcendental Phenomenology*, trans. David Carr, 269–99. Evanston, Ill.: Northwestern University Press, 1970. *Die Krisis der europäischen Wissenschaften und die transzendentale Phänomenologie*. Ed. Walter Biemel. The Hague: Martinus Nijhoff, 1954.

Ignatieff, Michael. "The Terrorist as Auteur." *New York Times Magazine*, November 14, 2004, pp. 50–58.

Ince, Kate. "Questions to Luce Irigaray." *Hypatia* 11, no. 2 (1996): 122.

Isidore of Seville. *Etymologiae. Patrologia Latina* 82. In *Patrologiae cursus completus*, ed. Jacques-Paul Migne. Paris, 1830.

Jay, Martin. *Marxism and Totality: The Adventures of a Concept from Lukács to Habermas*. Berkeley: University of California Press, 1984.

Jordan, Barry. "Refiguring the Past in the Post-Franco Film: Fernando Trueba's *Belle Époque*." *Bulletin of Spanish Studies* 76, no. 1 (1999): 139–56.

Kain, Philip J. *Schiller, Hegel, and Marx: State, Society, and the Aesthetic Ideal of Ancient Greece*. Montreal: McGill University Press, 1982.

Kant, Immanuel. *Critique of Pure Reason*. Trans. F. Max Müller. New York: Anchor, 1966. *Kritik der reinen Vernunft*. Frankfurt am Main: Suhrkamp, 1982.

―――. "The Vienna Logic." In *Lectures on Logic*. Trans. J. Michael Young. Cambridge: Cambridge University Press, 1992. 251–80.

Kaufmann, Doris. "Science as Cultural Practice: Psychiatry in the First World War and Weimar Germany." Trans. A. J. Wells. *Journal of Contemporary History* 34, no. 1 (January 1999): 125–44.

Kawashiwa, Ken C. "Capital's Dice-Box Shaking: The Contingent Commodification of Labor Power." *Rethinking Marxism: A Journal of Economics, Culture, and Society* 17, no. 4 (2005): 609–26.

Kearney, Richard, and Mark Dooley, eds. *Questioning Ethics: Contemporary Debates in Philosophy*. New York: Routledge, 1999.

Khanna, Ranjana. *Algeria Cuts: Women and Representation, 1830 to the Present*. Stanford: Stanford University Press, 2008.

―――. "*The Battle of Algiers* and *The Nouba of the Women of Mont Chenoua*: From Third to Fourth Cinema." *Third Text* 12, no. 43 (1998): 13–32.

Kintzler, Catherine. "Terreur et vertu: Métaphysique, morale et esthétique au comble du politique." In *La République et la terreur*, ed. Catherine Kintzler and Hadi Rizk, 3–20. Paris: Kimé, 1995.

Kojève, Alexandre. *Introduction to the Reading of Hegel: Lectures on the 'Phenomenology of Spirit.'* Ithaca. N.Y.: Cornell University Press, 1980. *Introduction à la lecture de Hegel*. Paris: Gallimard, 1947.

Laborde, Cécile. *Critical Republicanism: The Hijab Controversy and Political Philosophy*. Oxford: Oxford University Press, 2008.

Lacan, Jacques. "The Agency of the Letter in the Unconscious or Reason since Freud." In *Ecrits*, trans. Alan Sheridan, 146–68. New York: Norton, 1977.

―――. "Kant with Sade," trans. James B, Swenson, Jr., *October*, no. 51 (Winter 1989): 55–75. "Kant avec Sade." *Critique* 191 (1963): 291–313. Rpt. in *La philosophie dans le boudoir, Oeuvres complètes du Marquis de Sade*, ed. Gilbert Lely (Paris: Au cercle du livre precieux, 1966), 551–77, and in *Écrits* (Paris: Seuil, 1966), 119–148.

―――. *Le séminaire, Livre VII: L'éthique de la psychanalyse*. Paris: Seuil, 1986.

―――. *Le séminaire, Livre XX: Encore*. Paris: Seuil, 1975.

―――. *The Seminar of Jacques Lacan, Book II: The Ego in Freud's Theory*. Ed. Jacques-Alain Miller. Trans. Sylvana Tomaselli. New York: W.W. Norton, 1991.

Laclau, Ernesto. *Emancipation(s)*. London: Verso, 1996.

―――. *On Populist Reason*. London: Verso, 2005.

―――. "Why Constructing a People Is the Main Task of Radical Politics." *Critical Inquiry* 32 (Summer 2006): 646–80.

Laclau, Ernesto, and Chantal Mouffe. *Hegemony and Socialist Strategy*. London: Verso, 1985. 2d ed., 2001.

Laclau, Ernesto, and Lilian Zac. "Minding the Gap: The Subject of Politics." In *The Making of Political Identities*, ed. Ernesto Laclau, 11–39. London: Verso, 1994.

Laclau, Ernesto, Judith Butler, and Slavoj Žižek. *Contingency, Hegemony, Universality*. London: Verso, 2000.

Laqueur, Walter. *The Age of Terrorism*. Boston: Little, Brown, 1987.

Larise, Djuna. "Der aleatorische Materialismus: Ein theoretisches Projekt des spaten Althusser." *Synthesis Philosophica* 41, no. 1 (2006): 115–37.

Lazarus, Sylvain, ed. *Politique et philosophie dans l'oeuvre de Louis Althusser*. Paris: Presses Universitaires de France, 1993.

Lea, Henry Charles. *A History of the Inquisition of Spain*. New York: The Macmillan Company, 1922.

Le Blanc, G. "Etre assujetti: Althusser, Foucault, Butler." *Actuel Marx* 36 (2004): 45–62.

Leclaire, Serge. "L'analyste à sa place?" *Cahiers pour l'analyse* 1 (1966): 50–52.

Leed, Eric. *No Man's Land: Combat and Identity in World War*. Cambridge: Cambridge University Press, 1979.

Lerner, Paul. *Hysterical Men: War, Psychiatry, and the Politics of Trauma in Germany, 1890–1939*. Ithaca, N.Y.: Cornell University Press, 2003.

Lever, Ralph. *The Arte of Reason, Rightly Termed, Witcraft*. London: H. Bynneman, 1573.

Levin, Michael. "The Case for Torture." *Newsweek*, June 7, 1982. Online at http://www.coc.cc.ca.us/departments/philosophy/levin.html. Also in *The Norton Reader: An Anthology of Expository Prose*, ed. Linda H. Peterson and John C. Brereton. New York: W. W. Norton, 2003. 694–96.

Levinas, Emmanuel. *Otherwise than Being, or Beyond Essence*. Trans. Alphonso Lingis. The Hague: Martinus Nijhoff, 1981. *Autrement qu'être ou au-delà de l'essence*. The Hague: Martinus Nijhoff, 1978.

———. "Substitution." Trans. Alphonso Lingis. In *The Levinas Reader*, ed. Seán Hand, 88–125. Oxford: Blackwell, 1989.

Lewis, William S. *Louis Althusser and the Traditions of French Marxism*. Lanham, Md.: Lexington Books, 2005.

Levinson, Sanford, ed. *Torture: A Collection*. New York: Oxford University Press, 2004.

Lezra, Jacques. "Sade on Pontecorvo." *Discourse* 26, no. 3 (Fall 2005): 48–75.

Lezra, Jacques, ed. *Depositions: Althusser, Balibar, Macherey, and the Labor of Reading*. Special issue, *Yale French Studies* 88 (1995).

Lispector, Clarice. *Family Ties*. Trans. Giovanni Pontiero. Austin: University of Texas Press, 1972. *Laços de família*. São Paulo: Livraria Francisco Alves, 1961.

Loewe, Johann Karl Gottfried. "Das heilige Haus in Loretto." Op. 33, no. 2. *Legende*, 1:1834. From http://www.recmusic.org/lieder/get_text.html?TextId=6169.

López de Ayala Cedillo, Jerónimo. *Toledo en el siglo XVI, después del vencimiento de las comunidades: Discursos leídos ante la Real Academia de la historia en la recepción pública . . ..* Madrid: Hernández, 1901.

Lozano, Cristóbal de. *De los reyes nuevos toledanos.* Madrid, 1674.

Lukács, Gyorgy. *History and Class Consciousness.* Trans. Rodney Livingstone. Cambridge: MIT Press, 1972.

Luna, Miguel de. *La verdadera historia del Rey Don Rodrigo, en la qual se trata la causa principal de la perdida de España y de la conquista que de ella hizo Miramamolin Almançor Rey que fue del Africa, y de las Arabias* (Granada, 1592 and 1600). Facs. rpt. Ed. Luis F. Bernabé Pons. Granada: Editorial Universidad de Granada, 2001.

Luxon, Thomas H. "A Second Daniel: The Jew and the 'True Jew' in *The Merchant of Venice.*" *Early Modern Literary Studies* 4, no. 3 (January, 1999): 1–37.

Macey, David. "Thinking with Borrowed Concepts: Althusser and Lacan." In *Althusser: A Critical Reader*, ed. Gregory Elliott, 142–58. Oxford: Blackwell, 1994.

McGuinness, Brian, ed. *Wittgenstein and the Vienna Circle: Conversations Recorded by Friedrich Waismann.* Trans. Joachim Schulte and Brian McGuinness. New York: Barnes & Noble Books, 1979.

Macherey, Pierre. "Le leurre hégélien." *Le Bloc Note de la Psychanalyse* 5 (1985): 27–50.

———. *A Theory of Literary Production.* Trans. Geoffrey Wall. London: Routledge, 1978. *Pour une théorie de la production littéraire.* Paris: Maspero, 1966.

Majod, Anouar. *Unveiling Traditions: Postcolonial Islam in a Polycentric World.* Durham, N.C.: Duke University Press, 2000.

Marighella, Carlos. "Minimanual of the Urban Guerrilla." In *Manual of the Urban Guerrilla*, ed. and trans. Gene Hanrahan. Chapel Hill: Documentary Publications, 1985.

Markell, Patchen. *Bound by Recognition.* Princeton: Princeton University Press, 2003.

Martínez Guijarro, Juan (Silíceo, Siliceus). *Arithmetica Ioannis Martini, Scilicei, in theoricen et praxim scissa.* Paris, 1519.

Marx, Karl. "Bekenntnisse einer schönen Seele." "Neue Rheinische Zeitung," no. 145 (November 17, 1848). In Karl Marx and Friedrich Engels, *Werke*, 6:24–28. Berlin: Dietz Verlag, 1959. Translated in *Collected Works of Karl Marx and Friedrich Engels, 1848–49*, vol. 8, *The Journalism and Speeches of the Revolutionary Years in Germany*, 30–32. Moscow: International Publishers, 1980.

———. *Capital.* Vol. 1. Trans. Samuel Moore and Edward Aveling. New York: International Publishers, 1967.

———. *Critique of Hegel's Philosophy of Right.* Trans. Joseph O'Malley. Cambridge: Cambridge University Press, 1970.

Marx, Karl, and Friedrich Engels. *The German Ideology.* Amherst, N.Y.: Prometheus Books, 1998.

Marx, Werner. "The Life-World and the Particular Sub-Worlds." *Phenomenology and Social Reality: Essays in Memory of Alfred Schutz,* 62–72. The Hague: Martinus Nijhoff, 1970.

Marx-Scouras, Danielle. "Yacef Girls." *Maghreb Review* 21, nos. 3–4 (1996): 256–66.

Mather, Ronald. "Hegemony and Marxist Psychology." *Theory and Psychology* 13, no. 4 (2003): 469–87.

Matheron, François. "The Recurrence of the Void in Louis Althusser." Trans. Erin A. Post. *Rethinking Marxism* 10, no. 3 (1998): 22–37.

Matthison, Friedrich. *Erinnerungen von Friedrich von Matthison.* Vienna, 1817.

Meddeb, Abdelwahab. "La Bataille d'Alger à présent." *Cahiers du cinéma,* September 2004, 64–74.

Mellen, Joan. *Filmguide to 'The Battle of Algiers.'* Bloomington: Indiana University Press, 1973.

———. "An Interview with Gillo Pontecorvo." *Film Quarterly* 26 no. 1 (1972): 2–10.

Menéndez Peláez, Jesús. *Los Jesuitas y el teatro en el Siglo de Oro.* Gijón: Universidad de Oviedo, 1995.

Menéndez Pelayo, Marcelino. *Historia de los heterodoxos españoles.* Madrid: F. Maroto and Sons, 1881.

Merleau-Ponty, Maurice. *The Phenomenology of Perception.* Trans. Colin Smith. New York: Humanities Press, 1962. *Phénoménologie de la perception.* Paris: Gallimard, 1945.

———. *The Visible and the Invisible.* Trans. Ernesto Lingis. Evanston, Ill.: Northwestern University Press, 1968. *Le visible et l'invisible.* Paris: Gallimard, 1964.

Mernissi, Fatima. *Beyond the Veil: Male-Female Dynamics in Modern Muslim Society.* 1975; 2nd ed. Bloomington: Indiana University Press, 1987.

———. *La peur-modernité: Conflit Islam démocratie.* Paris: Albin Michel, 1992.

———. *Women and Islam: An Historical and Theological Enquiry.* Trans. Mary Jo Lakeland. Oxford: Blackwell, 1991.

Méthais, Pierre. "Contrat et volonté générale selon Hegel et Rousseau." In *Hegel et le siècle des lumières,* ed. Jacques D'Hondt, 101–48. Paris: Presses Universitaires de France, 1974.

Meyers, Charles S. "Contributions to the Study of Shell Shock." *The Lancet.* February 13, 1915, 316–20.

———. *Shell Shock in France, 1914–1918.* Cambridge: Cambridge University Press, 1940.

Milchman, Alan, and Alan Rosenberg. "Marxism and Governmentality Studies: Toward a Critical Encounter." *Rethinking Marxism* 14, no. 1 (2002): 132–42.

Miller, Jacques-Alain. "Suture (Elements of the Logic of the Signifier)." Trans. Jacqueline Rose. *Screen* 18, no. 4 (Winter 1977–78): 24–34. "La Suture." *Cahiers pour l'analyse* 1, no. 1 (Winter 1966), n 1, 37–49.

Minne, Danièle, Djamila Amrane, and Alistair Clarke. "Women at War." *Interventions* 9, no. 3 (2007): 340–49.

Mocnik, Rastko. "Ideology and Fantasy." In *The Althusserian Legacy*, ed. E. Ann Kaplan and Michael Sprinker, 139–56. London: Verso, 1993.

Montag, Warren. *Althusser*. New York: Palgrave/Macmillan, 2003.

———."Marxism and Psychoanalysis: The Impossible Encounter." *Minnesota Review* n.s. 23 (Fall 1984): 70–85.

———. "Materiality, Singularity, Subject: Response to Callari, Smith, Hardt, and Parker." *Rethinking Marxism* 17, no. 2 (2005): 185–90.

———. "Politics: Transcendent or Immanent? A Response to Miguel Vatter's Machiavelli after Marx." *Theory and Event* 7, no. 4 (2004); online at http://muse.jhu.edu/journals/theory_and_event/v007/7.4montag.html.

Montefiore, Alan. "Levinas and the Claims of Incommensurable Values." Special issue *Levinas and Politics*, ed. Simon Critchley. *Parallax* 8, no. 3 (2002): 90–102.

Moore, Lindsay. " 'Darkly as Through a Veil': Reading Representations of Algerian Women." *Intercultural Education* 18, no. 4 (2007): 335–51.

———. "The Veil of Nationalism: Frantz Fanon's 'Algeria Unveiled' and Gillo Pontecorvo's 'The Battle of Algiers.' " *Kunapipi: Journal of Post-Colonial Writing* 25, no. 2 (2003): 56–73.

Morrison, James C. "Husserl's 'Crisis': Reflections on the Relationship of Philosophy and History." *Philosophy and Phenomenological Research* 37, no. 3 (1977): 312–30.

Mott, Frederick W. *War Neuroses and Shell Shock*. London: Henry Froude and Hodder & Stoughton, 1919.

Mouffe, Chantal. *The Democratic Paradox*. London: Verso, 2000.

———. *The Return of the Political*. London: Verso, 1993.

Murphy, Martin. *St. Gregory's College, Seville, 1592–1767*. The Catholic Record Society, vol. 73. Southampton: Hobbs, 1992.

Musso y Pontes, José, Ed. *Diccionario de las metáforas y refranes de la lengua castellana*. Barcelona: N. Ramírez, 1876.

Nancy, Jean-Luc. *The Experience of Freedom*. Trans. Bridget McDonald. Foreword by Peter Fenves. Stanford: Stanford Univeristy Press, 1993. *L'Expérience de la liberté*. Paris: Galilée, 1988.

———. *The Inoperative Community*. Ed. Peter Connor. Trans. Peter Connor et al. Minneapolis: University of Minnesota Press, 1991. *La communauté désoeuvrée*. Paris: Christian Bourgeois, 1986.

Negri, Antonio. *Il dominio e il sabotaggio*. Milan: Feltrinelli, 1978.

———. "Machiavel selon Althusser." *Future Antérieur* (1997); online at http://multitudes.samizdat.net/Machiavel-selon-Althusser.

Neiman, Susan. *Evil in Modern Thought: An Alternative History of Philosophy*. Princeton: Princeton University Press, 2002.

Newton, Adam Zachary. "Versions of Ethics; or, the SARL of Criticism: Sonority, Arrogation, Letting-Be." *American Literary History* 13, no. 3 (2001): 603–37.

Ong, Walter J. *Ramus, Method, and the Decay of Dialogue*. Cambridge: Harvard University Press, 1958.

Orlando, Valérie. "Historiographic Metafiction in Gillo Pontecorvo's *La bataille d'Alger*: Remembering the 'Forgotten War.'" *Quarterly Review of Film and Video* 17, no. 3 (2000): 261–71.

Ortiz, Blas. *Descriptio templi toletani*. In *Collectio S.S. Patrum Ecclesiae Toletana*. Madrid, 1793.

Parker, Andrew. "The Other of Class." *Rethinking Marxism* 17, no. 1 (2005): 15–18.

Patell, Shireen R. K. "Pas de Substitution." *The New Centennial Review* 7, no. 2 (2007): 89–110.

Patočka, Jan. "The Husserlian Doctrine of Eidetic Intuition and Its Recent Critics." In *Husserl: Expositions and Appraisals*, ed. Frederick Elliston and Peter McCormick, 150–59. Notre Dame, Ind.: University of Notre Dame Press, 1977.

Pauvert, Jean-Jacques. *Nouveaux (et moins nouveaux) visages de la censure*. Paris: Les Belles Lettres, 1994.

Pauvert, Jean-Jacques, and Pierre Beuchot. *Sade en procès*. Paris: Mille et Une Nuits, 1999.

Pavlovic, Tatjana. *Despotic Bodies and Transgressive Bodies: Spanish Culture from Francisco Franco to Jesús Franco*. Albany: State University of New York Press, 2003.

Persons, Robert. *A Christian Directorie Guiding Men to Their Saluation*. The second edition of Robert Persons's *First Booke of the Christian Exercise*. Rouen: Fr. Persons's press, 1585.

———. *Nevves from Spayne and Holland Conteyning. An Information of Inglish Affayres in Spayne vvith a Conference Made Thereuppon in Amsterdame of Holland*. Antwerp: A. Conincx, 1593.

Pettit, Philip. *Republicanism: A Theory of Freedom and Government*. Oxford: Oxford University Press, 1997.

Piñuel, José Luis. *El terrorismo en la transición española*. Madrid: Editorial Fundamentos, 1986.

Pocock, John. *The Machiavellian Moment: Florentine Political Thought and the Atlantic Republican Tradition*. Princeton: Princeton University Press, 1975.

Poe, Edgar Allan. *Poetry and Tales*. Vol. 1 of *Edgar Allan Poe*. Ed. Patrick Francis Quinn. New York: Library of America, 1984.

Powell, Griffith. *Analysis Analyticorum Posteriorum*. Oxford: Joseph Barnes, 1594.

Preston, Paul. *Franco: A Biography*. New York: Basic Books, 1994.

Primo de Rivera, José Antonio. *Obras completas*. Ed. Agustín del Rio Cisneros. Madrid: Dirección general de informaciones públicas españolas, 1952.

Prochaska, David. "That Was Then, This Is Now: *The Battle of Algiers* and After." *Radical History Review* 85 (2003): 133–49.

Putnam, Hilary. *Ethics Without Ontology*. Cambridge: Harvard University Press, 2004.

Rahmani, Sina. "Said: The Last Interview." *Comparative Studies of South Asia, Africa, and the Middle East* 125, no. 2 (2005): 512–14.

Rancière, Jacques. "Althusser, Don Quixote, and the Stage of the Text." In *The Flesh of Words: The Politics of Writing*, trans. Charlotte Mandell, 129–46. Stanford: Stanford Unversity Press, 2004. "La scène du texte." In *Politique et philosophie dans l'oeuvre de Louis Althusser*, ed. Sylvain Lazarus. Paris: Presses Universitaires de France, 1993, 47–66.

Raymond, Pierre, ed. *Althusser philosophe*. Paris: Presses Universitaires de France, 1997.

Read, Jason. "Primitive Accumulation: The Aleatory Foundation of Capitalism." *Rethinking Marxism* 14, no. 2 (2002): 24–49.

Reid, Donald. "Re-Viewing *The Battle of Algiers* with Germaine Tillon." *History Workshop Journal* 60 (2005): 93–115.

———. "The Worlds of Frantz Fanon's 'L'Algérie se dévoile.'" *French Studies* 61, no. 4 (2007): 460–75.

Reinares, Fernando. *Violencia y política en Euskadi*. Bilbao: Desclée de Brouwer, 1984.

Reinhard, Kenneth. "Kant with Sade, Lacan with Levinas." *Modern Language Notes* 110, no.4 (1995): 785–808.

Ricoeur, Paul. *Husserl: An Analysis of His Phenomenology*. Trans. Edward G. Ballard and Lester E. Embree. Evanston, Ill.: Northwestern Univeristy Press, 1967.

———. "Otherwise: A Reading of Emmanuel Levinas's *Otherwise than Being, or Beyond Essence*." Trans. Matthew Escobar. Special issue *Encounters with Levinas*, *Yale French Studies* 104 (2004): 82–99.

Riera, Gabriel. "'The *Possibility* of the Poetic *Said*' in *Otherwise than Being* (Allusion, or Blanchot in Levinas)." *diacritics* 34, no. 2 (2004): 14–36.

Rivette, Jacques. "De l'abjection." *Cahiers du cinéma* 120 (June 1961): 54–55.

Roberts, Katherine A. "Constrained Militants: Algerian Women 'In-Between' in Gillo Pontecorvo's *The Battle of Algiers* and Bourlem Guerdjou's *Living in Paradise*." *The Journal of North African Studies* 12, no. 4 (2007): 381–93.

Rorty, Richard. *Contingency, Irony, Solidarity*. Cambridge: Cambridge University Press, 1989.

Rouse, Joseph. "Husserlian Phenomenology and Scientific Realism." *Philosophy of Science* 54, no. 2 (1987): 222–32.

Saavedra Fajardo, Diego. *Empresas políticas*. Ed. Manuel Fraga Iribarne. Salamanca: Editorial Anaya, 1972.

———. *Empresas políticas: Idea de un príncipe político cristiano*. Ed. Quintín Aldea Vaquero. Madrid: Editora Nacional, 1976.

———. *The Royal Politician Represented in One Hundred Emblems*. Trans. James Astry. London: 1700.

———. *Locuras de Europa*. Ed. José M. Alejandro. Salamanca: Editorial Anaya, 1965.

Sade, Donatien Alphonse François, Marquis de. *Philosophy in the Bedroom*. In *Justine, Philosophy in the Bedroom, and Other Writings*. Trans. Richard Seaver and Austryn Wainhouse. New York: Grove Press, 1965. *Philosophie dans le boudoir*. In *Oeuvres complètes du Marquis de Sade*. Ed. Gilbert Lely. Paris: Au cercle du livre précieux, 1966.

Said, Edward. "The Dictatorship of Truth: An Interview with Gillo Pontecorvo." *Cineaste* 25, no. 2 (2000): 24–25.

———. "The Quest for Gillo Pontecorvo." In Said, *Reflections on Exile and Other Essays*, 282–92. Cambridge: Harvard University Press, 2002.

Schabel, Chris. "Peter Aureol on Divine Knowledge and Future Contingents: *Scriptum in Primum Librum Sententiarum*, Distinctions 38–39." *Cahiers de l'Institut du Moyen-Âge Grec et Latin* 65 (1995): 63–212.

———. "Peter de Rivo and the Quarrel over Future Contingents at Louvain: New Evidence and New Perspectives (Part I)." *Documenti e studi sulla tradizione filosofica medievale* 6 (1995): 363–473.

———. "Peter de Rivo and the Quarrel over Future Contingents at Louvain: New Evidence and New Perspectives (Part II)." *Documenti e studi sulla tradizione filosofica medievale* 7 (1996): 369–435.

———. *Theology at Paris, 1316–1345: Peter Auriol and the Problem of Divine Foreknowledge and Future Contingents*. Aldershot: Ashgate, 2000.

Schiller, Friedrich. *Don Carlos*. Trans. Robert D. MacDonald. London: Oberon Books, 1995.

———. *Don Carlos*. Trans. A. Leslie and Jeanne R. Willson. In *Plays*. Ed. Walter Hinderer. New York: Continuum, 1983, 103–304.

———. *Don Carlos, Infante of Spain*. Trans. Charles E. Passage. New York: Ungar Publishing, 1959.

———. *Don Karlos, Infant von Spanien: Ein dramatisches Gedicht (Letzte Ausgabe 1805)*. Ed. Helmut Nobis. Frankfurt am Main: Suhrkamp, 2007.

———. *Schillers Don Karlos: Edition der ursprünglichen Fassung und entstehungsgeschichlicher Kommentar*. Ed. Paul Bockmann. Stuttgart: Ernst Klett Verlag, 1974.

————. *Dramen II*. Ed. Gerhard Kluge. Frankfurt am Main: Deutscher Klassiker Verlag, 1989, vol. 49.

Schiller's Works. Ed. and trans. Johann Gustav Fischer. Philadelphia: Barrie, 1883.

Schmitt, Carl. *The Concept of the Political*. Trans. George Schwab. Chicago: University of Chicago Press, 1996.

————. *Political Theology: Four Chapters on the Concept of Sovereignty*. Trans. George Schwab. Cambridge: MIT Press, 1985.

Schröckh, Johann Matthias. *Christliche Kirchengeschichte*. Leipzig: Engelhart Benjamin Schwickert, 1799.

Scott, Joan. *The Politics of the Veil*. Princeton: Princeton University Press, 2007.

Seneca. *Oedipus*. Ed. and trans. John G. Fitch. Cambridge: Harvard University Press, 2004.

Sepúlveda, Lorenzo de. *Romances nuevamente sacados de historias antiguas de la cronica de España compuestos por Lorenço de Sepulueda. Añadio[se] el Romance de la conquista dela ciu[dad] de Africa en Berueria, enel año M.D.[L.] y otros diuersos, como por la tabla [p]arece*. Anvers, 1580.

Shakespeare, William. *King Richard III*. Ed. J. Dover Wilson. Cambridge: Cambridge University Press, 1954.

————. *King Richard III*. Ed. Anthony Hammond. London: Arden, 1981.

————. *The Tragedy of King Lear*. In *The Complete Works of William Shakespeare*, ed. Stanley Wells and Gary Taylor, 1573–615. Oxford: Oxford University Press, 1988.

Shephard, Ben. *A War of Nerves: Soldiers and Psychiatrists, 1914–1994*. London: Jonathan Cape, 2000.

Sicroff, Albert A. *Les controverses des statuts de "pureté de sang" en Espagne du XVe au XVIIe siècle*. Paris: Didier, 1960.

Sirinelli, J.-F., and J.-P. Rioux, eds. *La Guerre d'Algérie et les intellectuels français*. Paris: Complexe, 1991.

Sloterdijk, Peter. *Critique of Cynical Reason*. Minneapolis: University of Minnesota Press, 1988.

Slyomovics, Susan. "'Hassiba Ben Bouali, If You Could See Our Algeria': Women and Public Space in Algeria." *Middle East Report* 192. *Algeria: Islam, the State and the Politics of Eradication* (1995): 8–13.

Smith, Andrew R. "The Limits of Communication; Lyotard and Levinas on Otherness." *Transgressing Discourses: Communication and the Voice of the Other*, ed. Michael Huspek and Gary P. Radford, 329–51. Albany: State University of New York Press, 1997.

Smith, Steven. *Reading Althusser: An Essay on Structural Marxism*. Ithaca, N.Y.: Cornell University Press, 1984.

Solanas, Fernando, and Octavio Gettino. "Towards a Third Cinema." *Afterimage* 3 (1971): 16–35.

Solinas, Franco. *The Battle of Algiers* (screenplay). Trans. PierNico Solinas and Linda Brunetto. In *Gillo Pontecorvo's 'The Battle of Algiers,'* ed. PierNico Solinas. New York: Scribner's, 1973.

Sophocles. *Oedipus Rex*. Ed. R. D. Rawe. Rev. ed. Cambridge: Cambridge University Press, 2006.

———. *The Plays and Fragments*. Ed. Lewis Campbell. Oxford: Oxford Univeristy Press, 1881. Facs. rpt. New York: Georg Olms Verlag, 2000. 2 vols.

———. *Women of Trachis*. In *Electra and Other Plays*, trans. David Raeburn, 14–62. London: Penguin, 2008.

Soriano, Ramón. *La mano izquierda de Franco*. Madrid: Planeta, 1981.

Sprinker, Michael. *Imaginary Relations: Aesthetics and Ideology in the Theory of Historical Materialism*. London: Verso, 1987.

Srivasta, Neelam. "Anti-Colonial Violence and the 'Dictatorship of Truth' in the Films of Gillo Pontecorvo." *Interventions*. 7, no. 1 (2005): 97–106.

———. "Interview with the Italian Film Director Gillo Pontecorvo, Roma, Italy 1 July 2003." *Interventions* 7, no. 1 (2005): 107–17.

Stora, Benjamin, and Mary Stevens. "Still Fighting." *Interventions* 9, no. 3 (2007): 365–70.

Suchting, Wal. "Althusser's Late Thinking about Materialism." *Historical Materialism* 12, no. 1 (2004): 3–70.

Terray, Emmanuel. "Headscarf Hysteria." *New Left Review* 26 (March-April 2004): 118–27.

Thakkar, Mark. "Gregory of Rimini and the Logic of the Future." M.A. thesis, Warburg Institute, 2004. Available online at http://users.ox.ac.uk/~ball2227/ .

Thirard, Paul Louis. "Pontecorvo est-il abject?" *Positif*, no. 543 (May 2006): 61–62.

Thomson, Judith Jarvis. *The Realm of Rights*. Cambridge: Harvard University Press, 1990.

———. "The Right and the Good." *Journal of Philosophy* 94 (1997): 273–98.

Trezise, Thomas. Editor's Preface. Special issue *Encounters with Levinas, Yale French Studies* 104 (2004): 1–3.

Tusell, Javier, and Genoveva García Queipo de Llano. *Carrero: La eminencia gris del régimen de Franco*. Madrid: Ediciones Temas de Hoy, 1993.

Varadharajan, Asha. "A Theoretical Afterword." *Modern Fiction Studies* 47, no. 1 (2001): 255–76.

Vatter, Miguel. "Althusser and Machiavelli: Politics after the Critique of Marx." *Multitudes* 13 (2003); online at http://multitudes.samizdat.net/Althusser-and-Machiavelli-Politics .

———. "Machiavelli after Marx: The Self-Overcoming of Marxism in the Late Althusser." *Theory and Event* 7, no. 4 (2004); online at http://muse.jhu.edu/journals/theory_and_event/v007/7.4vatter. html.

Vilarós, Teresa. *El mono del desencanto: Una crítica cultural de la transición española (1973–1993)*. Madrid: Siglo XXI, 1998.

Vizcaíno Casas, Fernando. *1973/El año en que volaron a Carrero Blanco*. Barcelona: Editorial Planeta, 1993.

Vuillemin, Jules. *Necessity or Contingency: The Master Argument*. Trans. Thomas Morran. Stanford: Center for the Study of Language and Information, 1996. *Nécessité ou contingence: L'Aporie de Diodore et les systèmes philosophiques*. Paris: Minuit, 1984.

Waite, Geoffrey. "On Esotericism: Heidegger and/or Cassirer at Davos." *Political Theory* 26, no. 5 (1998): 603–51.

Waismann, Friedrich, and Ludwig Wittgenstein. *Wittgenstein and the Vienna Circle: Conversations Recorded by Friedrich Waismann*. Ed. Brian McGuinness. Trans. Joachim Schulte and Brian McGuinness. New York: Barnes & Noble Books, 1979.

Waldenfels, Bernhard. "The Despised Doxa: Husserl and the Continuing Crisis of Western Reason." *Research in Phenomenology* 12 (1982): 21–38.

Wall, Thomas Carl. *Radical Passivity: Levinas, Blanchot, and Agamben*. Albany: State University of New York Press, 1999.

Wandel, Lee Palmer. *The Eucharist in the Reformation: Incarnation and Liturgy*. Cambridge: Cambridge University Press, 2006.

Weber, Max. *Economy and Society: An Outline of Interpretive Sociology*. 1968; rpt. Berkeley: University of California Press, 1978.

Weimann, Robert. "Thresholds to Memory and Commodity in Shakespeare's Endings." *Representations* 53 (Winter 1996): 1–20.

Widdowson, Peter. "Terrorism and Literary Studies." *Textual Practice* 2, no. 1 (1988): 1–21.

Willet, Andrew. *Hexapla in Danielem, that is, A Six-fold Commentarie vpon the Most Diuine Prophesie of Daniel*. Cambridge: Leonard Greene, 1610.

Williams, Raymond. *Marxism and Literature*. Oxford: Oxford University Press, 1977.

Wiltshire, Harold. "A Contribution to the Etiology of Shell Shock." *The Lancet*, June 17, 1916, pp. 1207–12.

Wittgenstein, Ludwig. "Lecture on Ethics." *The Philosophical Review* 74 (1965): 3–12.

Wolf, Frieder Otto. "The 'Limits of Dialectical Presentation' as a Key Category of Marx's Theoretical Self-Reflection.' *Capitalism Nature Socialism* 15, no. 3 (2004): 79–85.

Wood, Michael. *The Road to Delphi: The Life and Afterlife of Oracles*. New York: Farrar, Straus and Giroux, 2003.

Yacef, Saadi. *Souvenirs de la bataille d'Alger*. Paris: René Julliard, 1962.

Yacef, Saadi, and Hocine Mezali. *La Bataille d'Alger*. Paris: Éditions du Témoignage Chrétien, 1982.

Zambrano, María. *Filosofía y poesía*. Alcalá de Henares: Ediciones de la Universidad, 1993.

———. "Lo que le sucedió a Cervantes: Dulcinea." In *España, sueño y verdad*, ed. María Zambrano, 43–52. Barcelona: Editora y Distribuidora Hispano-Americana (E.D.H.A.S.A.), 1965.

Zerilli, Linda M. G. "This Universalism Which Is Not One." *diacritics* 28, no. 2 (1998): 3–20. Rpt. in *Laclau: A Critical Reader*, ed. Simon Critchley and Oliver Marchart, 88–111. London: Routledge, 2004.

Žižek, Slavoj. "Identity and Its Vicissitudes: Hegel's 'Logic of Essence' as a Theory of Ideology." In *The Making of Political Identities*, ed. Ernesto Laclau. London: Verso, 1994. 40–75.

———. "Kant and Sade: The Ideal Couple." *Lacanian Ink*, no. 13 (1998): 12–25.

Zoary, Fawzia. *Ce voile qui déchire la France*. Paris: Éditions Ramsay, 2004.

Abbot, George, 78
abject, abjection, 14, 26, 36, 138, 150, 163, 190, 194, 195, 196, 236, 254, 278, 279
accident, 24, 43, 54, 63, 70, 133, 158, 160, 171, 197, 202, 214, 220–21, 224, 254, 282; and contingency, 271; Franco's hunting, 56–61
act, 3–4, 41, 51–53, 61, 92, 183, 200, 222; and actor, 183, 204; and agent, 3, 19, 50, 207–8, 236; promiscuity of, 3–4. *See also* performative
Adorno, Theodor W.: and Max Horkheimer, 31, 269n; *Dialectic of Enlightenment*, 153–55, 269; and "positive concept of Enlightenment," 153–60
Adrizzoni, Michela, 275
Agamben, Giorgio, 28, 30, 34, 64, 91–103, 152, 232, 268; *Homo Sacer*, 91–103, 245; *Il Regno e La Gloria*, 245–46
Agirre, Julen. *See* Forest, Eva
Alcocer, Pedro de, 261
aleatory materialism, 28–29, 114, 255, 255–56, 268. *See also* contingency; matter; metonymy
Alford, Fred C., 230, 233
Alleg, Henri, 165, 271
allegory, 12, 36, 43, 82–84, 126, 131, 135, 138, 142, 145–46, 154, 168, 171, 201, 211, 214
Allen, William, 242
allusion, 11, 20–21, 137, 139, 144, 148–49, 215–17, 230, 231
Alonso Asenjo, Julio, 244
Al Qaeda, 42
Althusser, Louis, 18, 28, 30–32, 110–19, 254–68; "Contradiction and Over-determination," 124, 126–27, 260; *The Facts*, 140–45, 267–68; "Freud and Lacan," 261; *The Future Lasts*

Forever, 128, 140–45, 261–62, 267–68; "Is It Simple to Be a Marxist in Philosophy," 119, 257; "On Content in the Thought of G. W. F. Hegel," 30–31; *Philosophy and the Spontaneous Philosophy of the Scientists*, 260; *Reading Capital*, 113–15, 119, 124, 129–30, 139–40, 142, 255; "Rousseau: The Social Contract. (The Discrepancies)," 125–30, 142, 260–61
Amrane, Djamila, 277
Andersson, Nils, 271
antagonism, 15–16, 31, 40, 151–52, 159–64, 208, 238. *See also* politics; violence
anxiety, 24–29, 39, 75, 140–41, 143, 185, 198, 209, 218, 232, 235, 254. *See also* terror
aphrastos, 33, 231
aporia: aporetic of sovereignty, 30–33, 64–65, 72, 86, 125
Arbeloa, Victor M., 280
Arendt, Hannah, 27, 99, 108, 235–36, 246
Aretxaga, Begoña, 51–52, 239
Aristotle, 4, 70, 97–104, 207, 227–29, 246; on future contingent propositions in *Peri Hermeneia*, 4, 97–104, 246, 250–51; on reciprocity in *Nicomachean Ethics*, 227–29, 246
Arnaud, Georges, 271
Asad, Talal, 277
association, 16, 29, 33, 41, 110–11, 115, 228, 280; contingent, 152, 174, 222; rules of, 4, 13, 111. *See also* community; republicanism
attribute, 40, 42, 82, 117, 207; contingent or accidental, 43, 63, 69–70, 160–61; essential, substantial, or necessary, 86, 94–95, 240–41, 254

autobiography, 128, 140–49, 201, 254, 262, 267–68

autonomy, 2, 16, 30–31, 110–49 , 161–62, 227, 275. *See also* subject; subjectivity

Baeza, Alvaro, 239

Balibar, Étienne, 38, 141, 209, 237, 254–56; on Marx's "ontology of relation," 113, 132, 146

Bardavío, Joaquín, 238

Baudry, Leon, 246

Beck, Maximilian, 283

Benton, Ted, 255

Berchadsky, Alexis, 271

Bergo, Bettina, 233

Berlin, Isaiah, 19, 229

Bernasconi, Robert, 232

Bernet, Rudolf, 230

Bignardi, Irene, 276

Bilson, Thomas, 77, 243

bivalence, 4, 95–101. *See also* truth; logic

Blanchot, Maurice, 230–32

Blanco, Miguel Ángel, 59–61

Blundeville, Thomas, 71–72, 85–86, 240, 244

Bobbio, Norberto, 229

Bodin, Jean, 30, 64–71, 207, 240, 280

body, 19–21, 26, 81, 183, 186, 195, 196, 198, 226, 275; Carrero's and Franco's, 38–63; colonized body, 188, 193; concept of , concept and, 116, 138; and embodiment, 26, 32, 42, 54, 116–18, 124–35 , 143, 146–48, 168, 184, 200, 204, 215; father's divided or shared, 69–70; and flesh, 20, 42, 146, 168, 214–16, 221, 230, 246, 254; instrumental use of, 154–55; labile body, 146–47; and *materia*, 214–17; mother's undivided, 167–72; of the sovereign, 29, 75, 86; of the state, corporate body, 34–36, 45, 58, 126, 131, 207

Boethius, 70, 98, 240, 251

Bogacz, Ted, 234

Bollack, Jean, 225

Boltanski, Luc, and Eve Chiapello, 13, 226

border, bounds, 21, 46, 49–58, 91, 121, 125, 252, 277; of the body, 49, 63; of the city, 95–96; of the concept, 64, 96; of the country, 36; of narrative,

28; of the object, 27. *See also* exile; limit; suture

Bourdieu, Pierre, 32, 187–92, 278

Bourke, Joanna, 235

Branch, Raphaëlle, 271

Brody, D. H., 231

Brown, Edward M., 234

Brown, Norman O., 190

Browne, Thomas, 270

Bruni, Luigi, 238

Burke, Edmund, 38, 237

Butler, Judith, 225, 270

Caillé, Patricia, 273.

Calderón de la Barca, Pedro, 60

Campo Vidal, Manuel, 46, 52, 54–55, 239

capitalism, 63, 226, 256

Carter, Angela, 272

Castejón y Fonseca, Diego de, 250

cause, causality, 25, 40–42, 58, 60, 91, 107, 127, 146, 152–53, 172, 184, 214, 242, 245, 268; absent, 134, 140–41, 147, 22; metonymic, 114, 130, 139–41, 143, 145, 147; structural, 144, 139, 147, 149, 256. *See also* effect; effectivity

Cavarero, Adriana, 27, 235–36

cave of Hercules, 30, 88–104, 247–50

Caviglia, Francesco, 273

Cervantes, Miguel de, 88, 211–17, 263, 281–82

Chafiq, Chahla, 277

Chaitin, Gilbert, 269

Christ and christology, 30, 69, 76–79, 139, 220, 24; freedom of, 90, 100–102, 109, 247, 251, 253, 263–65. *See also* concept

Cicero, 205, 207, 280

citizen, citizenship, 6–7, 9–17, 22, 27, 39, 106, 113, 115, 275, 281

city, 1–14, 72, 59–60, 80, 98, 178–79, 209; borders or bounds of, 95–96; concept of, 113–18

Clarke, Alistair, 277

Clemente, Josep Carles, 44, 238

Cohen, Richard A., 230

Colletti, Lucio, 256

colony, colonial, colonization, 164–65, 199–201, 274, 276–79; Sadism and the violence of, 150–53, 173–93; and terror and European decolonization, 29, 32

Comellas, José Luis, 281

Comestor, Petrus, 76, 243

community, 4, 6, 12–13, 15, 30, 61, 145; and communitarianism, 19, 156, 164, 174, 269; as constituted, 157–58; divided or shared, 68–70; jokes and, 38; produced contingently, 164, 170; unwrought, 69, 156–60, 171–72

Conant, James, 283

concept, 110–49, 155–59; defective or weak, 33, 63–64, 110–12, 123–24, 165, 218, 221; definition of, 117, 122, 141–42; positive, 153, 155–56, 167–68, 269; relational or transactional, 18, 112, 121, 200; theological, 30, 65, 74, 88–89, 91, 131–33; and woman, 146–47, 157; wounded, 10, 12, 28–29, 72, 204, 222. *See also* idea; matter; norm, normativity

consequence, consequentialism, 3–5, 16

context, historical-cultural, 32, 79, 174, 208, 271; and normative contexts and normative concepts, 17–18, 20–23, 26, 132; and radical contextualization of decision, 161; as secret's text and context, 63; social, of a joke, 38; traces of, in concepts, 142. *See also* history, historicity

contingency, 4, 10, 31, 42–43, 89, 109, 150–72, 200, 219, 222, 270n, 271n, 282n, 283n; versions of concept of, 158–64; contingent associations, contingency and community, 152, 174, 222; contingency and historicity of concepts, 31, 115, 139–40, 145; and contractualism, 111; distinguished from fate/*tukhē*, 28; and distribution of sovereignty, 204; future contingent propositions, 4, 30, 90–109, 246, 247, 250, 251; and judgment, 121, 158, 199; past contingent propositions, 109; radical contingency, 176; and suture, 122; and transference, 129, 145

Cornell, Drucilla, 290

Corral, Pedro de, 105, 252–53

Covarrubias Orozco, Sebastián de, 246, 280–81

Covington, Francee, 276

Critchley, Simon, 15, 18, 24, 224, 226, 229, 232, 233

Crowther, Bowsley, 279

D'Amico, Robert, 282–83

Daney, Serge, 32, 194–97, 199, 279

Dante Alighieri, 5, 110, 156, 224, 270, 281

Danzig, Gabriel, 228–29

David, Alain, 232

Davis, Colin, 261–62, 267–68

death, 1, 9, 21, 23, 28, 171, 174, 258–59; and community, the finitude of others, 156–57, 195–98; death drive, 233; and power, sovereignty, and democracy, 34–62

decision: undecidability, 1–30, 35–36, 49, 83–86, 128, 130, 144, 161, 176–77, 183, 200–201, 256; sovereign, as exception, 30, 65–70, 90–109, 161. *See also* ethics; sovereignty

deconstruction, 27, 115, 120, 144–45, 159

definition, 164, 227; and predication, 82, 91–96, 99, 245–46; reciprocal, 114

Del Burgo, Jaime Ignacio, 238

Della Volpe, Galvano, 131, 138, 262–63, 267

De Man, Paul, 260, 262

democracy, 226, 229–30, 232, 233; Athenian, 125; liberal, 161; radical, 15–16, 159–60; transition to, 36, 43–44, 59. *See also* republicanism

deontology, 2, 15

Derrida, Jacques, 13, 28, 30, 64–72, 177, 240, 283; *Politics of Friendship*, 68; "Provocation: Forewords," 64–66, 68; *Rogues*, 68–70, 240; *Speech and Phenomena*, 68, 282–83

Dershowitz, Alan M., 235

destiny, fate, 1, 4, 8–9, 11–12, 26, 28, 73, 91, 98, 100, 104, 108, 131–34, 245–50, 263. *See also tukhē*

determination, overdetermination, underdetermination, 17–18, 34, 49, 57, 62, 64, 75, 77–79, 91, 109, 112–49, 151, 161, 164, 171, 192, 208, 255, 257, 258, 261–62, 268; and logical indeterminacy, 95, 97–99, 102, 108

D'Hondt, Jacques, 260

dialectic, 15, 62–63, 117–18, 126, 132, 150–72, 177, 205, 238, 251, 262–63, 267, 269; and contingency, 158–60, 164; dialectics of colonial sovereignty, 151, 175; *Dialectic of Enlightenment* (Horkheimer and Adorno),

153–55, 164, 269; and failure of dialectical logic, 150; materialist, 118;
and nondialectical materialism, 29;
radical democratic challenge to dialectical logics, 31; and reciprocity,
151–53; nondialectical concept of *res*
and *res publica*, 218; of transference,
262. *See also* history; matter;
reciprocity
*Diccionario de la lengua castellana (de Autor-
idades)*, 209, 210, 261
Diccionario de la lengua española, 209, 261
Di Febo, Giuliana, 236
distinction, indistinction, 6–7, 9, 13, 22–
23, 58, 63, 111–12, 117, 125, 155–56,
170, 200–201, 209, 225–26, 259–60;
and division, 77; and historicity of
the concept, 139; public-private, 167;
and sovereignty, 64; and terror,
trauma, 23–25, 235; between terror
and virtue, 40–41; zone of indistinction (and undecidability), 30, 91–96,
103
distribution, 9–10, 33, 77, 174, 227–28,
258; metaleptic, 107; of premises and
conclusions, 82; redistribution and
recognition, 16–17, 227, 229; of
positions of sovereign and slave, 10,
14–15, 27–28, 31; of sovereignty, 6,
64, 86, 204, 207, 208. *See also* divisibility, indivisibility; ethics; republicanism; sovereignty
divisibility, indivisibility, 63–87; logical
status of, 70, 87; of sacraments, 77; of
sovereignty, 30, 64–70, 79, 86–87,
89. *See also* sovereignty
division, 72–79, 84–86, 201, 241–44, 259;
of act, 3; from and within church,
76–78; of common substance,
father's body, 30, 69; as descant,
74–75; of the indivisible, 64; as logical procedure, 78–79, 84–86; of matter, 30, 221; political division, civil
war, 72–74, 84–86; republicanism as,
18; of sovereignty, 10, 84–86, 90;
between underived and derived laws,
68. *See also* divisibility, indivisibility
Dolar, Mladen, 262
Dooley, Mark, 238, 245
Dowd, Nancy Ellen, 280
Dreyfus, Hubert L., 246
DuBois, Page, 224, 226

Dullaert, Johannes (Jean de Jandun Dullardus), 104, 250–51

Edelglass, William, 231
Eder, M. D., 234
Edwards, Francis, 242
effect, effectivity, 50, 62, 184, 186; community-effects, 156–57, 164, 172; of
concept, 31; documentary, 199, 280;
and element, 113–49; literary effects,
130, 144–49; mythological recognition effect, 4; and sovereign decision,
98–99, 108; of terror, 25–26; of torture, 223. *See also* structure
Eissler, Kurt, 234
Elliott, Gregory, 114, 119, 226, 255, 256,
257
Elliston, Frederick A., 282
encounter, 14, 15, 25–26, 28, 114, 130,
138, 146–49, 152, 164, 216, 248,
278–79
enemy, 15, 21, 51, 65, 67, 237–38, 240
Engels, Friedrich, 124, 258, 266–67
enlightenment, 29, 30, 38, 55, 63, 89, 108,
137, 148, 150–72, 175, 189, 209–10,
240, 269. *See also* subject, subjectivity
ethics, 1–33, 177, 200, 225–26, 227–29;
classical, 16; Levinasian, 232–33;
postmodern, 15; psychoanalytic, 15;
republican, 39; terrible, ethic of terror 1–33; and value, 2; virtue, 15;
Wittgensteinian, 112–13, 225–26,
254
event, 4, 5, 6, 14, 25–26, 29, 30, 32, 34–
62, 64, 83, 97–98, 134, 144–45, 159,
171, 176, 178, 183–84, 200, 202, 204,
213–14, 217, 268; and act, 92,
128–30; and sovereign decision, 80–
82, 91–92, 94. *See also* contingency
example, exemplarity, 35, 43–44, 75, 83–
84, 86, 97–103, 194; Aristotle's sea-
battle, 98; bad or terrible, 5, 136,
211; and contingency, 162; and *exemplum*, 86, 189; and justification of
torture, 2, 4, 26, 223–24; literary, 5,
140; and secularization thesis, 66;
and sovereignty, 90, 94, 98–100, 103;
and succession, paternity, legitimacy,
83–84; exemplary terror, 125. *See also*
pedagogy
exile, 10, 12, 67, 76; and logic, 79–87;
religious, 67, 76, 79–87; republican,
202–22, 281

Fanon, Frantz, 32, 150–52, 164–65, 184, 189–92, 274–76, 278–79
fascism, 33, 35, 37, 52–53, 61, 154, 211, 269. *See also* violence
fear, 8, 104, 168, 198, 235, 248–50, 258–59; of the masses, 38–39, 209; distinguished from terror and anxiety, 24–26, 235
Ferretter, Luke, 255
Fischbach, Franck, 257
Forest, Eva (writing as Julen Agirre), 46, 48–49, 239
Forgacs, David, 273, 275
Foucault, Michel, 27, 34, 92, 246; "Confession of the Flesh," 246; *History of Sexuality*, 92, 246; *Society Must Be Defended*, 34
Franco, Francisco, 29, 34–62, 236–37, 239; and *franquismo*
Fraser, Nancy, 16–18, 64, 227, 229, 240
Frazer, James George, 69
Freud, Sigmund, 24–25, 34, 37–38, 68–69, 113, 137, 233–35, 237, 243–44, 258, 261, 268; *Beyond the Pleasure Principle*, 24–25, 233–35; *The Ego and the Id*, 137; *Jokes and Their Relation to the Unconscious*, 34, 37–38, 237; *Totem and Taboo*, 68–69
friend, 1–2, 66–67, 214, 217
Frodon, Jean Michel, 279
Fuente, Ismael, 239
Fuss, Diana, 278–79
future, 25, 27, 59, 64, 74, 76, 121, 177, 185, 190, 202, 216, 222, 241, 250–51, 271; future-contingent propositions, 4, 30, 90–109, 246, 247, 250. *See also* contingency

Gabler, Neil, 1
Gallop, Jane, 169, 272
Galston, William, 230
García, Javier, 239
García Blázquez, Félix, 212, 281
García Queipo de Llano, Genoveva, 237
Gaspard, Françoise, 277
genealogy, 28, 29, 36, 64, 76, 92, 128, 140, 142–44, 148–49, 198–99, 205, 208, 245, 261
Gettino, Octavio, 273–74
Giavarini, Laurence, 280
givenness, 17, 25, 40–41, 56, 116, 157–58, 218–19, 222

globalization, 1, 13, 16, 39, 57, 152, 226
González Gutiérrez, Cayo, 256
Gramsci, Antonio, 119, 258
Grosrichard, Alain, 261

Habermas, Jürgen, 28, 226, 259, 270
Hardt, Michael, and Antonio Negri, 31, 150–53, 157, 172, 175, 226, 268. *See also* Negri, Antonio
Harrison, Nicholas, 272–73, 280
Harvey, Charles W., 283
Hegel, G. W. F., 28, 30–31, 50, 117–20, 123–25, 130–40, 144–49, 152–53, 155, 176–77, 225–26, 232, 256–60, 262–63, 265, 267–70, 273; *Encyclopedia of Logic* ("Lesser Logic"), 117–18, 130, 133–34, 256, 259–60; *Phenomenology of Spirit*, 120, 258; *Philosophy of Right*, 117, 130–36, 139, 144, 148, 176–77, 260, 262–63, 265, 273; *Science of Logic* ("Greater Logic"), 152–53, 256, 268
Henninger, Max, 229
Herrero, Luis, 239
Hindess, Barry, and Paul Hirst, 120
history, historicity, 28–30, 32–33, 35–37, 41, 47, 49, 53, 56, 59–62, 75, 79, 83–87, 103, 107–8, 115–18, 147–48, 150–52, 173–77, 189, 198–99, 202–22; "absolute historicity" (Husserl), 220–21; historical break, 149; of classical logic, 97–100; of concepts, 115–16, 139–40; historical embodiment, 124; historicist hermeneutics, 17; literary, 214–15; nondialectical character of, 150–51; historical account of sovereignty, 64–65, 68–70, 89–94, 210; teleological historicity, 118; time of historical experience, 198; Tudor myth of, 72
Honneth, Axel, 16–17, 64, 226–27, 229, 240
Horkheimer, Max. *See* Adorno, Theodor W., and Max Horkheimer
Horozco, Sebastián de, 251
Hunter, Stephen, 276
Husserl, Edmund, 22, 28, 33, 89, 218–22, 282–83; "Vienna Lecture," 33, 218–22, 282–83

idea, 17, 116–17, 131–33, 142, 144, 147–49, 207–9, 215, 217, 221, 282–83,

259–60; of the father, 69–70; ideality and materiality, 43, 142, 144, 147–49, 267; regulative, 12–13. *See also* concept; matter

identification, 128–29, 148–49, 152, 162, 176, 192, 198–200, 204–5, 215–17; collective, 113; and the masses, 38–39; mythic, 204; reciprocal, 169; spectatorial, 195–96, 198–200. *See also* identity

identity, 11, 14–15, 17, 22, 26, 60, 94, 118, 120, 127–28, 135, 150–52, 157–58, 176, 185, 190, 204, 215–16, 227, 229, 257, 268, 270, 278; class, 13, 113; coincidence of identity and difference, 157–58; communitarian, 164; concept of identity to a concept, 122–23, 129–30, 142, 145; national, 55; postnational "European," 44; reciprocal construction of "European" and "colonial," 150; resistant, 190; tautologous logic of, 70–71. *See also* identification

indeterminacy, 34, 102, 108. *See also* determination

Inquisition, 135–37, 251–52, 266–67

institution, 15, 17, 19, 40, 42–43, 60–61, 65–68, 117, 124–25, 139, 143, 164, 204, 207–9, 227, 237–38

instruction, scene of, 5, 152, 165–72, 190. *See also* pedagogy

irony, 9–11, 124, 138, 149, 166, 171, 263, 273–74

Isidore of Seville, 76, 243

Jay, Martin, 269–70

Jerome, 77

jokes, *chistes*, 34–38, 42, 45, 52–53, 55–56, 62, 140–41, 143–44, 237, 267

justice, 16–17, 76, 207, 226–29, 232–33, 280

Kain, Philip J., 267

Kant, Immanuel, 31, 116–17, 122, 129, 130, 145, 150, 153, 158, 162, 169, 230, 256, 269, 272; *Critique of Pure Reason*, 116–17, 122, 129, 256; "Vienna Logic", 256

Kantorowicz, Ernst, 42

Kaufmann, Doris, 234–35

Kearney, Richard, 226, 233

Khanna, Ranjana, 183, 273–74, 276, 278

Khosrokhavar, Farhad, 277

Kintzler, Catherine, 40, 237

labor, 33, 46–47, 202; of the concept, 27, 30, 127, 131–35, 142, 146–47, 250–51; and globalization, 57; refusal of, 237–38; shared, 185; of working through, 10, 36

Laborde, Cécile, 179, 275

Lacan, Jacques, 31–32, 77, 110, 121–22, 127, 140–41, 143, 147, 150, 168–69, 230, 233, 243, 257, 259, 261, 262, 269, 272; *Écrits*, 259, 261; "Kant avec Sade," 150, 168–69, 269, 272; *Seminar of Jacques Lacan, Book II: The Ego in Freud's Theory*, 243; *Seminar of Jacques Lacan, Book VI: The Ethics of Psychoanalysis*, 269; *Seminar of Jacques Lacan, Book XX: Encore: On Feminine Sexuality, the Limits of Love and Knowledge*, 269

Lacan, Judith, 140–43

Laclau, Ernesto, 15, 152, 159–61, 226, 257, 258–59, 270; *Hegemony and Socialist Strategy*, 37, 114, 119–21, 141, 144–45, 238, 255, 257, 259, 261–62; and Chantal Mouffe, 31, 37, 114, 119–21,141, 144–45, 159, 160, 238, 255, 257, 258, 259, 261–62; and Lilian Zac, 258

Laqueur, Walter, 237

Larise, Djuna, 255

law, 14–15, 39–41, 50, 91, 96, 123–26, 139, 168–69, 228–29, 232, 237, 241–42; and the city, 7, 96; of the Father, 168–69; formality of, 40; immanent, 69, 119, 122, 258; Kantian moral, 269; "of movement" (Arendt), 27; and nature, 91, 228–29; of noncontradiction, 97; preservation of, 2; republican conception of, 16, 18–19, 227; and sovereignty, 67–69, and the will, 123–26, 259–60

Lazarus, Sylvain, 255–56, 258

Lea, Henry Charles, 251–52

Leclaire, Serge, 268

Leed, Eric, 235

Lenin, Vladimir Ilyich, 130

Lerner, Paul, 233–34

Lever, Ralph, vii, 82–84, 244–45

Levin, Michael, 1–6, 12, 20, 26, 223

Index   315

Levinas, Emmanuel, 20–24, 168, 224,
    230–33; "Substitution," 20–24,
    230–33
Levinson, Sanford, 224
Lewis, William S., 255
Lezra, Jacques, 254
liberalism, 26, 31, 44, 136, 161, 163, 214,
    216, 226, 229–30, 237–38. See also
    autonomy; ethics
libido, libidinization, 19, 54–55, 142–43,
    174. See also pleasure
Lispector, Clarice, 93, 246
Loewe, Johann Karl Gottfried, 133–34,
    263–65
logic, bivalent and nonbivalent, 4, 30, 70–
    72, 90–110
López de Ayala Cedillo, Jerónimo,
    249–50
Lozano, Cristóbal de, 30, 103–109,
    247–249n
Lukács, Gyorgy, 118, 121, 269–70
Lukasiewicz, Jan, 98
Luna, Miguel de, 252–53
Luxon, Thomas H., 243

Macey, David, 257, 261
Macherey, Pierre, 141, 254, 257, 258
Machiavelli, 65, 99, 114, 229, 240
Majod, Anouar, 277
Marighella, Carlos, 41–42, 238
Markell, Patchen, 17, 229
Martínez Guijarro, Juan (Silíceo, Sili-
    ceus), 30, 88, 104–109, 247–53
Marx, Karl, 18, 30, 31, 99, 110–49, 228,
    237, 254–67, 270, 277; Capital,
    113–15; Communist Manifesto, 130;
    Critique of Hegel's Philosophy of Right,
    130–39, 144–49, 263; The German
    Ideology, 266–67. See also dialectic;
    labor; matter
Marx-Scouras, Danielle, 184, 276
Matesa, 35, 45, 236
Mather, Ronald, 260
Matheron, François, 261
matter, materialism, 28–32, 43, 51, 52, 54,
    57–58, 111, 114, 125, 129, 130–49,
    214, 222, 261, 266–67; aesthetic,
    57–58; aleatory materialism, 114,
    255, 268; and body, 32, 52, 215, 217;
    and concept, 43, 149, 215; concept
    of, 111; critical rematerialization of

symbolic body, 52; cultural material-
    ism, 122; dialectical materialism, 15;
    divine, 130–49; division of, 30; and
    ideology, 52; materialism of the
    encounter, 28; literary materialism,
    31; Spanish materialism, 214; Spi-
    noza and, 114, 246; spontaneous
    resistance of, 147; woman and, 146–
    47, 227
Matthison, Friedrich, 263
McCormick, Peter, 282
McGuinness, Brian, 254
Meade, George Herbert, 16
Meddeb, Abdelwahab, 274–75
mediation and immediacy, 9, 14, 22, 37,
    45, 49, 50–51, 66, 100–101, 135,
    176–77, 192, 198, 200, 204, 209, 213,
    227–28, 235–36, 260; and colonial-
    ism, 176–77; immediacy of decision-
    ist judgment, 200; and fantasy of
    immaterial conception, 135; medi-
    ated identity to the concept, 118; and
    image, 204; immediate instance, 25;
    mythic immediacy, 26, 49, 222;
    immediately present knowledge,
    101–2, 109; and spectatorship, 184
melancholia, 28, 33, 204, 210–11, 216–
    17, 221–22, 233, 241, 273–74
Mellen, Joan, 173–77, 193, 198–200, 272–
    73, 276
Menéndez Peláez, Jesús, 244
Menéndez Pelayo, Marcelino, 247–50
Merleau-Ponty, Maurice, 218, 282
Mernissi, Fatima, 277
Méthais, Pierre, 259–60
metonymy, 114, 129–30, 134, 139–41,
    143, 145, 147, 170, 262, 273–74. See
    also contingency
Meyers, Charles S., 233–34
Mezali, Hocine, 275
Miller, Jacques-Alain, 121–23, 140–43,
    147, 243, 258–59
Minne, Danièle, 277
mirror, 51–52, 101–2; divine, 101–2; mir-
    ror-shot, 177–93, 199–200, 273–74
Mocnik, Rastko, 257
modernity, modernization, 6–7, 13, 26,
    28–30, 38–39, 102, 108–9, 148, 149,
    150–51, 174, 179, 183, 201, 207, 211,
    216–22, 245–46, 282; and colonial-
    ism, 150–51; and community, 155,
    174; and the concept, 116; and forms

of identication, 38–39; high modernism, 19; modern political subjectivity, 26; modern republic, 18–20, 26,
33, 204–5, 210, 281; resistance to,
137; and secularization, 28–30, 63–
67, 89–91, 95–97, 99; modern state,
51, 62
Montag, Warren, 260
Montefiore, Alan, 232
Moore, Lindsay, 273–74, 278–79
Mott, Frederick W., 233–34
Mouffe, Chantal, 15, 159–61, 226, 270.
  See also under Laclau, Ernesto
movement, *movimiento*, motility, 18, 27,
33, 34–62, 63–64, 79–87, 118–19,
126–31, 144, 179, 186, 188, 191,
195–98, 219–21, 235–36, 259, 263,
274, 279, 282. *See also* exile; traveling
shot
Murphy, Martin, 244
Musso y Pontes, José, 239
myth, 4–6, 11, 21–23, 26, 30, 33, 39–41,
62, 72, 88–89, 103, 108, 114–15,
118–19, 125, 132, 144, 153–55, 180,
204–5, 210–12, 217–22; mythic
posit, 39–41

name, 3–4, 8, 21–23, 26, 31, 51, 53–54,
57, 60–61, 65, 78–79, 92, 114, 126,
133, 135, 141, 143, 161, 170, 173–74,
205, 226, 227–29, 243–44, 262; and
anonymity, 14; for the event, 26; and
hegemony, 226, generated by the
state, 51; mythic, 21–23; and nominalism, 89, 92, 102, 104, 108, "Spanish Republic" as brand, 205
Nancy, Jean-Luc, 30, 64, 68–70, 270; *The
Experience of Freedom*, 68–71, 240;
The Inoperative Community, 156–58,
240, 270
narcissism, 179–80, 216–17
Narcissus, 179–80
necessity, 46–47, 64, 69–71, 98, 127–28,
131–32, 154, 162, 174, 206–7, 222;
and contingency, 158, 171, 219, 222,
257, 270; logical, 70, 98; natural,
46–47; spurious, 225–26; structural,
128; therapeutic, of literature, 127.
  See also contingency
negation, 150–54, 174, 188, 191, 247,
267; denegation, 128

Negri, Antonio, 19, 229, 237–38; and
Michael Hardt, 31, 150–53, 157,
172, 175, 226, 268
Nessus, cloak of, 20–23, 230–32
neurosis, 24, 233–35
nomos: and *physis*, 91–96, 99, 227–29. *See
also* law; nature
norm, normativity, 1–33, 40, 63, 111, 114,
117, 132, 139, 148–49, 161, 191, 199,
201, 205, 226–27, 241–42, 254; and
affect, 38; and fantasy, 199; formal,
201; and sovereign exception, 92–96,
99–100; weak, 63, 111. *See also* concept; value

object, objectality, 24–29, 87, 101–2, 116,
129, 131–33, 135, 147, 155, 158–61,
169, 172, 186, 189, 197–99, 213, 224,
233, 235; and concept, 122–23; and
contract, 167; defective, 59; discourse and metadiscourse of, 85, 87;
material, 110–11; mythic, 103; of
knowledge, 255–56, 258–59. *See also*
subject, subjectivity
Ong, Walter J., 245
ontology: "effectivist," 245–46; and ethics, 225–26; numerical, of the mass,
61; paradoxical, of the norm, 22;
political, 12, 219; of relation, 113,
132, 146, 254–255. *See also* theology,
political theology
organicism, 18, 29, 38, 42–43, 121, 131,
254–55
Orlando, Valérie, 274
Ortiz, Blas, 247–50
Orwell, George, 163, 271

pain, 2–12, 20, 26, 70, 154, 161, 167–69,
190, 222, 233
Patočka, Jan, 282
Pauvert, Jean-Jacques, 165, 272
Pavlovic, Tatjana, 239
pedagogy, 1, 31–32, 75, 78, 81–82, 124,
127, 142, 146–47, 151–58, 174–78,
183–200, 208, 219, 254, 276
performative act or utterance, 126
personification, 54, 129, 170; of finitude,
157; of pleasure, 170; of republicanism, 214, 217–18, 221–22; of sovereignty, 209–10
Persons, Robert, 28, 76–87, 242–45; *A
Christian Directorie Guiding Men to*

Their Saluation, 76–77, 79, 242–43; *Newes from Spayne and Holland*, 79–87, 244–45

Pettit, Philip, 19, 229

phenomenology, 38, 40, 84, 123, 125, 132, 152, 218–22; of embodiment, 125, 128; of national consciousness, 38; of terror, 40; transcendental, 218–22; of violence and instruction, 152

philosophy, 19, 23, 28, 33, 42, 90, 102, 104, 110–49, 158–59, 165–66, 177, 214–18, 221, 250–51, 253, 255–57, 272, 283; of the concept, 113, 130, 134, 139, 144, 146–49; of the encounter, 114; and the female philosopher, 214, 221; political, 23, 158–59, 166, 217; of terror, 42; transcendental, 19

Piñuel, José Luis, 238

pleasure, libidinization, 5–6, 34, 38, 55–56, 93, 153–72, 190, 222, 229, 251–52; and contingency, 163, 172, 222; of domination, 153–58, 190; of the joke, 34, 38; Sadean, 164–72

Pocock, John, 19, 229

Poe, Edgar Allan, 1, 12–13, 20, 222, 236; "The Fall of the House of Usher," 1, 222, 236; "The Premature Burial," 12–13, 20

police, policing, 19, 45, 52, 55, 58, 89, 111, 143, 173, 223–24, 251–52

political theology. *See* theology

politics, 14–16, 34, 99, 110, 151, 192, 226–27, 233, 240, 258–59; and affect, 45; associative, 14; biopolitics, 26, 58; and ethics, 15, 224n; necropolitics, 26; without onto-theology, 112; and theology, 99, 149; and violence, 159. *See also* republicanism; sovereignty; theology, political theology

populism, 42, 55–62, 226

Powell, Griffith, 240

predication, 22, 67, 70–72, 78–79, 82–83, 86, 97, 118, 131, 240, 247

Preston, Paul, 237

Prieto, Joaquín, 239

primal scenes, 14–15, 77, 135, 144, 146, 149; of philosophy, 144, 146; of political theology, 135, 149; of textual exegesis, 77

Primo de Rivera, José Antonio, 35, 42, 61, 238

production, 4, 30–31, 72, 75, 110–49, 157, 159, 222, 237–38, 255–56; of community-effects, 157; of concept, 30–31, 110–49; early modern cultural, 72, 75; of ideology, 121; of material objects, 110–11; and reproduction, 116, 121, 133, 135; of utterance versus of truth, 4. *See also* labor; matter.

Putnam, Hilary, 112, 225–26

Rabinow, Paul, 246

radical (as a modifier), 18–20, 159–61, 164, 210, 217–22

Rancière, Jacques, 110, 140–41, 143, 147, 254

rank: in logic, 82–83, 86–87

Read, Jason, 256

reciprocity, 16–17, 67, 117, 164–65, 169, 173–74, 183–84, 227–29n, 254–55, 267, 272–73; reciprocal concepts, 165; reciprocal counterviolence, 150–53, 157–58, 164–65, 174, 183–84, 189, 272–73; reciprocal definition, 114; reciprocal determination, 113–14, 254–55, 267; reciprocal identification, 169; reciprocal recognition, 16–17; refusal of, 188–93, 195–200

Reid, Donald, 275–76

Reinares, Fernando, 250

Reinhard, Kenneth, 230

relation, 14–19, 31, 33, 41, 51, 54, 82–83, 92, 114–16, 118–22, 131–33, 152–66, 199, 222; ontology of, 113, 132–33, 146, 254–55; political, 152–66; social, 118–22, 131. *See also* community; reciprocity

representation, 11–12, 31–33, 38–42, 49–50, 54, 56, 58, 67, 80–86, 89, 93, 95, 123, 134, 141, 146–49, 168–69, 174–77, 186–87, 192–93, 196, 208–11, 214–22, 226, 227–29, 241–42, 246, 273–74, 277–79; allegorical, 83–84, 214; concept as, 31, 116–17, 119–20, 131–32, 256; of constitutive antagonism, 160–61; of contingent association, 222; and contract, 155; of domination, 154–55, 164; and ethical judgment, 199–200; of exile, 210;

and explication, 85–86; representative government, 19, 38–42, 208–9; and masques, 81; of pain, torture, 20, 179; of political change, 37; and republicanism, 19, 38–42; spatial, of logical form, 82–83; and transference, 127; and the unrepresentable, 32; and veil, 278–79; and women, 146–47. *See also* allegory; concept

republicanism, 16, 26, 39–40, 125, 136, 148–49, 164–72, 202–22, 226, 229, 232, 236, 275–76, 280–81; and exile, 210–11, 216, 221, 281; radical, 18–20, 28–29, 31–33, 39–40, 42, 62, 63, 86–87, 164–72, 174, 177, 204–5, 208, 210, 215–18, 221–22

Ricoeur, Paul, 20, 230

Riera, Gabriel, 230–31

Rioux, J.-P., 271–72

Rivette, Jacques, 32, 194–99, 236, 279

Romanticism, 23–24, 63, 128

Rorty, Richard, 31, 161–64, 172, 270–71

Rousseau, Jean-Jacques, 124–29, 142–43, 259–62, 266

rule, 4, 7, 12, 13, 17, 20, 30–31, 78–79, 111–17, 122, 129, 145, 148, 157, 167, 188–89, 192; rules of association, 4, 13, 111, 188; rule following, 7, 20, 78, 111–12, 148. *See also* norm

Saavedra Fajardo, Diego, vii, 205–10, 280–81

sacrifice, 7, 22, 40–41, 60, 69–70, 72, 138, 148–49, 254

Sade, Donatien Alphonse François, Marquis de, 30–32, 150–72, 174–75, 230, 269, 272; *Philosophy in the Bedroom*, 31–32, 154–55, 165–72, 272

Said, Edward, 187, 278

Santa Casa of Loreto, 131–39, 144–49, 263, 266–67

Schabel, Chris, 247

Schiller, Friedrich, 110, 136–39, 146–49, 254, 266–67

Schmitt, Carl, 29–30, 64–71, 89, 91, 95–96, 99, 240, 245; *Concept of the Political*, 65–71, 240; *Political Theology*, 65–71, 89, 240, 245

Schröckh, Johann Matthias, 133, 139, 263–65

Scott, Joan, 278

secularization, 6–7, 28–30, 63–67, 87, 89–91, 100, 109, 151, 209, 275–77

semantic excess, surplus, 17–18, 20, 22, 26–27, 36, 40, 51–53, 55, 63–64, 139, 191, 205, 273. *See also* terror; value

Seneca, 6–14, 28, 214, 224–26

Sepúlveda, Lorenzo de, 252

set, 17, 23–24, 78, 83, 93–100, 113–14, 125, 144–47, 161, 185–86

Shakespeare, William, 28, 72, 245; *King Lear*, 90, 241, 245; *Richard III*, 72–79, 240–43

Shephard, Ben, 234

Sicroff, Albert A., 251

sign, empty or vacuous, 60–61

Sirinelli, J.-F., 272

Sittlichkeit (ethical life), 16, 130–31, 226–27

skin, 20–23, 52, 230–32. *See also* body

Sloterdijk, Peter, 145, 281–82

Slyomovics, Susan, 178, 275

Smith, Steven, 114, 255

Solanas, Fernando, 273

Solinas, Franco, 194, 271, 276–78

Sophocles, 4, 6–14, 21, 23, 28, 72, 225–26, 231; *Oedipus*, 4–12, 28, 225–26; *Trachiniae*, 10, 20, 23, 231

Soriano, Ramón, 57, 239

sovereignty, 6–14, 17, 27–33, 34–35, 63–87, 88–109, 110, 115, 130–31, 134, 137–38, 140, 151, 153, 161, 163–65, 174, 207–10, 222, 238, 240, 245–46, 250; sovereign's body, 28–29; and citizen, 9; dialectics of colonial, 151, 164, 175; divisible, 30, 33, 63–87, 204; logic of, of logic, 70–72, 78–79, 88–109, 110, 151, 174; multitudinous, 153, 157; popular, 207–10; sovereign pleasure, 31, 229; and slave, 7–8, 14–15, 27; sovereign subjectivity, 153, 163–65, 222, 226–27; wounded, 10–12, 27, 222. *See also* sublime, sublimity; theology, political theology; transcendence

Spinoza, Spinozism, 114, 130, 246, 257

Sprinker, Michael, 257, 260

structure, 31, 113–49, 155, 226, 255, 259, 283; of feeling, 36–37; and element, 31, 113–149, 255; and effect, 113–15, 120–22, 124, 141–42, 144, 149; and function, 116; Möbius strip, 94; of reciprocity, 227–28; systematic, of concept of sovereignty, 65, 67, 91, 94, 99,109; of the Trinity, 132; of truth, 11

subject, subjectivity, 15, 19, 26–28, 34, 38–39, 52, 71–72, 79, 86–87, 103, 118, 121–23, 131, 138, 142, 146, 153–55, 158, 166–69, 179, 203–4, 219–22, 223–24, 226–27, 230, 233, 257–59, 262; autonomous ethical, 111; articulating, 119–20; as citizen, 39; colonial, 176, 190, 278–79; and contract, 166–68, 174; and intersubjectivity, 15, 219, 221, 275–76, 282–83; rule-giving and rule-following, 148; and sovereign, 65, 71, 74, 90, 208; and subjection, 14, 26–27, 168–69; and subjectivism, 220. *See also* libido, libinization; object, objectality; sovereignty; structure; suture

sublime, sublimity, 23, 37–38, 40, 59, 63, 132

Suchting, Wal, 268

surface, 51, 94–98, 103; filmic, 198; mirror as, 179–80, 183; skin or flesh and, 49, 230; and topology, 94–98, 101, 109

suture, 7, 31, 33, 41, 51–53, 55, 58, 61, 79, 118–23, 130, 141, 143–44, 146–49, 171, 182, 199, 258–59

synthesis, transcendent, 42–43, 58, 61

Teresa of Ávila, 236

Terray, Emmanuel, 179, 275

terror, 1–6, 10, 12, 23–33, 36, 38–42, 51–53, 59, 61–62, 89, 109, 110, 135–39, 174, 195, 197–98, 222, 235–36; and concept, as concept, 31, 33, 64, 110; and event, 26; distinguished from fear and anxiety, 24–25, 235; and judgment, 1–6, 23; and radical republicanism, 19, 42, 63; "the Terror," 23, 38–39; and terrorism, 26–27, 40–42, 51–53, 59, 61–62, 63, 149, 177, 201, 222, 223–24; theologico-political, 135–39, 149. *See also* semantic excess, surplus; sovereignty; sublime, sublimity; terrorism

terrorism, 26–27, 32, 39–43, 51–52, 59, 61–62, 110, 149, 173–74, 177–79, 193, 200–1, 204, 222, 223–24, 237–38, 274–75

Thakkar, Mark, 247

theology, political theology, 28–30, 62, 65, 69, 74, 78, 89–91, 95–104, 108–9, 110, 112, 125, 130, 132–33, 135, 138–39, 146, 148–49, 161, 168, 172, 222, 225–26, 240, 245–46, 247, 250–51, 277

Thirard, Paul Louis, 279

Thomson, Judith Jarvis, 19, 230

thought, thinking. *See* terror

time, 3, 25–28, 33, 68–69, 73–75, 84–85, 95–96, 100–103, 108, 149, 174–75, 177, 184, 202–3, 210–11, 213, 217, 219–22, 241; filmic, 197–198; of the nation-state, 64–65; and reflection, judgment, 174–75, 177, 193; and republic, 210–11, 217, 221–22; and sovereign decision, exception, 68–69, 89, 95–96, 103; and terror, 25–28, 223–24; and untimeliness, 221

Toledo, 28, 30, 103–9, 213, 215, 248–53

Tomás y Valiente, Francisco, 60–61

topology, 28, 51–52, 55, 61, 83–84, 86, 89–96, 103, 110, 114–15, 148, 155, 157, 230–31, 245–46, 255; and invagination, 94–95. *See also* surface

torture, *tormento*, 1–6, 8, 10–11, 20, 26, 32, 96, 110, 135, 138, 163–65, 173, 175–76, 178–79, 193, 223–26, 271–73

totality, 118–23, 131–32, 155–56, 159, 269–70; of effects, 118–23, 145; and individual, 132; rejection of, 156, 159; without totalitarianism, 155. *See also* community; idea; universal, universals

tracking shot, dolly shot, traveling shot, vii, 32, 193–201, 279. *See also under* movement

tragedy, 6, 56, 81–82, 149, 225–26, 241–42, 244–45; and comedy, 12; and farce, 56; tragic heroism, 3. *See also* Alonso Asenjo, Julio; Seneca; Shakespeare, William; Schiller, Friedrich; Sophocles

transcendence, transcendent, 42–43, 49, 111, 131–32, 135; "Transcendental Analytic" (Kant), 116; transcendence of norms, 17; transcendental phenomenology, 218–22, 282; transcendent synthesis, 42–43, 58, 61;

transcendental tradition, transcendental philosophy, 19, 116–17, 130, 259. *See also* idea; phenomenology; sovereignty

transference, 123–30, 135, 143–47, 254–55, 261–62

translation, 5, 12, 21, 84, 113–14, 125, 132, 135, 150, 183, 188–89, 196–99, 206–7, 211, 213, 214–16, 225, 240, 246; *translatio imperii*, 133, 267; and untranslatability, 160–61

trauma, 24–25, 72, 75, 83, 115, 160, 217–18, 230, 233–34, 273–74

tukhē, 9–10, 28. *See also* contingency; destiny; fate

truth, 3–4, 9–11, 89–90, 98–101, 103, 107–8, 117, 131, 163, 226, 247–50, 259–60, 271–73; and torture, 3–4, 9–11, 20. *See also* logic; proposition

Tusell, Javier, 237

unconscious, 127, 187, 233, 259, 262, 268; and ideology, 261; and the joke, 34, 37, 237; and the secret, 63. *See also* libido, libidinization; subject, subjectivity

universal, universals, 6–7, 12–29, 77, 138, 150–51, 168–69, 174, 215, 217, 225–26, 229–30, 278–79; concrete, 132–33, 232; and general will, 259–60; and predication, 70–71, 82–83, 240; and psychoanalysis, 190–92; and terror, 23; weak or defective, 12–29, 33

unspeakable, unspeakability, 22–23, 27. *See also aphrastos*

value, 6–7, 16–20, 22, 37, 47, 52, 96, 103, 111, 148–49, 150, 159–62, 166, 174, 179–80, 186, 204–5, 224–26, 228–32, 243, 254; affect-value of terror, 41; ethics, 2; of fiction, 125; irreducible plurality of, 159–62; multiple-value logics, 98; normative, of weak concepts, 111; pedagogical, 83, 208, 254; surplus value or validity, 17–20, 22, 27, 55, 64. *See also* labor; norm, normativity; semantic excess, surplus

veil, *haik*, 32, 151, 178–99, 274–79

Vergés, Jacques, 283

Vilarós, Teresa, 45, 238

Virgil, 5

violence, 6–8, 10, 14–15, 19, 36, 40, 43, 45, 49, 51, 61, 67, 139, 142–44, 147, 149, 150–72, 177, 183, 186–92, 201, 216, 218, 235–39, 269, 272–73; and counterviolence, 151–56, 164–65, 173–74, 189; instituting, 159, 164, 192; of resemanticization, 187, 191; in social relations as such, 159–60, 164

Viroli, Maurizio, 229

Vizcaíno Casas, Fernando, 239

Voltaire (François-Marie Arouet), 139, 267

Vuillemin, Jules, 270

Waismann, Friedrich, 254

Wall, Thomas Carl, 232

walls: city's, 2–22, 50, 178–79, 217, 253; Belshaz'zar's, 76–78, 242–43; and concept, 26. *See also* border, bound; skin; surface

Wandel, Lee Palmer, 243

Weber, Max, 236

Weimann, Robert, 241

Widdowson, Peter, 249–50

Willet, Andrew, 242

Williams, Raymond, 36–37, 237

Wiltshire, Harold, 246

Wittgenstein, Ludwig, 92, 111–13, 157, 225, 227, 254

Wood, Michael, 90, 245

wordplay, 126, 130. *See also* jokes, *chistes*

Yacef, Saadi, 178, 183–86, 189, 193, 272–78

Zambrano, María, 28, 33, 211–22, 281–82; "What Happened to Cervantes: Dulcinea," 211–22, 281–82

Zerilli, Linda M. G., 206

Žižek, Slavoj, 29, 115, 257, 269, 270

Zoary, Fawzia, 277